HANDBOOK ON DEBT RECOVERY

INDIAN INSTITUTE OF BANKING & FINANCE

Revised and updated by Dr. A.C. Chug, former Chairman, M G B Gramin Bank (sponsored by State Bank Group) and vetted by Dr. R. Bhaskaran, former CEO, IIBF and former CGM, NABARD

Edition : 2023

Price : ₹ 540

Published by :
Taxmann Publications (P.) Ltd.

Sales & Marketing :
59/32, New Rohtak Road, New Delhi-110 005 India
Phone : +91-11-45562222
Website : www.taxmann.com
E-mail : sales@taxmann.com

Mumbai
35, Bodke Building, Ground Floor M.G. Road,
Opp. Railway Station, Mulund (W), Mumbai - 400 080
Mob. +91-9322247686, 9619668669, 7045453844/45/51
E-mail : sales.mumbai@taxmann.com; nileshbhanushali@taxmann.com

Regd. Office :
21/35, West Punjabi Bagh, New Delhi-110 026 India

Printed at :
Tan Prints (India) Pvt. Ltd.
44 Km. Mile Stone, National Highway, Rohtak Road,
Village Rohad, Distt. Jhajjar (Haryana) India
E-mail : sales@tanprints.com

Foreword

Debt recovery is a complex and often challenging process that requires a great deal of skill and expertise. Debt recovery agents are involved in recovering outstanding debts on behalf of creditors. The work done by the debt recovery agents is important for the smooth functioning of the banking and financial system.

This book has been prepared to serve as a comprehensive guide to debt recovery agents and the important role they play in the debt recovery process. It is developed to provide readers with a deep understanding of the debt recovery process and the various strategies and guidelines to be followed by the debt recovery agents. This book provides inputs on the collection/recovery function including basic information and principles underlying credit collection, procedures involved in the collection function, codes to be adopted by recovery agents, etc. with valuable tips, techniques, illustrative real-world examples, and best practices on the issue. The book also covers information on banking and banking products and legal aspects of recovery. As the Non-Banking Financial Companies (NBFCs) also play an important role in the banking & finance landscape, a new section on NBFCs has been added. The guidelines issued by the regulator have been reckoned while updating the book.

In addition, the book delves into the soft skills and attributes required to be a successful debt recovery agent. It provides insights into the techniques and methods required by debt recovery agents to communicate with debtors and improve collections. The book also highlights the ethical considerations and regulatory frameworks that govern the work of debt recovery agents. It explores the importance of treating debtors with respect and dignity and the consequences of engaging in unethical or illegal practices. The courseware has been developed by the Institute with the help of experts drawn from the banking and financial industry. The Institute acknowledges with gratitude the valuable services rendered by them.

This book will serve as an essential guide for all DRAs whether associated with banks or NBFC in their recovery process. It provides a comprehensive overview of the entire business of recovery and offers practical insights and advice for those seeking to engage the services of debt recovery agents.

We welcome suggestions for improvement of the book.

Mumbai

2023

BISWA KETAN DAS

Chief Executive Officer

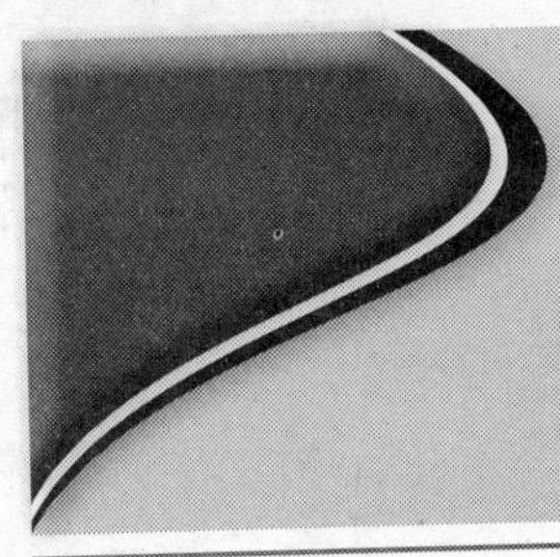

Syllabus

Module A - Basics of Banking

Features of Banking, Indian Financial System, Structure of Indian Banking System, Functions of Banks, Recent Trends, Various Customer Types, Banker-Customer relationship, Duties and Rights of bankers, Various deposit schemes and other services, procedure of account opening and KYC guidelines, Prevention of money laundering, Negotiable Instruments Act, 1881 and provision for payment and collection of cheques

Module B - Brief Outline of Various Products and Legal Aspects of Recovery

Debit and Credit Cards-types and features, principles of lending, credit score, types of loans and advances, priority sector advances, MUDRA scheme, CGTMSE, Securities- types and characteristics, creation of charge, loan documentation, types of loan documents, NPA-definition and income recognition and asset classification, legal aspects of loan recovery, SARFAESI Act, Recovery through Lok Adalat, Filing of Suits, DRT, Insolvency and Bankruptcy Code, 2016

Module C - Role in Loan Recovery and Soft Skills

Collection operations, Customer meeting etiquettes, anger management, DRA-legal and regulatory framework, roles and responsibilities of Debt Recovery Agents, rights of the loan defaulter, Integrated Banking Ombudsman Scheme, Debt Recovery Policy, Debt Recovery Procedure, Code of Conduct for DRAs, Soft Skills for recovery, Emotional Intelligence, Strategy for recovery, Credit counselling, rights and duties of recovery agents, Fair Practices code for lenders

Module D - Additional Reading on NBFCs

NBFCs-types and framework, loan types offered by NBFCs, Fair Practices Code for NBFCs

Recommended Reading

The Institute has prepared comprehensive courseware in the form of study kits to facilitate preparation for the examination without intervention of the teacher. An attempt has been made to cover fully the syllabus prescribed for each module/subject and the presentation of topics may not always be in the same sequence as given in the syllabus.

Candidates are also expected to take note of all the latest developments relating to the subject covered in the syllabus by referring to Financial Papers, Economic Journals, Latest Books and Publications in the subjects concerned.

Contents

MODULE A

BASICS OF BANKING

MODULE B

BRIEF OUTLINE OF VARIOUS PRODUCTS AND LEGAL ASPECTS OF RECOVERY

Page

MODULE C

DRA ROLE IN LOAN RECOVERY AND SOFT SKILLS

MODULE D

ADDITIONAL READING ON NBFCs

APPENDICES

MODULE

Basics of Banking

CHAPTER 1 Overview of Banking and Finance

1.1 OBJECTIVE

In this lesson the reader will learn about banks, functions of banks, various types of banks, types of customers, etc. Among the customers, it is important to know about the borrowers from banks and NBFCs who will be met by collection functionaries during collection work:

- An outline of banking and finance sector
- Various types of Banks in India
- Functions of banks
- Recent trends in banking

1.2 INTRODUCTION

People need banks and financial institutions to meet their savings, credit, investment, transactions and other financial needs. People would like to protect themselves against losses by taking insurance. Business persons would like to seek capital for business through credit from Banks. These requirements are met by banks, insurance companies, financial institutions, and others.

As per section 5(*b*) of the Banking Regulation Act, 1949, Banking is defined as "accepting, for the purpose of lending or investment, of deposits of money from the public, repayable on demand or otherwise, and withdrawal by cheque, draft, and order or otherwise". As per section 5(*c*) of the Banking Regulation Act, 1949 it is defined that "A banking company is a company which transacts the business of banking in India".

Banks accept money from public in the form of deposits. It is necessary that deposits are safe and returned as per terms of acceptance or when demanded by the depositor. To ensure this, banks carry on their business in a professional and safe manner. They take due care of monies accepted in the form of deposits. They lend money for various purposes. Banks are also involved in handling and putting through transactions on behalf of their customers and others. In order that banks function in an orderly manner and that depositors are protected, Banking and Financial Institutions are regulated by Reserve Bank of India. Institutions that come under RBI regulation are as under:-

(*a*) Commercial Banks

(*b*) Cooperative Banks

(*c*) All India Financial Institutions

(*d*) Non-Banking Finance Companies.

Traditionally, banks were involved only in deposits and credit giving facilities (loans and advances). Over the years, banks have increased the number of products they offer, some of which are:-

(*a*) Cash Management

(*b*) Investment Advisory

(*c*) Financial Planning

(*d*) Transaction Processing

(*e*) Equipment Leasing

(*f*) Foreign trade related services

(*g*) Credit Enhancement

(*h*) Escrow services.

In recent years, on account of digitalization, the use of products and facilities offered by banks and financial institutions has increased manifold.

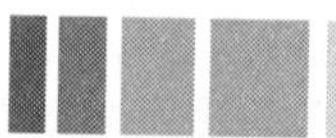

1.3 FEATURES OF BANKING

The following are the basic characteristics or the essential features of Banking:

- **Dealing in money**: Banks accept deposits from the public and provide the same as loans to the needy people. Banks also invest the money in various financial instruments.
- **Accepting Deposits**: Deposits could be in the form of current, savings and fixed/term deposit accounts. Deposits are accepted for various periods subject to certain terms and conditions. Savings and current accounts are transaction

accounts. Current and Savings account deposits are withdrawable by the account holder/customer by cheques, electronic transactions, etc. For this purpose, banks issue cheques, ATM cards or ATM cum Debit Cards and allow transactions through mobile banking. The deposits are usually withdrawable on demand *i.e.,* by presenting the cheque with the branch or putting through the transaction.

- **Sanctioning and issuing loans and advances**: Banks lend for various purposes. Loans could be in the form of cash credit, overdraft, term loans, bills discounting, letter of credit etc. Loans are repayable by the borrowers as per terms and conditions of loan. Loans are for specified periods. Banks charge interest and other fees/charges on loans.
- **Creating Money/Credit**: Money lent by the bank will be used in business and will be deposited by the recipient into the banking system. This creates a fresh chain of deposits and credit *i.e.* it ends up creating fresh credit. Thus, banks can create credit *i.e.,* creation of additional money for lending. This is a unique feature of banking.
- **Nature of Agent**: Besides the basic function of accepting deposits and lending money as loans, bank possesses the character of an agent because of its various agency services.

Though banks offer many services by nature of business, they are commercial in nature: They are 'for profit' organizations. Since all the banking functions are carried on with the objective of earning interest or fee or commission *i.e.* making profit, they are regarded as commercial institutions.

Following is a pictorial view of bank products:

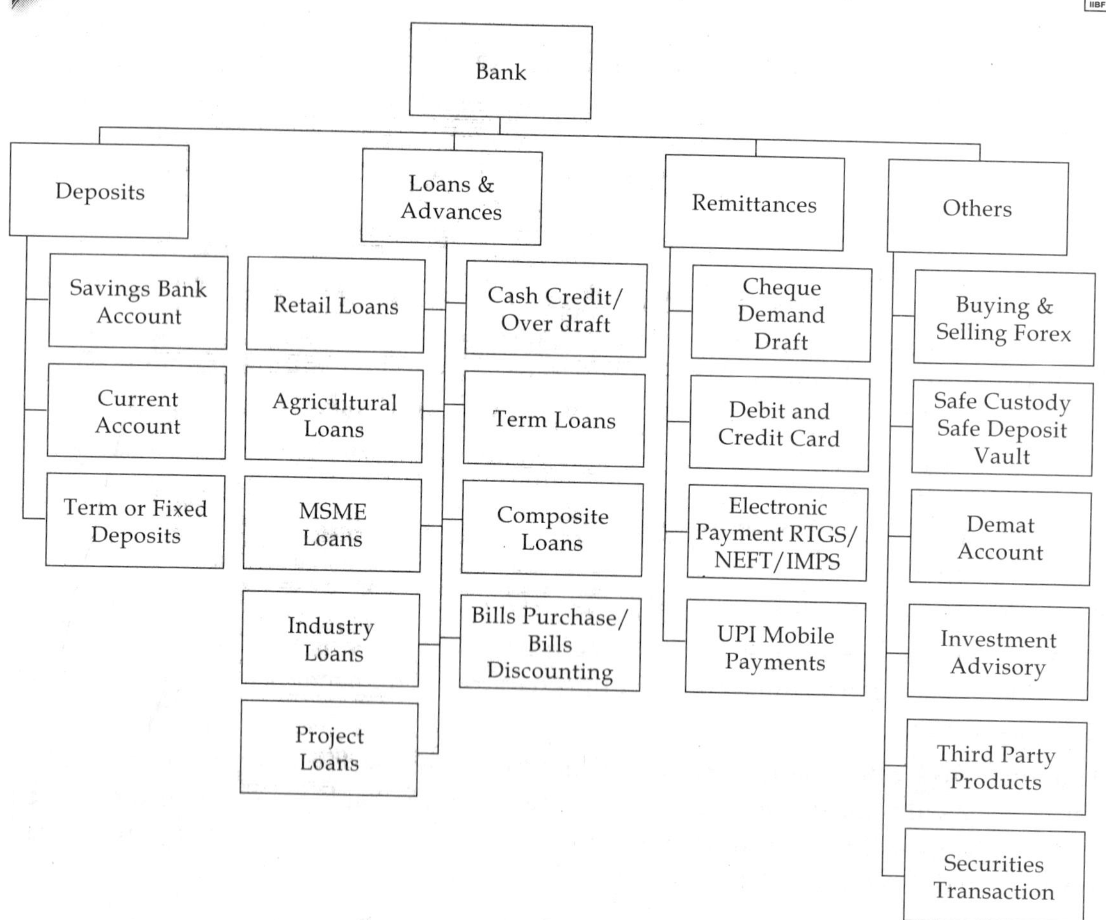

FIGURE 1.1 : DIAGRAMMATIC REPRESENTATION OF BANK PRODUCTS

From the picture above, it is easy to understand the role of banks in terms of deposits, loans, and remittances in an economy. Within the above, the major functions of banks are deposit and loans and advances. Let us learn about banks in detail.

An economy consists of savers of money and users of money. Bank accepts money from the savers and lends or invests it with the users. This is the **most important role of banks.** Savers of money could be individuals, insurance policy holders, investors (bonds etc.), firms, organisations, businesses, industries, etc. They keep money invested in banks and other financial institutions/instruments. Users are those who borrow money from banks and financial institutions for their personal or carrying out an economic activity like farming or manufacturing and/or business requirements.

Banks are part of the financial system of the country. The financial system consists of banks, financial institutions, insurance companies, mutual funds, and others.

1.4 INDIAN FINANCIAL SYSTEM

The Indian Financial System is one of the most important pillars of the economic development of our country. The financial services that are provided by the various Financial Institutions including banks, insurance companies, pensions, NBFCs, etc. constitute the financial system.

There are four main components of the Indian Financial System. This includes:

- Financial Institutions
- Financial Assets
- Financial Services
- Financial Markets

The Reserve Bank of India (RBI) is India's Central Bank Authority and regulatory body responsible for regulation of the Indian banking system. Its roles are as under:

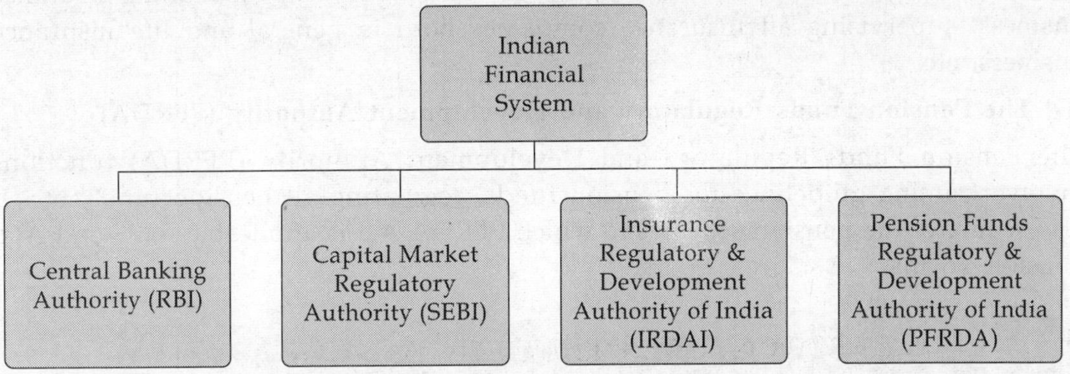

FIGURE 1.2 : FINANCIAL REGULATORS IN INDIA

(A) Central Banking Authority

Reserve Bank of India (RBI) is the Central Banking Authority of the country. Its various functions are as follows:

a. Monetary Control/controlling inflation

b. Supervision over Commercial Banks, NBFCs, Primary Dealers, Financial Institutions, Co-operative Banks, Clearing & Settlement System

c. Management of government debt

d. Banker to Government

e. Lender of last resort

f. Regulating money markets, etc.

(B) Capital Market Regulatory Authority

The Securities and Exchange Board of India (SEBI) is the Capital Market Regulatory Authority. Its functions consist of:

a. Equity market and debt market supervision and control;

b. Supervision over:

- Stock Exchanges
- Brokers
- Equity & Debt raisers
- Investment bankers (Merchant bankers)
- Foreign Institutional Investors, etc.

(C) The Insurance Regulatory & Development Authority of India (IRDAI)

The Insurance Regulatory & Development Authority of India (IRDAI) is engaged in drawing Regulatory Framework including rules and regulations for running insurance business, supervising all insurance companies both in general and life insurance business, etc.

(D) The Pension Funds Regulatory and Development Authority (PFRDA)

The Pension Funds Regulatory and Development Authority (PFRDA) functions involve framing guidelines for pension funds, regulating all pension funds, etc. It also regulates the pension schemes to which PFRDA Act is applicable- NPS and Atal Pension Yojana.

1.5 STRUCTURE OF INDIAN BANKING SYSTEM

1. Reserve Bank of India

Reserve Bank of India is the banking regulator and the Central Bank of our country. It was established on 1st April, 1935 under the RBI Act of 1934. As a regulator, it holds the apex position in the banking structure. RBI is the banker to banks and performs banking, regulatory, developmental, and promotional functions. It has powers to issue regulations and guidelines on banking and has the power to license, supervise and control the banking structure. It occupies the pivotal position in the monetary and banking structure of the country. Federal Reserve Bank of U.S.A, Bank of England in U.K. are central banks of the respective countries and are similar to the Reserve Bank of India.

RBI has the authority to formulate and implement monetary and credit policies. It is owned by the Government of India and has the monopoly power of issuing notes.

Functions of RBI are as under:

i. Announce and implement monetary policy - Monetary policy is *a set of policies and actions to control a nation's overall money supply. The objective of this policy is to control the money supply, manage inflation and achieve economic growth.*

ii. Regulation and supervision of the banking and non-banking financial institutions, including credit rating and credit information companies. Regulations aim to ensure financial stability and proper functioning of the banks.

iii. Regulation of money, foreign exchange, and government securities markets, etc.

iv. Manage issue of Government securities. Debt and cash management for Central and State Governments.

v. Management of foreign exchange reserves.

vi. Act as a Banker to banks: RBI can lend money to banks in need of support.

vii. Banker to the Central and State Governments: Manage Government business, payments, etc.

viii. Oversight of the payment and settlement systems including development of electronic payment systems.

ix. Currency management: Issue and management of currency

x. Developmental role: RBI is unique as it has a developmental function where it develops policies for economic development.

xi. Publishes reports on banking and finance and also data/statistics on banking and finance.

Chart. Indian Banking and Financial System[1]

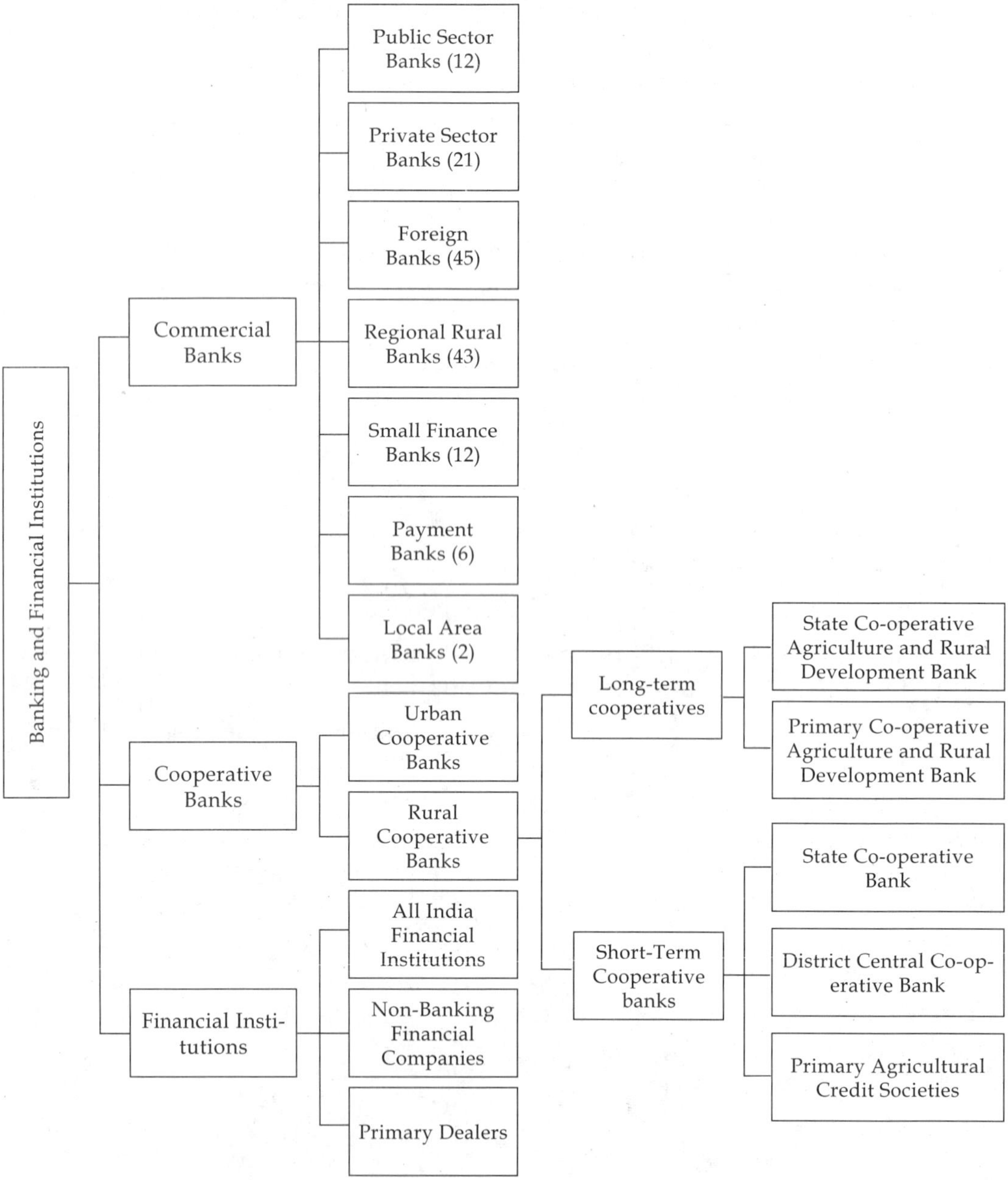

- Banking and Financial Institutions
  - Commercial Banks
    - Public Sector Banks (12)
    - Private Sector Banks (21)
    - Foreign Banks (45)
    - Regional Rural Banks (43)
    - Small Finance Banks (12)
    - Payment Banks (6)
    - Local Area Banks (2)
  - Cooperative Banks
    - Urban Cooperative Banks
    - Rural Cooperative Banks
      - Long-term cooperatives
        - State Co-operative Agriculture and Rural Development Bank
        - Primary Co-operative Agriculture and Rural Development Bank
      - Short-Term Cooperative banks
        - State Co-operative Bank
        - District Central Co-operative Bank
        - Primary Agricultural Credit Societies
  - Financial Institutions
    - All India Financial Institutions
    - Non-Banking Financial Companies
    - Primary Dealers

FIGURE 1.3: BANKING AND FINANCIAL SYSTEM

The Indian Banking and Financial system has a wide variety of institutions big and small and serves the length and breadth of the country. A brief description of the constituents of the banking and financial system is given in the following.

1. Source RBI, SCARB, PCARDB, PACS are not banks but part of the system/Grid.

2. Commercial Banks

Commercial banks are formed in the form of a company. As indicated earlier, these institutions accept deposit, issue loans and offer payment and settlement support to the business people and the public. There are a variety of commercial banks in India. However, all of them adopt branch banking model *i.e.,* the banks operate through their branches situated in various places in India. Now-a-days, branches and Head Office of the bank are well connected through core banking system and therefore, a customer of a bank can, subject to certain conditions, operate her/his/their account(s) from any of the branches. Typically, each commercial bank has a head office, zonal or regional offices and several branches. These institutions are "for profit" organizations.

Commercial banks in India are broadly classified as Public Sector, Private Sector, Foreign Banks, Small Finance Banks, Local Area Banks, Payments Banks and Regional Rural Banks:

Public Sector Banks: These include State Bank of India and 11 other banks which are owned by GOI (majority stake with GOI) and whose shares are also listed in the market. As indicated earlier, between 1969 and 1980, about 20 private banks were nationalized with the objective of using banks funds for the purpose of economic development. Subsequently, Government of India divested a portion of its share in the market and shares of majority of PSU banks were listed in the stock market. Recently, on account of financial stability norms, some of these banks have been merged in a process of consolidation. In view of this, there are currently 11 PSU banks and SBI. SBI is the largest bank of the country with a balance sheet size of over around Rs. 110 Lakh crore (as of March 2023).

Private Sector Banks: Private sector banks are those whose equity is held by private shareholders and government does not own any share capital or maybe a minor shareholder. Some of the private banks have come into existence after 1990. There are 21 private sector banks in India. HDFC Bank is the largest private bank. These banks are better capitalized, technology-driven, aggressive in business development and adopt a style of functioning comparable to foreign banks operating in India. These banks adopt a variety of delivery channels.

Foreign Banks: Foreign banks are commercial banks which are registered in foreign countries but doing business in India. While there are many foreign banks operating in India, their branch network is smaller and the most of them operate in metropolitan cities and State Capitals. Their operations are technology driven and a good part of their business comprises of corporate banking, foreign exchange, export/import finance and merchant banking.

Small Finance Banks: Small Finance banks (SFB) have come into being from 2015 after licensing norms were issued by RBI. The SFBs are expected to function with

an objective of achieving financial inclusion by offering basic banking activities to under-served sections including small business units, small and marginal farmers, micro and small industries and unorganized entities. These banks can accept deposits, issue loans and advances and offer other services to their customers. There are certain restrictions on the products and services they can offer. They cannot do all activities like a full-fledged commercial bank. As per RBI guidelines, they are required to extend 75 per cent of its Adjusted Net Bank Credit (ANBC) to the sectors eligible for classification as priority sector lending (PSL) by RBI. Further, in order to ensure that the bank extends loans primarily to small borrowers, at least 50 percent of its loan portfolio should constitute loans and advances of up to Rs. 25 lakh.

Payments Banks: A payments bank is a bank with restricted or limited functions. It can accept deposits and do transactions (remittances and payments) and other services but cannot grant loans and advances or handle credit. Whereas there is no limit on the amount of deposit, or the type of deposit accepted from individuals and others by other banks, payments banks cannot accept deposits of more than Rs. 2 lakh. They are allowed to provide only demand deposit (*i.e.*, current and savings account) and not term deposits. In essence, these banks have the objective of being focused on payments and settlements. These banks can offer remittance services, mobile payments/transfers/purchases and other banking services like ATM/debit cards, net-banking and third-party fund transfers. They cannot issue Credit Cards.

The list of payments banks in India are as follows:

1. Airtel Payments Bank Ltd.
2. India Post Payments Bank Ltd.
3. FINO Payments Bank Ltd.
4. Paytm Payments Bank Ltd.
5. Jio Payments Bank Ltd.
6. NSDL Payments Bank Limited.

Regional Rural Banks (RRBs): Regional rural banks (RRBs) cater to the basic banking and credit needs of people in rural and semi-urban areas such as small farmers, agricultural labourer's, artisans and MSMEs. These banks are jointly owned by the Government of India (50%), the State Government concerned (15%) and the sponsoring commercial bank (35%). Some time back, there were 196 RRBs. Over the years, due to consolidation, the number of RRBs has reduced in number. The main objective of an RRB is to develop the rural economy. Their borrowers include small and marginal farmers, agricultural labourers, artisans, etc. Agricultural lending constitute around 70 per cent of total loans and advances of these banks. There are 43 Regional RRBs in India as on December 31, 2022.

Local Area Banks: Local Area Banks (LABs) were licensed with the objective of mobilizing rural savings and strengthening institutional credit mechanisms in local areas. These banks have a small area of operation of three districts. As of March 2022, only two LABs were operational in the country as follows:

- Coastal Local Area Bank (operating in A.P);
- Krishna Bhima Samruthi Local Area Bank Ltd. (at present operating in Telangana, Andhra Pradesh and Karnataka).

3. Co-operative Banks

Co-operative Banks in India have become an integral part of the success of Indian Financial Inclusion story. Co-operative banks work on the principle of co-operation and mutual help. Unlike commercial banks, these are not companies but registered under the Co-operative Societies Act. A cooperative society/bank is owned by its members.

The structure of co-operative network in India can be divided into 2 broad segments -

(*a*) **Urban Co-operative Banks**: Urban Co-operatives Banks can be divided into scheduled and non-scheduled. Both the categories are further divided into multi-state and single-state. Many of these banks fall in the non-scheduled and single-state category. Banking activities of Urban Co-operative Banks are monitored by RBI. Registration and Management activities are managed by Registrar of Co-operative Societies (RCS). These RCSs operate in single-state and Central RCS (CRCS) which operate in multiple states.

(*b*) **Rural Co-operatives**: The rural co-operatives can be divided into short-term and long-term structures. The short-term co-operative banks are generally three-tiered operating in different states. These are:

(*i*) State Co-operative Banks - They operate at the apex level in states

(*ii*) District Central Co-operative Banks - They operate at the district levels

(*iii*) Primary Agricultural Credit Societies - They operate at the village or grass-root level.

Likewise, the long-term structures are further divided into - State Co-operative Agriculture and Rural Development Banks (SCARDBs) which operate at state-level and Primary Co-operative Agriculture and Rural Development Banks (PCARDBs) which operate at district/block level.

The rural banking co-operatives have a complex monitoring structure as they have a dual control which has led to many problems. Various reforms have been put in place to ensure that these institutions are run and managed on professional lines.

At present, all banking activities of co-operative banks are regulated by a shared arrangement between RBI and NABARD. All management and registration activities are managed by Registrar of Cooperative Societies of the state.

1.6 FUNCTIONS OF BANKS

A bank offers a number of financial services and products to its clients. It is easy to understand a bank from the various services it offers. The following is the illustrative list of services normally extended by banks to their customers:

(*i*) A bank accepts deposits from the public in the form of Savings, Current and/ or Term Deposits.

(*ii*) It allows a customer to remit money or funds from one place to another in the form of Demand Draft or Money transfer. These days, banks also offer to remit funds through electronic channels *viz.* NEFT/RTGS/IMPS, UPI, etc.

(*iii*) It accepts instructions from the customer and makes, on their behalf, payment for utilities such as electricity bill, school fees, etc.

(*iv*) It accepts tax payments on behalf of government.

(*v*) It lends money for business, agriculture, purchase of house, purchase of vehicles, etc.

(*vi*) It transacts (buying and selling of foreign currency) in foreign exchange and helps business people and others receive or pay in foreign currency for their export or import respectively. It buys and sells foreign currency as per the customer's needs.

(*vii*) It offers safe deposit vault facilities for safe keeping of the customer's valuables.

(*viii*) It provides facilities like Internet Banking, Mobile Banking, ATM machines, cash deposit machines, cheque collection machines, etc. which allow the customers to transact from their accounts round the clock.

(*ix*) It offers Credit/Debit card facilities which help customers make payments for their purchases. It is also possible to borrow money by using credit cards.

(*x*) Banks also sell mutual fund and insurance products.

The above functions of banks can be broadly classified as (*a*) Core or Traditional Functions and (*b*) Other Functions.

1.6.1 Core or Traditional

(*a*) Acceptance of Deposits:

The core activity of a bank is acceptance of deposits and maintenance of such deposit accounts is the core activity in any bank. Banking as defined in the Banking Regulation Act, 1949 means accepting deposits of money, for the purpose of lending or investment, from the public, repayable on demand or otherwise, and withdrawable by cheque, draft, order or otherwise. Thus, mobilisation of adequate deposits form a major resource and mainstay of a Bank.

The various deposit accounts can be broadly categorised into (*a*) Demand Deposits and (*b*) Term Deposits. Demand Deposit means a deposit which is withdrawable on demand and they are broadly of two types - (*a*) Savings Account and (*b*) Current Account. Term Deposit means a deposit received by the Bank for a fixed period withdrawable normally after the expiry of the fixed period. Term Deposits can be normally categorised into - (*a*) Fixed Deposits and (*b*) Recurring Deposits. Term Deposits constitute the largest portion of a bank's funds.

(*b*) Loans and Advances:

Banks have to pay interest on the deposits at agreed rates of interest. In addition, they have to meet their operational expenses. Therefore, banks have to invest/lend the money and earn interest. Lending money by way of loans and advances of various kinds is thus an important traditional function of a bank. The funds mobilized, in the form of deposits are deployed by a bank as loans and advances to earn profits by way of interest spreads, *i.e.*, the differential between the average interest rates on loans and on deposits. The interest income from loans and advances forms a major source of a bank's operating profit.

Banks lend in the form of Working Capital such as Cash Credits, Overdrafts, Demand Loans and for capital expenditure in the form of Term Loans. Based on the borrower's profile, loans can be classified as Corporate Loans, SME advances, Agricultural Loans, Retail Loans, Foreign Currency Loans, Educational Loans, Vehicle Loans, etc. Loans are also classified on the basis of security. Security could be in the form of surety, pledge of Bank's Deposit receipts, shares and debentures, assignment of Life Insurance policies, mortgage of immovable property, hypothecation of plant and machinery, raw material, etc. A loan account with security is known as secured loan whereas a loan without security is known as unsecured loan (clean advance).

In order to repay depositors on demand and pay interest on borrowed funds and deposits, banks expect that all the borrowers who take the loans are prompt in payment of interest and repayment of principal amount. However, it is possible that on account of number of reasons, the interest and principal may get defaulted and become overdue. Loans and advances which remain overdue for more than a stipulated period is known as 'Non-Performing Assets' (NPAs). NPAs cause loss of income (interest not being paid or recovered) and in some cases loss of the principal (amount lent). Lending, therefore, calls for good credit appraisal and requires adequate care, caution and supervision/monitoring by the bank to prevent loans turning overdue and eventually into NPAs. Collection or recovery of dues/overdues is important for sustaining the viability of banks in which the DRAs play an important role.

(*c*) Remittance Services:

Customers have to make payment for purchases in the place of their business or in the place of business of the vendor/seller. This calls for movement of money from place to place. However, it may not be possible for a buyer to move from place to

place for making payments. Nor will it be economically viable to carry large sums of money from place to place. It is, therefore, necessary that a good payment and settlement system should exist for enabling trade and commerce in the country. Banks perform the job of payment and settlements in the financial market. In this regard, Banks have branch network spread across various cities/regions/states. Some banks have branches and correspondent banks overseas as well. This network enables the banks to remit funds of their customers, if needed, from one place to another in the same country or overseas by mail/telegraphic/electronic funds transfer or by issuing bank drafts. Banks charge appropriate fee from the remitting person for the service rendered. Remittance of funds by banks is fast, safe, secure and cheap as compared to other modes of funds transfer, like post office money order (which is generally for small sums of money for personal use), physical transfer of money, etc.

1.6.2 Other Functions

(*a*) Miscellaneous Services:

In addition to the above-mentioned core functions, banks also render other services, which are useful to customers, business firms and members of the society. These services include safe deposit lockers, safe custody of important documents/valuables, trade finance services *viz.* letters of credit and guarantees, collection of outstation cheques/bills/hundies, furnishing opinion reports on their customers, agency services for Government business, correspondent, trusteeship and executor's business. Banks also engage in sale of third party products like insurance (both life & general), mutual funds, demat accounts and investment advisory services. Banks charge a commission or fee on such services, which provides them with non-interest income adding to their profits.

(*b*) Electronic Banking:

With the introduction of computers in Indian banks and with the advent of ATMs, banking services are provided across the banks. Customers need not necessarily visit a branch to do banking transactions when they provide them with telebanking or remote-banking facilities. This type of banking is called electronic banking, and this banking channel is becoming popular with individuals as well as corporate entities in India.

The electronic Banking Channels include:

(*i*) **Automated Teller Machines:** ATMs are electronic banking outlets, which allow customers to perform primary banking transactions without the help of any bank representative or teller. It is a machine that can be treated as a mini bank branch. There are host of banking activities that can be performed through ATMs such as:

- Withdrawal of cash
- Make Balance Inquiry

- Obtain Mini statement
- Open fixed deposit
- Transfer Funds
- Pay credit card bills
- Request for Cheque book.
- Update Mobile No./Aadhaar No.
- Recharge Mobile phones
- Pay Insurance Premium
- Pay utility bills
- Deposit cash
- Deposit cheques

(ii) **Cards:** A payment card is a usually a plastic card—that allows its user to make an electronic payment. The most common types of payment cards are credit cards and debit cards. All types of cards are uniquely linked to some or other types of account at the back end. This account can be with a banking entity/ non-banking entity which has issued the card. There are various types of cards in circulation in market issued by banks/non-bank entities.

(iii) **Internet Banking:** With easy access to the Internet and the World Wide Web (WWW), banks are increasingly using the internet as a channel for receiving instructions and delivering their products and services to their customers. This form of banking is referred to as Internet Banking, although the range of products and services offered by different banks vary in their content and sophistication.

Customers can visit the bank's page from their own PCs/Phones or from some other PCs/mobiles. They can register and link their account via the branch. The branch then enables internet banking facility. The bank provides ID and Password for login. On login attempt, the Internet banking server verifies its database for the login details, and then, permits login if those tally. The software links the customer to his CBS account, and he/she can then transact as per menus in the webpage.

(iv) **Mobile Banking:** Mobile phones, as a medium for extending banking services, have attained greater significance. Wider coverage of mobile phone networks, has made this medium an important platform for extending banking services to every segment including unbanked segment. Banks are permitted to offer mobile banking services (through SMS, USSD or mobile banking application).

Some of the common services offered through mobile banking are:

Account Balance Enquiry, Account Statement Enquiries, Cheque Status Enquiry, Cheque Book Requests, Fund Transfer between Accounts, Fund transfer across

Banks through IMPS/UPI etc., Credit/Debit Alerts, Utility Bill Payments like Electricity/Water/Mobile, Recent Transaction History Requests, Various other transaction Alerts, Train/Bus/Flight Bookings, Demat portfolio Management, Tax payments, Buy Life Insurance and General Insurance.

(v) **Tele Banking:** By using a telebanking facility, customers can dial up the Bank's designated telephone number, which is connected to the Bank's server. By dialling his identification number, the customer will be able to avail of some banking services using a secure PIN. The Telebanking software will be interactive with the customer asking him to dial the code number of the service required by him/her and suitably answer him/her.

A customer can access his balance and place an order for the statement of accounts, cheque books and a few selected services through this tele(phone) banking. Some of the services that can be availed with telebanking facility are:

- Balance Inquiry
- Last few transaction details
- Request for a cheque book online
- Stop payment of any cheque
- Initiate fund transfers to self-account
- Generate ATM PIN
- Get the interest certificate
- Get the Deposit Interest Certificate
- Update mobile information or mail ID

This facility is now being served through Voice assistants/Bots using Artificial Intelligence to help the Customer in availing banking services.

(vi) **Electronic Payment Systems:** Clearing Systems have undergone a massive change due to Information and Communication Technology.

The introduction of MICR clearing was the first step towards the process of automated settlement. Reserve Bank of India decided to introduce Cheque Truncation System (CTS) in India to improve the efficiency of the Cheque Clearing Cycle. In the CTS scenario, the physical instrument is truncated at presenting bank end (either at branch level or service branch level). The images & data of collected instruments captured at presenting bank would travel electronically to the drawee bank for processing on the same day. The return cycle would be completed on the next day & settlement is completed on the completion of the return cycle. The customer would get funds on completion of the settlement process.

The use of electronic media is one of the prerequisites for a true EFT system. Phenomenal progress has been made with the introduction of various EFT systems in the country.

National Electronic Fund Transfer (NEFT) System facilitates an efficient, secure, economic, reliable and expeditious system of funds transfer and clearing in the banking sector throughout India, and relieves the stress on the existing paper-based funds transfer and clearing system. NEFT enables the transfer of Funds on a 24 × 7 basis across Banks and transfer can happen through various delivery channels. Real-Time Gross Settlement (RTGS) System is an electronic payment system where Payment instructions are processed on a 'continuous' and 'REAL-TIME' basis and settled on a GROSS or Individual basis without netting the debits against credits. Payments so effected are 'final' and 'irrevocable' settlement is done in the books of RBI.

Electronic Banking is significantly less costly, less error prone and more efficient than traditional banking. Anywhere and Anytime Banking has made banking convenient to the customers.

1.7 RECENT TRENDS IN BANKING

The banking sector is laying greater emphasis on providing improved services to their clients and also upgrading their technology infrastructure, in order to enhance the customer's overall experience as well as give banks a competitive edge. The recent trends in the banking sector can be summarized as follows:

(i) **Risk Management:**

The banking sector drives the economy and plays an important role in utilising effectively to attain maximum productivity. This process involves risk which needs to be identified and managed. Risk refers to an undesirable or an unplanned event involving finances that can result in failure of the investment or reduced earning. It may be possible that the entire or partial investment may be lost.

Risk Management involves management of the risks by forecasting, analysing and making estimations based on historical trends. This includes taking corrective measures to reduce the impact of the risks. Examples of financial risks are high inflation, volatility in capital markets, recession, volatility, bankruptcy, etc.

The major types of risk in the banking industry are:

Liquidity Risk: In situations where an institution is unable to meet its financial commitments or is able to do so only by external borrowing, it leads to liquidity risk. This may be caused due to assets turning into NPAs.

Market Risk: This risk arises when the value of investment might decrease due to changes in factors governing a market. This risk is mostly related to factors governing the market such as recession that impacts the entire market and not restricted to a single industry.

Credit or Default Risk: This type of risk arises when borrowers fail to meet its obligations in accordance with the signed contract. Loans are the major source of income for the banks and in case of default, they are the obvious source of credit or default risk for most banks. Amongst all type of risk, credit risk is the most significant risk typically in the Indian banking sector where NPA size is significantly high.

Operational Risk: This type of risk arises due to breakdown in the internal procedures, people and systems or from external events. Banks are the custodians of public funds and are exposed to a higher volume of global financial interlinkages and involves high level of automation in rendering banking and financial services.

(ii) **Customer Service**:

Customer service in banking is a critical aspect that significantly influences a bank's reputation, customer loyalty, and overall success. With the banking industry being highly competitive, providing exceptional customer service is paramount for retaining existing customers and attracting new ones. The significance of customer service can be summarised as:

- **Customer Retention and Loyalty:** Exceptional customer service fosters customer loyalty and trust, encouraging clients to stay with the bank for the long term.
- **Brand Reputation**: Positive experiences shared by customers can enhance the bank's brand image, attracting new clients and reinforcing its position in the market.
- **Competitive Advantage:** In today's highly competitive banking landscape, providing outstanding customer service sets a bank apart from its rivals and can influence customers' choices when selecting a financial institution.
- **Customer Acquisition:** Happy customers are more inclined to engage in cross-selling and up-selling opportunities, leading to increased revenue streams for the bank.
- **Complaint Resolution**: Efficient and empathetic handling of customer complaints is vital. Promptly addressing and resolving issues not only retains dissatisfied customers but also provides an opportunity to turn a negative experience into a positive one, thereby strengthening customer relationships.
- **Personalization and Customisation:** Effective customer service enables banks to understand their customers' needs and preferences better. With this knowledge, banks can offer personalized solutions and tailored products that cater to individual customer requirements.

- **Technology Integration:** In the digital age, customer service extends beyond in-person interactions. Successful banks integrate technology to enhance customer service through various channels, such as online banking, mobile apps, chatbots, and social media platforms.
- **Compliance and Trust:** Strong customer service reinforces compliance with industry regulations and ethical standards. Building trust with customers is essential for maintaining the security and confidentiality of their financial information.

(*iii*) Income Recognition and Asset Classification (IRAC):

Banks are also subject to strict Income Recognition, Asset classification and Provisioning norms (IRAC or NPA norms) and cannot:

a. Earn or accrue interest on amounts that are NPA and

b. Make provisions for amount in default.

In view of this, collection of loans past due (overdue) *i.e.* defaulted amount is important. This debt collection is also a sensitive function. Non-repayment of loans and non-repayment of instalments in time from customers could be due to genuine reasons, want on, or deliberate default. All these defaults end up impacting the balance sheet and bank's financial position. All these issues could result in aggressive collection efforts which may cause inconvenience to the customers. Making aggressive collection from genuine customers who have temporary difficulties could impact customer service.

In view of the above, appropriate customer service, adherence to code of conduct by banks/NBFCs are monitored by RBI. Banks in turn monitor collection agents. In recent years, this monitoring has been tightened. Banks should ensure that customer service is appropriate.

(*iv*) Financial Inclusion:

"Financial inclusion is the process of ensuring access to financial services and timely and adequate credit wherever needed by vulnerable groups such as weaker sections and low-income groups at an affordable cost (The Committee on Financial Inclusion, Chairman: Dr. C. Rangarajan). RBI announced financial inclusion as an important agenda in the year 2008.

The objective is to make every eligible individual in rural, semi-urban, urban, and metropolitan household who did not have a bank account to OPEN a savings account and avail banking and financial services. For this purpose, a Basic Savings Bank Deposit Account (BSBDA), also called small account has been introduced which calls for simplified KYC and which does not have any minimum balance stipulation.

Financial Inclusion aims to bring poor and low income and disadvantaged groups into the banking fold by providing them access to banking services at affordable cost.

The objective of schemes such as Pradhan Mantri Jan Dhan Yojana (PMJDY), Pradhan Mantri Jeevan Jyoti Scheme, Pradhan Mantri Suraksha Bima Yojana is to provide financial products to all such people who have been excluded so far from banking facilities.

For achieving financial inclusion banks are allowed to use the services of Business Correspondents (BCs) who are linked to the core banking system of the banks. BCs have access to POS and mini-ATM's.

The availability of ICT based transactions has helped in financial inclusion. Using services of Business Correspondents and Business Facilitators for providing banking services in the remotest areas has proved to be successful. Financial inclusion also includes credit inclusion, which is attempted through OD accounts in BSBDA, KCC and GCC.

(*v*) Increased Use of Technology:

In the last decade, banks have adopted many technologies to improve their service, make changes in the products and also reduce cash transactions. Digital channels of payments by banks in transactions, back-office functions, launch of UPI, etc. have considerably changed the way banks operate and function. Customers do not have to go physically to the Branch for their transactions but do their transactions at home or nearby commercial establishment or through mobile 24×7 digitally, which in the past was limited to banking hours. Technology has enabled off-site banking through ATMs, internet banking, mobile banking etc. Another important change -post lock down due to covid- is how the retail sector business has slowly shifted to online mode of orders and payments. All these have changed the way customers access banking services.

(*vi*) Consolidation of Banks:

The number of PSU banks has come down due to consolidation. The promoter banks have also merged their RRBs in each respective state due to which the number of RRBs has also come down to 43. This has been achieved by consolidation of banks keeping in view the financial stability aspects. Some of the private banks have also merged with large sized banks. A higher capital base, which could be possible through consolidation, will thus allow higher lending to borrowers. Other perceived benefits from Consolidation are increased efficiency and profitability.

(*vii*) Non-Banking Financial Companies:

Shadow Banking is a term used to describe bank like activities (mainly lending) that take place outside the banking sector. The role of shadow banking is carried by NBFCs which access funds from commercial banks for on-lending. In this regard, as per RBI guidelines, NBFCs can originate and distribute loans for commercial banks and also do Co-lending with commercial banks. This will help improve the outreach of small loans, group loans, etc. For this purpose, the majority of regulatory guidelines for commercial banks and NBFCs have been made similar.

(*viii*) Central Bank Digital Currency:

Central Bank Digital Currency (CBDC) refers to a digital form of national currency issued and regulated by a country's central bank. CBDC is essentially the digital equivalent of physical cash and is intended to be used as a legal tender for transactions and payments. In India, RBI has launched India's fiat digital currency on a pilot basis in the FY 2022-23. The CBDCs have been implemented through two different models:

- **Retail CBDC** which is accessible directly to the general public and can be used for day-to-day transactions. Individuals and businesses can hold and use this digital currency through digital wallets or mobile apps, allowing them to make purchases, pay bills, and conduct other financial transactions digitally.
- **Wholesale CBDC** which has been designed for use by financial institutions and banks for interbank transactions and settlement purposes. It facilitates more efficient and faster interbank transfers and can have potential benefits for the financial system's stability.

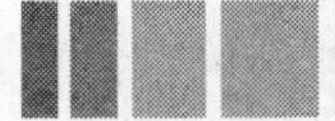

1.8 LET US SUM UP

Banks are financial institutions licensed by RBI. They accept deposits. Public need various products and services of banks to manage their savings and credit needs. Banks accept and lend money to people. They offer Current, Savings and Fixed Deposits. Amounts in current and savings deposits can be withdrawn by cheques, ATM cards, drafts, etc. Banks also deal with credit. They lend in the form of loan, cash credit, overdraft, etc. Banks are commercial in nature and Profit-making organizations.

There are different types of banks based on the ownership and activities namely Public Sector Banks, Private banks, Foreign Banks, Small Finance Banks, Co-operative Banks and RRBs functioning in our country. Banks are regulated by RBI which is the central bank of our country. It performs many functions such as regulating the banks, managing issue of currency, foreign exchange reserves. It has the responsibility for monetary policy as well.

Banks perform some core functions like accepting deposits and lending. Other functions of banks include:

(*a*) Transactions which can be done through cheques, ATMs, RTGS, IMPS etc.

(*b*) Accepting payment of taxes

(*c*) Offer locker, vault facilities

(*d*) Selling insurance, mutual funds, etc.

Banks have played an important role in the lives of consumers for a long time. There have been many recent developments with new focus areas such as:

(*a*) Financial Stability (*b*) Customer Service (*c*) Income Recognition and Asset Classification (*d*) Financial Inclusion (*e*) Increased Use of Technology (*f*) Consolidation of Banks (*g*) Non-Banking Financial Companies (*h*) Central Bank Digital Currency

1.9 KEY WORDS

RBI, Banking, deposits, loan, public sector, private sector, foreign banks, co-operative banks, financial inclusion, basic savings bank deposit account, financial stability, RTGS, IMPS, NEFT, remittances, NBFCs.

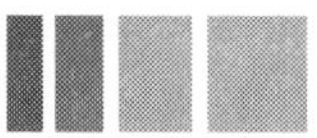

1.10 CHECK YOUR PROGRESS

1. Principal functions of banks are:
   (*a*) Accepting deposits
   (*b*) Lending and investments
   (*c*) Non-fund business and remittance services
   (*d*) All of above
2. IDBI is a ---------
   (*a*) Private Bank
   (*b*) Nationalised Bank
   (*c*) Public Sector Bank
   (*d*) Development Bank
3. Payment Banks can accept deposits ---------- (complete the sentence):
   (*a*) Of any type and also without any ceiling
   (*b*) Term deposits only
   (*c*) Demand deposit only but there is no upper limit for it
   (*d*) Demand deposits having balance not exceeding Rs. 2 Lakh per customer
4. Which of the following statements is True in reference to Small Finance Banks?
   Small Finance Banks are required to give finance ________________
   (*a*) Minimum 75% of total loans to Priority sector.

(*b*) Maximum Loan amount per borrower can be sanctioned up to Rs. 50 Lakhs.

(*c*) To small businesses, organized sector and low income households.

(*d*) To all segments except Export.

5. Regional Rural Banks can open its branches:

(*a*) Anywhere in the state wherein it has its Head Quarters

(*b*) Anywhere in the state but non-customer related offices can be opened anywhere in the country

(*c*) Anywhere in the country

(*d*) Only in the Govt. notified area (Districts)

1.11 ANSWERS TO CHECK YOUR PROGRESS

1.	(*d*)	2.	(*a*)	3.	(*d*)	4.	(*a*)	5.	(*d*)

CHAPTER

2 Banker-Customer relationship

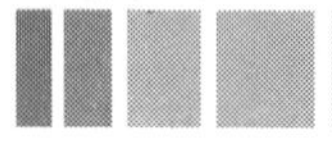

2.1 OBJECTIVES

Collection agents have to meet various customers for the purpose of collecting dues. It is important to know, in this regard, type of customers and their general characteristics so that interaction with them is more effective and smoother. In this lesson readers will learn:

- Who is a customer?
- Various types of customers
- Different types of lender-customer relationship
- Duties of a bank
- Maintaining secrecy: Precautions to be adopted while disclosing information
- Furnishing of information: important aspects

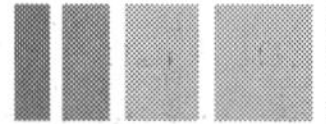

2.2 INTRODUCTION

A customer is "a person or entity that maintains an account and/or has a business relationship with the bank". This definition applies to financial institutions like NBFCs as well as other businesses. In the Prevention of Money Laundering Act, a customer has been defined as a person "who is engaged in a financial transaction or activity with a reporting entity" which could be a bank or NBFC or other financial institution.

An important consideration which determines a person's status as a customer is the nature of his/her dealings with a financial institution namely a bank or NBFC. The dealings or activities must be relating to the business of banking/NBFC namely accepting of deposits, lending money, doing a transaction, etc.

Thus, to constitute a customer the following essential requisites must be fulfilled.

- A bank account - Savings, Current or fixed deposit or loan account. NBFC customers must also have a bank account as repayment of loans happen through Cheque or remittance through bank account.
- The dealing between the banker and the customer must be of the nature of banking business.

Customer of a Bank: A customer of a bank could be a real person or legal person namely firm, Joint Stock Company, a society, or any separate legal entity.

2.3 VARIOUS TYPES OF CUSTOMERS

Customers are categorized in different types based on their relationship with financial institutions.

2.3.1 Individuals

An individual who is above 18 years of age being of sound mind and not disqualified from contracting by any law to which he is subject, can open a deposit account in terms of (Sec. 11 of Indian Contract Act, 1872). An individual can also take loans from NBFCs and also invest in term deposits of NBFCs which are approved by RBI to accept deposits.

Individuals of 18 years and above age can take loan from banks or NBFCs. Person less than 18 years cannot enter into a legally binding agreement.

2.3.2 Joint Accounts

When more than one individual opens an account, it is called a joint account. Generally joint accounts are opened by two individuals though there is no bar on more than two individuals opening the accounts. In case of joint accounts, it is necessary to clearly give the operational instructions as to whom all will operate the accounts and how the balance in the account is to be paid if the account is closed.

For ease of operations in the account, the account holders will have to give instructions to the bank about who would be operating the account. Such accounts can be operated by anyone of the account holders or jointly by two or more account holders. The operating instructions given by the joint account holders should be explicit, unambiguous and would be accepted as per the original wish confirmed by all in writing. Normally, the types of operational instructions in case of deposit accounts could be:

(1) **'Either or survivor'**, where in the account can be operated by any one of the joint holders and in the event of closure of account, the deposit can be repaid to anyone and in the event of death of a joint holder to the survivor,

(2) '**Former or survivor**', wherein the account will be operated only by the first named depositor and the balance will be payable to only the first named depositor or if the first named is deceased, the survivor, as the case may be,

(3) **'Both jointly or survivor',** wherein the account will be operated jointly and the money repayable to both jointly and the survivor, if any one of the joint holders is deceased,

(4) '**Any two jointly or last survivor**' wherein the number of account holders is more than two and any two will operate the account. On decease of all the account holders, the money's repayable to the last survivor

In case of loans taken by individual - the individual uses the loan and is responsible for repayment.

In the case of loans by two or more borrowers *i.e.* jointly, both or all the borrowers are individually and severally (jointly) liable for the full amount of loan. Thus, if one of the persons does not pay, the other(s) will have to pay the full amount of dues. As such, in case of joint borrowers, banks/lenders do not indicate the share of each borrower. Banks or NBFCs will not agree for any statement or condition which would indicate that each of the signatory is only partially responsible for the loan.

2.3.3 Illiterate Persons

Illiterate persons, who cannot sign, are allowed to open savings account (without cheque facility) or fixed deposit account. Current account is not generally opened for such persons. Withdrawals are permitted in the account through withdrawal slip on production of the passbook and after verification of the thumb impression and against proper identification of the account holder. Now-a-days withdrawals by ATM cards and mobile banking are also allowed. Illiteracy does not mean inability to understand or execute digital transactions. Additionally, banks undertake financial literacy programmes for such individuals.

If an illiterate person were to take a loan from any financial institution, then it would be necessary to explain the terms and conditions in the presence of witness and record the same. As per law there is no bar on issuing loans to illiterate customers.

2.3.4 Minors

A person who has not completed 18 years of age is considered as a minor, irrespective of the fact that a guardian of this person or his estate is appointed by the Court before he completes 18th year. According to the Indian Contract Act, 1872, a minor is not capable of entering into a valid contract and a contract entered into by a minor is void ab initio (i.e. from the beginning).

A banker should, therefore, be very careful in dealing with a minor and take the following precautions:

(*i*) A savings/fixed/recurring bank deposit account can be opened by a minor of any age through his/her natural or legally appointed guardian.

(*ii*) Minors above the age of 10 years may be allowed to open and operate savings bank accounts independently, if they so desire. upon completion of KYC formalities.

(*iii*) On attaining majority, the erstwhile minor should confirm the balance in his/her account and if the account is operated by the natural guardian/legal guardian, fresh operating instructions and specimen signature of erstwhile minor should be obtained and kept on record for all operational purposes.

(*iv*) Banks are free to offer additional banking facilities like internet banking, ATM/debit card, cheque book facility etc., subject to the safeguards that minor accounts are not allowed to be overdrawn and that these always remain in credit.

2.3.5 Blind Persons

Blind persons are competent to enter into a contract. They can open and maintain any type of bank accounts. However, following precautions are to be taken while opening and maintaining such accounts:

(*i*) Various risks in operations of the account should be explained to the account holder

(*ii*) Joint account with close relative can be opened

(*iii*) Cash receipts and payments should be made in presence of witness preferably bank customer

(*iv*) Account opening form etc. should be stamped "blind person"

(*v*) For withdrawal of the amount, he/she should come personally.

2.3.6 Proprietorship concerns

A business or enterprise carried out by an individual in his/her own name or singly is known as Sole Proprietorship. This is the oldest and the most common form of business. In this case a single individual owns, manages, and controls the business. Often the funds of business and personal funds are mixed.

A proprietor can borrow in his own name and open a bank account in his own name or the given name for the business. He is the owner of the business, and all profits accrue to him. If he were to take a loan, he is personally responsible for repayment of loan. In India majority of the bank loans and majority of NBFC loans are given to household sector which consists mainly of individuals and proprietorships. This includes business, retail, and personal loans.

2.3.7 Partnership firms

A Partnership is defined under Section 4 of the Indian Partnership Act, 1932, as "the relationship between persons who have agreed to share the profits of business carried on by all or any of them acting for all."

The Partnership Act does not provide for the compulsory registration of a firm. However, from the lenders perspective registration is necessary as an unregistered firm cannot sue others for any cause relating to the firm's business whereas it can be sued by the outsiders irrespective of its registration. Lending to unregistered firms could face difficulty as the partnership may not be able to recover its dues which could affect the quality of the loan.

The minimum number of partners in a partnership firm is two. The maximum number of partners prescribed by the Central Government is 50 and u/s. 464 of the Companies Act is 100.

Lenders/Bankers should ensure that the following requirements are complied with while lending to and opening account for partnership:

(1) The account is opened in the name of the firm and the forms/documents are signed by all the partners of the firm.

(2) A copy of the Partnership Deed executed by all the partners (whether registered or not) is obtained and kept with the lender.

(3) Partnership letter signed by all the partners is obtained to ensure their several and joint liabilities. The letter governs the operation of the account and is to be adhered to accordingly.

(4) The account has to be signed 'for and on behalf of the firm' by all the authorized partners and not in an individual name.

(5) A cheque payable to the firm cannot be endorsed by a partner in his name and credited to his personal account.

(6) In case the firm is to furnish a guarantee to the bank, all the partners have to sign the document.

(7) If a partner (who has furnished his individual property as a security for the loan granted to the firm) dies, no further borrowings would be permitted in the account until an alternative for the deceased partner is arranged for, as the rule in Clayton's case operates.

2.3.8 Limited Liability Partnership

Limited Liability Partnership (LLP) is a body corporate and a legal entity separate from its partners. The provisions of Indian Partnership Act, 1932 shall not be applicable to LLPs, since LLP is in the form of a body corporate. An LLP has to be incorporated with a minimum of two persons. Limited Liability Partnership, a legal form available world-wide, was introduced in India with effect from April, 2009. It is governed by Limited Liability Partnership Act, 2008.

Main features:

- LLP is a legal entity separate from its partners and it can own assets in its name, sue and be sued.
- It has perpetual succession (unlike normal partnership, death of partner does not affect the LLP)
- Unlike corporate shareholders (who cannot individually manage the company) partners have the right to manage the business directly.
- One partner is not responsible or liable for another partner's misconduct or negligence except in certain cases.
- Liability of the partners is limited to the extent of his/her contribution in the LLP. No exposure of personal assets of the partner, except in cases of fraud.
- LLP should have minimum 2 partners. Out of the two individuals, at least one of them should be resident of India. There is no limit on maximum No. of partners.
- Partners can be resident individuals, a company, or an LLP.
- The business objective should be for profit.
- The rights and duties of partners in LLP are governed by an agreement between partners. The partners have the flexibility to devise the agreement as per their choice.
- LLP shall maintain annual accounts. Audit of accounts is required if the contribution exceeds Rs. 25 Lakh or annual turnover exceeds Rs. 40 Lakh.
- Registrar of Companies (RoC) shall be having authority over the incorporation of LLP

The LLPs are eligible to avail loans from the banks and NBFCs. The account and documentation formalities are like that of partnership.

2.3.9 Limited Company

Limited Companies are governed by the Companies Act, 2013. A Company is incorporated under the Companies Act, 2013 and is a separate entity from its members.

There are four types of the companies:

(1) Public Limited Company (2) Private Limited Company (3) Government Company (4) One Person Company.

1. Private Limited Company:

A private limited company is one which has the following characteristics:

(*i*) It has a minimum of two members and a maximum of 200 members.

(*ii*) A private company restricts the rights of members to transfer their shares.

(*iii*) It prohibits any invitation to the public to subscribe to its shares and debentures.

(*iv*) Does not invite general public to invest deposits in the company

(*v*) No minimum paid-up capital is required.

(*vi*) It can commence business upon incorporation without obtaining any Certificate of commencement of business; etc.

A private company is an ideal form of organization when a business is to be expanded at a large scale without involving large number of shareholding groups.

2. Public Company:

According to Companies Act, a "public limited company" means which :

(*a*) is not a private company;

(*b*) need not maintain any minimum paid-up capital

A public company has the following traits:

(*i*) It is formed with a minimum of seven members.

(*ii*) It invites general public to subscribe to its shares.

(*iii*) There is no restriction on the maximum number of members.

(*iv*) It permits the transfer of shares.

(*v*) It must allot shares within 120 days from the issue of prospectus.

(*vi*) Certificate of commencement of business is required for commencement of business, etc.

3. Government Company:

A "Government company" means any company in which not less than fifty-one per cent of the paid-up share capital is held by the Central Government, or by any State Government or Governments, or partly by the Central Government and partly by one or more State Governments, and includes a company which is a subsidiary company of such a government company.

4. One Person Company:

One Person Company (OPC) introduced by Companies Act, 2013, is a new form of business entity. OPC is a hybrid of sole-proprietor and company form of business, that enables sole-proprietors to enter into a corporate framework.

Features of OPC:

The following are the important features of the One Person Company (OPC)

- OPC is one type of company distinct from its owner.
- OPC has only one person as a member/shareholder.
- There is no minimum requirement of paid-up share capital for OPC.
- Any person whether an Indian or not can form an OPC whereas previously NRIs were not allowed to incorporate OPCs. He will hold entire shareholding of the company. A person can be a shareholder in only one OPC at any given time *i.e.* he cannot have two different OPCs in his name.

The Shareholder is to nominate another person who shall become the shareholders in case of death/incapacity of the original shareholder. Such nominee is to give consent for being appointed as the nominee for the sole shareholder. Only a natural person, who is an Indian citizen and resident in India can be a nominee. If the nominee becomes the member of an OPC or is already a member of another OPC, he has to decide within 6 months with which OPC he shall continue. The nominee can be changed any time.

2.3.10 Joint Hindu Family or Hindu Undivided Family (HUF)

Under Hindu Law, an HUF is a family (business unit) which consists of all persons lineally descended from a common ancestor and includes their wives and unmarried daughters. An HUF cannot be created by a contract. It is created automatically in a Hindu Family. As per the law when a Hindu dies, leaving a business it passes on to the heirs and property becomes the Joint Hindu Family property. The eldest member is called 'Karta' and the members (male as well as female) of the family are called 'coparceners'. HUF cannot be admitted as a partner in a partnership firm. Hindu Undivided Family (HUF) is treated as a 'person' under Section 2(*31*) of the Income Tax Act, 1961 and HUF is a separate entity for the purpose of assessment under the Act.

HUF can open an account in its name and borrow in its name. The HUF is responsible for the repayment of loans and its assets can be attached for loans due if any. The property of HUF is distinct from the property owned in individual names of the co-

parceners. The Karta has the authority to borrow money for the family or ancestral business. In the eye of law, in case a loan is granted to HUF, coparcener's liability is limited to the extent of their interest in the joint property. The Hindu Succession (Amendment) Act, 2005 has given equal rights to male and female in the matters of inheritance. As a result, a daughter also acquires status of coparcener in a HUF. In view of this, in the absence of any male member or all male member(s) is/are minor, a Hindu female member can become Karta/manager of HUF.

Following precautions to be taken while dealing with such accounts:

1. HUF letter should be signed by the Karta and all the major coparceners.
2. The account is to be operated by the 'Karta' only.
3. Names of the minor coparceners should be kept on record and on attaining the majority a fresh letter of HUF duly signed by all to be obtained.
4. Death, Lunacy, insolvency of the members does not affect the operations in the account.

2.3.11 Trust, Associations, Clubs, Societies

Non-profit entities viz. Trusts, Associations, Societies and Clubs (TASC) are allowed to open their accounts. These entities need to be registered as per the respective State Acts in this regard. However, banks need to exercise caution in case accounts of non registered entities are being opened. While opening an account in the name of registered body, following documents should be obtained:

(1) Copy of Certificate of Registration.
(2) Copy of trust deed or byelaws, rules, and regulations.
(3) Copy of resolution of the trustees/managing committee/governing body etc.
(4) A list of the members of the trust/managing committee.
(5) No advance including temporary overdraft (TOD) should be permitted.

2.4 DIFFERENT TYPES OF BANKER-CUSTOMER RELATIONSHIP

When a bank, NBFC or a Fintech lends to a borrower, it enters a legal relationship. Following are the implied relationships that one can enter:—

Creditor-Debtor: This is a relationship between the customer having a deposit account, where the depositor is the creditor, and the banker is the debtor. NBFCs cannot accept deposits except term deposits that too only if approved by RBI. If NBFC accepts deposit, the Creditor- Debtor relationship prevails.

Debtor-Creditor: When the customer avails a loan or an advance, then his relationship with the lender/banker is one of the debtor-creditor. The borrower is the debtor and the lender/banker a creditor.

Beneficiary-Trustee: If a customer keeps certain valuables or securities with a bank for safe-keeping or deposits a certain amount of money for a specific purpose, the banker, besides becoming a bailee, is also a trustee. The money or the securities so kept are not at the disposal of the bank. The banker cannot utilize those moneys or securities at his pleasure as the money does not belong to him. The security given by the borrower to the lender as collateral for the loan comes under this relationship.

Principal-Agent: Banks provide ancillary services such as collection of cheques, bills etc. They also undertake to pay regularly, as per standing instructions, the electricity bills, phone bills, Insurance premium, etc. of the customer. The relationship arising out of these ancillary services is that of principal-agent between the customer and the bank.

It is important to note that the proceeds of the cheques sent for collection, which are in transit, not credited to the customer's account do not become the money of the lender/banker till such time as they are credited into the customer account.

Lessee-Lessor: Banks provide safe deposit lockers to the customers who hire them on lease basis. The relationship, therefore, is that of lessee (Customer) and lessor (Bank). This can also be called as licensee and licensor. Technically a bank leases out the locker space for the use of clients. The bank is not responsible for any loss that arises to the lessee in this form of transaction except where the loss could be attributed to the negligence of that bank.

Indemnifier-Indemnified: The customer is indemnifier, and the bank is indemnified. A contract by which one party promises to save the other from loss caused to him by the conduct of the promisor himself or the conduct of any other person is called a contract of indemnity.

In the case of banking, this relationship happens in transactions of issue of duplicate demand draft, fixed deposit receipt, etc. The underlying point in these cases is that the customer will compensate the Bank of any loss arising from the wrong/excess payment.

Bailer and Bailment: A bailment is the delivery of goods in trust. A bank may accept the valuables of its customer such as documents, and securities for safe custody. In such a case the customer is the Bailer, and the bank is bailee. As per section 148 of Indian Contract Act, 1872 the delivery of goods from one person to the other for some purpose with a condition or contract that the goods will be returned when the purpose is accomplished is bailment.

Pledger and Pledgee: When a customer pledges goods and documents as security for an advance, he then becomes a pledger, and the lender/bank becomes the pledgee.

The pledged goods are to be returned intact or in original condition to the debtor if advance repaid by the debtor.

Mortgagor and mortgagee: Mortgage is the transfer of an interest in specific immovable property for the purpose of securing the payment of money advanced or to be advanced by way of loan. When a customer mortgages specific immovable property with the lender/bank as security for advance, the customer becomes mortgagor, and the bank is the mortgagee. Mortgage may not involve change of possession of the item mortgaged.

Each of the above relationship has certain duties and responsibilities. The relationships is diagrammatically presented as below:

Transactions	**Relationship**	
	Bank	**Customer**
Deposit Account with bank	Debtors	Creditors
Loan from the Bank	Creditors	Debtors
Locker	Lessor	Lessee
Safe custody of Articles	Bailee	Bailor
Collection of Bills/Cheques	Agent	Principal
Purchase of DD/MT/TT	Debtors	Creditors
Payment of Draft	Trustee	Beneficiary
Pledge of goods	Pledgee	Pledger
Mortgage	Mortgagee	Mortgager
Standing instruction	Agent	Principal
Article left by the bank	Trustee	Beneficiary
Hypothecation of goods	Hypothecatee	Hypothecator
Assignment of securities	Assignee	Assignor
Indemnity	Indemnifier	Indemnified

FIGURE 2.1 : BANK-CUSTOMER RELATIONSHIP

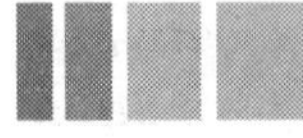

2.5 DUTIES OF A LENDER/BANK

(1) Duty to maintain the secrecy about customer's account

(2) Duty to honour the cheque

(3) Duty to maintain record of transactions and issue passbook, statement of account etc.,

(4) Duty to collect the Cheques, bills, etc. and accept payments through electronic or digital mode

2.5.1 Lenders/Bank's duty to maintain secrecy of customer's accounts

When a person opens an account in a bank, he/she should be sure that information regarding the account be it deposits or loans, remain a matter of knowledge only between the lender or bank and the borrower or account holder. Thus, one of the principal duties of the financial institution is to maintain complete secrecy of customer's account. This obligation to maintain secrecy continues even after the customer's account is closed. If the institution makes an unwarranted disclosure of their customer's account to any other person, even a close relative of the customer, it is liable to compensate the customer. However, the lenders/bank's obligation of keeping the secrecy of the customer's account is subject to some conditions and not absolute. There are certain circumstances in which the lender/banker is entitled or required to make disclosures about a customer's account.

Let us understand the conditions under which a banker is justified in making disclosure.

i. **Disclosures permitted by Law:**

Legally an NBFC/Lender/Bank is justified to disclose any information about the customer's account when it is statutorily required to do so under:

- Income-tax Act, 1961
- Companies Act, 1956/2013
- Bankers Book Evidence Act, 1891
- Reserve Bank of India Act, 1934. RBI requires lenders/banks to share specific customer information with credit bureaus. It may ask for details of defaulted accounts, etc.
- Foreign Exchange Management Act, 1999
- Gift-tax Act, 1958
- Right to Information Act, 2005.

ii. **Under expresed or implied consent of the customer:**

When an account is opened with a bank, there is an implied contract between the customer and the Bank that the bank will not disclose any information relating to customer's account without customers' consent. Wherever a customer permits this information can be disclosed it is necessary to obtain the customer's consent before disclosing the information. The consent can be expressed or implied. For example, a customer may permit giving information about his/her account to a prospective guarantor or customer dealing with him in his business.

In case of loans, it is necessary that the customer is made aware that the lender could share the information about loans, dues, defaults, etc. to the collection agents or employees for contacting the borrower and collecting the amounts. It would be better if this is indicated specifically and accepted by the customer.

Also, information could be shared with the advocates/lawyers once it has been decided to take legal recourse to recovery/collection.

iii. **Disclosure in the bank's interest:**

A bank or lending institution can disclose information when it is essential to protect its own interest, legally. For instance, if there is any dispute between the customer and the lender/banker, regarding balance standing or due in the account of the customer or if there is a loan in default, then the lender/bank will be justified in revealing the information to the guarantor or to a solicitor for initiating legal proceedings in the court of law.

The sharing of information between a bank and DRA, business correspondent/ facilitator will fall under this head. It is necessary that the information shared with agent is exclusive and not to put to other uses.

iv. **Disclosure in Public/National interest:**

Banker may be required to make disclosure in the interest of the nation and public at large. Public interest may be considered only according to the prevailing circumstances.

2.5.2 Precautions to be adopted while disclosing information

Collection function involves sharing of information with collection agents and they in turn share it with the customer. It is important that collection agents share information only with the customers (borrowers) and with their family that too only if the borrower has consented for the same. Sharing important information with other agencies or others or on any digital platform can lead to poor collection efficiency and termination of duties. Such acts can cause reputation risk for the borrower and tarnish the image of the bank/NBFC as well.

A banker should exercise due caution while disclosing the financial status information of his customers. Undue or irrelevant information may make the bank liable for compensation. Besides that, due to use of such information by the third party, bank may suffer loss. It is, therefore, necessary, wherever permitted to note the following points:

i. **Only data or facts should be revealed:** Only such facts as are evident from the customer's account to be revealed. In other words, the disclosure should not be based on hearsay or rumours. Lender should not add interpretation or opinion.

ii. **Statement should be in general:** Banker/lender should give information about the customer's financial position in a general form. Terms commonly said and understood in the banking industry like 'ordinary, 'fair', good', excellent, 'satisfactory, 'unsatisfactory; 'in the ordinary course of business', etc., may be used for describing the means, credit standing of a customer. IBA has introduced a standard format for opinion reports. Based on worth of the person/entity the means or worth could be indicated as High or Medium or Low.

iii. **Secrecy should be maintained by the recipient also:** The banker should clearly state while giving the information that the recipient should maintain absolute secrecy of information furnished.

iv. **Confidentiality of Information:** It is the practice among lenders/bankers to state while sharing information about customers with others, other lenders or bankers that the information is being furnished in strictest confidence and that the institution giving the information is not responsible and liable for the information so given, further making it explicit that the recipient should also treat it as confidential.

v. **Information should not be given to persons out of context and without proper justification:** If any person not directly concerned with a customer solicits information on his account, the request from such a person is out of context and hence the banker should not make disclosure.

2.5.3 Furnishing of Opinions: Important Aspects

One of the important duties of a bank is to submit an opinion report on its customer if asked for by a fellow banker. A lender/banker is also required to obtain credit reports or opinion from other bankers before processing application for credit facilities if the customer has been banking with the other bankers earlier. While obtaining guarantees from a third party, not known to the bank or while sanctioning bills purchase/discount/book debts facility, etc. lender may call for opinion report from other banks/agencies.

2.6 RIGHTS OF A LENDER

A lender has primary rights namely:

(*i*) Right of Lien

(*ii*) Right of Set-Off

(*iii*) Right of Appropriation and

(*iv*) Right to act as per mandate given by the customers

2.6.1 Right of General Lien

Lien is the right of a creditor to retain possession of goods and securities belonging to the debtor till the debts due to creditor are paid. This right is available only on goods and securities and not on balances in the accounts. A lien can be Particular Lien or General Lien.

A General Lien gives the creditor a right to retain the goods and securities belonging to the debtor for all dues payable by him/her. This right is available only to bankers, factors, and attorneys. Banker's Lien is a general lien. This is an implied pledge because the banker has right to retain as well as sell goods of the borrower, in banks' possession after giving him/her reasonable notice.

A lender (NBFC) can exercise the right of lien subject to the conditions that (*a*) the goods and/or securities and debt are in the same right and same capacity (*b*) the loan is due or overdue and lawful, and (*c*) reasonable notice has been given by the lender to the debtor. It is important to note that the right of Lien is available only on the goods and securities received in the ordinary course of business.

Sec. 171 of the Indian Contract Act, 1872 gives a right of General Lien to the Lender.

2.6.2 Right of Set-Off

Right of Set-Off is the right to combine two or more accounts having debit and credit balance. This right is not provided by any Act. It is available due to implied contract. This right arises when two parties are debtor as well as creditor to each other *i.e.*, one account is in debit and another account is in credit. For banks, this right arises when it wants to combine its loan due from a borrower with his/her deposit accounts. For exercising right of set-off following conditions should be satisfied:

i. Both accounts should be in same right and same capacity. For example, a Term deposit in joint names cannot be used to set-off against a retail loan on a single name.

ii. The debt should be due and not accruing due. This means future due cannot be recovered under set-off process. For example, a customer has balance in his/her deposit account and has taken a retail loan where instalments are due in future. The balance in FD account cannot be set off against future instalments due.

iii. Reasonable notice should be given or sent to the depositor before exercising set off.

iv. If the amount is kept under trust (safe custody), the bank cannot exercise the right against a debit balance on another account.

v. The account of a sole proprietor (of a trading firm) and his individual account cannot be combined.

vi. No right of set-off is available in Joint accounts.

2.6.3 Right of Appropriation

The customer, who deposits the amount, has a right to clarify the purpose and account against which the credit is to be given by the banker. It means it is the duty of the customer to specify the nature of the transactions. If he fails to mention the purpose, then banker has a right to adjust the credit against any debit/dues. This is called the right of appropriation.

The bank has the right of appropriation when there are two or more debts owing from a borrower and the latter makes a payment to the bank. In such cases the appropriation should be done :-

(*i*) Specific intimation or under circumstances implying that the payment is to be applied to discharge of some particular debt, the payment should be appropriated accordingly.

(*ii*) Where there are no intimation and the borrower omitted to mention, the creditor can appropriate at his discretion to any lawful debt actually due and payable to him from the debtor.

(*iii*) Where neither the party makes any appropriation, the payment shall be applied in discharge of the debts in the order of time, whether they are or are not barred by the law in force for the time being as to the limitation of suits.

(*iv*) Application of famous Clayton's case (1816) where it was ruled that in case of current accounts, payment in the absence of any express indication to the contrary by the customer, are presumed to have been appropriated to the debit items in order of date. Thus, the appropriation of payments in order of dates is known as "Rule in Clayton's case."

RULE IN CLAYTON'S CASE

The Rule was laid down in [*Devaynes* v. *Noble* (1816) 35ER 767, 781; (1816) I Mer. 529, 572]. It is applicable in case of loans such as cash credit and overdraft where the customer deposits and withdraws money from the account frequently. As per this rule, the order in which the credit entry will set off the debit entry is the chronological order. This means that the first item on the debit side will be the item to be discharged or reduced by a subsequent item on the credit side.

The rule operates in case of :

- death or insolvency or insanity of a borrower(s),
- death, insolvency, insanity, retirement of partner,

- insolvency of guarantor or revocation of guarantee by the guarantor in a loan account,

The existing debt due from the borrower is adjusted if subsequent credit is allowed. If fresh debits are allowed, these are considered a fresh loan and the bank cannot recover such debt from the assets of the deceased, retired or insolvent partner and may ultimately suffer the loss if the debt cannot be recovered from the remaining partners.

Example: A firm's loan account is showing a debit balance of Rs. 3 Lakh when notice of death of one partner is received. Bank however, allows operations by surviving partners. A sum of Rs. 1 Lakh is debited to the account and Rs. 0.50 Lakh is credited. The debit balance now is Rs. 3.50 Lakh. The legal heirs are liable or Rs. 2.50 Lakh (3 Lakh minus 0.50 Lakh).

How to stop operation of the Clayton's rule: To avoid the operation of the rule, the bank should stop the operations in the account and break the account. Thus, the liability of the deceased or insolvent partner at the time of his death, retirement or insolvency is determined/crystallized and his estate may be liable.

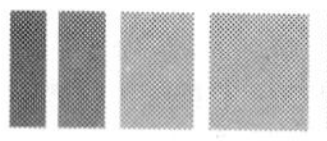

2.7 GARNISHEE ORDER

Provision relating to Garnishee order are under Sec. 60 of the Code of Civil Procedure, 1908. The procedure is described in Rule 46 of order XXI of the Schedule to the Code of Civil Procedure.

'GARNISHEE ORDER' is an order issued by a court on the request of a creditor for attachment of funds of the Judgment debtor available with his bank. The creditor is called Judgment creditor. The debtor is called the judgment debtor and the Bank (the judgment debtor's debtor) on whom the order is served, is called Garnishee.

When the Garnishee order is received, the relationship between the banker and customer is suspended temporarily if the balance in the account is less than amount of order. Bank has no obligation to pay cheques issued by the depositor.

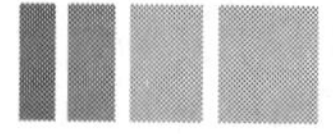

2.8 INCOME TAX ATTACHMENT ORDERS

Income Tax Authorities can issue attachment orders for recovery of Govt. dues, revenue, or tax etc. On receipt of this order, banker/lender is required to remit the desired amount to income tax authorities. An order without mentioning the amount is not a valid order.

Attachment Order is different from Garnishee order in following respects namely:

(*i*) Attachment Order applies to money deposited in the account after receipt of order also till it is fully satisfied whereas Garnishee order does not apply to subsequent deposits.

(*ii*) Attachment Order in single name applies to joint accounts also proportionately unless the contrary is proved whereas Garnishee order in single name does not apply to joint accounts.

(*iii*) However, right of set off is available to bank before applying the order.

(*iv*) If banks fail to comply with Attachment Order, it will be liable under the order and be deemed as the assessee in default.

(*v*) When both Garnishee order and Attachment Order are received simultaneously, priority should be given to attachment order.

2.9 CLOSING AN ACCOUNT

When an account is closed, the lender/bank must return customers documents that have been given by him/her for the purpose of loan or account. These documents must be given back in good condition. Further if the customer has pledged some valuables or mortgaged property the lender will have to take steps to return the same within a specified time.

Closure of account brings the contractual relationship to a close.

2.10 LET US SUM UP

From individual to companies, many types of customers who can open a bank account or take a loan from an institution. Customers that can be classified depending on the interaction of customers with the bank:

(*a*) Individual - Individuals who are 18 years and above can open a bank account.

(*b*) Joint account - When one or more individuals open an account, it is called a joint account.

(*c*) Illiterate account - Individuals who cannot read/write can also open a bank account and take loan with their thumb impression for documentation.

(*d*) Proprietorship concerns - A business carried out by an individual in his/her own name is called sole proprietorship.

(*e*) Partnership firms - People who have agreed to share profits of business carried out by the members.

(*f*) Limited Liability Partnership - Partnership in which some or more partners have limited liabilities.

(*g*) Private limited company - A private company owned by minimum 2 and maximum 200 members.

(*h*) Joint Hindu family - Consists of a family business which descendants of a family can run.

(*i*) Clubs/Associations - Membership of clubs is given to members only.

Based on these types of customers, there are different types of Lender-customer relationships like Creditor-Debtor; Debtor-Creditor; Beneficiary-Trustee and more. As a lender, banks also have many duties to fulfil. Some important duties of Banks include:

1. Duty to maintain secrecy about customer's account.
2. Duty to collect cheques, bills, etc.
3. Duty to maintain record of transactions.

Lender's/bank's duty to maintain secrecy of customer's accounts: When a person opens an account in a bank, the bank and the borrower need to maintain complete secrecy and confidentiality of the customer's information. Banks often must disclose information to authorities based on certain conditions and these conditions are listed below:

(*a*) Disclosures permitted by Law : Sometimes banks need to justify information based on different acts of law.

(*b*) With consent of the customer : Banks can disclose information based on the consent received from customers.

(*c*) Amongst bankers: Sometimes data is shared with other banks for reference purposes.

(*d*) Disclosure in banks and national interest: Data is shared often to safeguard the interest of the bank or the national reputation.

Some Precautions to be adopted while disclosing information:

1. Only data or facts should be revealed.
2. Statement should be in general.
3. Secrecy should be maintained by the recipient.
4. Confidentiality of information.

Submitting opinion reports in a genuine and authentic manner is also a responsibility given to Banks.

2.11 KEY WORDS

Different types of customers, lender customer, mortgage, indemnifier, Bailor-bailee, proprietorship, partnership, garnishee, attachment orders, right of set-off, right of appropriation

2.12 CHECK YOUR PROGRESS

1. The term Customer has been defined in:
   (*a*) Negotiable Instruments Act
   (*b*) RBI Act
   (*c*) Banking Regulation Act
   (*d*) PMLA 2005
2. When a banker allows overdraft to his customer, the relationship between his customer and him is that of:
   (*a*) Bailor and Bailee
   (*b*) Lessor and Lessee
   (*c*) Debtor and Creditor
   (*d*) Creditor and Debtor
3. When a customer takes a locker in the bank, what is the relationship between the bank and the Customer?
   (*a*) Lessor and Lessee
   (*b*) Principal and Agent
   (*c*) Trustee-Beneficiary
   (*d*) None of the above
4. When does the Banker-Customer relationship stand terminated?
   (*a*) On the death of the customer
   (*b*) On customer becoming lunatic
   (*c*) On customer being declared insolvent
   (*d*) All of the above
5. In deposit accounts, the main relationship between bank and customer is:
   (*a*) Creditor-bank, Debtor-customer
   (*b*) Debtor-bank, Creditor-customer
   (*c*) Agent-Principal
   (*d*) Both (*a*) and (*b*)
6. Bailor-Bailee relationship is applicable in:
   (*a*) Cash deposited with cashier by customer
   (*b*) Safe deposit locker

(c) Demand draft issued by bank

(d) Keeping articles in safe custody with bank

7. What relationship is created when the bank collects a cheque in clearing?

(a) Clearing member and Principal

(b) Agent and Principal

(c) Collecting Bank and Holder

(d) None of the above

8. Attachment Order in respect of bank accounts is issued by:

(a) RBI

(b) Ombudsman

(c) IBA

(d) Tax Authorities

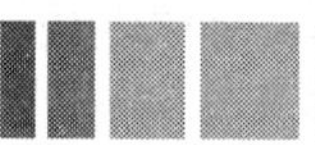

2.13 ANSWERS TO CHECK YOUR PROGRESS

1.	(d)	2.	(c)	3.	(a)	4.	(d)	5.	(b)	6.	(d)	7.	(b)	8.	(d)

CHAPTER

3 Various Deposit Schemes and Other Services

3.1 OBJECTIVES

Debt Recovery Agents are the extended arms of the bank and it is important to have a basic understanding of the important deposit products of the bank. After reading this chapter, the reader would understand:

- Types of Deposits
- Remittances
- Safe Deposit Lockers and Safe Custody of Articles

3.2 INTRODUCTION

Banks provide various types of services to its clients. Acceptance of deposits is one of its important functions. Banks have developed numerous deposit schemes which serve the needs of every clientele. Names of deposit schemes may vary from bank to bank but broadly, there are two types of deposits. One is demand deposit and the other is term deposit. Other services provided by banks like remittances, collection of cheques and bills, safe deposit lockers and safe custody of articles are widely used by its customers and, therefore, knowledge about these services is also important.

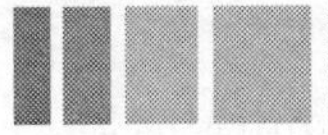

3.3 TYPES OF DEPOSITS

Deposits of banks are broadly classified into three categories:

(*i*) Demand deposits which are repayable on demand by the customers. These comprise of:

- Current account deposits
- Savings bank deposits

(*ii*) Term deposits that are repayable on maturity dates as agreed between the customers and the banker. These deposits comprise of:

- Fixed deposits
- Recurring/Cumulative deposits

(*iii*) Hybrid deposits or flexi deposits which combine the features of demand and term deposits. These deposits have been introduced by some banks to meet customers' financial needs and convenience and are known by different names in different banks.

3.4 DEMAND DEPOSITS

(*i*) *Current Accounts* : A current account is a form of demand deposit with facility of multiple deposits and withdrawals. In current account, withdrawals are allowed any number of times depending upon the balance in the account or upto a particular agreed amount and shall also be deemed to include other deposit accounts which are neither savings deposit nor term deposits. Since such deposits are repayable on demand, they constitute the demand liabilities of the bank.

Current accounts, particularly suit the requirements of business, trading, limited companies, institutions, public authorities and public corporations, etc. whose banking transactions happen to be numerous on every working day.

The main features of current accounts are:

- There are no restrictions on the number and amount of withdrawals/ deposits. Hence, this account is maintained for the purpose of business activity.
- Cheque book facility is provided to each current account holder. Withdrawals are permitted by cheques. There is no restriction on the number of cheques that can be transacted in a day.
- Balances in the current accounts do not earn any interest. Banks are not allowed to pay interest or brokerage in any form to the current account holders.
- The account holder gets periodical statements of accounts from the bank giving the details of transactions for customer's verification and record. The statement of account would show date-wise the entire debit and credit transactions and balances, as recorded in the bank's ledger account of the customer.

(*ii*) *Savings Bank Accounts* : Savings bank deposit (designated as Saving bank account) means a form of deposit account primarily meant for developing the habit of saving among the public. In addition to getting nominal interest on the balance in the account, the depositor has the freedom to withdraw the amount deposited as and when he/she desires subject to certain restrictions on the number of withdrawals. The relationship between the bank and the depositor is essentially that of "debtor and creditor" respectively. Savings bank accounts should be maintained in accordance with the Bank's rules framed for the conduct of such accounts and also in conformity with the directives issued by the RBI from time to time.

Savings accounts can be opened by individuals, guardians (on behalf of their minor children/wards), minors above the age of 10 years, trusts, HUF, etc.

The Savings bank accounts are of two types:

(*a*) Accounts with cheque book facility in which withdrawals are permitted by cheques drawn in favour of self or other parties. The payees of cheques can receive payment in cash at the drawee bank branch or through their bank account *via* clearing or collection. The account holder may also withdraw cash by filling up withdrawal form or in ATM.

(*b*) Accounts without cheque book where withdrawals are permitted to the account holders only at the drawee bank branch by filling up a withdrawal form or letter accompanied with the account passbook. In such accounts, third parties cannot receive payments.

The main features of Savings bank accounts are as follows:

- Withdrawals are permitted on demand of the account holder by presentment of cheques or withdrawal form/letter. However, cash withdrawals in excess of the specified amount per transaction/day (the amount varies from bank to bank) require prior notice to the bank branch. Banks stipulate certain restrictions on the number of withdrawals per month/quarter, amount of withdrawal per day, minimum balance to be maintained in the account on all days, etc. and levy fee/penalty for violations of these rules. These rules are different for different banks. The rationale of these restrictions is that the savings bank account should not be used like a current account, as it is primarily intended for keeping and accumulating the savings.
- Banks pay interest on the daily balance maintained in the account at the prescribed rate. Banks are free to decide interest rate on Savings Bank account. Presently most of the banks are paying between 2.5% to 4% per annum interest on these accounts on daily balance basis. The interest can be paid on monthly/quarterly/half yearly/yearly intervals as per the policy of the bank.
- No overdraft (payment in excess of the credit balance) is allowed in a savings bank account, as there cannot be any debit balance in savings account.
- Most of the banks provide to every savings bank account holder a passbook wherein date-wise debit/credit transactions and credit balances are shown as per the customer's ledger account maintained by the bank. These days, banks

offer computer generated statement of account as per the convenience of the account holder.

Under electronic banking, a customer can access the account through internet by using a customer ID number and password assigned to him/her by the bank. The electronic banking enables the customer to transfer funds from one account to another, verify the transactions in the account etc. Now-a-days, customers can also get their account statement through e-mail. Customer can transact his account through the Mobile App of the concerned bank by using his mobile internet service.

Basic Savings Bank Deposit Account (BSBDA)

The Basic Savings Bank Deposit (BSBDA) Account, also called small account was designed as a savings account which offers certain minimum facilities, free of charge, to the holders of such accounts, being part of better customer service. Banks offer 'Basic Savings Bank Deposit Account' with the following minimum common facilities to all their customers:

i. The 'Basic Savings Bank Deposit Account' is a normal banking service available to all.

ii. This account does not have the requirement of any minimum balance.

iii. The services available in the account include deposit and withdrawal of cash at bank branch as well as ATMs; receipt/credit of money through electronic payment channels or by means of deposit/collection of cheques drawn by Central/State Governments agencies and departments.

iv. While there is no limit on the number and value of deposits that can be made in a month, account holders will be allowed a maximum of four withdrawals in a month, including ATM withdrawals.

v. Facility of ATM card or ATM-cum-Debit Card.

vi. The above facilities are provided without any charges. Further, no charge is to be levied for non-operation/activation of in-operative 'Basic Savings Bank Deposit Account'.

vii. Banks are free to evolve other requirements including pricing structure for additional value-added services beyond the stipulated basic minimum services on reasonable and transparent basis and applied in a non-discriminatory manner.

viii. The 'Basic Savings Bank Deposit Account' are subject to RBI instructions on Know Your Customer (KYC)/Anti-Money Laundering (AML) for opening of bank accounts issued from time to time. If such account is opened on the basis of simplified KYC norms, the account would additionally be treated as a 'Small Account' and would be subject to conditions stipulated for such accounts.

ix. Holders of 'Basic Savings Bank Deposit Account' are not eligible for opening any other savings bank deposit account in that bank. If a customer has any other existing savings bank deposit account in that bank, he/she will be required to close it within 30 days from the date of opening a 'Basic Savings Bank Deposit Account'.

3.5 TERM DEPOSITS

3.5.1 Fixed Deposits

"Fixed Deposit or Term Deposit" is a time deposit for a fixed period and which is withdrawable only after the expiry of the said fixed period. It does not include deposits withdrawable at notice. Fixed deposits are repayable on the fixed maturity date along with the principal and agreed interest rate for the period. Unlike current accounts and savings account, no operations are allowed to the customer in the fixed deposit account.

The main features of fixed deposits are as follows:

- Fixed deposits are accepted for specified periods at specified interest rates as mutually agreed between the depositor and the banker at the time of opening the account. Since, the interest rate on the deposit becomes contractual, it cannot be altered even though the interest rate could change - upward or downward - during the period of the deposit.
- Banks offer varying interest rates for different maturities as decided by their ALCO Commitee. The maturity-wise interest rates in a bank will, however, be uniform for all customers subject to two exceptions - high value deposits above certain cut-off value and deposits of senior citizens (above the specified age normally 60 years) may be offered higher interest rate.
- Minimum period of fixed deposit is 7 days and maximum period for which a bank may accept a deposit is, presently 10 years. Those term deposits which are held for periods of 6 months and less are called Short-Term Deposits or Short Deposits.
- A deposit receipt is issued by the bank branch accepting the fixed deposit-mentioning thereon the depositor's name, principal amount, maturity period and interest rate, dates of the deposit and maturity, etc. The deposit receipt is not a negotiable instrument nor is it transferable like a cheque.
- Banks generally agree to the customer's request for premature closure of deposits at their discretion, to accommodate the depositors' request for meeting emergent expenses. In such cases, interest is paid for the period the deposit was actually with the bank (period between the date of deposit and premature closure). The rate of interest payable in such cases of premature closure would be less as banks generally charge a penalty for withdrawal of deposits on premature basis.

- Banks also may grant overdraft/loan against the security of their fixed deposits to meet emergent liquidity requirements of the customers. The interest on such facility will be 1% to 2% higher than the interest rate offered on the fixed deposit against which the loan is taken.
- Banks are required to calculate and credit the interest payable on the deposits on a quarterly basis. However, for the convenience of the depositors, banks pay interest at different desired intervals namely monthly, quarterly, half yearly or yearly. Banks may compound the payable interest even after less than three months at times, the customer opts to reinvest the interest, in which case, the final payment on maturity is at compound rate of interest. Banks give different names to such deposits for easy identification both by the bank and also the depositor.

3.5.2 Recurring Deposits

"Recurring Deposits" or "Cumulative Deposits" are deposits, where the inputs are in equal monthly instalments and the output, on maturity, is in one lump sum. The main features of these deposits are:

- The customer deposits a certain sum of amount as per pre-fixed frequency (generally monthly/quarterly) for a specified period (12 months to 120 months). A few banks have introduced flexible recurring deposit account, in which the customer may deposit more than the pre-decided amount on monthly basis with certain stipulations of maximum amount limit.
- The interest rate payable on recurring deposits is pre-fixed and the rate of interest will be the same as payable in fixed deposit for the period for which the recurring deposits are made.
- The total amount deposited along with the interest is repaid on the maturity date. Depositor can take a loan or advance against the deposits or to have the deposit prepaid before the maturity, for meeting emergent expenses. In the latter case, the interest rate payable by the bank would be lower than the contracted rate and some penalty would also be charged.

3.6 INSURANCE OF BANK DEPOSITS BY DEPOSIT INSURANCE AND CREDIT GUARANTEE CORPORATION (DICGC)

Each depositor in a bank is insured up to a maximum of Rs. 5,00,000 (Rupees Five Lakh) for both principal and interest amount held by him in the same capacity and same right. No premium is charged from customer for the purpose. Individual Banks who are registered with DICGC bears the insurance premium cost.

The DICGC insures all deposits such as savings, fixed, current, recurring, etc. deposits except the following types of deposits:

- Deposits of foreign Governments;
- Deposits of Central/State Governments;
- Inter-bank deposits;
- Deposits of the State Land Development Banks with the State co-operative bank;
- Any amount due on account of and deposit received outside India;
- Any amount, which has been specifically exempted by the corporation with the previous approval of Reserve Bank of India.

3.7 REMITTANCES

Funds Remittance means transfer of money from one party to another, either inland or overseas. In banking, there are multiple remittance products both traditional as well as electronic channels.

In banking transactions, instruments like demand drafts (or, banker's draft) and travellers cheques are used frequently by customers and the public. All these are issued by banks and are similar to the negotiable instruments (*i.e.*, cheque, or bill of exchange, or promissory note) as defined in Negotiable Instruments Act, 1881. The features of these other instruments are as follows:

3.7.1 Banker's Drafts

A banker's draft (or demand draft) is a payment order issued by one branch of a bank upon other branch, instructing the drawee branch to pay the specified sum of money to the specified person. A demand draft is always drawn, payable to order. A demand draft resembles a bill of exchange, the only difference being that in the former, the drawer (bank) and the drawee (bank) are same. The definition of bill of exchange in NI Act does not state that the drawer and drawee have to be different. It merely states a bill of exchange should be signed by the maker and that the drawee should be a 'certain person'. A bank draft can therefore be treated as a bill of exchange and also a cheque since it is payable on demand and is drawn on a banker.

Demand drafts provide another mode of transfer of money from one account to another at different centres. A demand draft is a negotiable instrument payable to a certain person or to the order thereof, drawn by one branch of a bank on another branch of the same bank, or specific branch of another specific bank with which the drawer bank has draft-drawing agency arrangements. The drawer bank, drawee bank and the beneficiary are three parties to a bank draft. The amount payable to

the beneficiary is definite and certain because the drawee is a bank that is expected to honour its obligation on presentment of the draft.

Draft is issued by the drawer branch after realizing the entire amount plus the exchange or fee related to the amount of the draft from the applicant. Drafts provide float funds to the bank (drawer and drawee) as there would always be time gaps between the issuance and presentment of drafts for payment at the drawee branches.

Remittance of Funds for Value Rs. 50,000 and above:

Banks should ensure that any remittance of funds by way of demand drafts/mail transfers/telegraphic transfers or any other mode and issue of travellers cheques for value of Rs. 50,000 and above is effected only by debit to the customer's account or against cheques or other instruments tendered by the purchaser and not against cash payment.

3.7.2 Electronic Funds Transfer

Traditionally, the funds were transferred by banks from one party to another by mail transfer and telegraphic transfer, the latter being faster than the former. In both kinds of transfer, banks use the post & telegraph departments' services and use certain codes to ensure confidentiality and safety in transmission of the messages.

Now, in the electronic system of communication, the transmission is much faster and safer. Almost all banks have started the following systems for funds transfer:

(*i*) **SWIFT:** The Society of Worldwide Inter-Bank Financial Telecommunication is an international society for enabling international electronic fund transfer between member banks world-wide. Most of the commercial banks in India are members of this society. The member banks are connected through a high-speed closed-user group communication system. Structured and codified messages are sent by the remitting bank to the receiving bank for crediting the beneficiary's account with it. The inter-bank settlement of account is done *via* the correspondent banks. The funds' transfer system is fast, secure and efficient.

(*ii*) **Remittances through RTGS:**

RTGS is an inter-bank funds transfer system, where funds are transferred as and when the transactions are triggered (*i.e.* real time). The acronym 'RTGS' stands for 'Real Time Gross Settlement'. RTGS system is a funds transfer mechanism where transfer of money takes place from one bank to another on a 'real time' and on 'gross' basis. 'Real Time' means the processing of instructions at the time they are received; 'Gross Settlement' means that the settlement of funds transfer instructions occurs individually. It is a safe and secure system for funds transfer. The minimum amount to be remitted through RTGS is Rs. 2 lakh and there is no upper ceiling of the amount.

The remitting customer has to furnish the following information to a bank for effecting a RTGS remittance:

1. Amount to be remitted
2. His account number which is to be debited
3. Name of the beneficiary bank
4. Name of the beneficiary customer
5. Account number of the beneficiary customer
6. Sender to receiver information, if any
7. The IFSC Number of the receiving branch.

The beneficiary customer can obtain the Indian Financial System Code (IFSC) code from his branch. The IFSC code is also available in the cheque leaf. This code number and bank branch details can be communicated by the beneficiary to the remitting customer. At present, all the bank branches in India are not RTGS enabled.

(*iii*) **Remittances through NEFT:**

National Electronic Funds Transfer (NEFT) is a nation-wide centralised payment system owned and operated by the Reserve Bank of India (RBI). The NEFT Service helps in the seamless transfer of funds from one branch to another without any delays or procedural hassles. Like RTGS, RBI has introduced another type of funds transfer system called NEFT (National Electronic Funds Transfer). The operations and functions of the system are similar to RTGS.

BENEFITS OF NEFT:

- Round the clock availability on all days of the year.
- Near-real-time funds transfer to the beneficiary account and settlement in a secure manner.
- Pan-India coverage through large network of branches of all types of banks.
- Positive confirmation to the remitter by SMS/e-mail on credit to beneficiary account.
- Penal interest provision for delay in credit or return of transactions.
- No charges to savings bank account customers for online NEFT transactions.
- Besides funds transfer, NEFT system can be used for a variety of transactions including payment of credit card dues to the card issuing banks, payment of loan EMI, inward foreign exchange remittances, etc.
- Available for one-way funds transfers from India to Nepal upto a limit of Rs. 2 Lakhs for account holders and upto a limit of Rs. 50,000 for non-account holders.

- There is no limit imposed by the RBI for funds transfer through NEFT system. However, banks may place amount limits based on their own risk perception with the approval of its Board.

This facility can be availed only by account holders of a bank since both the beneficiary as well as applicant account number should be compulsorily mentioned in the NEFT application form. The NEFT system is available round the clock throughout the year on all days, *i.e.*, on 24x7x365 basis. NEFT presently operates in batches on half-hourly intervals throughout the day. In case of non-availability of NEFT for any reason, appropriate message will be broadcasted by RBI to all system participants. NEFT provides a maximum timeline of two hours from the batch settlement within which beneficiary's account should be credited.

(*iv*) Remittance through Mobile Phones as well as Internet Banking and ATM:

(*a*) Immediate Payment Service (IMPS):

Immediate Payment Service (IMPS) was launched by NPCI on 22nd November, 2010. It offers an instant, 24×7, interbank electronic fund transfer service through mobile phones as well as internet banking & ATMs. In the process of remittances across the bank there are four stakeholders *i.e.* (*i*) Remitter (Sender), (*ii*) Beneficiary (Receiver), (*iii*) Banks & (*iv*) National Financial Switch - NPCI.

In order to remit fund through IMPS, the sender should use either mobile banking or internet banking to send money. The receiver mobile number should be registered with his bank and the money is credited to receivers account instantly.

For registration the Remitter must register for mobile banking and get Mobile Money Identifier (MMID) & Mobile Banking PIN (MPIN) for initiation of a transaction. MMID is a 7-digit number, to be issued by the bank to the customer upon registration and the beneficiary must register his/her mobile number with the bank account and get MMID. A remitter can initiate an IMPS transaction by sending an SMS to his bank typing the beneficiary Mobile Number, Beneficiary MMID and Amount. The receiver will get an SMS confirmation for the credit of his account. National Payments Corporation of India (NPCI), is facilitating the Interbank Mobile Payment Service (IMPS).

(*b*) National Unified USSD Platform (NUUP):

Mobile banking is one of the most potent modes for increasing reach of banking facilities to the masses. Today, mobile phones have become a household device in India, with almost 900 million mobile phones connection. Mobile banking service can be initiated using SMS–an unencrypted service, considered unsafe - or using mobile banking app.

Though very interactive, the major problem with mobile banking apps is that these can be used only on smart phones. Less than 40% of Indian users have compatible smartphone handsets and GPRS connection on their mobile phone, as required by this system.

To offer banking facility to basic feature phones, an alternative solution on USSD platform is available. Customers can avail USSD solution through any mobile phone on GSM network, irrespective of make and model of the phone. This does not require any application to be downloaded on customer's mobile phone and need for GPRS connectivity. USSD is user friendly so it is easy to communicate and educate customers as well. USSD alleviates the need for application download and is more secure than SMS channel.

Banking customers can use this service by dialing *99#, a "Common number across all Telecom Service Providers, (TSPs)", on their mobile and transact through an interactive menu displayed on the mobile screen. Using *99#, a customer will be able to access both financial like fund transfer as well as non-financial services like balance enquiry and mini-statement of bank account, at his/her own convenience.

Key services that NUUP will offer include, interbank account to account fund transfer, balance enquiry, mini statement besides host of other services.

A notable inclusion in the NUUP service is a new addition in the form of Query Service on Aadhaar Mapper (QSAM). Under this feature a user can come to know about his/her AADHAAR seeding status with the banks, a service that will find tremendous utility for the government's direct subsidy disbursals programme.

(*c*) Aadhaar Enabled Payment System (AEPS):

AEPS is a banking product which allows online interoperable financial inclusion transaction at PoS (Micro-ATM) or Kiosk Banking through the Business Correspondent of any bank using the Aadhaar authentication.

Presently, four Aadhaar enabled basic types of banking transactions are available *i.e.* (*i*) Enquiry, (*ii*) Cash Withdrawal, (*iii*) Cash Deposit & (*iv*) Aadhaar to Aadhaar Funds Transfer. For undertaking AEPS transaction by customer, two inputs *i.e.* IIN (Six Digits Number Identifying the Bank to which the customer is associated) & Aadhaar Number are required.

(*d*) Aadhaar Payments Bridge System (APBS):

The Aadhaar Payments Bridge System enables the transfer of payments from Government and Government Institutions to Aadhaar-enabled accounts of beneficiaries at banks and post offices.

Every Government Department or Institution that sends EBT and DBT/DBTL payments to individuals simply needs to prepare a file containing the Aadhaar number and amount and submit it to their accredited bank. The accredited bank then processes the file through an interoperable Aadhaar Payments bridge and funds are credited into the accounts of beneficiaries. Upon receiving incoming funds, the beneficiary's bank will notify him or her through an SMS or any other communication channel that is established between the bank and the customer.

(*e*) **Unified Payment Interface (UPI):**

Unified Payment Interface (UPI) is a payment mechanism that allows users to link more than one bank account in a single smartphone app (of any participating bank) merging several banking features, seamless fund routing & merchant payments into one hood and make fund transfers without having to provide IFSC code or account number seamlessly.

This is a real-time payment system where funds are credited instantly on a real-time basis.

How Does UPI Work:

The user will only have to use a virtual address, known as a Virtual Payment Address (VPA) or personal QR code to carry out any transaction. UPI has been developed by the National Payments Corporation of India (NPCI) and is regulated by the Reserve Bank of India (RBI).

The below-mentioned things are required to transfer funds *via* UPI:

- A smartphone
- An active bank account
- The mobile number must be active and linked to the bank account
- Internet connection.

UPI is slowly becoming the most preferred form of digital payment. The UPI interface is compatible with most banks and many digital wallets and payment applications are embracing UPI. Some of the most popular apps include Google Pay, Paytm, PhonePe, BHIM UPI, etc.

Participants in UPI:

- Payer PSP
- Payee PSP
- Remitter Bank
- Beneficiary Bank
- NPCI

- Bank Account holders
- Merchants

(*f*) UPI 123:

UPI as mentioned above has emerged as one of the fastest growing payment platforms in the world. NPCI has developed the UPI 123PAY to facilitate UPI transactions by feature phone user without internet connection and the product was launched on 8th March 2022, by Shri Shaktikanta Das, Governor, Reserve Bank of India.

UPI 123PAY is an instant payment system for feature phone users who can use Unified Payments Interface (UPI) payment service in a safe and secure manner. Through UPI 123PAY, feature phone users will now be able to undertake a host of transactions based on four technology alternatives. They include calling an IVR (Interactive Voice Response) number, app functionality in feature phones, missed call based approach and also proximity sound-based (NFC) payments.

(*i*) UPI payment through pre-defined IVR number:

Customers (Users) are required to initiate a secured call from their registered feature phone to a pre-defined IVR number and complete UPI on-boarding formalities to be able to start making financial transactions without internet connection. IVR provides multiple language options, users can avail this service in their preferred language.

(*ii*) Payment through Missed Call:

Missed call-based approach will allow feature phone users to access their bank accounts and perform transactions like transferring and receiving funds, regular purchases, bill payments etc. by giving a missed call on the number displayed at the merchant's place. At the time of billing, the merchant will create a token with the customer's mobile number and the bill amount of her/his purchase. Customer then need to give a missed call to the number prescribed by the merchant and immediately, the customer will receive an incoming call from 08071800800 asking to authenticate the transaction by entering UPI PIN. This product is having easy IVR based preemptive on-boarding that completes within two minutes. First time user has to call IVR and enter area PINCODE to get language selection option. After IVR will ask user name, then first time OTP will be used for verification. After OTP verification, user has to provide last six digits of debit card, expiry date and debit card PIN, etc. for verification. After verification, user will be prompted to set UPI PIN of his/her choice. Person-to-person (P2P) payment user need to call a pre defined number and select the option for payment.

(*iii*) Feature phone where payment functionality implemented by OEM:

UPI app on feature phone has been developed by few payments banks in association with Fintech companies. In this type, the solution providers will need to partner with the feature phone mobile manufacturers (OEM) to enable a native payment app developed in embedded C language (or as supported). Look and feel of this app is similar to smart phone based app but has certain limitations to the feature phone. On-boarding is almost similar to smart phone as all options are made available in the app itself.

3.7.3 Bhim UPI

Bharat Interface for Money (BHIM) is a payment app that lets you make simple, easy and quick transactions using Unified Payments Interface (UPI). You can make direct bank payments to anyone on UPI using their UPI ID or scanning their QR with the BHIM app. You can also request money through the app from a UPI ID.

Pioneered and developed by National Payments Corporation of India (NPCI), BHIM has been conceived and launched by the Hon'ble Prime Minister of India, Narendra Modi on 30th December, 2016 to bring in Financial Inclusion to the nation and a digitally empowered society.

The various features of BHIM UPI are as follows:

- **Send Money**: This feature enables a user to send money using Virtual Payment Address (VPA) or combination of Account Number and IFSC or even by scanning QR code.
- **Request Money**: This feature enables a user to initiate a collect request by entering Virtual Payment Address (VPA). Additionally, through BHIM App, one can also transfer money using Mobile if it is registered with BHIM or *99#. Also, it is mandatory that the customers mobile number is linked with the bank account.
- **Scan & Pay**: Customers can pay by scanning the QR code through 'Scan & Pay' and generate QR codes in the app for making payments.
- **Transactions**: This option allows a user to check transaction history. It also highlights pending UPI collect requests (if any) so that a user can approve or reject the payment requests. There is a report issue tab if a customer is willing to raise any complaint pertaining to transactions.
- **Profile**: Profile option helps the user to view the static QR code and Payment addresses created. The QR code is downloadable and could be shared through various messenger applications like WhatsApp, Email, etc.
- **Bank Account**: Using this Option, a customer can check the bank account which is linked with the BHIM App along with PIN status. Customer can set/change the UPI PIN, bank account linked with BHIM App by clicking 'Change Account' tab provided in the menu. This feature also helps a user to check their account balance.

3.7.4 Bharat QR

One more addition to the various means of digital transactions is Bharat QR which is a QR based payment solution and can be used to make P2M (Person to Merchant) digital payments. This means that one can directly scan the Bharat QR code deployed at merchant's or seller's place, using any Bharat QR enabled mobile application. Bharat QR is a new transformative way to pay with the mobile phone and there is no need to carry any cash.

The features and benefits of Bharat QR is as follows:

Secure : It is as secure as making a payment *via* UPI as the card details or bank details are not exposed to any third party.

Interoperable : It allows use of any apps that support Bharat QR and pay using all types of Cards (*via* Visa, MasterCard, Amex or Rupay) or BHIM-UPI.

No additional charges : No additional charge is applicable to customer for using Bharat QR to make payments.

In short, Bharat QR is an alternate channel of payment which can be downloaded from any QR enabled mobile banking app. This code can be scanned using any payment app at the shop and select the mode of payment and process the payment accordingly. Once the payment is successful, both the remitter and the merchant will receive a notification for the successful transaction.

3.8 SAFE DEPOSIT LOCKERS

Banks provide Safe Deposit Lockers facility to the public at the selected branches. For this purpose, the banks arrange strong rooms, preferably at the ground floor or underground, equipped with safe deposit lockers. These lockers are of different sizes and are hired to the public at a rent which varies in Metro, Urban, Semi-urban and Rural centres. The rent is revised from time to time.

3.9 SAFE CUSTODY OF VALUABLES AND DOCUMENTS

Safe custody of valuables and important documents have been traditional service rendered by banks, on a fee basis. The customers have faith in their banks about the safety, security and confidentiality of the valuables kept with them. As these requirements are rarely met elsewhere, banks have been the main repositories of customers' valuables. A contract contrary to the right of banker's general lien comes into existence and the banker is placed in the position of a bailee. The procedure generally followed by the banker in this regard is as follows:

(*a*) The articles for safe custody may be handed over to the banker either openly or in a sealed cover or box. If the contents are told to the banker, the same are to be recorded into Safe Custody Register. The banker issues a receipt for the valuables deposited with him for safe custody and the signature of the customer is obtained on the counterfoil or the duplicate copy.

(*b*) At the time of withdrawal of the valuables, the receipt issued by the bank to the customer should be duly discharged by him and surrendered to the bank. In case the receipt is lost by the customer. A letter of indemnity is to be obtained from him and the discharge of the customer is obtained on a duplicate receipt.

(*c*) If the customer has not declared the contents of the box handed over to the banker for safe custody, the banker must record the description of the boxes, etc., in a Register of Boxes.

(*d*) The customer is required to give exclusive possession over the valuables to the banker and the latter should have sole right over them.

3.10 SMALL SAVINGS SCHEMES (LAGHU BACHAT YOJANA)

Small savings instruments are promoted and managed by the Central Government to provide opportunities to the citizens to save regularly. The products are made available easily at post offices and selected branches of Public and Private Sector banks. They generally provide returns that are usually higher than bank fixed deposits and also come with a sovereign guarantee and tax benefits.

A few popular small savings schemes are as follows:

3.10.1 Public Provident Fund (PPF)

The Public Provident Fund (PPF) scheme is one of the most popular and safest investment options that is available in the country. Contributions made towards the scheme are also tax exempt under Sec. 80C of the IT Act.

The PPF account can be opened at post offices and selected branches of public sector and private sector banks and the duration of the scheme is 15 years. Individuals are allowed to increase the duration of the scheme by a further 5 years. The rate of interest is declared by the Central Government every year and the interest is compounded on a yearly basis. The minimum contribution in the scheme is Rs. 500 and maximum contribution is Rs. 1.5 lakh on a yearly basis.

3.10.2 Sukanya Samriddhi Yojana (SSY)

The Sukanya Samriddhi Yojana is a government saving scheme to benefit a girl child who is ten years or less. A parent or guardian can open a maximum of 2 accounts. The principal amount qualifies for a deduction, and the interest is tax-free. The account matures after 21 years of investment or at the event of the marriage of a girl child.

3.10.3 Atal Pension Yojana

The Atal Pension Yojana (APY) is a government pension scheme and mainly focused on providing old age security to the unorganised workers who are not covered under any of the social security schemes. The scheme provides the subscribers with a fixed pension ranging between Rs. 1000 to Rs. 5000 depending upon the amount opted by the subscriber at the time of enrollment. The APY subscriber can enroll in the scheme between the age of 18 years and 40 years. The contribution level varies as per the conditions which is low if the subscriber joins the scheme early and might increase if he/she joins late. After the subscriber reaches the age of 60 years, the pension amount is paid till death. After the death of the subscriber, the spouse is eligible for availing the same benefits provided by the pension. The corpus left behind after death of both husband and wife will be returned to the nominees.

3.10.4. Senior Citizens Savings Scheme (SCSS)

The SCSS was launched by the Central Government with the objective of helping individuals who are 60 years and above. Individuals who are between the ages of 55 years and 60 years and have chosen for Voluntary Retirement Scheme (VRS) can also open the SCSS account with the Post Ofiice and selected branches of public and private sector banks.

The duration of the SCSS is 5 years and the rate of interest under the scheme is declared by the Government. The minimum in the scheme Rs. 1,000 and the maximum investment is Rs. 15 lakh. Under Section 80C of the Income-tax Act, tax deductions are available for investments made towards the scheme.

3.11 PAYMENT AGGREGATORS AND PAYMENT GATEWAYS

Payment Aggregators (PAs) and Payment Gateways (PGs) are intermediaries playing an important function in facilitating payments in the online space. According to RBI guidelines, Payment Aggregators are entities that facilitate e-commerce sites and merchants to accept various payment instruments from the customers for completion of their payment obligations without the need for merchants to create a separate payment integration system of their own. PAs facilitate merchants to connect with acquirers. In the process, they receive payments from customers, pool and transfer them on to the merchants after a time period. On the other hand, Payment Gateways are entities that provide technology infrastructure to route and facilitate processing of an online payment transaction without any involvement in handling of funds.

By using the services of a payment aggregator, the client can achieve all forms of payment acceptance *i.e.* credit/debit card, QR codes, UPI, Aadhaar Pay, net banking, e-wallets, bank transfers, SMS payments, as well as cash and cheque under one interface. However, payment gateway is a software service that allows e-commerce businesses to process transactions on their website/app through payment mechanisms *viz.* credit/debit cards, net-banking, e-wallets and UPI.

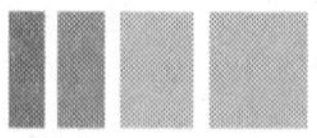

3.12 LET US SUM UP

Acceptance of deposits from customers is one of the main functions of banks. Almost all banks have same types of deposit products, but with different names. Basically, there are two types of deposits- one is Demand Deposit and the other is Term Deposit. Balances in current and savings bank accounts are the part of demand deposits and similarly, fixed deposits and recurring/cumulative deposits are the part of term deposits. Ancillary services of banks include remittances/funds transfer, safe deposit lockers, safe custody of articles and collection of cheques and bills. Electronic banking has increased the speed, accuracy and reliability of remittance system. Mobile banking has become very popular for funds transfer. Funds can be transferred through ATMs also. Small savings instruments like PPF, SCSS, Sukanya Samriddhi, APY are managed by the Central Government to provide opportunities to the citizens to save regularly.

3.13 CHECK YOUR PROGRESS

1. Savings accounts contain some restrictions regarding................
   (*a*) Number of withdrawals per quarter
   (*b*) Amount of withdrawals per transaction in ATM
   (*c*) Number of deposits into the account per quarter
   (*d*) Both (*a*) and (*b*) above
2. Overdraft is allowed generally by banks in.....................
   (*a*) Saving accounts
   (*b*) Term deposit accounts
   (*c*) Current accounts
   (*d*) Recurring deposit accounts

3. A bank's Fixed Deposits is characterized by..................
   (*a*) Interest rate as agreed with the customer at the time of the deposit
   (*b*) Fixed period of the deposit
   (*c*) Periodical Payment of interest
   (*d*) All of the above
4. Fixed deposits cannot be.......................
   (*a*) Renewed for a further period on maturity date
   (*b*) Transferred to third parties
   (*c*) Prepaid before the maturity date
   (*d*) Cannot be pledged to the bank as security
5. A Recurring Deposit account requires the customer to ....
   (*a*) Deposit any amount at specified intervals for a specified period
   (*b*) Deposit a fixed amount at will for a specified period
   (*c*) Deposit a fixed amount at specified intervals for any period
   (*d*) Deposit a fixed amount at specified intervals for a specified period
6. Interest on savings bank can be paid:
   (*a*) on any interval as per bank's own approved policy
   (*b*) on half yearly intervals only
   (*c*) on yearly intervals only
   (*d*) on quarterly intervals only
7. Demand Deposits are those which can be withdrawn:
   (*a*) On Request
   (*b*) On Sanction by Manager
   (*c*) On Demand
   (*d*) On Persuasion
8. Current account deposits are not entitled to ____________
   (*a*) Cheque book above 100 leaves
   (*b*) Monthly Statements
   (*c*) Cash Payments
   (*d*) Interest

9. In saving account deposits, interest is paid on ____________ balance in the account:
   (*a*) Maximum
   (*b*) Average
   (*c*) Daily
   (*d*) Last Balance at the end of month

3.14 ANSWERS TO CHECK YOUR PROGRESS

1.	(*d*)	2.	(*c*)	3.	(*d*)	4.	(*b*).	5.	(*d*)	6.	(*a*)	7.	(*c*)
8.	(*d*)	9.	(*c*)										

CHAPTER

4 Account Opening and Operations in Accounts

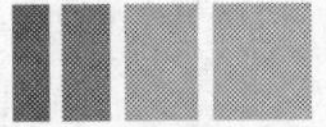

4.1 OBJECTIVES

After reading this chapter, the reader would understand:

- Procedure of opening an account
- Operations in accounts
- Guidelines on preventing money laundering
- Important terms on "Interest"

4.2 INTRODUCTION

Any person who wants to open an account with a bank, will have to submit certain documents to prove his identity and residential/office address. In general terms, this procedure in banking terms is called "Know Your Customer" (KYC). RBI has stipulated "Officially Valid Document" (OVD) for various types of customers. These guidelines are aimed to check money laundering which is an undesirable process wherein the origin of funds generated by illegal means (blood diamonds, terrorism, drug trafficking, illegal arms trade, corruption, extortion, etc.) is concealed. The purpose of money laundering is to route the moneys so generated through the banking systems of various countries and transferred to various entities such that moneys can be invested in legitimate activities. By routing the same through the banking system, it becomes clean/white (gets laundered). The issue of generation of illegal money and routing the same into legal channels is not new but it used to be mostly confined to the economies where it is generated. However, of late, this has become a grave danger to the humanity because of usage of this channel by terrorists to fund terrorist activities. Improved IT usage in banking transactions where a face-to-face contact with customer is missing, has also made it difficult to detect money laundering. Thus, the money laundering activity has become a menace not only to the economies of the world but also to the security and peace of humanity.

4.3 PROCEDURE FOR OPENING AN ACCOUNT

4.3.1 Submitting Account Opening form and other prescribed documents

Any person who wants to open an account with the bank, has to enter into a contract with the bank by filling in the prescribed Account Opening Form in physical form or online. At the same time banks are required to obtain certain documents including his recent photograph from the new customer as a proof of his identity and proof of residence as per "Know Your Customer" (KYC) policy of the bank and RBI guidelines. Account opening form is a proposal by the new customer which a bank will accept only on fulfilling certain conditions.

4.3.2 'Know Your Customer' (KYC) guidelines of RBI

KYC establishes the identity and residential address of the customers by specified documentary evidences. One of the main objectives of KYC procedure is to prevent possible misuse of the banking system for money laundering and financing of terrorist activities. RBI has stipulated that banks should show strict adherence to 'KYC' guidelines and monitoring of cash transactions based on prescribed norms (above specified amounts). The 'KYC' guidelines, issued by RBI, reinforce the existing customer identification practice of banks. KYC guidelines have to be compulsorily adhered by banks in regard to all of their customers who maintain domestic or non-resident rupee or foreign currency accounts with them. This would prevent money from illegal and/or undesirable sources coming into the banking system. Accounts opened by individuals, group of individuals, companies, firms, religious trust accounts and non-religious trust accounts, etc. should be subjected to KYC procedure.

Documents to be obtained:

(A) Accounts of individuals:

As per RBI guidelines, the "Officially Valid document" (OVD) are enlisted as (*i*) passport, (*ii*) driving license, (*iii*) Voter's Identity Card issued by the Election Commission of India, (*iv*) job card issued by NREGA duly signed by an officer of the State Government, (*v*) letter issued by the Unique Identification Authority of India containing details of name, address and Aadhaar number and letter issued by National Population Register containing details of name and address. Customers, at their option, shall submit one of the six OVDs for proof of identity and proof of address.

In cases where OVD furnished by the customer does not have the updated address, the following documents or the equivalent e-documents can be considered to be OVDs for limited purpose of proof of address:

- Utility bill which is not more than 2 months old of any service provider (electricity, telephone, postpaid mobile phone, piped gas, water bill)
- Property or municipal tax receipt
- Pension or family Pension Payment Orders (PPOs) issued to retired employees by Government Departments or Public Sector Undertakings if they contain the address
- Letter of allotment of accommodation from employer issued by State Governments or Central Government Departments, statutory or regulatory bodies, public sector undertakings, scheduled commercial banks, financial institutions and listed companies and leave and license agreements with such employers allotting official accommodation.

  In such cases where the account has been opened with limited KYC as above, the customer shall submit OVD with current address within a period of three months of submitting the documents specified above.
- The e-KYC service of Unique Identification Authority of India (UIDAI) shall be accepted as a valid process for KYC verification under the PML Rules, as the information containing demographic details and photographs made available from UIDAI. As a result, e-KYC process is treated as an 'Officially Valid Document', and transfer of KYC data, electronically to the bank from UIDAI, is accepted as valid process for KYC verification.
- One recent photograph; and
- such other documents pertaining to the nature of business or financial status specified by the Regulated Entity (RE) in their KYC policy shall also be called for.

  RBI has also issued guidelines with respect to Video based Customer Identification Process (V-CIP) procedure, an alternate method of customer identification with facial recognition and customer due diligence by an authorised official of the bank or financial institution by undertaking seamless, secure, live, informed - consent based audio-visual interaction with the customer to obtain identification information required for CDD purpose, and to ascertain the veracity of the information furnished by the customer through independent verification and maintaining audit trail of the process. Such processes complying with prescribed standards and procedures shall be treated on par with face-to-face CIP as per RBI master directions.

Small Accounts

Those persons who do not have any of the 'officially valid documents' can open 'small accounts' with banks. A 'small account' can be opened on the basis of a self-attested photograph and putting her/his signature or thumb print in the presence of an official of the bank. Such accounts have limitations regarding the aggregate credits (not more than Rupees one lakh in a financial year), aggregate withdrawals (not more than Rupees ten thousand in a month) and balance in the accounts (not more than Rupees fifty thousand at any point of time). These small accounts would be valid normally for a period of twelve months. Thereafter, such accounts can be allowed to continue for a further period of twelve more months, if the account holder provides a document showing that she/he has applied for any of the officially valid document, within twelve months of opening the small account. The period of operationality of the small accounts will be as per the notification made by the Central Government.

(B) Accounts of companies:

The following details to be obtained:

(*i*) Name of the company
(*ii*) Principal place of business
(*iii*) Mailing address of the company
(*iv*) Telephone/Fax Number
(*v*) Type of business
(*vi*) Contact Details (Contact No./Mail ID)
(*vii*) Signatory Details

Documents to be obtained:

(*i*) Certificate of incorporation and Memorandum & Articles of Association (*ii*) Resolution of the Board of Directors to open an account and identification (KYC) of those who have authority to operate the account (*iii*) Power of Attorney granted to its managers, officers or employees to transact business on its behalf (*iv*) Permanent Account Number of the company (*v*) Address proof of the company (*vi*) Documents, as specified by RBI for KYC purpose, relating to beneficial owner, the managers, officers or employees, as the case may be, holding an attorney to transact on the company's behalf.

(C) Accounts of partnership firms:

(*i*) Legal name
(*ii*) Address
(*iii*) Names of all partners and their addresses
(*iv*) Telephone numbers of the firm and partners
(*v*) Type of business
(*vi*) Mode of Operation

Documents to be obtained:

(*i*) Registration certificate (if applicable) (*ii*) Partnership deed (*iii*) Power of Attorney granted to a partner or an employee of the firm to transact business on its behalf (if applicable) (*iv*) Any officially valid document identifying the partners and the persons holding the Power of Attorney and their addresses (*v*) Address proof (*vi*) Documents, as specified by RBI for KYC purpose, relating to beneficial owner, managers, officers or employees, as the case may be, holding an attorney to transact on its behalf.

(D) Accounts of trusts & foundations:

(*i*) Names of trustees, settlers, beneficiaries and signatories

(*ii*) Names and addresses of the founder, the managers/directors and the beneficiaries

(*iii*) Telephone numbers/Mail ID

Documents to be obtained:

(*i*) Copy of Trust Deed alongwith Certificate of registration (*ii*) Power of Attorney granted to transact business on its behalf (*iii*) Any officially valid document to identify the trustees, settlers, beneficiaries and those holding Power of Attorney, founders/ managers/directors and their addresses (*iv*) Resolution of the managing body of the foundation/association (*v*) Address proof of trust (*vi*) Permanent Account Number or Form No. 60 of the trust (*vii*) Documents, as specified by RBI for KYC purpose, relating to beneficial owner, managers, officers or employees, as the case may be, holding an attorney to transact on its behalf.

(E) Accounts of Proprietorship Concerns:

For Proof of the name, address and activity of the concern:

Any two of the following documents or entity proofs would suffice. These documents should be in the name of the proprietary concern. The banks have the discretion to accept only one of the two documents as activity proof while opening accounts of sole proprietary firms in certain cases where the banks are satisfied that it is not possible to furnish any two documents out of the prescribed as activity proof. In such cases, the banks, however, would have to undertake contact point verification, collect such information as would be required to establish the existence of such firm, confirm, clarify and satisfy themselves that the business activity has been verified from the address of the proprietary concern.

Officially valid documents:

- Registration certificate
- Certificate/license issued by the Municipal authorities under Shop & Establishment Act, or Trade License issued by Municipal Authorities
- Sales and income-tax returns
- GST Certificate

- Certificate/registration document issued by Sales Tax/Service Tax/Professional Tax authorities.
- License issued by the Registering authority like Certificate of Practice issued by Institute of Chartered Accountants of India, Institute of Cost Accountants of India, Institute of Company Secretaries of India, Indian Medical Council, Food and Drug Control Authorities, registration/licensing document issued in the name of the proprietary concern by the Central Government or State Government Authority/Department, etc. Banks may also accept IEC (Importer Exporter Code) issued to the proprietary concern by the office of DGFT as an identity document for opening of the bank account, etc.
- Utility bills such as electricity, water, and landline telephone bills in the name of the proprietary concern.

The list of registering authorities is only illustrative and therefore includes license/certificate of practice issued in the name of the proprietary concern by any professional body incorporated under a statute, as one of the documents to prove the activity of the proprietary concern.

4.3.3 Electronic Know Your Customer (e-KYC)

In the year 2013, RBI permitted e-KYC as a valid process for KYC verification under Prevention of Money Laundering (Maintenance of Records) Rules, 2005. In order to reduce the risk of identity fraud, documentary forgery and have paperless KYC verification, UIDAI has launched its e-KYC services. Under the e-KYC process under the explicit consent of the customer and after his or her biometric authentication from UIDAI database individual basic data comprising name, age, gender and photograph can be shared electronically with Authorised users like Banks, which is a valid process for KYC. The aforesaid process is paperless and has made the account opening of customers having Aadhaar number much easier. Almost all the banks have either adopted this process or in the advance stage of putting the system live. The e-KYC process would be used in large scale for opening accounts in future.

Banks are required to monitor the transactions in new accounts at least for a period of six months and report any suspicious transactions to the designated authority who is Government of India. Even in the case of other accounts, banks are required to monitor the transactions. If there is any suspicion about any account being used for money laundering activity, the same should be reported to the Government of India through proper channel without at the same time alerting the customer. In any case, cash transactions of over Rs. 10 Lakhs are required to be reported to the RBI (FIU-IND) on a fortnightly basis.

4.3.4 Digital Locker

Digital Locker (Digi-Locker) is an initiative of the Ministry of Electronics & IT (MeitY) under Digital India Corporation (DIC).It provides access to authentic virtual documents. It is a digital document wallet where one can store his documents such as driving licence, PAN card, Voter ID, policy documents, etc. He can upload the documents and keep these safe when he signs up for a Digilocker account. He gets a dedicated cloud storage space that is linked to his Aadhaar number. The digital locker helps eliminate use of physical documents and enables sharing of e-documents across government agencies *via* a mechanism to verify the "authenticity" of the documents online.

There are following four simple steps to open a Digi-locker online:

Step 1: Visit the Digi-Locker website. You can access the Digilocker at digilocker.gov.in. You can even download the application from the play/app store on your mobile phone. Further, you can use Aadhaar number to create a digital locker account *via* visiting Digi-locker website. Make sure that your current phone number is registered with the Aadhaar number.

Step 2: Click on 'Sign Up'. Enter your full name, date of birth, mobile number (registered with Aadhaar). Make a security PIN and enter an email ID.

Step 3: Enter your Aadhaar Number. Once you enter your unique 12-digit Aadhaar number, you will get two options – One Time Password (OTP) or Fingerprint - you can use any options to proceed further.

4.3.5 Periodic Updation of KYC

(*a*) Banks should carry out on-going due diligence with respect to the business relationship with every client and closely examine the transactions in order to ensure that they are consistent with their knowledge of the client, his business and risk profile and, wherever necessary, the source of funds. Parameters of risk perception are clearly defined in terms of the nature of business activity, location of customer and his clients, mode of payments, volume of turnover, social and financial status etc. to enable categorisation of customers into low, medium and high risk.

(*b*) Full KYC exercise should be done at least every two years for high-risk individuals and entities.

(*c*) Full KYC exercise should be done at least every ten years for low risk and at least every eight years for medium risk individuals and entities since opening of the account/last KYC updation.

(*d*) confirmation (obtaining KYC related updates through e-mail/letter/telephonic conversation/forms/interviews/visits, etc.), should be completed at least every two years for medium risk and at least every ten years for low-risk individuals and entities.

(*e*) Fresh photographs and full KYC should be obtained from minor customers on their becoming major.

Banks need not seek fresh proofs of identity and address at the time of periodic updation, from those customers who are categorised as 'low risk', in case of no change in status with respect to their identities and addresses. A self-certification by the customer to that effect should suffice in such cases. In case of change of address of such 'low risk' customers, they could merely forward a certified copy of the document (proof of address) by mail/post, etc. Banks should not insist on physical presence of such low- risk customer at the time of periodic updation.

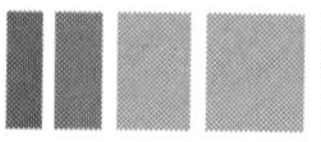

4.4 PHOTOGRAPHS OF DEPOSITORS

Banks should obtain and keep on record photographs of all depositors/account holders in respect of accounts opened by them subject to the following clarifications:

(*i*) The instructions cover all types of deposits including fixed, recurring, cumulative, etc.

(*ii*) They apply to all categories of depositors, whether resident or non-resident.

(*iii*) The banks should obtain photographs of all persons authorised to operate the accounts *viz.,* Savings Bank and Current Accounts without exception.

(*iv*) The banks should also obtain photographs of the 'Pardanashin' women.

(*v*) The banks may obtain two copies of photographs and obtaining photocopies of driving license/passport containing photographs in place of photographs would not suffice.

(*vi*) The banks should not ordinarily insist on the presence of account holder for making cash withdrawals in case of 'self' or 'bearer' cheques unless the circumstances so warrant. The banks should pay 'self' or 'bearer' cheques taking usual precautions.

(*vii*) Photographs cannot be a substitute for specimen signatures.

(*viii*) Only one set of photographs need to be obtained and separate photographs should not be obtained for each category of deposit. The applications for different types of deposit accounts should be properly referenced.

(*ix*) Fresh photographs need not be obtained when an additional account is desired to be opened by the account holder.

(*x*) In the case of operative accounts, *viz.* Savings Bank and Current accounts, photographs of persons authorised to operate them should be obtained. In case of other deposits, *viz.,* Fixed, Recurring, Cumulative, etc., photographs of all depositors in whose names the deposit receipt stands may be obtained except in the case of deposits in the name of minors where guardians' photographs should be obtained.

4.5 SPECIMEN SIGNATURE

Specimen signature of the customer is obtained on the account opening form in the presence of the bank staff and it is attested by an authorized bank officer in the form itself. A customer is recognized mainly by his/her signature on the cheques/ vouchers and these are compared with the specimen signature on record to verify the genuineness of the customer's signature. In respect of credit/debit cards and ATM cards, customers are given specific PIN numbers by the banks. Customers are expected to use the initial PIN and replace the same with their own PIN. Specimen signature and PIN are essential to ensure safety of customers' funds.

In the case of illiterate customers, banks take the thumb impression for identification purposes.

4.6 POWER OF ATTORNEY

At times, a customer/depositor would like to transact his/her business through another person. Banks accept this arrangement for which a power of attorney or mandate is essential. Power of Attorney (POA) is a document, duly stamped as per the Indian Stamp Act, given by a customer to his/her banker, authorizing his/her attorney or agent named therein, to operate the account. Power of attorney could be general or specific. Few banks also follow the process of obtaining the mandate declaration instead of POA.

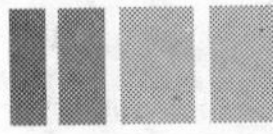

4.7 NOMINATION

At the time of opening an account in a single name, banks advise the customer to indicate the nominee to whom the amounts are payable in the event of death of depositor/s. The effect of a valid nomination is that in the event of death of the sole depositor or all depositors, the amount lying in the account will be returned to the nominee without any further legal formality. The procedure of nomination is as under:

(1) A single depositor may nominate, in the prescribed manner, a person to whom, in the event of death of the depositor, the amount to his credit may be paid by the banking company.

(2) In case of a joint account, all the depositors together may nominate a person to whom, in the event of demise of all the joint depositors, the amount to their credit may be paid by the banking company. Thus, the nominee's right

to receive deposit money arises only after the death of all depositors. There cannot be more than one nominee in respect of a joint account.

(3) A nomination can be made in favour of an individual only and not association, societies, trusts or any organization or their office-bearers.

(4) Facility is available to all types of deposit accounts, including the accounts opened for credit of pension.

(5) Such nomination confers upon the nominee the right to receive the amount of deposit from the banking company. On the death of the depositor/all the joint depositors, the nominee shall become entitled to all the rights of the latter to such deposit, to the exclusion of all other persons.

(6) If the nominee is a minor, the depositor/depositors may also appoint any person to receive the amount of deposit in the event of his death during the minority of the nominee.

(7) The nomination may be varied or cancelled by the depositor in the prescribed manner. In case of a joint account variation or cancellation of a subsisting nomination can be made by all the surviving depositors acting together.

(8) On making payment under the provisions of this section, the banking company shall be fully discharged from its liability in respect of the deposit.

(9) The right or claim of any other person against the nominee, to whom any payment is made under this section, shall not be affected by such payment.

(10) No other person shall be able to get notice of his claim to such deposits to the banking company. Nor shall the banking company be bound by such notice even though expressly given to it.

4.8 PREVENTION OF MONEY LAUNDERING

Money laundering is the illegal process of making large amounts of money generated by criminal activity, such as drug trafficking or terrorist funding, appear to have come from a legitimate source. The money from the criminal activity is considered dirty, and the process "launders" it to make it look clean. Money laundering needs to be curbed. As a member of the international financial system, our country is also serious about and committed to curbing this. Moreover, international investment flows do not happen in those countries, which have not implemented the measures for prevention of money laundering. The Government of India has enacted, in the year 2002, Prevention of Money Laundering Act (PMLA). According to this, any person who either directly or indirectly attempts to indulge in or knowingly assists or unknowingly is a party or is actually involved in any process or activity connected with the proceeds of crime and projecting it as untainted property shall be guilty of offence of money laundering.

In order to combat money laundering in India, the PMLA, 2002 has following three main objectives:

- Preventing and controlling money laundering;
- Confiscation and seize of the property obtained from the laundered money; and
- Dealing with any other issue related with money laundering.

Provisions of Prevention of Money Laundering Act, 2002 necessitate banks to:

- Know and understand the customers and their financial dealings better which in turn would help the bank to manage risks prudently.
- Put in place appropriate controls for detection and reporting of suspicious activities in accordance with acceptable laws and laid down procedures.
- Comply with applicable laws and regulatory guidelines.
- Take necessary steps to ensure that the bank staff is adequately trained in the above required procedures.

4.8.1 Money Laundering - Stages and Types

The process of laundering money typically involves three steps: placement, layering, and integration:

- **Placement** surreptitiously injects the "dirty money" into the legitimate financial system.
- **Layering** conceals the source of the money through a series of transactions and bookkeeping tricks.
- In the final step, **integration**, the now-laundered money is withdrawn from the legitimate account to be used for whatever purposes the criminals have in mind for it.

4.8.2 Role of Banks

As per proverb 'prevention is better than cure', banks are required to initiate steps to prevent the money laundering at the first stage itself which means 'do not accept funds the sources of which are not satisfactorily explained'. This can be done only if banks know the financial details of the customer. Banks are required to know the actual identity of the customer, his financial background and the likely volume of transactions in the account before accepting him as a customer such that transactions can be monitored to verify that the Bank a/c is not used for illegal transactions. KYC procedure is important both for deposit and loan transactions.

4.9 RBI GUIDELINES IN REGARD TO OPERATIONS IN ACCOUNTS

4.9.1 Savings Bank Accounts

(*a*) **Savings Bank Rules:**

As many banks are now issuing statement of accounts in lieu of pass books, the Savings Bank Rules must be annexed as a tear-off portion to the account opening form so that the account holder can retain the rules.

(*b*) **Minimum balance in Savings Bank Accounts:**

At the time of opening the accounts, banks should inform their customers in a transparent manner the requirement of maintaining minimum balance and levying of charges, etc., if the minimum balance is not maintained. Any charge levied subsequently should be transparently made known to all depositors in advance with one month's notice. The banks should inform, at least one month in advance, the existing account holders of any change in the prescribed minimum balance and the charges that may be levied if the prescribed minimum balance is not maintained. Banks are not permitted to levy penal charges for non-maintenance of minimum balances in any inoperative account.

(*c*) **Issuance of Pass books to Savings Bank Account holders (Individuals):**

A pass book is a ready reckoner of transactions and is handy and compact and as such, is far more convenient to the small customer than a statement of account. Banks may either offer passbook facility or bank statement as per customer choice.

(*d*) **Providing monthly statement of accounts:**

(*i*) Banks should ensure the prescribed periodicity while sending statement of accounts.

(*ii*) The statements of accounts for current account holders may be sent to the depositors in a staggered manner instead of sending by a target date every month. The customers may be informed about staggering of the preparation of these statements.

(*e*) **Issuing of cheque books:**

Banks may issue cheque books with larger number of (20/25) leaves if a customer demands the same. Bank should issue only "payable at par"/"multi-city" CTS 2010 Standard cheques to all eligible customers without extra charges. Banks cannot charge their savings bank account customers for issuance of CTS-2010 standard cheques when they are issued for the first time.

4.9.2 Term Deposit Account

(*a*) Issue of term deposit receipt:

Bank should issue term deposit receipt indicating therein full details, such as, date of issue, period of deposit, due date, applicable rate of interest, etc. Many banks have introduced the facility of on-line issuance of TDR and in such cases customer can himself convert the balances kept in savings/current account into term deposit. He can also take print of e-receipt for his record. Term deposits should be freely transferable from one branch.

Advance instructions from depositors for disposal of deposits on maturity may be obtained in the application form itself. Wherever such instructions are not obtained, banks should ensure sending of intimation of impending due date of maturity well in advance to their depositors as a rule.

Any change in interest rate on deposits should be displayed at the Notice Board of the branch as well as its official website.

(*b*) Method of calculation of interest:

Banks are free to decide the periodicity of the payment of interest for the purpose of compounding the interest. Further, on deposits repayable in less than three months or where the terminal quarter is incomplete, interest should be paid proportionately for the actual number of days reckoning the year at 365 days. Some banks are adopting the method of reckoning the year at 366 days in a Leap year and 365 days in other years.

(*c*) Premature withdrawal of term deposit:

A bank, on request from the depositor, should allow withdrawal of a term deposit before completion of the period of the deposit agreed upon at the time of making the deposit. Banks have the freedom to determine its own penal interest rate of premature withdrawal of term deposits. While prematurely closing a deposit, interest on the deposit for the period that it has remained with the bank will be paid at the rate applicable to the period for which the deposit remained with the bank and not at the contracted rate. No interest is payable, where premature withdrawal of deposits takes place before completion of the minimum period prescribed.

Banks have the discretion to disallow premature withdrawal of a term deposit in respect of bulk deposits of Rs. crore and above of all depositors, including deposits of individuals and HUFs. Banks have the discretion to offer differential interest rates based on whether the term deposits are with or without premature-withdrawal facility. (Bulk deposits for banks raised to Rs. 2 crore from Rs. 1 crore by RBI to provide more operational freedom to lenders to raise funds) (*d*) **Acknowledgement by banks at the time of submission of Form 15G/15H:**

Banks are not required to deduct TDS from depositors who submit declaration in Form 15G/15H under Income-tax Rules, 1962. However, it has been brought to our notice that despite submission of Form 15G/15H by customers, Banks should give an acknowledgement at the time of receipt of Form 15G/15H.

4.9.3 Acceptance of cash over the counter

Some banks have introduced certain products whereby the customers are not allowed to deposit cash over the counters and also have incorporated a clause in the terms and conditions that cash deposits, if any, are required to be done through ATMs.

Banking, by definition, means acceptance of deposits of money from the public for the purpose of lending and investment. As such, banks cannot design any product which is not in tune with the basic tenets of banking. Further, incorporating such clauses in the terms and conditions which restrict deposit of cash over the counters also amounts to an unfair practice.

Banks, therefore, should ensure that their branches invariably accept cash over the counters from all their customers who desire to deposit cash at the counters. Further, they should not incorporate clauses in the terms and conditions which restrict deposit of cash over the counters.

4.9.4 Fixing service charges by banks

While fixing service charges for various types of services like charges for cheque collection, etc., banks should ensure that the charges are reasonable and are not out of line with the average cost of providing these services. Banks should also take care to ensure that customers with low volume of activities are not penalised. If a particular service is provided free at home branch, the same should be available free at non-home branches also. There should be no discrimination as regards intersol charges between similar transactions done by customers at home branch and those done at non-home branches.

Banks may levy charges for sending SMS alerts to customers but such charges should be on actual usage basis.

4.9.5 Banking hours/working days of bank branches

Banks should display business hours (for the purpose of transactions by the customers) at each branch. The business hours for banking transactions other than cash, may be till one hour before close of the working hours.

No particular banking hours have been prescribed by law and a bank may fix, after due notice to its customers, whatever business hours are convenient to it *i.e.,* to work in double shifts, to observe weekly holiday on a day other than Sunday or to function on Sundays in addition to the normal working days, subject to observing normal working hours for public transactions. There should not be infringement of any other relevant local laws such as Shops and Establishment Act, etc.

Further, the provisions, if any, in regard to the banks' obligations, to the staff under the Industrial Awards/Settlements, should be complied with. Clearing House authority of the place should also be consulted in this regard.

The banks' branches in rural areas can fix the business hours (*i.e.* number of hours, as well as timings) and the weekly holidays to suit local requirements. A list of non-cash transactions are given below:

Non-voucher generating transactions:

i. Issue of pass books/statement of accounts;

ii. Issue of cheque books;

iii. Delivery of term deposit receipts/drafts;

iv. Acceptance of share application forms;

v. Acceptance of clearing cheques;

vi. Acceptance of bills for collection.

Voucher generating transactions:

i. Issue of term deposit receipts;

ii. Acceptance of cheques for locker rent due;

iii. Issue of travellers cheques;

iv. Issue of gift cheques;

v. Acceptance of individual cheques for transfer credit.

4.9.6 Complaints/suggestions box

Complaints/suggestions box should be provided at each office of the bank. Further, at every office of the bank a notice requesting the customers to meet the branch manager may be displayed regarding grievances, if the grievances remain un-addressed.

Complaint book with perforated copies in each set may be made available to customers, so designed as to instantly provide an acknowledgement to the customers and an intimation to the Controlling Office.

4.9.7 Printed material in trilingual form

Banks are required to make available all printed material used by retail customers including account opening forms, pay-in-slips, pass books, etc., in trilingual form *i.e.*, English, Hindi and the concerned Regional Language.

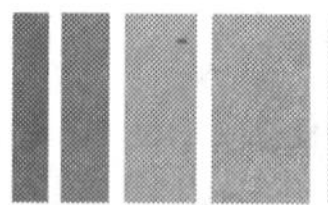

4.10 SOME IMPORTANT TERMS RELATING TO INTEREST RATES

Interest is the price paid by the banks to the depositor for the deposits it has accepted or paid by the borrower to the bank for the loans and advance he/she has taken from the bank. The interest rate applicable for each type of deposit or loan is specified as a percentage. Although the price of credit is generally stated as rate of interest, the amount of interest paid or earned on deposits or payable on loans depend upon a number of other factors, including the method used to calculate interest.

4.10.1 What is interest?

Interest is the price that someone pays for the temporary use of someone else's funds. Interest can also be said to be the compensation that someone receives for temporarily giving up the ability to spend money. Without interest, lenders would not be willing to lend or temporarily give up the ability to spend, and savers would be less willing to defer spending. To repay a loan, a borrower has to pay interest, as well as the principal amount originally borrowed.

When money is advanced by a bank, the borrower usually pays a price in consideration of the loan to the bank, till it is repaid (to the bank). This price is called 'Interest'. Similarly, a bank pays interest at agreed rates on deposits accepted by it.

4.10.2 Equated Monthly Instalment (EMI)

The most commonly adopted method of repayment of loan now is EMI, where the principal and interest is repaid through monthly instalment over the fixed tenure of the loan. It is fixed on the basis of the loan amount, interest rate and the tenure of loan.

The formula for calculation of EMI given the loan amount, tenure and interest is:

$EMI = P \times r \times (1 + r)^n = P \times r \times (1 + r)^{n/}\{(1 + r)^{(n-1)}$

where:

P = principal (amount of loan),

r = rate of interest per month

(*e.g.*: if interest rate per annum is 10% then 10/(12×100))

n = No. of instalments

By using the above formula, the EMI will be calculated.

4.11 MARGINAL COST OF FUNDS BASED LENDING RATE

As per the extant guidelines, all rupee loans sanctioned and credit limits renewed w.e.f. April 1, 2016 will be priced with reference to the Marginal Cost of Funds based Lending Rate (MCLR). MCLR has been the internal benchmark rate for banks since then. MCLR has to be a tenor-linked rate with reset clause at least once in a year. For the customer, the MCLR that is prevailing on the day the loan is sanctioned will be in application till the next reset even if the benchmark rate changes. While calculating the MCLR, it has been clarified by RBI that, banks have to factor incremental cost of funds and not the average cost.

The MCLR will comprise of:

a. Marginal cost of funds;

b. Negative carry-on account of CRR;

c. Operating costs;

d. Tenor premium.

Marginal Cost of funds

The marginal cost of funds will comprise of Marginal cost of borrowings and return on net-worth.

Negative Carry on CRR

Negative carry on the mandatory CRR which arises due to return on CRR balances being nil, will be calculated as under:

Required CRR x (marginal cost)/(1- CRR)

The marginal cost of funds arrived will be used for arriving at negative carry on CRR.

Operating Costs

All operating costs associated with providing the loan product including cost of raising funds will be included under this head. It should be ensured that the costs of providing those services which are separately recovered by way of service charges do not form part of this component.

Tenor premium

These costs arise from loan commitments with longer tenor. The change in tenor premium should not be borrower specific or loan class specific. In other words, the tenor premium will be uniform for all types of loans for a given residual tenor.

Since MCLR will be a tenor linked benchmark, banks shall arrive at the MCLR of a particular maturity by adding the corresponding tenor premium to the sum of Marginal cost of funds, Negative carry-on account of CRR and Operating costs.

Accordingly, banks shall publish the internal benchmark for the following maturities:

a. overnight MCLR,

b. one-month MCLR,

c. three-month MCLR,

d. six-month MCLR,

e. one-year MCLR.

In addition to the above, banks have the option of publishing MCLR of any other longer maturity.

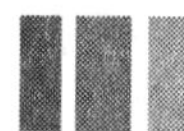
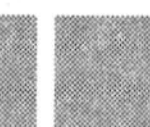

4.12 LET US SUM UP

Any person who wants to open an account with a bank has to submit certain prescribed documents to prove the identity and residence/office address. This procedure is aimed to check money laundering which is an undesirable process wherein the origin of funds generated by illegal means is concealed only to be retrieved later through the banking systems of various countries and transferred to various entities such that moneys can be invested in legitimate activities. RBI has stipulated certain guidelines in regard to operation in accounts and providing good customer service. Banks are liable to follow these guidelines. It is the duty of banks to honour the cheques issued by its customers if otherwise in order. Bank is liable for the fraudulent debits in the accounts of its clients.

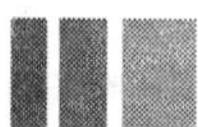

4.13 KEY WORDS

Anti-Money Laundering (AML), Know Your Customer, placement, layering, integration, risk management, Marginal Cost of Funds based Lending Rate (MCLR)

4.14 CHECK YOUR PROGRESS

1. Money Laundering refers to:

   (*a*) Conversion of assets into cash

   (*b*) Conversion of Money which is illegally obtained

   (*c*) Conversion of cash into gold

   (*d*) Conversion of assets into cash

2. One of the important steps in Money Laundering is:
   (*a*) Placement & Layering
   (*b*) Organisation & Controlling
   (*c*) Depositing & Withdrawing
   (*d*) Backward & Forward integration
3. Which one of the following is an Officially valid document available to the bank for customer identification?
   (*a*) Election ID card
   (*b*) Ration card
   (*c*) Photograph
   (*d*) Bank statement of account
4. Objectives of KYC:
   (*a*) to ensure appropriate customer identification
   (*b*) to monitor transactions of suspicious nature
   (*c*) if loan given, it would not be a NPA
   (*d*) to create a data base of customers
5. In the case of safe deposit locker taken on lease by two persons jointly which is to be operated also jointly:
   (*a*) Only one nomination will be accepted
   (*b*) They can nominate two persons separately
   (*c*) Nomination is not permitted
   (*d*) Nominee cannot be a minor

4.15 ANSWERS TO CHECK YOUR PROGRESS

1.	(*b*)	2.	(*a*)	3.	(*a*)	4.	(*a*)	5.	(*b*)				

CHAPTER

5 Provisions of NI Act for Payment and Collection of Cheques

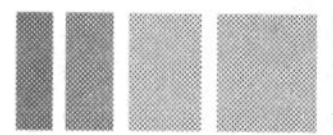

5.1 OBJECTIVES

After reading this chapter, you should be able to understand:

- Meaning of a cheque and bills of exchange
- Legal aspects of Collection of Cheques/Bills of Exchange
- Legal aspects of payment of cheques
- RBI directives relating to payment and collection of cheques

5.2 INTRODUCTION

The Negotiable Instruments Act, 1881 lays down the law relating to payment of a customer's cheque by a banker and the protection available to a banker. The relationship between a banker and customer, being debtor-creditor relationship, the banker is legally bound to pay the cheques drawn by his customer.

This duty on the part of the banker, to honour his customers' mandate, is laid down in Section 31 of the Negotiable Instruments Act. Collection of cheques, bills of exchange and other instruments on behalf of a customer is an important service rendered by a bank to his customer. Section 131 provides protection to collecting bankers on completion of certain requirements.

5.3 CHEQUES

Savings and current account holders are issued cheque book. Each cheque book contains a specified (10/25/50/100) number of cheque leaves. A customer can use the cheques book to direct the bank to make payments from his/her account.

As per the definition, a cheque is a bill of exchange drawn on a specified banker and not expressed to be payable otherwise than on demand. This means that a cheque is an instrument that is exclusive to the banking system and no other institution is empowered to operate a checkbook system.

A cheque has three parties:

- The drawer is the account holder signing the cheque;
- The drawee is always the bank (branch where the account holder maintains his account); and
- The payee is the beneficiary who will receive the amount mentioned in the cheque. In case of cheques payable to self-*i.e.*, the account holder drawer and payee will be the same.

Other features of a cheque may be described as follows:

5.3.1 Cheques should be in writing

A cheque should be in writing (by ink pen or ballpoint pen, or printed, but not in pencil as the writing can be easily erased or altered). A cheque can be written by another person, and not necessarily by the drawer only. It should contain:

(*a*) Drawer's signature: The cheque must be signed in ink by the account holder as per the specimen signature on record with the bank branch. If the signature of the drawer differs materially, the cheque may be returned by the banker, to protect the customer's interest from possible forgery.

(*b*) Date of the cheque: A cheque must be dated as the date constitutes a material element of a cheque. A holder of an undated cheque may fill in the date while presenting it for payment. A post-dated cheque cannot be paid before its due date. As per the banking practice in India, a cheque presented after the expiry of 3 months from its written date (called a stale cheque), cannot be paid unless it is revalidated by the drawer under his signature.

(*c*) Amount of cheque: In the printed cheque forms of all banks, there are two spaces for writing the amount of the cheque - in figures and in words. While both these requirements have not been laid down in law, it has become a banking practice not to pay a cheque written only in figures, as the amount written only in figures can be easily altered by the holder or any other person. However, a banker can pay a cheque written only in words or where the amount in words and figures mutually differs, after consulting the drawer, who can later remove the deficiency.

(*d*) Writing the cheques in any language: All cheque forms are printed in Hindi and English. The customer may, however, write cheques in Hindi, English, or the concerned regional language.

(*e*) Acceptance of cheques bearing date as per the National Calendar (Saka Samvat) for payment: The government of India has accepted Saka Samvat as National Calendar with effect from 22 March, 1957 and all Government statutory orders, notifications, Acts of Parliament, etc. bear both the dates *i.e.,* Saka Samvat as well as Gregorian Calendar. An instrument written in Hindi having a date as per Saka Samvat calendar is a valid instrument. Cheques bearing date in Hindi as per the National Calendar (Saka Samvat) should, therefore, be accepted by banks for payment, if otherwise in order. Banks can ascertain the Gregorian calendar date corresponding to the National Saka calendar to avoid payment of stale cheques.

5.3.2 Other points for cheques

a. *Cheque "Drop Box" Facility for Collection of Cheques* : Both the drop box facility and the facility for acknowledgement of the cheques at regular collection counters should be available to the customers and no branch should refuse to give an acknowledgement if the customer tenders the cheques at the counters. Banks should ensure that customers are not compelled to drop the cheques in the drop-box.

b. *Issuance of CTS-2010 Standard cheques only* : All banks have been advised by RBI to issue fresh chequebooks only which comply with CTS-2010 standards to facilitate the electronic processing or collection of cheques.

c. For local cheques, credit and debit shall be given on the same day or at the most the next day of their presentation in a clearing. Ideally, in respect of local clearing, banks shall permit usage of the shadow credit afforded to the customer accounts immediately after closure of relative return clearing, and in any case, the withdrawal shall be allowed on the same day or maximum within an hour of commencement of business on the next working day, subject to usual safeguards.

d. Timeframe for collection of cheques drawn on State Capitals/major cities/other locations are to be 7/10/14 days respectively. If there is any delay in collection beyond this period, interest at the rate specified in the Cheque Collection Policy (CCP) of the bank will be paid. In case the rate is not specified in the CCP, the applicable rate shall be the interest rate on Fixed Deposits for the corresponding maturity.

e. Banks shall not decline to accept outstation cheques deposited by their customers for collection.

f. Now a days, almost all banks are on the CBS platform: Banks are providing cheques to their customers which are payable "at par" at all branches of the bank. Therefore, the volume of collection of outstation cheques has decreased to a real extent.

g. Collection of Account Payee Cheque : Prohibition on Crediting Proceeds to a Third-Party Account: RBI has directed the banks not to credit the 'account payee' cheque to the count of any person other than the payee named therein. Accordingly, banks should not collect account payee cheques for any person other than the payee constituent.

h. Time-limit of a cheque: Banks should not make payment of cheques/drafts/pay orders/bankers cheques, bearing that date or any subsequent date if they are presented beyond the period of three months from the date of such instrument.

i. Cheques/Instruments lost in transit/in clearing process/at paying banks branch: Banks should follow the following guidelines regarding cheques lost in transit:

  a. In respect of cheques lost in transit or the clearing process or at the paying bank's branch, the bank should immediately bring the same to the notice of the account holder so that the account holder can inform the drawer to record stop payment and can also take care that other cheques issued by him are not dishonoured due to non-credit of the amount of the lost cheques/instruments.

  b. The responsibility of such loss lies with the collecting banker and not the account holder.

  c. The banks should reimburse the account holder-related expenses of obtaining duplicate instruments and interest for the reasonable delay that occurred in obtaining the same.

  d. If the cheque/instrument has been lost at the paying bank's branch, the collecting banker should have a right to recover the amount reimbursed to the customer for the loss of the cheque/instrument from the paying banker.

5.4 CHEQUE TRUNCATIONS (CTS)

Cheque truncation is a system between the clearing and settlement of cheques based on electronic images. This form of clearing does not involve any physical exchange of instruments. Bank customers would get their cheques realized faster as local cheques are cleared almost the same day as the cheque is presented to the clearing house, while intercity clearing happens the next day. Besides the speedy clearing of cheques, banks also have the additional advantage of reduced reconciliation and clearing fraud. In this cheque truncation system, the movement of the physical instruments is curtailed at a point in the clearing cycle, beyond which the process is completed, purely based only on the electronic data and images of the cheques.

Benefits of Cheque Truncation:

- Speeding up the collection of cheques
- Enhancing the customer experience/service,
- Reducing the scope for clearing related frauds,
- Minimizing the cost of collection of cheques,
- Reducing the reconciliation work.

Returning dishonoured cheques:

Banks should return/dispatch dishonoured instruments to the customer promptly without delay, in any case within 24 hours.

5.5 CROSSING OF CHEQUES

The effect of crossing a cheque is that the cheque will be payable not in Cash, but through the bank by credit to the account of the payee:

(*a*) General Crossing: A cheque may be crossed by the drawer/issuer and holder by drawing on its face two parallel transverse lines simply, either with or without the words 'not negotiable' or 'and company' or 'account payee. These are examples of "general crossing" and in such cases, the drawee banker shall not pay it otherwise than to a banker.

(*b*) Special Crossing: A special crossing consists of an addition of the name of a bank across the face of a cheque with or without two parallel transverse lines. The effect of such crossing is that the drawee bank shall not pay the cheque otherwise than to the bank to whom it is crossed or his collection agent. This means that a specially crossed cheque must be routed through an account with the named bank.

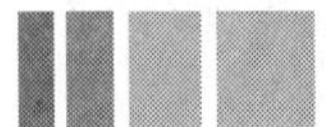

5.6 ENDORSEMENTS

A cheque can be made payable to a bearer or the order of the payee. Bearer cheques can be encashed by the payee or the bearer of the cheques. An order cheque must be paid to the specified payee or his/her endorsee. In such cases, it is essential to identify the payee and validity of the endorsement.

A cheque payable to the order can be negotiated only by endorsement and delivery. Endorsement is made on the back of the instrument, or by attaching a slip of paper (allonge) if the space on the instrument is not enough. The following are the main requirements for endorsement:

(*i*) Signature of the endorser without adding any words is adequate to constitute an endorsement.

(*ii*) The endorsement must be made by the payee or by all the payees jointly.

(*iii*) A stranger cannot endorse an instrument unless he is a holder in due course.

(*iv*) An endorsement cannot be partial as to only a part of the amount of the instrument.

5.7 CARE WHILE ACCEPTING CHEQUES FOR REPAYMENTS

Things to check while accepting cheques :

1. Full name of the payee
2. Valid date
3. Check amount entered is in both number and text
4. Check the signature

It should be noticed that if there are more than one payee – *e.g.*, "Pay to the order of ABC and XYZ" – all payees must endorse the cheque.

A cheque can be deposited into a joint account with only one of the joint owners signing the cheque.

Once the cheque is endorsed, unless there are written restrictions, the cheque becomes a "bearer" instrument so that anyone can cash it.

5.8 CUSTOMER LIABILITIES IF A CHEQUE IS DISHONOURED/BOUNCED

Definition: A cheque falls under the dishonoured category when a payee cannot successfully encash the payor's cheque. A drawer/payor is the one who issues a cheque to the payee. The payee deposits this cheque in the bank. If the bank refuses to pay the amount mentioned on the cheque, the cheque is dishonoured.

The payee must inform the payor of the dishonoured cheque and ask them to inquire about its reason. If the payor believes that the cheque will be honoured a second time, it can re-submitted within three months from the date on it. However, if the cheque bounces again, the payor can face legal action.

Cheques can get dishonoured due to multiple reasons:

i. Insufficient funds

ii. Mismatched signature

iii. The date on the cheque

iv. Damaged cheque

v. Overwriting.

5.9 BANKER'S OBLIGATION TO HONOUR THE CHEQUES

Deposits accepted by a banker are his liabilities repayable on demand or otherwise. The banker is, therefore, under a statutory obligation to honour the customer's cheques in the usual course. Section 31 of the Negotiable Instrument Act of 1881, lays down that:

- The drawee of a cheque having sufficient funds of the drawer in his hand properly applicable to the payment must compensate the drawer for a loss or damage caused by such default.
- Though the primary relationship between a banker and his customer is that of a debtor and creditor or *vice versa,* the special features of this relationship noted above, impose the following additional obligations on the banker:

  Thus, the banker is bound to honour his customer's cheques provided the Following conditions are fulfilled:

  a. There must be sufficient funds for the drawer in the hands of the drawee

  b. The funds must be properly applied to the payment of the cheque

  c. The banker must be duly required to pay.

A banker is bound to honour the cheques only when he is required to pay. This means that the cheque, complete and in order, must be presented for payment within three months. On the expiry of this period, the cheque is treated as stale and the banker dishonours the cheque. Similarly, a post-dated cheque is also dishonoured by the banker because the order of the drawer becomes effective only on the date given in the cheque.

5.10 ERRONEOUS DEBITS ARISING ON FRAUDULENT OR OTHER TRANSACTIONS BANKS SHOULD BE VIGILANT

Banks are required to adhere to the guidelines and procedures for opening an operating deposit account to safeguard against unscrupulous persons reaching accounts mainly to use them as a conduit for fraudulent encashment of Payment Instruments.

However, given a receipt of continuous complaints of fraudulent encashment by unscrupulous persons opening deposit accounts in the name like already established concern/s resulting in an erroneous and unwanted debit of drawers' accounts, banks should remain vigilant to avoid such lapses and issue necessary instructions to the branches/staff.

5.11 COMPENSATING THE CUSTOMER

a. In case of any fraud, if the branch is convinced that an irregularity/fraud has been committed by its staff towards any constituent, the branch at once acknowledges its liability and pays the just claim

b. In cases where banks are at fault, the banks should compensate customers without objection,

c. In cases where neither the bank is at fault, nor the customer is at fault, but the fault lies elsewhere in the system, then also the banks should compensate the customers (up to a limit) as part of a Board approved Compensation policy.

5.12 SECTIONS 138 TO 148 OF NI ACT

Dishonour of cheque for insufficiency, etc., of funds in the Account: Criminal offence.

Where any cheque drawn by a person on an account maintained by him with a banker for payment of any amount of money to another person out of that account for the discharge, in whole or in part, of any debt, is returned by the bank unpaid, either because of the amount standing to the credit of that account is insufficient to honour that or it exceeds the amount arranged to be paid from that account by an agreement made with that bank, such person shall be deemed to have committed an offense and shall, without prejudice to any other provision of this be punished with imprisonment for a term which may extend to two years with a fine which may extend to twice the amount of the cheque, or both.

An offense under the NI Act shall be deemed to have been committed, if the following conditions are satisfied (Section 138):

- Cheque must have been drawn by the drawer in favour of a payee bank account for payment of a legally enforceable debt either in part, or full
- The cheque must have been returned by the Banker to the payee or in due course due to:
    - (*a*) insufficient balance in the account of the drawee or
    - (*b*) it exceeds the arrangement he had with the bank.

The provision requires fulfilment following additional conditions:

- Cheque must be presented within its validity period.

- Written Notice must be given demanding payment of the cheque within 30 days from the date of receipt of debit advice notice. Such written notice must be issued within 30 days from the date of receipt of intimation of dishonour memo from the bank, and
- Drawer fails to pay the dishonoured cheque amount within 15 days date of receipt of the notice.

In these cases, cause of action arises only on failure of the drawer to pay demanded sum within the notice period and on the expiry of the notice period.

The procedure for filing a complaint: A complaint must be filed within 30 days from the date of cause of action *i.e.,* not before the expiry of the notice period nor after 30 days from the date of cause of action. The Apex Court in the case of *MSR Leathers* v. *Palanniappan,* reversed its earlier judgment in *Sadanandan Bhadran* v. *Madhavan Sunil Kumara* and held that a payee or holder of a cheque can now issue a statutory notice to the drawer each time the cheque is dishonoured on subsequent presentations and institute proceedings based on a second or successive statutory notice as well.

Thus, there is a trend in recent judgments of the Supreme Court in interpreting the law relating to cheque bouncing cases more in favour of the complainant. Similarly, other recent judgments expressed a view that strict interpretation should not help dishonest drawers of the cheque.

Directors of companies and partners of firms have been fastened with stricter onus by the Supreme Court in cheque-bouncing cases. It ruled that notice of dishonour of cheques to the company is sufficient, and there is no need to serve separate notices on the directors.

The directors are supposed to know about the dishonour when the company gets the notice. There is sufficient time, nearly 75 days, to find which directors are responsible for the fault, and therefore, there is no need to prolong the process by serving notices to each director or partner.

Cognizance of offence:

Section 142 of the Act starts with "Notwithstanding anything contained in Code of Criminal Procedure, 1973" and mandates that no court shall take cognizance of the offense unless a complaint in writing is given by the payee or holder in due course and such complaint must be made within one month from the date of cause of action.

The effect of this *non-obstante* clause is that NI Act overrides the provisions of CPC to the extent stated in the NI Act. This section also permits belated complaints filed after the prescribed period provided the complainant satisfies the court with sufficient grounds for late filing.

Summary Trial:

Section 143 permits summary trial and it also starts with a *non obstante* clause.

The contents can be summarized as follows:

- It gives power to judicial magistrate of First class or a Metropolitan Magistrate to try 138 cases summarily.
- It specifies that provisions of Sections 262-265 of CrPC shall apply, as far as may be, to summary trials. In other words, discretion has been given to the Magistrate to apply or not to apply provisions of CrPC depending on the facts of the case. However, in practice it is not exercised.
- Trial shall be conducted from day to day until its conclusion unless the Court finds justifiable reasons for the adjournment of the trial beyond the following day. Courts must record reasons in writing for adjourning to a later date. Further courts shall make an endeavour to conclude the trial within 6 months.

Mode of service of summons:

Section 144 deals with mode of service of summons on the accused. It specifies that:

- Summons may be served at the place where the accused or witness ordinarily resides or carries on its business or personally works for gain.
- Summons can be served by speed post, or such courier service authorized by the court of sessions and in case of refusal/receipt by any authorized person, court may declare it is duly served.

Evidence on affidavit:

Section 145 provides that complainant can give evidence on affidavit. Even though the NI Act specifically provides for this, some Magistrates mechanically follow strict compliance of the provisions of sections 261-265 of CrPC. This is one of the main causes for abnormal delay in completion of trial. The complainant is made to appear twice at the pre-summoning stage and post-summoning stage for cross examination or re-examination which really does not serve any meaningful purpose in Section 138 cases but contributes to the delay in the conclusion of trial. It the accused who takes the maximum benefit out of such procedural delays.

5.13 LET US SUM UP

Savings and current account holders are issued cheque book. The cheque is an instrument with an unconditional order, addressed to the banker. It is signed by the person who has deposited cash in the bank.

A cheque can be made payable to a bearer or to the order of the payee. Bearer cheques can be encashed by the payee or the bearer of the cheques. The crossing of the cheque is an instruction to the paying banker to pay the amount to a specific person. The crossing of the cheque secures the payment by the banker.

A banker is bound to honour his customer's cheques provided there is sufficient funds of the drawer in the hands of the drawee and such funds can be applied for the payment of the cheque.

In case of any fraud, if the bank is convinced that an irregularity has been committed by its staff towards any constituent, the branch should acknowledge its liability and pay the just claim towards it.

The relationship between a banker and customer, being debtor-creditor relationship, the banker is bound to pay the cheques drawn by his customer. Where a cheque drawn by a person on an account maintained by him with a bank for payment of any amount of money to another person from out of that account for the discharge, in whole or in part, of any debt or other liability, is returned by the bank unpaid, either because of the amount of money standing to the credit of that account is insufficient to honour the cheque or that it exceeds the amount arranged to be paid from that account by an agreement made with that bank, such person shall be deemed to have committed an offence and shall, without prejudice, to any other provisions of the NI Act, be punished with imprisonment for a term which may extend to two years, or with fine which may extend to twice the amount of the cheque, or with both.

5.14 KEY WORDS

Cheques, Crossing, Honouring of cheques, Cheque truncation, crossing of cheques, N.I. Act, dishonoured cheque, endorsements.

5.15 CHECK YOUR PROGRESS

1. The validity of a cheque/draft is:
   (*a*) Six months
   (*b*) Three months
   (*c*) Nine months
   (*d*) Twelve months
2. An "account payee" crossed cheque can be:
   (*a*) Paid-in cash over counter.
   (*b*) Credited in the account of the endorsee.
   (*c*) Credited in the account of the payee only.
   (*d*) Ignored because it has no legal cognizance.
3. The "special crossing" of a cheque means:
   (*a*) When it bears the name of a bank between two transverse lines.
   (*b*) That the cheques is to be credited in the account of payee only.

(*c*) That it has certain conditions which are to be fulfilled before presenting it for payment/collection.

(*d*) That it can be paid in cash over counter.

4. Section 131A of the Negotiable Instruments Act extends the protection granted to a banker while:

   (*a*) Receiving payment of a cheque and drafts.

   (*b*) Making payment of a cheque and drafts.

   (*c*) Endorsing payment of a cheque and drafts.

   (*d*) All of the above

5. The duties of collecting bank to claim protection has been laid down under the:

   (*a*) Indian Contract Act

   (*b*) Banking Regulation Act

   (*c*) Negotiable Instruments Act

   (*d*) Banking Companies Rules

6. If a bank pays a cheque wherein signatures of the customer are forged, the bank will:

   (*a*) Not be held liable

   (*b*) Not be held liable if the forgery in signatures is not visible in general course

   (*c*) Be held liable

   (*d*) Contact the drawer of the signature and ask him to change the signatures on record so that in future such incidence should not take place

5.16 ANSWERS TO CHECK YOUR PROGRESS

1.	(*b*)	2.	(*c*)	3.	(*a*)	4.	(*a*)	5.	(*c*)	6.	(*c*)		

MODULE B

Brief outline of various products and Legal Aspects of Recovery

CHAPTER

6

Credit Cards and Debit Cards

6.1 OBJECTIVES

After going through this chapter, the reader would be able to understand:

- the various types of cards that are available in the Indian market
- features of these credit cards and debit cards
- ATMs and Micro-ATMs

6.2 INTRODUCTION

Payments for purchases can be made in cash, or by cheques or cards. In respect of cash there is the limitation that bigger payments cannot be made in cash on account of the need to carry bulk. Cheques are not often accepted as the credit standing of the person issuing cheques is not apparent. In such circumstances credit cards come in handy and are used in making payments for day -to- day purchases and expenses.

Now-a-days, plastic money in the form of credit cards has become a preferred mode of payments and has wide acceptance among public. With the increasing use of the credit cards, the financial system is moving more towards cashless transactions.

In the recent years our country has seen rapid growth in the use of cards. However, currently the use of credit facility under the card has not been high as use of credit cards seems restricted to small value and mostly personal transactions. The international credit card giants, *viz.* Visa International, Master Card International and Amex are already present in India and banks issue the cards in collaboration with them.

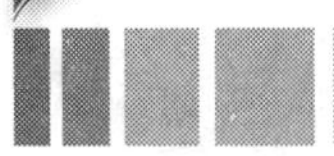

6.3 CARDS

A card is small plastic card of size 8.5 cm by 5.4 cm issued by a bank in association with one or more of the three card companies or Rupay Card in association with NPCI. The name of the card holder, card number and the validity period are embossed on the face of card. Further on every card the name, account number of the holder, and the end of the month up to which the card is valid will also be encrypted. In addition, the reverse of the card contains a three-digit security-number which is to be kept in confidence and used as a measure to establish that the user is in possession of the card while carrying out the transaction. The card issuer should normally get the card holder to sign on the specimen signature panel in his presence before parting with the credit card. The limit up to which the cardholder can make purchases in a month, known as the card limit is also informed to the card holder. A part of this limit is permitted to be used for withdrawing cash for emergency purposes and service fee for such withdrawals is levied. Many banks also have credit cards, which double up as ATM cards.

There are different types of cards some of which are discussed below:

1. Charge card
2. Debit card
3. Credit card
4. Smart card or Chip card
5. Restricted card/Member card
6. ATM Card

6.3.1 Charge Card

Charge card is a typical variety of credit card. In these cards, transactions by the card holder are accumulated over a period of time generally a month, and the total amount is charged, *i.e.*, debited to the account of the card holder. The card holder is given about 20 to 50 days' time to credit his account in case there are insufficient funds in his account at the time of debit.

Since the transactions are only accumulated and charged when the holder is expected to pay the amount, such cards are called charge cards.

6.3.2 Credit Card

This is the same as a charge card where the transactions are charged to the account with the total value of transactions debited to the card holder's account once in a month. The difference between the credit and charge card is that in case of charge card, the amount becomes payable immediately on the debit to the account. In case of credit cards, the cardholder is sent a bill indicating the dues and he/she has the option to pay the entire amount as soon as the bill is received on due date or choose to pay only certain percentage of the amount billed in which case the card holder gets credit to extent of remaining amount, *i.e.*, he/she can pay it in monthly instalments later. Whereas no fee is levied if the full amount billed is paid within a given due date, a service fee is charged on the amount of payment which is deferred. Whereas charge card would warrant maintaining an account with the concerned bank, the dues on the credit card can be paid by any cheque. Credit card holder need not maintain an account with the card issuer bank.

It is expected that the cardholder makes the payment of the billed amount within the stipulated due date or seek instalments as offered by the card company. Generally, card companies will indicate in the bill the minimum amount payable to avail the instalments. The bill will also indicate the rate of interest or fee payable if the card holder seeks to pay in instalments.

A credit card provides consumers with access to a line of credit. Consumers make payments using their card and receive a bill at the end of the billing cycle. The card issuer usually demands a minimum payment against the outstanding balance, but, beyond this, the customer can choose how much of the bill he/she wishes to repay. Any balances not repaid within the interest-free period offered by the issuer, attracts interest at the rate stipulated by the card issuer.

Like other loans and advances credit card dues also may be defaulted. Thus, Credit Cards might cause credit risk for the banks. Given that credit card holders could be dispersed in a large geographical area where the card issuing bank may not have reach and some of card holders may not have accounts with the bank the card issuing banks have to select the Card Clients after thorough appraisal.

Collection of card dues should also be done carefully and methodically. Banks, credit card subsidiaries of banks and card companies use call centres and collection/ recovery agents in managing card dues.

There are a number of parties involved in the credit card business. They are:

(*i*) Card Holder: The person on whose name the card has been issued

(*ii*) Card Issuing Bank: This is the bank which identifies the customer and issues the card. This bank will raise a bill on the customer as per agreed billing schedule

(*iii*) Merchant: Is the person who has accepted payment through the credit card for services rendered or goods sold.

(*iv*) Merchant Bank or Acquiring Bank: Once the card is swiped in the shop, the merchant will seek credit from his/her bank. The bank which reimburses the merchant is known as the merchant bank.

(*v*) The Merchant Bank will claim the payment from the card issuing bank. This is known as the collecting bank.

(*vi*) VISA or Master Card or Rupay Card (NPCI) are the companies which run the credit card operations and they capture all deals and settle the dues among the different intermediaries.

Salient features of credit cards:

- Credit Cards are accepted globally through their affiliation with Visa, Master Card, etc.
- Credit Cards are issued with limits of usage called "Card Limit" which fix the upper limit upto which the cards can be used. Within the overall limit, limits on cash withdrawal through ATMs are fixed which will be equal to or less than the total card limit. While the overall limit can be used at any point of time without any charges, for withdrawal of cash, finance charges are recovered depending upon the frequency of withdrawal.
- Credit cards have a regular billing cycle and billing date and due date of payment is decided from the billing date. The period after which payment is to be made after the billing date is called as the free credit period and will be usually **between 20 days and 50 days** and differ across banks.
- To induce usage of cards, reward points are awarded based on the amount and type of usage. Reward points vary for different classes like Silver, Gold, Platinum, Titanium, etc.,
- Another promotional concept is in vogue now for usage of credit cards. The concept of "CashBack Offer" was introduced in credit cards to promote more usage by incentivizing the usage.
- The payment for the usage of the card after the credit period and on the due date can be paid in different ways such as in full on or before the due date or in instalments, etc.
- Cards are issued with photos also as add on feature
- Some banks offer free personal accident insurance cover for the card holders ranging from Rs. 1 Lakh to Rs. 10 Lakh depending on the type of card, etc.
- RBI has announced in June, 2022 that it will allow credit cards to be linked with the Unified Payments Interface (UPI). This would begin with RuPay credit cards issued by the RBI-promoted National Payments Corporation of India (NPCI). Basic objective of linking credit cards to UPI is to provide customers with wider choice of payments.

Period of credit – An illustration:

Mr. X holds a Credit card and made a transaction on 3rd September. He received his Credit card statement dated 2nd October. He is required to pay the Credit card outstanding in 22 days from the date of statement. How many days credit he would receive in the instant case?

(*a*) 20 days

(*b*) 22 days

(*c*) 50 days *

(*d*) 30 days.

(Answer: October 2nd statement shows the credit card usage for the previous month *i.e.*, from 3rd September to 2nd October. Which is equal to 28 + 2 = 30 days. Credit available in Oct. *i.e.*, from 3rd October to 22nd October = 20 days. So total period of credit available is 50 days *i.e.*, the maximum credit period available in Credit card scheme)

ADVANTAGES OF A CREDIT CARD

The advantages of credit card system to various concerned are as under:

To the card holder:

- It is convenient for a card holder to carry a credit card in his/her wallet and make payment towards travel or purchase. It allows the card holder to draw cash too.
- It inculcates a sense of financial discipline in them.
- It provides a proof of purchase through banking channels to strengthen the card holders' position in case of disputes with sellers, etc.
- It also allows giving spending power to add-on members.
- It also extends additional facilities like insurance cover/discount, etc.

To the merchant establishment:

- Increase in sales because of increased purchasing power of the card holder due to credit available to the card holder.
- Preferred by a card holder to another who does not accept cards.
- Merchant establishments can avoid provision of direct credit to customers.
- Systematic accounting since sale receipts are routed through banking channels.
- Advertising and promotional support on a national scale.
- Development of a prestigious clientele base.
- Assured and immediate settlement/payment.
- Avoidance of all costs and security problems involved in handling cash.

To banks:

- Scope and potential for better profitability out of share earned from the traders' turnover.

- Helps in establishing banking relationship with new customers.
- This also provides additional customer service to the existing clients.
- Better network spread of cardholders and their increased use means higher popularity and image for the banks.
- Savings of expenses on cash holding/stationery printing and manpower to handle clearing transactions.

6.3.3 Debit Cards

Debit cards are similar to the credit cards. The only difference in this card is that the amount of dues from the card holder for each and every transaction is debited from cardholders account as soon as each transaction is notified to the issuer.

A debit card provides access to a cardholder to funds in his/her bank account. It can be used to make purchases and to withdraw cash from ATMs. Debit cards offer consumers a facility to pay with own existing funds, subject to balance available in the account, while providing all the security and convenience that comes with a plastic card.

The characteristics of Debit Cards differ vastly from Credit Cards. As already explained, Credit Cards define the concept of "Buy Now, Pay Later" but Debit Cards explain the concept of "Buy Now and Pay Now". The important aspect of Debit Card is that at the point of purchase itself, the payment is made directly from their account balances.

RuPay Debit cards:

RuPay is a new card payment scheme launched by the National Payments Corporation of India (NPCI), to offer a domestic, open-loop, multilateral system which will allow all Indian banks and financial institutions in India to participate in electronic payments. "RuPay", the word itself has a sense of nationality in it. "RuPay" is the coinage of two terms Rupee and Payment. RuPay Cards address the needs of Indian consumers, merchants and banks. The benefits of RuPay debit card are the flexibility of the product platform, high levels of acceptance and the strength of the RuPay brand-all of which will contribute to an increased product experience.

The main features are as under:

- Lower cost and affordability
- Customized product offering
- Protection of information related to Indian consumers
- Provides electronic product options to untapped/unexplored consumer segment

6.3.4 Contactless Debit and Credit Cards

A Contactless card is a faster way to pay with a credit or debit card for purchases under Rs. 5000/- (increased from Rs. 2,000/- to Rs. 5,000/- w.e.f. 1-1-21) at participating stores. Instead of dipping (or swiping) the card at the billing counter, simply wave or tap the card on the contactless terminal and pay without entering a PIN (for amount under Rs. 5,000/-). The key advantage is that; this card can ensure the transaction gets completed in one tenth the time taken by an existing credit card

HOW DO THEY WORK?

These cards work on near-field communication (NFC) technology, which employs radio transmission to ascertain contact when the cards are tapped or waved near a terminal. These enable customers to make payments by waving or tapping the cards instead of swiping them. After this, one needs to enter one's PIN to complete the transaction. If needed, these cards can also be used in the traditional way – by swiping or dipping. Reserve Bank of India (RBI)'s guidelines allow to process contactless transactions below Rs. 5000 without a PIN.

WHAT ARE ITS BENEFITS?

It increases the ease and convenience of transactions. Moreover, the speed at which the transaction can be carried out is almost double that of traditional cards.

ARE THEY SECURE?

It is claimed that these cards are very secure because unlike the cards in use now, these do not have to be handed over to the merchant and so is always in one's sight.

However, there have been skimming attacks on these cards in some countries where they had been introduced. In certain instances, fraudsters have been able to skim the data using mobile applications. But then, experts say these threats are present even in the regular cards.

6.3.5 Smart Cards

A Smart Card is an electronic device about size of a credit card, containing electronic memory and possibly an embedded Integrated Circuit (IC). This data is usually associated with either value or information, or both and is stored and processed within the card's chip. The IC contains memory, may contain a processor, and communicates with the external world through contacts on the surface of the card. Smart card is a versatile payment tool that can offer great value for the cardholder. It offers the highest level of security for payment cards. The size, position and utility of the contacts are specified by an international standard (ISO 7816), so that cards can interact with a variety of equipment. Some cards have a photo of the holder printed on the card which also serves the purpose of identification in case of need.

6.3.6 Member Card

This is used exclusively by members of a club or a chain of hotels. For example, the Taj Card, is a card issued by the Management of Taj Group of Hotels to be used by patrons of their hotels. The cards are for use in their hotels only. Similarly, there are many other types of cards where the usage is exclusive to the members of a group or establishment.

6.3.7 ATM Card

An ATM is a computerised machine that provides customers of banks the facility of accessing their accounts for dispensing cash and to carry out other financial & non-financial transactions without the need to visit the bank branch. These are cards issued to the savings account holders for drawing cash from ATM Machines which can be placed in the branch or off site. Some of the debit/credit cards are also used as ATM cards. The ATMs ensure availability of cash 24 hours and the customer need not visit the branch for small transactions.

A full-fledged ATM (e-lobby) is well-equipped to perform the following functions:

- Deposits/Withdrawals, Personal Identification Number (PIN) changes, Requisition for cheque books, Statement of accounts, Balance enquiry, Inter account transfer within the bank between accounts of same customer or different customers of the bank at the same centre or different centres within the country, Inter Bank Funds Transfer, Transfer of Funds between the bank's customers and customers of other banks, mail facility for sending written communication to the bank, Utility payments like Electricity bill, Telephone bill, etc., Issue of railway tickets and Product Information.

Reconciliation of transactions at ATMs failure:

a. The prescribed time-limit for resolution of customer complaints is 5 working days from the date of receipt of customer's complaint. If a bank fails to re-credit the customer's account within 5 working days of receipt of the complaint, it will entail payment of compensation to the customer @ Rs. 100 per day by the issuing bank. This compensation will be credited to the customer's account automatically without any claim from the customer, on the same day when the bank affords the credit for the failed ATM transaction.

b. Any customer is entitled to receive such compensation for delay, only if a claim is lodged with the issuing bank within 30 days of the date of the transaction.

c. The number of free transactions permitted per month at other bank ATMs to Savings Bank account holders are inclusive of all types of transactions, financial or non-financial.

d. All disputes regarding ATM failed transactions shall be settled by the issuing bank and the acquiring bank through the ATM System Provider only.

6.3.8 Micro-ATMs

Micro ATM is a device that is used by Business Correspondents (BC) to deliver basic banking services. The platform enables Business Correspondents to conduct instant cash transactions. Micro-ATMs are biometric authentication enabled hand-held devices. In order to make the ATMs viable at rural/semi-urban centers, low-cost Micro-ATMs need to be deployed at each of the Bank Mitra location. This would enable a person to instantly deposit or withdraw funds regardless of the bank associated with a particular Bank Mitra/Business Correspondent:

- This device is based on a mobile phone connection and would be made available to every Bank Mitra/Business Correspondent. Customers would have to get their identity authenticated and withdraw or put money into their bank accounts. This money will come from the cash drawer of the Bank Mitra/ Business Correspondent.
- Essentially, Bank Mitras act as bank for the customers and all they need to do is verify the authenticity of customer using customer's UID. The basic transaction types to be supported by micro-ATM are deposit, withdrawal, fund-transfer and balance enquiry. Micro-ATM offers one of the most promising options for providing financial services to the unbanked population. Micro-ATMs would have various options of authentication like biometric, PIN based etc. and it would also be used as mobile ATMs to enable transactions near the door step of the customers. The Micro-ATMs offer an online interoperable, low-cost payments platform to everyone in the country.

6.4 LET US SUM UP

Credit Card is plastic money with pre-set limits based on the credit score of the customer and can be used across merchant establishments for payment of purchases and in ATMs for withdrawal of cash. The operational process of a credit card starts from the card issue, matures into card usage and closes with the payment of credit card dues. The credit period available in Credit card scheme is 20–50 days depending upon the usage. Apart from being a delivery channel of the banking services, credit cards issued by banks are also a good source of credit delivery. Due to advancement of technology and easy accessibility to credit they provide for card users, they have gained popularity and wide acceptance in the market today. It is, no doubt, a novel way of providing value added services to bank customers. If used prudently, they offer a bundle of benefits to card users. To prevent the customers from falling into a debt trap and consequent harassment from the recovery agents of the card issuers,

Reserve Bank of India has come out with well-documented policy guidelines called "Fair Practices Code" for banks. The characteristics of Debit Cards differ vastly from Credit Cards. As already explained, Credit Cards define the concept of "Buy Now, Pay Later" but Debit Cards explain the concept of "Buy Now and Pay Now". There are different types of cards such as credit card, debit card, charge card, etc. With the increasing use of credit cards, the society is moving towards cashless transactions or plastic money.

6.5 KEY WORDS

Debit card, Charge card, Credit card, Smart card, ATM card, RuPay Card, Contactless/ card

6.6 CHECK YOUR PROGRESS

1. The difference between the credit and the debit card is:
   (*a*) Your account gets debited immediately on using a credit card
   (*b*) Your account gets debited immediately on using a debit card
   (*c*) Your account does not get debited immediately on using a debit card
   (*d*) None of the above
2. Credit risk to the bank is high from the:
   (*a*) credit card holders
   (*b*) debit card holders
   (*c*) both of the above
   (*d*) none of the above
3. The bank which pays the merchant for the transactions is called as:
   (*a*) issuer bank
   (*b*) clearance bank
   (*c*) acquiring bank
   (*d*) none of the above
4. Disadvantages to Credit Card holders:
   (*a*) Over Spending ending in Debt Trap
   (*b*) Frauds due to loss or theft of cards
   (*c*) Forged signatures
   (*d*) All of the above

5. One of the following statement is not true with respect to credit cards:
   (*a*) The card issuing banks would not be responsible for fulfilment of KYC requirements, where agents solicit business.
   (*b*) While issuing cards, the terms and conditions for issue and usage of a credit card should be mentioned in clear and simple language.
   (*c*) Card issuers should quote Annualized Percentage Rates (APR) on card products.
   (*d*) The card issuing bank/NBFC can unilaterally upgrade credit cards and enhance credit limits without prior intimation to the borrower.

6.7 ANSWERS TO CHECK YOUR PROGRESS

1.	(*b*)	2.	(*a*)	3.	(*c*)	4.	(*a*)	5.	(*d*)				

CHAPTER

7 Various types of Loans and Advances

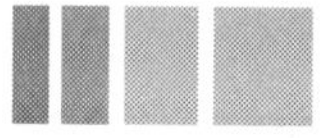

7.1 OBJECTIVES

At the end of the chapter, the student would be able to learn the features of:

(*a*) Cardinal principles of lending

(*b*) Credit Scoring

(*c*) Various types of advances:

- (*i*) Housing loans
- (*ii*) Vehicle loans
- (*iii*) Loans for purchase of consumer durables
- (*iv*) Personal loans
- (*v*) Education loans
- (*vi*) Agricultural loans
- (*vii*) Loans to Micro, Small and Medium Enterprises (MSMEs)

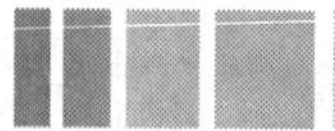

7.2 INTRODUCTION

The commercial banks accept deposits and simultaneously lend money to the people who require it for various purposes. Banks lends funds for business purposes, cultivation of crops and allied activities, and also for housing, education and purchase of consumer durables, etc. The major part of the deposits received by banks is lent out, and a large part of their income is earned from interest on such lending. There is a considerable difference between the rate of interest which the commercial bank grants on deposits, and the rate they charge on loans and advances. It is this difference which constitutes the main source of bank earnings. Retail Banking Products can be broadly classified into retail liability products, retail assets products, and other products/services. Liability products are basically Savings, Current and Term Deposit Accounts. Retail assets products are loans such as Home Loans, Vehicle Loans, Education Loans, Personal Loans, Credit Card Receivables, and other Retail Loans. Other Products/Services broadly cover the beyond product facilities tagged to the products and services, such as Debit Cards, ATM Cards, Internet Banking, Mobile Banking, Third Party Products like Insurance, Mutual Funds, Demat Services, etc.

In this Unit, we will briefly describe the salient features of important retail credit products *viz.* housing loan, vehicle loans, loans for purchase of consumer durables, personal (consumption) loans, overdrafts, loans. In this lesson, you will also learn cardinal principles of lending, credit scoring and about the procedure of getting loans and advance for various purposes from the banks.

7.3 CARDINAL PRINCIPLES OF LENDING

The business of lending is not without certain inherent risks, especially when the lending banks depend largely on the borrowed funds. The cardinal principles of lending are, therefore, as follows:

(*a*) Safety

(*b*) Liquidity

(*c*) Profitability

(*d*) Purpose

(*e*) Diversification of Risks

(*f*) Security

(*a*) Safety:

Safety first is the most important principle of good lending. When a banker lends certain money, he has to ensure that the advance is safe and that the money lent will comeback. While banks are, no doubt, traders in money; the money lent does not belong to them but to the public, *i.e.*, the depositors. The banker is a custodian of public funds and lends money which has been entrusted to his care by the depositor and which is to be repaid in accordance with the tenure of the deposit. The repayment of loans depends upon the borrower's (*i*) capacity to pay, (*ii*) willingness to pay, (*iii*) income generation. The banker must, therefore, take utmost care in ensuring that the enterprise or business, for which a loan is sought, is a sound one and the borrower is capable of carrying it out successfully.

(*b*) Liquidity:

It is to be seen that money lent is not going to be locked up for a long time. The money should return to the bank as per the repayment schedule. Banks are having Asset liability management by which they can manage liquidity of fund received from depositors and can lend accordingly.

(*c*) Profitability:

A fair return on investment is essential so also in the case of lending by banks. Banks are commercial organisations and profit earning is the objective of the banks in order to pay adequate dividends to the stakeholders. The interest margin of three to four per cent between lending and borrowing is essential to meet their administrative expenses. While looking at profitability, it is prudent for a banker to look at the overall profitability from all businesses undertaken for a customer instead of applying the test of profitability against each component of business or service offered separately. Possibly a banker may not be earning a desirable return on a service undertaken for a customer, while he may be more than compensated in respect of another service or business undertaken for the same customer. It is, therefore, advisable to have a Customer Profitability Analysis (CPA) done when the banker is engaged in more than one service or business for a customer, this is all the more necessary not only to assess the profitability of the operation/business *vis-à-vis* a customer but also to enable a banker to decide on as to what length he can go in parting with a portion of profit and offer a competitive rate for the customers. Such an analysis will be very helpful to the banker in pricing his product whether it is in lending or offering a service to a customer.

In the current context of the availability of freedom to a banker in the matter of pricing credit and services, a very conscious and a careful exercise is called for on his part in order to strike a proper balance between the twin aims of making a desirable level of profit and at the same time offering a competitive price for the product/service offered. This is the kind of approach that is required of a banker in order to bring new customers to his fold while retaining the existing customers. Hence, there is a direct relationship between profit and pricing of credit or service offered by a banker.

(*d*) Purpose:

Loans for undesirable and speculative purposes cannot be granted. Although the earnings on such business activities may be higher, even then a bank cannot resort to these loans.

(*e*) Diversification of Risks:

It means that the banker should not grant advances to only a few business houses, undertakings, cities, industries or regions. It should be ensured that the advances are diversified in a good number of customers.

(*f*) Security:

The security offered against the loans may consist of a large variety of items. It may be plot or land, building, flat, shop, ornaments, insurance policies, shares, debentures, bonds, etc. There may be cases where there is no security except the personal security. The banker must realise that it is only a cushion to fall back upon in case of need. The security and its adequacy alone should not form the sole consideration for judging the suitability of a loan. Of course, the security, if accepted, must be adequate and readily marketable, easy to handle and free from encumbrances.

7.4 THE 5 "Cs" OF CREDIT

Extending credit to a customer is about taking on a certain level of risk. There is no secret formula or mathematical equation that ensures you're making the right decision. But by applying the 5 Cs of Credit, you can at least, make an informed one.

A. Character:

What do you know about the customer? Has he exhibited integrity in former business dealings? Does he keep his word? One way to handle those of questionable integrity is to get references. What are other business contacts saying about him? The important thing is, a person can have the ability to pay, but if they don't keep their word or are in some way untrustworthy, they are a risk you don't want to take. It's obvious that those who betray trust aren't good candidates for extended credit.

B. Collateral:

By taking a lien, you're staking a claim to your customer's assets. In that case, you become their secured creditor. It goes without saying that you don't want to go back and re-claim products you've sold to your customer in the event that he doesn't pay back his loan. But by using a security agreement and financial statement, that's exactly what you can do.

C. Capacity:

Capacity is all about cash flow. Most businesses experience the ebbs and flows of cash flow right along with the nation's economic health (or lack thereof). Even the most responsible and conscientious customer can experience a turn of events that throws a kink in the works. But the bottom line is, can your customer still pay you even when there's a temporary hitch in his cash flow?

D. Capital:

What's your customer's net worth? By comparing several financial statements, you'll be able to see any trends upward or downward. If net worth is increasing each year, then capital is being put into the company.

E. Conditions:

The economy and market conditions play a role in everything across the board in business. For certain customers, tough economic times can be particularly challenging. When conditions are good, orders come in and the money flows. When they're not, the customer is not prepared for the eventuality and may react to it by letting some bills slide. When that happens, it's time to tighten up your policies.

To determine which of your customers is the bigger risk to you, start by taking into consideration the 5 C's of Credit. It's a great beginning point before you make any credit decisions.

7.5 CIBIL AND IMPORTANCE OF SIMILAR CREDIT SCORING SYSTEM

Every formal lender is required to know the credit worthiness of an applicant. This can be assisted by a few Credit Information Companies like CIBIL which are licensed by RBI. Trans Union CIBIL Ltd., earlier known as Credit Information Bureau Ltd., is among the leading credit information companies in India. Incorporated in 2000, it is popularly known as CIBIL credit bureau. The bureau gathers and maintains records of your payments related to credit products such as loans and credit cards. Lenders, financial institutions like banks and non-banking finance companies submit your credit records to CIBIL every month. The credit bureau uses this information and computes your CIBIL score and creates a detailed credit report. Lenders use this report and score to measure your creditworthiness and assess whether you can repay the borrowed amount.

This bureau is licensed by the Reserve Bank of India (RBI) and is overseen by the Credit Information Companies (Regulation) Act of 2005. It has more than 2,400 members including banks, financial institutions, non-banking financial companies, and housing finance companies. The credit bureau maintains credit records of more than 550 million consumers and businesses.

What is a CIBIL Score?

A CIBIL score is a 3-digit number that represents creditworthiness of a person. It ranges from 300-900. The closer one's score is to 900, the better the chances are of his getting a loan or a credit card approved. A higher score suggests that he is a responsible borrower and have a good credit history. As per general standards, a score of 750 and above gives his quicker access to loans and credit cards.

What makes CIBIL Score?

There are four main factors that make up the score:

Payment History	30%
Credit Exposure	25%
Credit Type and Duration	25%
Other Factors	20%

What are the Factors that affect my CIBIL Score?

(*a*) Payment History:

One of the biggest factors that affects one's CIBIL score is payment history. He should make it a priority to pay his credit card bills as well as loan EMIs on time. Avoid late payment of bills at any given time as it will bring down his score. As per a recent CIBIL analysis, a 30-day delinquency can reduce his CIBIL score by 100 points.

(*b*) Total Amount of Debt:

The total amount of debt one has at a given point of time has a major effect on his CIBIL score. Credit utilisation ratio is the amount of credit used by him in proportion to his combined credit limit. He should maintain a low credit utilisation ratio at all times to get a high score. As per experts, it is advised to use only up to 30% of your total credit limit.

(*c*) Length of the Credit:

A long credit history helps to improve one's score. It suggests that he has a good experience with handling credit. Lenders prefer offering credit to people who have a rich history because it makes assessing him as a borrower, easier. Therefore, it is advised to avoid closing old cards as he will lose out on the long credit history and good repayment behaviour associated with it.

(*d*) Type of Credit and Duration:

It is important to have a decent credit mix. Maintaining a healthy balance of secured and unsecured credit helps to boost his CIBIL score. He needs to make sure that he does not have high secured credit or unsecured credit and instead try and maintain a good balance of both.

(*e*) Total Credit Inquiries:

He should avoid making multiple credit inquiries within a short period of time. When he inquires to a bank or a financial institution about a loan or a credit card, the lender will pull out his CIBIL report. Such an inquiry is called a "hard inquiry" and it has a negative impact on his score. Multiple credit inquiries can bring his score down. Therefore, it is advised to inquire for credit only when he actually needs it. Meanwhile, when he checks his own score or report, it is called a "soft inquiry". He can check his report multiple times and it will not have any effect on his CIBIL score as soft inquiries are not recorded on his report.

How to Improve CIBIL Score?

In order to improve one's CIBIL score, he needs to be consistent in paying bills on time and be a responsible borrower. Here are some of the ways that will help improve one's score.

- **Use Credit Lines Responsibly:**

  At the end of the day, any money from a line of credit is borrowed money. He needs to repay it to his lender, with or without interest, depending on the type of credit line, and his repayment behaviour. So, he should use his credit card, loan amount, or any other type of borrowing wisely. Also, he should not use or borrow more than he can afford to repay. This could lead him into a debt-trap.

- **Avoid Late or Missed Payments:**

  Apart from being charged late payment fees on his late payments, this repayment behaviour will also get reported to the credit bureaus, affecting his creditworthiness. If he has multiple credit card payments and loan EMIs to make, it is advised to set up payment reminders or due date alerts to get more organised. This way he never forgets making his payment. He could also set up a direct debit arrangement with his lender, where his payments get automatically deducted from his savings/current account on the due date. This way, he will never have to worry remembering due dates, or about late or missed payments.

- **Maintain a Low Credit Utilisation Ratio:**

  As mentioned earlier, he should ideally not exceed 30% of his total credit card limit. This is especially important if he applies for a home loan in the future. When he applies for a home loan, banks will assess his debt-to-income (DTI) ratio. This ratio evaluates his total debt with respect to his total income. If his debt exceeds 50% of his income, banks are more likely to reject his application. Another reason why he should maintain a low credit utilisation ratio is to not appear credit hungry. If most of his expenses are being borne by his credit lines, he will appear as a borrower who is unable to manage their expenses on his own.

- **Make Sure to Close Accounts Instead of Settling:**

  If he has defaulted on any payments in the past, it will be reflected in his credit history and will bring his CIBIL score down. He should make sure to pay off the unpaid amount and close the account instead of opting for a settlement. He should ensure that the account gets a 'closed' status. Also, it is best to get a formal closure certificate from the lender for the account.

- **Review your Credit Report:**

  He should check his credit report periodically to understand his credit health. This should be done to ensure that his credit report is free of any errors related to his credit accounts. This is important because any incorrect information recorded on his report could bring down his score through there is no fault of his own. It is important to identify and rectify such errors at the earliest.

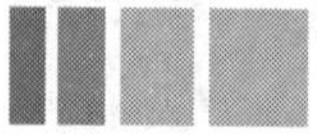

7.6 TYPES OF LOANS AND ADVANCES

Credit facilities are broadly classified into two types as follows:

1. Fund based credit facilities
2. Non-Fund based credit facilities

7.6.1 Fund Based Credit Facilities

Fund based credit facilities involve outflow of funds from the banks meaning thereby that the money of the bank is lent to the customer. They can be generally of following types:

1. Loans:
   (*a*) Demand/Short-Term Loans
   (*b*) Medium and Long-Term Loans
   (*c*) Bridge Loans
2. Advances:
   (*a*) Cash Credit
   (*b*) Overdrafts
   (*c*) Bills finance
      (*i*) Bills Purchase
      (*ii*) Bills Discounting
   (*d*) Export Finance
      (*i*) Pre-shipment Credit
      (*ii*) Post-shipment Credit.

7.6.2 Non-Fund Based Credit Facilities

In the business of lending, a banker also extends non-fund based facilities. Non-fund based facilities do not involve immediate outflow of funds. The banker undertakes a risk to pay the amounts on happening of a contingency. Non-fund based facilities can be of following types among others:

(*a*) Bank Guarantees
(*b*) Letter of Credit
(*c*) Co-acceptances
(*d*) Underwriting and credit guarantee

The terms and conditions, the rights and privileges of the borrower and the banker differ in each case.

7.6.3 Working Capital and Term Loans

The type of loan that a borrower need will depend upon the need of the borrower namely whether the funds are required for meeting the day-to-day expenses or for

investment in plant and machinery, etc. The loan for meeting day to day business/ trading/manufacturing activities is known as Working Capital Finance. These loans take the form of Cash Credit or Overdrafts. The investment loans are granted as term loans.

(*a*) Cash Credit System:

Under the system, the banker specifies a limit, called the cash credit limit, for each customer, up to which the customer is permitted to borrow against the security of tangible assets or guarantees. The customer withdraws from his cash credit account as and when he needs the funds and deposits any amount of money which he finds surplus with him on any day. The cash credit account is thus an active and running account to which deposits and withdrawals may be affected frequently.

(*i*) The banker fixes the cash credit limit after taking into account several features of working of the borrowing concern such as production, sales, inventory levels, past utilization of such limits, etc. The banks are thus inclined to relate the limits to the security offered by their customers.

(*ii*) The advances sanctioned under the cash credit arrangement are technically repayable on demand and there is no specific date of repayment.

(*b*) Term Loans:

(*i*) Under the term loan facility, credit is given for a definite purpose and for a predetermined period. Normally, these loans are repayable in instalments. Funds are required for single non-repetitive transactions and are withdrawn only once.

(*ii*) Term loans are utilized for establishing expanding or modernizing a manufacturing unit by acquiring of fixed assets.

(*c*) Difference between Cash Credit System and Term Loan:

The major difference between term loans and working capital finance lies in the purpose of the finance, the type of assets created out of it and the form in which the advance is made by the bank. The other differences are:

(*i*) Term loans are utilized for establishing, expanding or modernizing a farming and service enterprise by acquisition of fixed assets, while the working capital finance is utilized for cultivation and operating purposes resulting in the creation of current assets for production and the sale of final produces or finished goods.

(*ii*) Term loans are usually of medium or long-term duration and are repayable in monthly, quarterly or half yearly instalments over an agreed period of time. As against this, the working capital finance is generally availed for crop cultivation in a farming enterprise or in cash credit (hypothecation) accounts in a production or service enterprise, with frequent drawings and repayments within the time period fixed and is repayable on demand.

(*iii*) Term Loans are secured by Mortgage or Hypothecation of plant and machinery, etc. whereas working capital loans are secured by hypothecation of raw material/stocks or inventory, standing crop, etc.

7.7 RETAIL LOANS

There has been a sharp growth of Retail loans - both in the number and amount especially in the last five years. The main reasons/features of such growth are:

(*i*) Fast growing population of the middle- income class, coupled with fast rising income levels of middle and higher classes, in the country. These population groups mainly comprise of salaried employees, self-employed professionals, traders and businessmen forming SMEs (Small and Medium Enterprises)

(*ii*) Other demographic factors like workers migration to cities/metros and increasing population of entrepreneurs, self-employed professionals, women workers have led to the concentration of retail loans in metros and second tier cities.

(*iii*) The number of loans for vehicles (bikes, three wheelers, and cars), houses, consumer durables and other consumption needs has increased significantly across the country due to issues such as poor public transport system and the fast-growing middle class population.

(*iv*) Exponential growth in credit cards usage and the resultant over-due receivables from a large number of customers in scattered locations.

The typical products offered in the Indian retail-banking segment are housing loans, loans for purchase of consumer durables, auto loans, personal loans, credit cards and educational loans. The loans are marketed under attractive brand names to differentiate the products offered by different banks. The loans are generally issued with a repayment period of five to seven years with housing loans going for a longer duration of say 20 years.

SEGMENTS AND TARGET GROUPS OF RETAIL LOANS

The Retail Loans mainly comprise the following sub-segments and their target customer groups are:

(*i*) Home loans to salaried and self-employed professionals. Home loans account for about half of total retail loans.

(*ii*) Auto loans (car and two wheelers) to salaried and self-employed professionals. This sub-segment accounts for about one third of total retail loans.

(*iii*) Loans/advances against shares to High Net-worth Individuals (HNIs), businessmen and traders.

(*iv*) Personal loans to salaried, self-employed professionals and traders/businessmen. These loans, for consumption needs and unsecured (*i.e.,* without tangible security), are granted on the basis of income flows or net worth of the individual borrowers.

(*v*) Credit card receivables from salaried, self-employed professionals and traders/ businessmen.

7.7.1 Housing Loans

Loans granted by the banks and housing finance companies for purchase of flat, purchase of land and construction of house and for modernization or renovation of existing homes, etc. are classified as housing finance/loans.

Housing is a basic need of every family and majority of the population of the country does not still own houses. Almost every individual need own house. Companies also need funds to buy housing colonies for allotting houses to their employees. In this background there has been good demand for housing loans. Housing/Home loans account for about half of total retail loans of banks. The amount of loans issued by the banks and outstanding there against has been increasing very rapidly during the last 7 years.

In the recent years, there has been an upward movement in the salary packages of the youngsters taking up jobs. This coupled with the availability of an IT package to handle home loan appraisal on the basis of score card and capability to handle large number of borrowers has been the reason for the rapid growth of home loan portfolio. The possibility of securitization has also increased the banks appetite for retail and home loan portfolio.

The scope of growth in housing loans is enormous. The salient features of home loans are as follows:

(*i*) **Purpose**: Purchase/construction/upgradation/extension etc. of houses.

(*ii*) **Amount of Loan**: Will cover cost of land and construction or price of the flat and interior decoration.

(*iii*) **Type of Borrower**: Single or Joint or corporate.

(*iv*) **Period of Loan/Term**: Medium (3-5 years) to very long period (15-20 years), depending on cash flows and choice of the borrower.

(*v*) **Interest Rate**: Fixed/floating rate. Currently home loans are granted at lowest interest rate among all retail products.

(*vi*) **Security**: First Mortgage (Equitable or Registered) of the land/house or other immovable property (being purchased/constructed or already built) by the borrower in favour of the bank.

(*vii*) **Registration**: The mortgage charge is registered with Registrar of Properties.

(*viii*) **Guarantee**: Taken in cases where margin is low or net worth of the borrowers as assessed is inadequate.

(*ix*) **Documents**: Term Loan Agreement, Guarantee letter in case of personal guarantee and all other documents specified by respective banks.

(*x*) **Repayment**: Repayment is generally in the form of EMI (equated monthly instalments) for the period of loan. EMI includes both interest and principal. EMI is fixed on the basis of borrower's cash flow which is analysed at the time of sanction of loan. In respect of flats where the construction takes time, banks may stipulate that the borrower has to pay the interest on the prescribed periodicity till the house is constructed and possession obtained. Once the possession is obtained or after a lapse of a given period after the release of the full loan, whichever is earlier, the banks may stipulate the payment through EMI.

(*xi*) **Step up Repayment**: It is seen that some banks offer lower EMI in initial years and higher EMI in later years, when the cash inflows are expected to increase. This is known as step up loan.

Levy of foreclosure charges/pre-payment penalty:

Banks cannot charge foreclosure charges/pre-payment penalties on home loans on floating interest rate basis.

As per extant norms, a fixed rate loan is one where the rate is fixed for entire duration of the loan. Hence, the Dual Rate/Special Rate home loans sanctioned by banks cannot be treated as fixed rate loans.

Banks are also not permitted to charge foreclosure charges/pre-payment penalties on all floating rate term loans sanctioned to individual borrowers. In some of the public/private sector banks pre-payment/foreclosure charges are levied in case the housing loan is taken over by some other bank/Housing finance companies.

7.7.2 Vehicle Loans

Vehicle Loans or, Auto loans (car, two/three-wheelers) account for about one-third of total retail loans in the country. The amount of loan outstanding for vehicle loans is next only to housing sector. This portfolio has also grown very fast in recent years. The demand for car and two-wheeler loans come from professionals and self-employed persons. Due to shortage of public transport system, demand for loans for auto-rickshaws and car-taxis is also increasing in most cities. The salient features of vehicle loans are as follows:

(*i*) **Purpose**: Purchase of vehicles (2/3/4 wheelers) for personal use or as taxi loans for small duty vehicles which are issued under Small Road Transport Operator Scheme.

(*ii*) **Period/term of Loan**: The maximum period of loan in the case of new 4 wheelers is 7 years and for new 2 two wheelers, it is 5 years. For Second hand vehicles, the repayment period depends on the estimated income/cash flows and nature/cost of vehicle, but generally maximum period of loan in such cases does not exceed 3 years.

(*iii*) **Interest Rate**: Generally floating-rate is charged on the loan and the rate is higher than housing loan.

(*iv*) **Security**: Hypothecation charge in favour of bank on the vehicle purchased out of bank finance.

(*v*) **Registration**: Hypothecation charge is registered with the Road Transport Commissioner's office.

(*vi*) **Guarantee**: Surety or personal guarantee is stipulated in the case of loan for taxis or in other cases also as per the scheme of the different banks.

(*vii*) **Repayments**: EMI Repayment can be more frequent. Longer period (lower EMI) is extended to some sectors. In the case of auto rickshaw loans fortnightly repayments are accepted.

7.7.3 Loans for Purchase of Consumer Durables

Loans granted by banks (term loans) and finance companies (usually, NBFCs) for purchases of white goods like mobiles, refrigerators, washing machines, TVs, music system, micro wave/electric ovens, other kitchen equipment, etc. are classified in this category. Generally, the loans are for periods of less than 4 years. These loans attract a higher rate of interest than home loans.

In the case of hire purchase finance, the title to the goods passes to the purchaser only on payment of the last instalment. In the case of term loans, it vests in the purchaser after payment of the price and therefore the goods are hypothecated in favour of the lender.

In the case of default of instalments, the Hire purchase transaction gives the right of repossession to the vendor as the title is still with the vendor. As against this, in the case of loan which is supported by a hypothecation there is, for the lender, the need to follow the due process of law before taking possession of the goods. It should be added that even HP vendor has to comply with certain legal formalities such as issue of notice about intention to repossess, etc. The salient features of consumer durables loans are as follows:

(*i*) **Purpose**: Purchase of white goods.

(*ii*) **Repayment term**: 18-48 months, depending on the cost/nature of the product and income/cash flows of the borrower.

(*iii*) **Repayment**: EMI

(*iv*) **Interest Rate**: Floating. The rate is higher than home/vehicle loans

(*v*) **Security**: Hypothecation of the assets purchased

(*vi*) **Guarantee**: Generally not required, unless income/cash flow of the borrower is not adequate.

7.7.4 Consumption (Personal) Loans

Personal Loans are basically unsecured in nature and are backed by personal guarantees only. These loans are for purposes which are not specific about end use. Generally, the purpose does not include purchase of goods/property as in foregoing loans. Being generally clean loans without any tangible security, they are granted to individuals/businessmen with good net worth. The salient features of personal loans are as follows:

(*i*) **Purpose:** Travel, marriage or other function/event requiring large expenses

(*ii*) **Loan term**: Short-term loan or Demand loan or overdraft.

(*iii*) **Repayment**: EMI or as agreed upon.

(*iv*) **Interest Rate**: Floating rate. The rate is higher than other loans in retail segment.

(*v*) **Security**: No tangible security. Banks may ask for tangible security in cases where the net worth or income/cash flows may not be adequate.

(*vi*) **Guarantee**: Required, if net worth/cash flows are not adequate and tangible security is not available.

(*vii*) **Other**: Granted mostly to people in high income bracket among salaried, self-employed professionals, and businessmen. Quantum of finance is linked with monthly/annual income of individual proponent.

7.7.5 Overdrafts

Overdrafts are granted in the Current accounts, whereby a customer can over-draw (*i.e.,* in excess of the credit balance) up to a sanctioned limit as per his/her cash requirements. It is a running account and interest is charged only on the debit balances, generally on daily product basis. The interest rate is highest in retail loans segment. The salient features of overdrafts are as follows:

(*i*) **Purpose**: Omnibus or general purpose, for meeting contingencies and *ad hoc* cash requirement

(*ii*) **Term**: Payable on demand of the bank

(*iii*) **Interest**: Floating rate - Highest rate in Personal (or retail) segment.

(*iv*) **Security**: Generally unsecured. But liquid (movable) security (*e.g.*, fixed deposit receipts, bonds/certificates issued by RBI/FIIs/Post offices) is asked for in cases of large amount and/or long period requirements.

(*v*) **Guarantee**: Generally not required if above said security requirements are met.

(*vi*) **Other**: Documentation is very easy and quick for existing account holders.

7.7.6 Credit Card Dues

Several banks issue both debit cards and credit cards directly or through their subsidiaries/affiliates. Both these cards allow cash-less purchases of goods and services, which are convenient and safe and these are the prime reasons for their increasing usage in cities and metros. While credit card allows certain free credit period, in the case of debit cards the card holders account is debited instantaneously with the purchase transactions. After the initial free credit period between the bill date and due date, the card companies also allow credit/time to the card holders to make payments in instalments. If the customer delays the payment beyond the free period or due date of bill the bank will charge interest on dues. In the recent years, credit card over-dues have substantially increased. Since the debtors are in large numbers and are located far and wide, the collection work is out-sourced by many card issuers. The salient features of credit cards dues are as follows:

(*i*) **Free credit period**: Up to 20–50 days from purchase date (depending on the billing cycle).

(*ii*) **Statement Date**: Monthly Statement date is fixed. It shows particulars of all purchases made *via* the credit card during the previous monthly period, payments made and the balance payable.

(*iii*) **Payment- Due Date**: Fixed date of payment each month.

(*iv*) **Over-dues**: If payments of dues are not made within the due date of payment, then these are called overdues. Interest rate on overdues is levied at rates ranging between 20% to 42% p.a. (vary from bank to bank) plus taxes. Some credit card companies offer unsecured loan to the card holders for repaying the credit card dues, to be repaid *in* 6-10 EMIs at stipulated interest rate (generally higher than clean overdraft rate, but lower than credit card overdues rate). The advantage of such a loan is that it converts the credit card dues into a short-term loan repayable in some instalments. As such, there will not be over-dues so long as the loan instalments are paid in time.

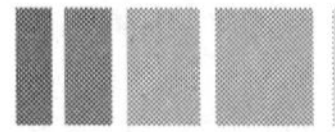

7.8 AGRICULTURAL FINANCE

The credit needs of a farmer are met through broad categories of advances *viz.*, direct finance and indirect finance. Based on the period of credit, direct finance is classified as short-term loans and medium/long-term loans.

7.8.1 Short-term loans

Loans repayable up to 18 months are termed as short- term loans. This includes: crop loan and the limits sanctioned through Kisan Credit Cards scheme for raising crops, loan against gold ornaments for agricultural purposes.

7.8.2 Medium/long-term loans

The period of credit under this category is generally thirty-six months and more. This includes loan for the purpose of minor irrigation, farm/land development, farm mechanization, plantation and horticulture, allied activities such as dairy farming, sheep/goat rearing, piggery and rabbit farming, poultry farming, fisheries, sericulture, bee-keeping, mushroom cultivation, bio-gas plants, etc. Indirect finance includes credit for financing distribution of fertilizers, pesticides, loans granted to Electricity Boards for energizing of pump sets under Rural Electrification Corporation (REC) Scheme, finance for construction and running storage facilities in the producing areas, loans to individuals, institutions or organizations who undertake spraying operations, advances to State Corporations for onward lending to weaker section etc.

Certain important types of agricultural loans are given below.

7.8.3 Crop loan

The purpose of the crop loan is to facilitate the agriculturists to carry on seasonal operations, *i.e.,* to meet the expenses for raising of seasonal crops including the cost of seeds, fertilizers and pesticides, irrigation charges, labour charges, etc. Agriculturists, tenant farmers and share croppers who actually cultivate the lands, farmers - small/ marginal (SF/MF) and others are eligible for loans. The amount of loan for the farmer is worked out based on the cost of cultivation. Generally full amount of cost of cultivation or about 40% of the produce value is financed. Banks estimate the loan required by using the scale of finance deteremined by district level technical committees taking into account various inputs that are needed for crop cultivation in that area. The crop loans do not have a direct margin but it is expected that the labour and other inputs are met by the farmers.

Crop loan for one crop could be extended by way of a demand loan repayable as and when the crop is harvested and sold. As such the normal period of loan may not exceed one year. Sugarcane crop loans are for 18 months in view of the longer gestation period.

7.8.4 Agricultural term loans

Purpose: Agricultural term loans are provided for the purchase of assets (farm machinery, bullocks, sheep, etc.), creation of assets (orchard development, poultry, dairy development, etc.) connected with rural activities under agriculture, horticulture, plantation, sericulture, animal husbandry, fisheries, etc., where the loan amount is repayable over a period of time not exceeding three years.

Eligibility: All categories of farmers and agricultural labourers are eligible for term loans.

A few types of agricultural term loans are given below:

7.8.4.1 Land Development

Credit for land development projects, in the form of finance to cultivators is given for better productivity. Loans under this head cover various activities like land clearance (removal of bushes, trees, etc.), land levelling and shaping, bench terracing for hilly areas, contour stone walls, staggered contour trenches, disposal drains, reclamation of saline/alkaline soils and fencing, etc.

7.8.4.2 Minor Irrigation

Credit for the creation of irrigation facilities from underground/surface water sources are covered under minor irrigation scheme. All structures and equipment connected with the proposed facility are also financed. Loans also cover various activities like digging of new wells (open/bore wells), deepening of existing wells (traditional/bore), energizing of wells (oil engine/electrical pump set), laying of pipe lines, installing drip/sprinkler irrigation system and lift irrigation system.

7.8.4.3 Farm Mechanization

Credit for the purchase of farm equipment and machinery for agricultural operations. The scheme covers activities ranging from purchase of tractors and accessories, trailers, power tillers, combine harvesters, power sprayers, dusters, threshers etc.

The eligibility for purchase of other farm equipment is dependent on the income generated by the agricultural activity undertaken by the borrower. In case the farmer holds less than the specified acres of land, it is to be ensured that the tractor can be deployed/used for minimum 1000 hours in a year to make the proposal economically viable.

7.8.4.4 Horticulture Finance

Loans for development of fruit orchards like mango, chikoo, guava, grapes, pomegranate, apple, litchi, etc., as well as short-term fruit crops (banana, pineapple, etc.), flowers in open and greenhouses (roses, carnation, chrysanthemums, ,asmine, etc.) and vegetable crops (potato, tomato, brinjal, gourds, peas, etc.) are financed.

7.8.4.5 Land Purchase

Loan is given to small and marginal farmers/landless labourers for purchase of agricultural land. The land purchased with the bank finance will be mortgaged as security. No other security will be insisted upon.

Repayment: In respect of term loans, normally repayment of loan will be monthly/ half yearly/yearly instalments depending on the harvest of the crops, its marketing and liquidity created by the agricultural activity undertaken over a period of ten years. Adequate gestation period is allowed for activities such as creation of minor irrigation structure, development of land etc.

7.8.5 Kisan Credit Card Scheme

Kisan Credit Card Scheme aims at providing adequate and timely credit support from the banking system under a single window to the farmers for their cultivation & other needs as indicated below:

a. To meet the short-term credit requirements for cultivation of crops

b. Post-harvest expenses

c. Produce marketing loan

d. Consumption requirements of farmer household

e. Working capital for maintenance of farm assets and activities allied to agriculture, like dairy animals, inland fishery, etc.

f. Investment credit requirement for agriculture and allied activities like pump sets, sprayers, dairy animals, etc.

Note: The aggregate of components "(*a*) to (*e*)" above will form the short-term credit limit portion and the aggregate of components under "(*f*)" will form the long-term credit limit portion.

Eligibility:

i. All Farmers – Individuals/Joint borrowers who are owner cultivators

ii. Tenant Farmers, Oral Lessees & Share Croppers

iii. SHGs or Joint Liability Groups of Farmers including tenant farmers, share croppers, etc.

7.9 ADVANCES TO MSME

MSME stands for Micro, Small, and Medium Enterprises. In accordance with the Micro, Small, and Medium Enterprises Development (MSMED) Act in 2006, the prescribed criteria for classification of Micro, Small and Medium enterprises based on the investment in plant and machinery and annual turnover under each category of enterprise is as under:

Type of enterprise	Investment in Plant and Machinery	Annual Turnover
Micro	Rs. 1 Crore	Rs. 5 Crore
Small	Rs. 10 Crore	Rs. 50 Crore
Medium	Rs. 50 Crore	Rs. 250 Crore

Basically, there are three types of business activities:

(*a*) Service Sector

(*b*) Retail Traders

(*c*) Manufacturing Activity

All commercial banks in place loan policies governing extension of credit facilities for the MSME sector. Banks sanction limits after proper appraisal of the genuine working capital requirements of the borrowers keeping in mind their business cycle and short-term credit requirement. As per Nayak Committee Report, working capital limits to SSI units is computed on the basis of minimum 20% of their estimated turnover up to credit limit of Rs. 5 Crore.

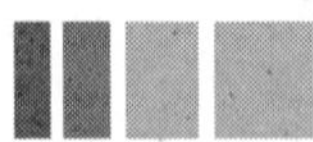

7.10 PRADHAN MANTRI MUDRA YOJANA

Micro Units Development & Refinance Agency Ltd. (MUDRA) is a new institution set up by Government of India to provide funding to the non-corporate, non-farm sector income generating activities of micro and small enterprises whose credit needs are below Rs. 10 Lakh.

The MUDRA loans are extended under following three categories:

a. Shishu-Loans upto Rs. 50,000/-

b. Kishore-Loans from Rs. 50,001/- to Rs. 5 Lakh

c. Tarun-Loans from Rs. 5,00,001/- to Rs. 10 Lakh

More focus would be given to Shishu. Accordingly, all advances granted on or after 8th April, 2015 falling under the above category are classified as MUDRA loans under the PMMY.

All Non-Corporate Small Business Segment (NCSBS) comprising of proprietorship or partnership firms running as small manufacturing units, service sector units, shopkeepers, fruits/vegetable vendors, truck operators, food-service units, repair shops, machine operators, small industries, food processors and others in rural and urban areas, are eligible for assistance under Mudra.

Bank branches facilitate loans under Mudra scheme as per customer requirements. Loans under this scheme are collateral free loans.

Mudra Loans could be availed for the following:

Vehicle loan: Commercial vehicle loan, Car loan and Two-wheeler loan for business purpose

Business Instalment Loan (BIL): Loan for working capital requirement, buying plant and machinery, renovating offices, etc.

Business Loans Group Loans (BLG) and Rural Business Credit (RBC)

7.11 PRIORITY SECTOR ADVANCES

Priority Sector advances means loans to those sectors which the Government of India and Reserve Bank of India **consider as important for the development of the basic needs of the country and are to be given priority over other sectors**. The banks are mandated to encourage the growth of such sectors with adequate and timely credit.

The categories under priority sector are as follows:

i. Agriculture
ii. Micro, Small and Medium Enterprises
iii. Export Credit
iv. Education
v. Housing
vi. Social Infrastructure
vii. Renewable Energy
viii. Others

The targets and sub-targets set under priority sector lending, to be computed on the basis of the Adjusted Net Bank Credit (ANBC)/Credit Equivalent of Off-Balance Sheet Exposures (CEOBE) as applicable as on the corresponding date of the preceding year are as under:

Commercial Banks:

- Total Priority Sector - 40 percent of ANBC or CEOBE whichever is higher.
- Agriculture - 18 percent of ANBC or CEOBE, whichever is higher; out of which a target of 10 percent prescribed for Small and Marginal Farmers (SMFs).
- Micro Enterprises - 7.5 percent of ANBC or CEOBE, whichever is higher.
- Advances to Weaker Sections - 12 percent of ANBC or CEOBE whichever is higher,

Foreign banks with less than 20 branches:

- Total priority sector advances: 40 percent of ANBC or CEOBE whichever is higher; out of which up to 32% can be in the form of lending to Exports and not less than 8% can be to any other priority sector.

- No targets for Agriculture, Micro Enterprises and advances to weaker sections.

Regional Rural Banks:

- Total priority sector advances: 75 percent of ANBC or CEOBE whichever is higher;
- Agricultural advances: 18 percent ANBC or CEOBE, whichever is higher; out of which a target of 10 percent is prescribed for SMFs
- Micro enterprises: 7.5 percent of ANBC or CEOBE, whichever is higher
- Advances to weaker sections: 15 percent of ANBC or CEOBE, whichever is higher

Small Finance Banks:

- Total priority sector advances: 75 percent of ANBC or CEOBE whichever is higher;
- Agricultural advances: 18 percent ANBC or CEOBE, whichever is higher; out of which a target of 10 percent is prescribed for SMFs
- Micro enterprises: 7.5 percent of ANBC or CEOBE, whichever is higher
- Advances to weaker sections: 12 percent of ANBC or CEOBE, whichever is higher

The following loans are also to be included in Priority Sector Advances:

- All loans to units in the Khadi and Village Industries sector are eligible for classification under the sub-target of 7.5 percent prescribed for Micro Enterprises under priority sector as mentioned above.
- Loans to individuals for educational purposes, including vocational courses, not exceeding Rs. 20 lakh will be considered as eligible for priority sector classification. Loans currently classified as priority sector will continue till maturity.
- Loans to individuals up to Rs. 35 lakh in metropolitan centres (with population of ten lakh and above) and up to Rs. 25 lakh in other centres for purchase/ construction of a dwelling unit per family provided the overall cost of the dwelling unit in the metropolitan centre and at other centres does not exceed Rs. 45 lakh and Rs. 30 lakh respectively.
- Loans up to Rs. 10 lakh in metropolitan centres and up to Rs. 6 lakh in other centres for repairs to damaged dwelling units conforming to the overall cost of the dwelling unit
- Bank loans to any governmental agency for construction of dwelling units or for slum clearance and rehabilitation of slum dwellers subject to dwelling units with carpet area of not more than 60 sq.m.

- Bank loans for affordable housing projects using at least 50% of FAR/FSI for dwelling units with carpet area of not more than 60 sq.m.
- Bank loans to HFCs (approved by NHB for their refinance) for on-lending, up to Rs. 20 lakh for individual borrowers, for purchase/construction/reconstruction of individual dwelling units or for slum clearance and rehabilitation of slum dwellers
- Bank loans up to a limit of Rs. 30 Crore to borrowers for purposes like solar based power generators, biomass-based power generators, wind mills, micro-hydel plants and for non-conventional energy based public utilities, *viz.*, street lighting systems and remote village electrification etc., will be eligible for Priority Sector classification. For individual households, the loan limit will be Rs. 10 lakh per borrower.
- Loans not exceeding Rs. 1.00 lakh per borrower provided directly by banks to individuals and individual members of SHG/JLG, provided the individual borrower's household annual income in rural areas does not exceed Rs. 1.00 lakh and for non-rural areas it does not exceed Rs. 1.60 lakh, and loans not exceeding Rs. 2.00 lakh provided directly by banks to SHG/JLG for activities other than agriculture or MSME, *viz.*, loans for meeting social needs, construction or repair of house, construction of toilets or any viable common activity started by the SHGs.
- Loans to distressed persons [other than distressed farmers indebted to non-institutional lenders] not exceeding Rs. 1.00 lakh per borrower to prepay their debt to non-institutional lenders.
- Loans up to Rs. 50 crore to Start-ups, as per definition of Ministry of Commerce and Industry, Govt. of India that are engaged in activities other than Agriculture or MSME.

Common guidelines for priority sector loans:

Banks should comply with the following common guidelines for all categories of advances under the priority sector.

Rate of interest: The rates of interest on bank loans will be as per directives issued by Department of Regulation (DoR), RBI from time to time.

Service charges: No loan related and *ad hoc* service charges/inspection charges should be levied on priority sector loans up to Rs. 25,000/-. In the case of eligible priority sector loans to SHGs/JLGs, this limit will be applicable per member and not to the group as a whole.

Receipt, Sanction/Rejection/Disbursement Register: A register/electronic record should be maintained by the bank wherein the date of receipt, sanction/rejection/ disbursement with reasons thereof, etc. should be recorded. The register/electronic record should be made available to all inspecting agencies.

Issue of acknowledgement of loan applications: Banks should provide acknowledgement for loan applications received under priority sector loans. Bank Boards should prescribe a time limit within which the bank communicates its decision in writing to the applicants.

7.11.1 Credit Guarantee Fund Trust for Micro and Small Enterprises (CGTMSE)

CGTMSE is an initiative of the Government of India in collaboration with the Ministry of Micro, Small and Medium Enterprises (MSME) and the Small Industries Development Bank of India (**SIDBI**) launched on 30th August, 2000. It is a Trust which provides the financial institutions with credit guarantee to provide loans to SMEs and MSMEs.

The basic aim of CGTMSE is to encourage first-time entrepreneurs to establish SMEs and MSME, considered to be the bulwark of the Indian economy by availing of collateral-free loans from eligible financial institutions. The guarantee covers default by the borrower to repay the advance. Thus, the CGTMSE scheme primarily envisages the provision of loans to first-generation entrepreneurs so that they can flourish in the competitive environment without the burden of security or third-party guarantees. In turn, the financial institutions are provided cover for the absence of security to fund SMEs and MSMEs promoted by small Indian businessmen up to a certain limit.

Features of the Credit Guarantee Scheme:

One of the key objectives of **CGTMSE coverage** is the focus on the creation of a robust credit relief system that promotes better credit flow to SMEs and the MSME sector. The stand out features of the CGTMSE scheme is:

- Guaranteed repayment of 75% or 85% in some cases for the defaulted principal loan amount up to Rs. 50 lakh in the case of Micro Enterprises.
- The maximum guarantee is 75% for loan amounts greater than Rs. 50 lakh but under Rs. 1 crore.
- Provides 85% repayment for loans up to Rs. 5 lakh to micro-enterprises.
- The guarantee amount for repayment is 80% of the loan amount in case the MSME unit is in the North East Region (including Sikkim, UT of Jammu & Kashmir and UT of Ladakh).
- The guarantee amount goes upto 85% in the case of women entrepreneurs/SC/ST entrepreneurs/MSEs situated in Aspirational District/ZED certified MSEs/Person with Disability (PwD)/MSE promoted by Agniveers
- The repayment procedure or **CGTMSE loan recovery** covers the entire loan amount inclusive of the interest component for a period of 3 months and/or the entire outstanding loan amount along with the accrued interest from

the suit filed date or the day when the loan turns into an NPA, whichever is lower.

- Rehabilitation of business units if the failure is beyond the control of the management to the extent of Rs. 1 crore as support to the lender for assistance in resuscitating the enterprise.
- **Maximum Guarantee Cover:**

<table>
<tr><th rowspan="3">Category (including Trading activity)</th><th colspan="3">Maximum extent of Guarantee Coverage</th></tr>
<tr><th colspan="3">where credit facility is</th></tr>
<tr><th>Upto Rs. 5 lakh</th><th>Above Rs. 5 lakh & upto Rs. 50 lakh</th><th>Above Rs. 50 lakh & upto Rs. 200 lakh</th></tr>
<tr><td>Micro Enterprises</td><td>0.85</td><td>0.75</td><td rowspan="2">0.75</td></tr>
<tr><td>MSEs located in North East Region (incl. Sikkim, UT of Jammu & Kashmir and UT of Ladakh)</td><td colspan="2">0.8</td></tr>
<tr><td>Women entrepreneurs/SC/ST entrepreneurs/MSEs situated in Aspirational District/ZED certified MSEs/Person with Disability (PwD)/MSE promoted by Agniveers</td><td colspan="3">0.85</td></tr>
<tr><td>All other category of borrowers</td><td colspan="3">0.75</td></tr>
</table>

CGTMSE Scheme Eligibility Criteria:

As per the CGTMSE guidelines, a credit guarantee is deemed to back a borrower with collateral and third party guarantee free advance. Under the scheme, the member lending institution which can be an NBFC also, who lend to the SME and MSME sector are eligible for a maximum credit cap of Rs. 2 crores, which in any case is meant to cover a large proportion of the loan amount. The eligibility norms prescribed both for the credit providers and borrowers are:

- **Lending Institutions:** It covers the whole gamut of scheduled commercial banks, specified Regional Rural Banks, SIDBI, NSIC, NEDFi, SFB and NBFCs who lend to the specific sector and have entered into an agreement with CGTMSE or the Trust for the purpose.

7.12 LET US SUM UP

Retail Banking is defined as doing banking business with individual customers. With liberalization in the early nineties, the Indian economy started growing fast. Helped by the huge inflow of foreign investments into India, the liquidity in the banking system has improved. On the other hand, liberalization has led to increased incomes and purchasing power with people accompanied by aspiration for a better lifestyle.

As an off-shoot, the retail lending in banks has, of late, grown leaps and bounds. Today's retail banking sector is characterized by three basic aspects *viz*: multiple products, multiple channels and multiple customer groups.

Of retail loans extended by banks, home loans and consumer loans form a major percentage. With the growth in employment and the per-capita income and savings, the demand for housing has also gone up. Related ancillary services include credit cards, remittances, selling of mutual fund and insurance products and depository services.

A hassle-free approach to buying a house for a salaried employee is to take a home loan from banks or housing finance companies. The related procedures for raising a home loan and the practices the banks follow while sanctioning such loans are explained in this Unit. Following the home loans, the demand for consumer loans is increasing also corresponding to the increase in the living standards of the people. So is the case with personal loans and the demand for credit cards. The details of the personal and consumer loans are also provided in this Unit. There are various methods of assessing working capital need of an enterprise.

The credit needs of a farmer are met through broad categories of agricultural advances *viz.*, direct finance and indirect finance. Based on the period of credit, direct finance is classified as short-term loans and medium/long-term loans. Direct finance to agriculture is provided to farmers for short-term purposes like cultivation of crops or for other medium/long-term purposes like, among others, land development or for augmenting water resources. A novel offering by banks to farmers for meeting their cultivation needs and other non-farm requirements, including consumption needs in timely manner and without any procedural delay by banks is Kisan Credit Cards. With these cards, farmers can draw amounts from banks whenever needed by them and up to a pre-fixed limit or purchase needed inputs from suppliers as per their convenience. Finance is also provided by banks for undertaking allied activities like dairy development, poultry farming, bee-keeping, sericulture, piggeries, pisciculture, sheep/goat rearing, etc. Indirect finance to agriculture includes credit for distribution of fertilizers and other inputs used by farmers in agricultural operations. Finance for construction and running of ware-house facilities in the producing areas and advances to State Electricity Boards for energizing wells in villages and to State corporations for onward lending to weaker sections also come under this category.

7.13 KEY WORDS

Hire purchase, due date, term loan, consumption loan, credit card, working capital, maximum permissible bank finance, Turn-over method, Business cycle.

7.14 CHECK YOUR PROGRESS

1. A Housing loan is granted against the security of:
   (*a*) Pledge of the house financed
   (*b*) Hypothecation of the house financed
   (*c*) Mortgage of the house financed
   (*d*) Lien of the house financed
2. The term 'EMI' in a housing or vehicle loan is calculated on the basis of:
   (*a*) Principal of the loan
   (*b*) Principal and Interest on the loan
   (*c*) Interest on the loan
   (*d*) Principal and Processing charges on the loan
3. Housing loans are granted for:
   (*a*) Short-term
   (*b*) Medium-term
   (*c*) Long-term
   (*d*) Either (*b*) or (*c*)
4. A vehicle loan is granted against the security of:
   (*a*) Pledge of the vehicle financed
   (*b*) Hypothecation of the vehicle financed
   (*c*) Mortgage of the vehicle financed
   (*d*) Hypothecation of all assets of the borrower
5. A loan for a refrigerator is granted against the security of:
   (*a*) Pledge of the item financed
   (*b*) Hypothecation of the item financed
   (*c*) Mortgage of the item financed
   (*d*) Mortgage of all assets of the borrower
6. Maximum loan limit under Kisan Credit Card Scheme to marginal farmer is:
   (*a*) Rs. 1,00,000
   (*b*) Rs. 50,000
   (*c*) Rs. 40,000
   (*d*) Rs. 20,000

7. Advances to Micro Enterprises upto Rs. 5 crore is assessed by adopting:
   (*a*) Business Cycle Method
   (*b*) Drawing Power Method
   (*c*) Turn-Over Method
   (*d*) Cash Budget Method

7.15 ANSWERS TO CHECK YOUR PROGRESS

1.	(*c*)	2.	(*b*)	3.	(*d*)	4.	(*b*).	5.	(*b*)	6.	(*b*)	7.	(*c*)

CHAPTER

8 Securities and Modes of Registering or Recording Securities

8.1 OBJECTIVES

By reading this unit, the candidates will be able to know:

(*a*) different types of securities generally taken by bankers while lending

(*b*) the characteristics of these securities, and

(*c*) get an insight into how banks create their charges on different securities.

8.2 INTRODUCTION

Banks are financial intermediaries where public resources are mobilized in the form of deposits and borrowings and used in lending and investment. Bankers take utmost care to see that they get back the money lent to various types of customers as per the repayment schedule along with interest. To safeguard the advance, bankers normally take securities which will enable them to recover in case the customers commit default.

Various types of securities could be offered to banks by the customers. These could be classified as immovable security and movable security, etc.:

i. Land and building including agricultural land, plant and machineries embedded to earth, etc., come under the category of immovable securities/properties.

ii. Whereas, finished goods/raw material, agricultural produces (including standing crops in the field), farm machinery like tractors, power tillers, combine harvesters, vehicles, agricultural implements, gold ornaments, Life Insurance Policies, etc., come under the category of movable securities.

iii. Accounts receivables, known as **book debts**, other trade receivables could also be taken as security.

In the case of finished goods and raw material, which are hypothecated, banks use a percentage of their value for arriving at the drawing limit for cash credit and overdraft accounts. The securities may be classified into:

- **Personal**
- **Tangible**
- **Primary**
- **Collateral**

(*i*) Personal security indicates the personal liability of the customer or the surety/ guarantor. In such a case, banks have a recourse to the customer (property and other assets) over and above the assets hypothecated or pledged. A third-party surety is a personal security. In case of personal security, like other collaterals it is not necessary for the bank to first exhaust other securities before seeking payment from the collateral. Banks will seek to utilize that security first which has a reasonable chance of realization and is less costly to invoke and less time consuming.

(*ii*) Tangible security is something that can be realized by a sale or transfer *e.g.*, land, goods, stock, crops, etc. In the case of land and building there exist registration procedures and need to prove that the security has indeed been given to the bank by the customer for use in case of default or recall of account. Once the bank decides to use the tangible security it is necessary to maintain it in good condition.

(*iii*) Primary security is one that is regarded as the main security cover for an advance and is normally the assets that are created out of the loan or credit. For example, standing crops in the field in the case of crop loan; stock for cash credit in the case of working capital finance. A mortgage of the house in case of housing loan, though often called collateral, is a primary security. It must be added that in financial institutions availability of mortgaged security is often referred to as collateral.

(*iv*) Collateral security is the security other than the primary security lodged with the bank by the customer or by a third party.

Whatever may be the nature of the securities, the banker, while accepting the securities, must ensure that :

(*i*) The securities are saleable, whenever the need arises, in the case of default by customers.

(*ii*) The value of the securities is ascertainable at any time from reliable sources, to fix the drawing limit, saleable value, etc.

(*iii*) The value of the security is not subject to heavy fluctuation as otherwise banks must fix a higher percentage of margin.

(*iv*) The title to the securities is with the customer and is easily transferable without, as far as possible, without going through lengthy legal formalities.

8.3 CREATING A CHARGE ON THE SECURITY

For a loan a security must be formally and properly taken over by the bank. This is achieved through documentation and registration. The following are the methods usually resorted to by the banker for the purpose of creation of charge. The method to be selected amongst others is also dependent on the nature of the securities offered:

i. Pledge
ii. Hypothecation
iii. Lien
iv. Assignment
v. Mortgage

The method of creating charge over a security depends upon the nature of security and the nature of charge. For example, when a bank gives a loan against the security of gold ornaments, it takes the possession of the ornaments under pledge, whereas for issuing advance against the security of a vehicle it will be hypothecation and in case of a home loan the house will be mortgaged. The following are the methods of creating charge.

8.3.1 Pledge

Pledge is when a customer hands over the security to the banker to be kept in latter's control. **Section 172 of Contract Act** defines pledge as "The bailment of goods as security for payment of a debt or performance of a promise is called pledge." The bailor is in this case is called the 'pawnor' and the bailee is called 'pawnee'.

Essential features of a Pledge:

Pledge is bailment of goods by the debtor to the creditor with an intention to create a charge thereon as security for the debt. Important conditions to be complied with for constitution of a valid pledge are:

- There should be bailment of goods which implies that goods should be **delivered** by the debtor/customer (pledger) to the lender/creditor (pledgee). The delivery could be actual physical delivery or constructive delivery as in case of documents of title to goods.
- The bailment must be signed by the debtor or by an authorised person on behalf of the debtor.

- The delivery of goods must be with an intention of the parties to create security for a debt or performance of a promise.

In pledge, the ownership of the goods remains with the customer whereas physical control over these goods will be exercised by the bank. The customer has a right to get the goods returned to him after repayment of debt.

In case of default by the customer, bank can sell the goods after giving a reasonable notice of sale as required under Section 176 of the Indian Contract Act. Notice must clearly indicate the intention of the lender/pledgee to sell the security. The notice is compulsory before the sale can be affected. If the bank realises more amount than its dues by such sale, the excess amount realised will have to be paid to the customer. However, if there is any shortfall *i.e.,* the amount realised is not sufficient to clear the dues of the customer to the bank, then, the bank can proceed against the customer in a court of law for recovery of such shortfall or balance.

The goods pledged to the bank may sometimes be required by the customer for some purpose or undertaking a small process. The documents of title to goods deposited with the bank in the pledge account namely transport receipt may be required to take delivery from the port/railway etc. In such situations the bank may temporarily part with the security on the customer signing a 'Trust Receipt'. In such cases, the possession of pledged security legally remains with the bank and the customer keeps those security 'in trust' for the bank during that temporary period. This facility is sometimes given by the bank as a sub-limit of pledge account for operational convenience.

8.3.2 Hypothecation

Pledge takes away the control over the goods from the customer which may not be practicable as the customer would require certain goods under his control to continue its manufacturing and/or trading activities. Pledge involves frequent access to pledged goods. Take for example cotton bales pledged and kept in a godown. Every time the customer needs cotton for manufacture of yarn or cloth the bank will have to release cotton and to that extent reduce the drawing limit in the cash credit account.

Instead, if the goods are hypothecated by the bank (*a*) there will be no need to release goods frequently and (*b*) the drawing limit can be worked based on stock statement submitted by the customer. For this it is necessary that an equitable charge, in favour of the bank over the goods is created without parting with the possession of the goods. A charge on a property for a debt where neither ownership nor possession is passed on to the creditor is known as 'hypothecation charge'. Hypothecation agreements obtained by banks generally have a clause under which hypothecation can be converted into a pledge at, a later date.

Under SARFAESI Act hypothecation is defined as "a charge in or upon any movable property, existing or future, created by a borrower in favour of a secured creditor without delivery of possession of the movable property to such creditor, as a security for financial assistance, and includes floating charge and crystallization into fixed charge on movable property."

This form of charge is ideal from the point of view of the customer as he is always in control of goods offered as security to the bank. In case of default by the customer, the bank may take possession of goods and convert it to pledge - subject to suitable notice to the customer- not withstanding any clause with this effect being included in the hypothecation agreement. If the customer were not to agree then the bank will have to move a court of law for taking physical possession of goods or their attachment before judgment.

Hypothecation charge extends to all the goods and movable properties with the customer as per the agreement of hypothecation and operations in these accounts are permitted based on stock statement, submitted by the customer periodically usually every month. Hypothecation may, however, also be created as a fixed charge over a particular machinery/vehicle, etc.

8.3.3 Lien

Lien means the right of the creditor to retain the goods or securities of the debtor, which are in his possession, until the debt due from the debtor is paid. It does not require any specific agreement to support this right. The lien may be (*a*) general lien which confers the right to retain any goods for a general balance of account or (*b*) lien where goods can be retained by the creditor for a specific or debt only. The person exercising general lien has only a right to retain the goods till the dues are paid and may not be able to sell those goods.

8.3.3.1 Types of lien

Particular Lien : In case of a particular lien the creditor gets the right to retain possession of only those goods or securities for which the dues have arisen and not for other dues. For example, a watch-repairer can withhold the delivery of watch until his charges of repairing the watch are paid to him.

General lien : A general lien gives the right to the lender/creditor to retain the possession of a said item till all amounts due from debtor are paid or discharged. This is available to lenders, bankers, factors, wharfingers, attorneys of High Court and Insurance Policy agents.

Negative Lien or No Lien : In certain cases, the customers may have immovable or other assets which they do not offer as collateral security to secure their loans for one reason or the other. But when the customers give an undertaking to the banks stating that (*a*) they are owners of a particular asset which is free from charges and (*b*) that they shall either not dispose of the asset or will not create charge on the asset, without concurrence of the bank, such undertaking is known as a no-lien or negative lien. This type of lien has no legal force. As such if assets are disposed of by the customer without informing the bank – the lender/bank cannot claim any remedy in a court of law.

Lender/Banker's Right of Lien: Banker has right of general lien against his customers. Bank can retain/sell the securities available in different loans for repayment of all loans. Features of Lender/banker's general lien:

i. **Implied pledge and right of sale:** To create general lien, no special contract is required. It is always implied unless there is contract to the contrary, if any. The right to sell is also available under bank's right of lien because a banker's general lien tantamount to an implied pledge.

ii. **Limitation:** The right of lien is not restricted or barred by Law of Limitation. In view of this though there is no legal recourse in such cases (time barred) the bank can recover time barred debts also.

iii. **Ownership & possession:** Though the possession is with the bank, but the ownership remains with owner when a banker exercises this right.

iv. **Conversion to lien:** If it is indicated through an agreement or otherwise that a particular security was obtained for a particular debt only, the general lien gets converted into lien.

v. **Criminal action:** When the banker exercises his right of general lien, no criminal action is available because there is no criminal intention behind it.

The lender or banker's lien, however, does not extend to:

(*a*) Securities or valuables lying in the locker rented to the customer.

(*b*) Securities deposited upon a particular trust.

(*c*) Securities deposited to secure a specific loan.

(*d*) Securities left with the banks after an advance against them has been repaid/ adjusted.

(*e*) Securities left inadvertently with the bank.

No specific letter of lien agreement is necessary as the banks enjoy the right of lien under the Contract Act. However, in some cases the bank may obtain a specific letter of lien so that the customer is not able to contend later that the securities were deposited by him for a specific purpose inconsistent with the lien.

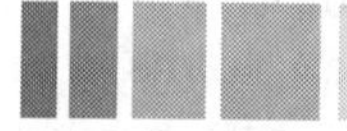

8.4 ASSIGNMENT

Assignment refers to the transfer of some or all property rights and obligations associated with an asset, property, contract, etc. to another entity through a written agreement. 'Actionable claims' can be assigned to a bank by customers. Section 130 of the Transfer of Property Act, 1882, permits such assignment to anyone except to a judge, a legal practitioner, or an officer of the Court of Justice. Section 3 of the Act defines; an 'actionable claim' as a claim which is not (*a*) a debt secured by mortgage of immovable property or (*b*) by hypothecation or pledge of movable property, or to any (*c*) beneficial interest in movable property not in the possession, either actual or constructive, of the claimant, which the civil courts recognize as affording ground for relief. In view of the above, a customer may assign the following to the banker for securing loans:

- the book debts or account receivable,
- money due from Government department or semi-government organization, and
- life insurance policies.

8.5 MORTGAGE

Mortgage is a mode of charge associated with immovable property. Immovable property shall include land, benefits to arise out of land and things attached to the earth or permanently fastened to anything attached to the earth. Immovable property does not include standing timber, growing crops or grass. It also provides explanation to the term "attached to the earth" which means:

(*a*) rooted in the earth, as in case of trees and shrubs,

(*b*) imbedded in the earth, as in case of walls or buildings, or

(*c*) attached to what is so imbedded for the permanent enjoyment of that to which it is attached.

A similar definition of immovable property has been given by Section 2(6) of the Registration Act, 1908 as under:

> 'Immovable property includes land, buildings, hereditary allowances, rights to ways, lights, ferries, fisheries or any other benefit to arise out of land and things attached to the earth or permanently fastened to anything which is attached to the earth but not standing timber, growing crops nor grass.'

A point in case may arise in respect of machinery. Machinery which is not permanently attached to the earth and can be shifted to other place will not be considered as immovable property. But if machinery is permanently attached to the earth in, a manner that it cannot be removed from there, it shall be considered as immovable property.

Section 58 of the Transfer of Property Act, 1882 defines mortgage as a transfer of interest in a specific immovable property for the purpose of securing an existing or future debt. The person transferring the interest is known as 'mortgagor' and the person to whom the interest is transferred is known as 'mortgagee'. Indian law recognises six different types of mortgages as under:

i. Simple Mortgage

ii. Equitable Mortgage

iii. Mortgage by Conditional Sale

iv. Usufructuary

v. English

vi. Anomalous

Out of the above the two most acceptable forms of mortgages namely Simple Mortgage and Mortgage by Deposit of Title Deeds (Equitable Mortgage) are discussed here under. These are the two mortgages which Banks generally prefer.

8.5.1 Mortgage by deposit of title deeds or equitable mortgage

Section 58(*f*) of the Transfer of Property Act defines equitable mortgage as mortgage created by depositing title deeds of an immovable property to secure a debt, existing or future. Three basic conditions to constitute a valid equitable mortgage are:

(*i*) Delivery of title deeds (original) by the mortgagor to the bank.

(*ii*) Existence of a debt, existing or future.

(*iii*) Intention of the mortgagor to create a mortgage on that property to secure the debt.

No equitable mortgage can be created if any of the above three conditions' is not complied with. This form of mortgage is very popular because it does not require finalisation of any mortgage deed and its subsequent registration which requires payment of heavy stamp duty. Mortgage is created simply by depositing the title deeds with the bank with an intention to create a security and no other agreement etc. is strictly required. Equitable mortgage can, however, be created only at places as notified by government in this regard. In some States there exist levy of stamp duty for equitable mortgage as well.

8.5.2 Simple Mortgage

Section 58(*b*) of Transfer of Property Act, 1882 relates to simple mortgage in which the mortgagor personally binds himself to pay the debt and agrees that in the event of non-payment by him, the mortgager may cause the mortgaged property to be sold and the proceeds of sale be applied in repayment of debt. The possession of mortgaged property, however, remains with the mortgagor. The mortgagee does not have an absolute right to sell the property in case of default but must seek intervention of the court.

A formal mortgage deed will be executed for creation of a simple mortgage. This must be registered with the registrar of land and properties after payment of necessary stamp duty which will have to be borne by the customer.

In all forms of mortgages, the mortgagor has a right of redemption on payment of the debt after it has become due. The mortgagor also has a right to inspect the documents of title to goods and make copies of or extracts from the title deeds which are in the custody of the bank.

In the event of the customer's default in repayment of the advance granted against immovable property, the lender may bring it for sale. However, it can be done only through appropriate legal process. Normally, lender/banks must file a suit before the civil court for recovery if the amount due in the loan account is less than Rs. 20 lakh and, before the Debt Recovery Tribunal (DRT) if the amount due is Rs. 20 lakh and above. However, under the provisions of the Securitization and Reconstruction of Financial Assets and Enforcement of Security Interest (SARFAESI) Act, 2002, banks can sell the immovable property taken under mortgage, without intervention of the court after observing certain formalities mentioned in the Act. Because of this right of sale without the court intervention, this type of security has gained importance now and viewed with favour by banks.

8.6 RIGHT OF SET OFF

Set off is the right of combining of accounts between a debtor and a creditor to arrive at a net balance payable to one or the other. Set off in relation to bank means his right to apply the credit balance in customer's account towards liquidation of debit balance in another account of the customer provided both the accounts are maintained by him in the same capacity. The right may not be considered as absolute, and the bank may be required to give a notice for exercising his right of set off. The right of set off can be applied by the bank only if the following conditions are met:

a. The liability of the customer is for a sum which is certain,

b. The repayment of debt is due, and

c. Both the accounts are held by the customer in the same capacity.

The right of set off should, however, not be exercised arbitrarily and a notice for combining the accounts must invariably be served by the bank on the customer

8.7 RIGHT OF APPROPRIATION

Sections 59 to 61 of the Indian Contract Act, 1872 contains provisions regarding the right of appropriation of payments in some cases. Right of appropriation is vested in the debtor, who makes a payment to his creditor to whom he owes several debts. He can appropriate the payment by:

a. an express intimation or

b. under circumstances implying that the payment is to be applied to the discharge of some debt.

If the creditor accepts such payment, it must be applied accordingly. For example, A owes B several debts, including Rs. 1,000 upon a promissory note which falls due on 1st December, 1986. He owes B no other debt of that amount. On 1-12-2020 'A' pays 'B' Rs. 1,000. The payment is to be applied to the discharge of the promissory note.

If the debtor does not intimate or there are no other pointers or indicators as to which debt the payment is to be applied, the right of appropriation is vested in the creditor. He may apply it as his discretion to any lawful debt due and payable to him from the debtor (Section 60) Further, where neither party makes any appropriation, the payment shall be applied in discharge of each proportionately (Section 61).

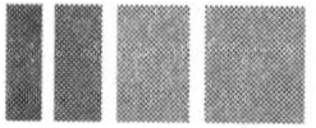

8.8 TYPES OF SECURITIES

While discussing the security processes a number of underlying items to be mortgaged or otherwise secured has been discussed. In the following some of the items are discussed in brief.

8.8.1 Land (including agricultural land) and buildings

The nature of charge created on immovable properties like land and buildings while taking them as security to the advance granted by banks is known as mortgage. Immovable properties are accepted by lending banks both as primary and collateral securities. The following are important aspects of mortgages.

8.8.1.1 Examination of Title to the property

Before an immovable property is accepted as security, the ownership or title to the customer over the said property should be examined by the lender's/bank's lawyer to ascertain that the person in whose name the property stands has a good, valid, subsisting, and marketable title over the property. It may also have to be ensured that the property is free from any encumbrances (*i.e.*, it is not mortgaged to someone else) and is not subject to any litigation or attachment from any Court or Statutory authorities. It is advisable for the lender/bank to inspect the property offered as security to ensure the correctness of the particulars given by the proponent/customer. The lender/banker may also make inquiry through independent sources to satisfy the customer's ownership of the property.

8.8.1.2 Documents to be taken from the Mortgagor

(*a*) All material documents of title, like the sale deed/gift deed/will/partition deed that convey the title in his/her favour.

(*b*) Parent documents for the prescribed period to ascertain the flow of title. Some lender/banks call for parent documents for thirty years.

(*c*) Encumbrance certificate, normally for thirteen years to see, if any encumbrance subsists on the property. It is advisable to apply for an encumbrance certificate for the property through the bank's advocate to avoid possible manipulation.

(*d*) Tax receipts for the property to evidence the possession of the property by the proposed mortgagor.

(*e*) If the property offered is standing in the name of a minor, permission of the competent court to encumber the property.

(*f*) Search report, if the immovable property belongs to a company, to ascertain any charge is subsisting on the property.

(*g*) Normally, lender/banks take an opinion from their panel advocate regarding the clear, good, and marketable title of the proposed mortgagor over the property. The advocate should see that the documents produced are genuine and not forged/fabricated. The opinion so rendered should be clear and unconditional and should certify that a valid enforceable mortgage can be created by the proposed mortgagor over the property.

(*h*) The Title verification report should also indicate the list of documents to be obtained by the bank at the time of creation of mortgage.

8.8.1.3 Valuation of property

When a loan or advance is allowed against the security of an immovable property, it is necessary to get it valued by an approved valuer. Valuation must be conservative, realistic and should be on a forced sale basis. While valuing the property, the following may be taken into consideration:

(*a*) Location of land and the consequent location value with four boundaries.

(*b*) Age of the building and its present strength

(*c*) The nature of its construction

(*d*) Taxes paid

(*e*) Extent (Area in acres etc.) of the land and the building area

(*f*) Cost incurred for building construction.

8.8.1.4 Leasehold properties

If the land is leasehold, it is necessary to ascertain whether the terms of the lease permit the customer to assign or transfer by way of mortgage, the leasehold rights in the land. It must be ensured that the repayment of loan by the customer does not extend beyond the period of lease.

8.8.2 Raw material, Agricultural Produce etc.

Banks advance loans routinely against the security (hypothecation) of the raw material, work in progress etc., and also agricultural produces/goods, agricultural inputs like fertilizers, pesticides, etc. In case of manufacturing company, the assistance by the bank may take the shape of loan, key cash credit/Pledge (in case of produce pledge) or open cash credit. When the possession of the goods is with the banker, the nature of charge created is a pledge. One of the main and the most essential requirement of a pledge is the actual or constructive delivery of the goods pledged to the pledgee (in this case the banker). The term 'constructive delivery' means that there is no need for physical transfer of goods from the custody of the pledger to the pledgee. An agreement of pledge may be implied from the nature of transaction or the circumstances of the case.

When the possession of goods is not given or obtained, the nature of charge created is hypothecation.

Hypothecation differs from mortgage in two respects:

i. Firstly, mortgage relates to immovable property whereas hypothecation relates to movables.

ii. Secondly, in a mortgage, there is transfer of interest in the property to the creditor but in hypothecation there is only obligation to repay money and no transfer of interest is involved. Ownership and possession remain with the customer.

iii. In the case of pledge and hypothecation, the title in the goods is not transferred to the bank.

PRECAUTIONS FOR ADVANCE AGAINST GOODS:

(*a*) No advance should be made for speculation or hoarding purposes.

(*b*) The goods charged to the bank should have been fully paid. This is to avoid loss of charge on the property on account of the rights of the unpaid seller.

(*c*) The age of the stock should be reasonable. Otherwise, the stock may not be saleable in the market.

(*d*) The ownership of the goods should be ensured by verifying the original paid invoices.

(*e*) As the price of goods/raw material pledged may vary from time to time the bank should always stipulate and maintain an appropriate margin.

(*f*) If the customer has own goods apart from pledged goods, then he/she should segregate the goods while storing in the godown.

(*g*) The goods should be, adequately insured.

(*h*) The valuation of stock under hypothecation will be based on cost price or market price whichever is less.

8.9 ADVANCES AGAINST LIFE INSURANCE POLICIES

Life insurance policies are acceptable either as a primary or collateral security for an advance.

Before making an advance against Life Policies the points to be taken into consideration are:

i. the policy must be in force and the premium paid up to date. The latest premium receipt must be kept on record by the lender/bank.

ii. the original policy should be with the lender/bank. It should be seen if it is duly stamped and signed by the issuing authority.

iii. the policy should be free from restrictive/onerous clauses.

iv. the insurance company should have admitted the age of the assured.

Generally, the following life policies are not acceptable as security:

(*a*) Children endowment policy

(*b*) Policies taken out specifically for purposes like estate duty

(*c*) Children deferred policy

(*d*) Policies with nominations under section 6 of the Married Women's Property Act.

Banks lend against the life policies based on the current surrender value. Surrender value is the amount which the insurance company will pay if the policy is surrendered on any day before maturity of the policy.

8.9.1 Assignment of the policy

Assignment is the process in which the life policy is assigned to the lender or bank entitling the later to claim the surrender value in case of default by the customer. The assignment should be obtained by indicating words to that effect. Assignment should be witnessed by a person. Nominee under the policy need not join in assigning the policy as nomination under the policy is automatically cancelled in the event of assignment of the policy. The assignment shall not be operative as against the insurance company until the notice in writing of assignment is given to the insurance company either by the assignor or by the assignee.

In case of death of the life assured, the assignee becomes entitled to receive the policy amount. When the advance is repaid, the policy must be reassigned in favour of the policyholder.

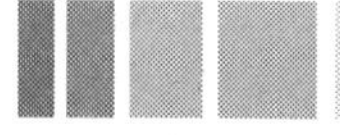

8.10 LOANS AGAINST TERM DEPOSITS

Banks often lend against their term deposits, such as fixed deposits, cumulative deposits, recurring deposits, etc. The nature of a facility granted against the security of term deposits may either be a loan or an overdraft. The nature of charge created while granting this type of facility is a pledge.

Normally banks lend up to ninety per cent of the deposit amount/accrued value of the deposit maintained with the bank.

The rate of interest charged on the loan would be one per cent or two per cent above the interest rate offered on the deposit.

The customer can repay the loan out his/her sources on any date before the maturity. If not paid, in full before the maturity of the deposits, only the balance amount over and above the loan amount and interest due thereon if any will be paid to the party. If there is any shortfall in the maturity proceeds of deposit in meeting the loan repayment commitment, the party must pay the same to the bank.

Normally, no loan can be granted against the security of deposit receipt standing in the name of a minor. However, if the loan is sought by the guardian for the necessities of the minor depositor, the bank may consider it on getting from the guardian an undertaking letter to the effect that the proceeds of loan would be utilized only for the necessities of the minor depositor.

While granting the facility, banks get the deposit receipt duly discharged by the deposit holder. In case, of more than one deposit holder, all of them should discharge the deposit receipt. The depositor/s should also execute necessary loan documents. In case of more than one depositor, all of them should execute the documents or one of them on the strength of authorization letter given by the depositors who is/are not executing the loan documents.

Loan given to a sole proprietor against deposits in the name of the proprietary concern is not treated as a third-party loan, whereas loan granted to a partner against the deposits in the name of the firm is classified as third-party loan. In the latter case interest shall be charged not at one or two per cent over the rate of interest on deposit but at commercial rates.

In case of premature closure of deposits (on which loan has been granted), the interest should be 1-2% over the actual rate of interest applicable for the prematurely closed deposit.

Loan can be granted against deposits receipt of other branches of the same bank. However, before granting of loan, lien should be noted in the records of the deposit branch. No loan should be granted against the security of TDRs of other banks

Where a loan is sought by a company, against its deposits, a Board Resolution authorizing the company to raise the loan should be obtained. Unlike other loans of the company there is no need, in the case of loans against deposit, to register the charge with the ROC.

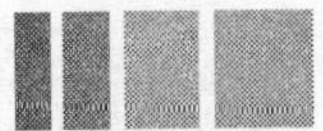

8.11 LOAN AGAINST GOLD ORNAMENTS

NBFCs/Banks give loans against gold ornaments (jeweller) for personal or business needs of individuals, MSME etc. Farmers are given gold loans for non-agricultural purposes. The nature of charge created while giving this type of loan is a pledge. Some banks allow an overdraft also against the security of gold ornaments, gold bonds:

(*a*) The amount of loan on ornaments depends upon the market value and purity of the gold. Normally lender's banks keep a margin of around thirty percent on the market value of the ornaments. The amount lent *vis-à-vis* the value is arrived by a Loan to value ratio. There are some regulatory prescriptions on LTV which could vary from time to time.

(*b*) The rate of interest varies with the purpose of the loan.

(*c*) On closure of the loan, the ornaments should be returned to the pledger or his/her authorized representative.

(*d*) Even after the closure of a loan, the lender/banker can, by exercising right of general lien retain the possession of the ornaments, if any other loan is due/overdue loan in the name of the customer. Suitable notice must be given to the customer.

(*e*) Normally lender/banks appoint appraisers/valuers for the purpose of appraising the purity of the gold ornaments.

(*f*) The loan granted under this category is also subject to NPA norms.

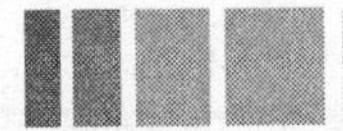

8.12 LOAN AGAINST SHARES AND BONDS

Banks grant advances against the security of shares, debentures, or bonds to individuals subject to the following conditions:

(*i*) **Purpose of the Loan**: Loan against shares, debentures and bonds should be granted to individuals to meet contingencies and personal needs or for subscribing to new or rights issues of shares/debentures/bonds or for purchase in the secondary market, against the security of shares/debentures/bonds held by the individual.

(*ii*) **Amount of advance**: Loans against the security of shares, debentures and bonds should be minimum Rupees one lakh and not exceed the limit of Rupees ten lakhs per individual if the securities are held in physical form and Rupees twenty lakhs per individual if the securities are held in dematerialized form. Such loans are meant for genuine individual investors, and banks should not support collusive action by a large group of individuals belonging to the same corporate or their inter-connected entities to take multiple loans to support stock-broking activities of the connected firms. Such finance should be reckoned as an exposure to capital market.

(*iii*) **Margin**: Banks should maintain a minimum margin of 50 per cent of the market value of equity shares/convertible debentures held in physical form. In the case of shares/convertible debentures held in dematerialized form, a minimum margin of 25 per cent should be maintained. These are minimum margin stipulations and banks may stipulate higher margins for shares whether held in physical form or dematerialized form. The margin requirements for advances against preference shares/non-convertible debentures and bonds may be determined by the banks as per Board approved policy.

Advances to Share and Stock Brokers/Commodity Brokers:

(*i*) Banks and their subsidiaries do not undertake financing of 'Badla' transactions.

(*ii*) Share and stock brokers/commodity brokers are provided need-based overdraft facilities/line of credit against shares and debentures held by them as stock-in-trade. A careful assessment of need-based requirements for such finance is done taking into account the financial position of the borrower, operations on his own account and on behalf of clients, income earned, the average turnover period of stocks and shares and the extent to which the broker's funds are required to be involved in his business operations. Large scale investment in shares and debentures on own account by stock and share brokers with bank finance, is not encouraged. The securities lodged as collateral should be easily marketable.

(*iii*) The ceiling of Rupees 10 Lakh/Rupees 20 Lakh for advances against shares/debentures to individuals will not be applicable in the case of share and stock brokers/commodity brokers and the advances would be need based.

8.13 LET US SUM UP

Bankers take different types of securities for safeguarding their advances. Each type of security has its own features. Securities are pledged against a loan to financial lending institutions. There are different types of securities like (*a*) Immovable - land, plant machineries, etc. (*b*) Movable - goods, raw materials, agricultural produce, (*c*) Book debts- account receivables (*d*) Personal securities - personal liability of the customer (e) tangible securities - any security that can be realized by a sale or transfer physically (*f*) Primary - main security cover for an advance and (*g*) Collateral-security other than primary security.

The method of creation of a charge on these securities varies according to the type. In this the charge of pledge and hypothecation applies to movable properties. In the case of pledge, the possession of the property is transferred, and it is not so in the case of hypothecation. In both these cases, ownership does not change. Among the various mortgages, the mortgage by deposit of title deeds and simple mortgage are usually taken by banks. Banks' charge on insurance policies is created by way of assignment. Though banks generally grant loans against its own deposits, no loans are given against minor's deposit, unless the guardian states that the loan is meant for the minor's necessities.

8.14 KEY WORDS

Immovable property, Goods, Inspection of goods, Personal Guarantee, Assignment, Constructive Delivery, Simple Mortgage, Mortgage by Deposit of Title Deed, Notified Centre

8.15 CHECK YOUR PROGRESS

1. The nature of charge created while advancing against LIC policy is:
   - (*a*) Assignment
   - (*b*) Lien
   - (*c*) Pledge
   - (*d*) Set off
2. Loan against minor's term deposit:
   - (*a*) can be granted if the documents are signed, if the minor has completed the age of 14 years
   - (*b*) cannot be granted under any circumstances as the minor does not have the contractual capacity

(*c*) can be granted to the guardian of the minor, if it is for the necessities of the minor

(*d*) can be granted only with the permission of the Court.

3. State True or False:

(*a*) In the case of assignment of LIC Policy as a security to an advance, the assignment is not complete unless a notice of assignment is given to the insurance company.

(*b*) To above notice of assignment may be given either by the assignor or by the assignee.

(*c*) There is less risk for the bank when hypothecation charge created by a company is registered with the ROC.

(*d*) One of the essential requirements of a pledge is the actual or constructive delivery of the goods pledged by the pledger to the pledgee.

(*e*) Limitation period for filing suit for sale of an immovable property is thirty years from the date mortgage debt becomes due.

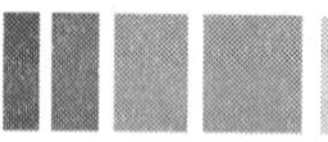

8.16 ANSWERS TO CHECK YOUR PROGRESS

1.	(*a*)	2.	(*c*)	3.	(*a*) T (*b*) T (*c*) T (*d*) T (*e*) F

CHAPTER

9 Loan Documentation

9.1 OBJECTIVES

After studying this unit, you will be able to know the following:

(*a*) Importance of loan documentation

(*b*) Procedure for obtaining proper and error free documents to secure the advances made by a bank

(*c*) Execution of documents

9.2 INTRODUCTION

Documentation is one of the vital areas in the credit portfolio of a bank. The purpose of taking documents is to fix the terms and conditions between the bankers and the borrowers, to identify the borrowers, to identify the securities, to count the period of limitation, to enable to resort to legal remedies in case of need and so on. There are certain enactments such as Indian Contract Act, Partnership Act, Companies Act, Indian Registration Act, Limitation Act, Indian Stamps Act, etc., which directly impact/ affect the bankers' loan documentation. While taking documents for a credit facility, the provisions of these enactments are to be kept in mind. Non-compliance of any of the provisions of any of these enactments may affect the validity of documents. For example, if a loan is given to a minor other than for his/her necessities, the documents executed may not be enforceable in a court of law, as a contract with a minor is *ab initio void* as per the provisions of the Indian Contract Act.

The most important aspect of sanctioning a loan after due credit appraisal is proper documentation *i.e.*, signing of various agreements to secure the loan before disbursing the credit. The following are important points about documentation:

i. Disbursements should be done only after completion of documents. Disbursement may be in phases for term loans and for fresh working capital loan whereas the enhancement in working capital limits may be released in stages or in line with other members of Joint venture agreement if it is lent under consortium arrangement.

ii. Documents are to be signed by the customer or the authorized representatives of the customer and by the guarantor/s if the loan is secured by 3rd party guarantee in the presence of authorized representative of the lender.

iii. Necessary documents are also obtained for creation of charge in case of limited companies for filing charge with ROC within 30 days of execution of the document.

iv. Similarly appropriate documents should be obtained for collateral security and if the collaterals are offered by a third party, his/her guarantee must be ensured.

v. Documents need to be properly stamped as per Stamp Act at the place of execution.

vi. Date of execution of documents should never be earlier than the date of stamping the documents.

vii. Place of execution should be properly mentioned and be witnessed by the lender's authorized signatory in evidence of the documents being signed in his/her presence.

viii. Agreements/Documents must be filled in before signing. As a rule, no blank/ partially filled documents should be signed by the customer/guarantor. Documents should not be signed under coercion, and it must be ensured that person signing the document has signed it with his/her free will.

ix. All agreement/document that are required to be registered with the Sub-registrar should be done within the prescribed time limit.

x. Partners should sign the documents in their capacity as partner, by affixing the official stamp of the partnership.

xi. It is preferable that standard covenants should be a part of the documents and pre-disbursal conditions should necessarily be a part of the documents in case of project loans.

xii. Wherever third-party guarantees are stipulated as a condition by the lender while sanctioning the loan, appropriate agreement/documents must be signed by the guarantor. In case of default after serving due legal notice by the lender; legal action can be initiated against the guarantor for recovery of dues since the liability of the customer (principal debtor) and guarantor are co-extensive. If recovery is made by initiating legal action against only the guarantor, then guarantor steps into the shoes of the lender and can recover the dues from the customer by initiating legal action against him.

xiii. In case of limited companies and other legal entities, the promoters/Directors or trustees personal guarantee is insisted upon to secure the loan. Personal guarantee of promoter/Directors holding the majority shares are usually insisted upon and in case of default their names are advised to RBI and CIBIL as defaulters in respect of default by the company. No commission or fees should be paid by the company to its directors for standing as a guarantor and it should be stipulated as one of the conditions in the documents to be executed by the customer.

xiv. In case of multiple banking arrangement, each lender may have standard set of documents which is obtained by the lender.

xv. For any properties mortgaged to Bank/NBCs, registration of the property with CERSAI in their central registry need to be ensured. This rule is applicable to housing loans, mortgage loans, etc.

xvi. For vehicle loans/two-wheeler loans, in addition to documents for hypothecation of the vehicle/two-wheeler, charge need to be registered with the local Regional Transport Authority (RTA).

xvii. In the case of loans, against life insurance policies, the policies need to be assigned by the customer in favour of the lenders and suitable documents be obtained from the customer assigning the policies in favour of the lenders. The assignment should be, subsequently registered with the concerned insurance company before loan is disbursed.

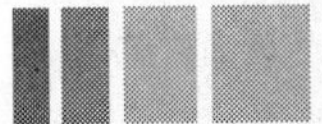

9.3 DIFFERENT TYPES OF LOAN DOCUMENTS

The documents taken by a banker for a loan may be:

(*a*) Demand Promissory Notes (DPN)

(*b*) Agreements

(*c*) Forms

9.3.1 Demand Promissory Notes

Where no specification for a fixed period for the repayment of loan is given, the bankers obtain Demand Promissory Note (DPN). In DPN, the borrower makes a promise to the banker to repay the loan amount on demand with agreed rate of interest. The form of DPN should be in conformity with section 4 of the Negotiable Instruments Act, 1881. The form of a DPN varies normally to suit the situation such as fixed rate of interest, floating rate of interest, single borrower, joint borrowers, joint and several borrowers, public/private Ltd. companies etc. DPN attracts a stamp duty as per Indian Stamp Act. The rate of stamp duty on DPN is uniform throughout India. As per section 35 of the Indian Stamp Act, if a DPN is unstamped or under-stamped, the defect cannot be rectified even by paying a penalty at a later date. Such a DPN cannot be admissible as evidence in a court of law. It must be ensured that the DPN is duly filled in and stamped before the borrower signs it.

9.3.2 Agreements

The form of an agreement should be in conformity with the Indian Contract Act. The terms and conditions are set out in the agreement. The amount of loan, rate of interest, rate of penal interest, percentage of margin, period of repayment, rights of the bankers in case of default of loan, details of security/securities charged are included in the agreement. The agreements attract stamp duty as per Indian Stamp Act. The rate of stamp duty on agreements varies from State to State. Bankers use different forms of agreement such as pledge agreement, hypothecation agreement, term loan agreement, clean loan agreement, guarantee agreement, etc. The stamp duty is different for different type of agreements. The agreement duly filled in and stamped, is checked before the party signs it. Banks take steps to ensure that the borrower understands the terms of the loan and the covenants of the agreement clearly and without any doubt so that the parties do not dispute the agreement at a later date.

9.3.3 Forms

Forms are not in the nature of promise or agreement. These are obtained to specify clearly the intention of the borrower. For example, when a loan is granted against the security of a fixed deposit standing in joint names, one of the depositors gives an authorisation to the other to raise a loan on the deposit. Such an authorisation is taken in a printed form. Similarly, when a payment is to be made out of loan proceeds to a supplier of goods, a letter from the borrower authorising the bank to pay the proceeds by means of draft or bankers cheque, is taken by means of a form. Yet another example of a form would be a letter from the guardian of a minor stating that the loan against the minor's deposit will be used only for the minor's necessities. This is in view of the fact that no loan can be granted against a minor's deposit, as the minor has no capacity to contract.

Such forms are used as part of documentation to prove the intention of the borrowers. These are also called undertakings or authorisations.

9.4 DOCUMENTATION PROCEDURE

For a document to be error free and proper, the steps to be followed are:

9.4.1 Selection of correct set of documents

Documents to be taken and the process vary depending upon the nature of facility and type of person. The document prescribed for a cash credit facility may not be used for a term loan facility. Similarly, a document meant for an individual borrower cannot be used for a company or partnership borrower. As the bankers have pre-printed forms of documents, it should be ensured that the correct set of documents, which are relevant for the particular facility and borrower are used. It is preferable that the documents are printed in the local vernacular language for better understanding.

9.4.2 Stamping

The next aspect of documentation is stamping. A document shall be stamped in accordance with the Indian Stamp Act as amended by the concerned State Governments. Indian Stamp Act contains provisions regarding time of stamping for instruments executed in India and out of India. A document executed in India shall be stamped before or at the time of execution. Section 12 of Indian Stamp Act provides for cancellation of adhesive stamp so that the same cannot be used again. Any instrument bearing an adhesive stamp which has not been cancelled so that it cannot be used again, shall be deemed to be unstamped.

9.4.3 Writing or Filling the document

The next aspect of documentation procedure is filling. As bankers are generally using the pre-printed formats of documents with blanks in appropriate places, it is necessary to fill these blanks as per the terms of sanction of the credit facility before execution. Once the document is executed, it becomes a concluded contract and any subsequent filling by bank without the consent of the executants will invalidate it. The document should be filled and completed without any alteration, overwriting or cutting. The entire document shall be filled with same ink, in same handwriting and by same person in single sitting. Otherwise, it may give rise to a suspicion that the document is filled, subsequent to the execution.

9.4.4 Execution

After filling, the next step in the documentation procedure is the execution or signing of the document. It should be ensured that the signature in the document tallies with the signature as appearing in the application for the loan and also with the specimen signature, in case the party maintains a deposit account with the bank. In case of execution in the representative capacity of sole proprietor or partner or director or agent or trustee or executor, etc., the fact should be clearly mentioned. Similarly, in case document is taken for a loan sanctioned to a minor borrower for his/her necessity; the signature of the guardian is to be obtained for self and as guardian of the minor borrower. Normally, bankers take the signature of the executants in all the pages of the documents, so that they may not take a plea later that the contents of the pages were not known. In case the document contains any alteration, overwriting or cutting, it must be authenticated with the full signature of the executants. The documents shall be executed in the presence of bank officials and the fact of execution of documents with the date and time of execution, the details of documents executed, the fact of having explaining the contents of the documents in the language known to the executants shall be recorded in a register with the signature of two bank officials so that in case of any dispute regarding execution of documents, this register may be produced as evidence before appropriate authority in case of dispute in a court of law at a later date.

9.4.5 Legal Formalities

In some cases, after execution of the document, certain legal formalities are required to be undergone. For example, in case of advances to limited companies against its assets, the required forms are to be presented to the Registrar of Companies (RoC) within a period of 30 Days from the date of execution. However, under Section 77 (Companies Act, 2013) RoC may on application by the company, allow the registration of charge within 300 days (30 days + additional period of 270 days) with additional fees. Similarly, in the case of creation of registered mortgage, the mortgage deed is presented for registration before the Registrar of Assurances within four months from the date of execution of the deed. If these formalities are not observed, then the bank may have to loose priority over the security. The documents may not be admissible as evidence before the competent authority. This process is called registration of charge created.

9.4.6 Keeping documents valid

The documents taken by banks for a credit facility do not have perpetual life. The provisions of Limitation Act apply to them. The Limitation Act prescribes the period of limitation for different types of documents/charges. For example, the period of limitation for a DPN is three years from the date of execution. If a loan is not repaid within the period of limitation, then the bank has to get fresh document/s or revival letter for extending the period of limitation as per the provisions of Limitation Act. As per section 18 of the Act, when the borrower acknowledges the debt before the expiry of period of limitation, then the life of the document is extended by one more period from the date of such acknowledgement. As per section 19 of the Act, if the borrower or his duly authorised agent makes any part payment towards the loan before the expiry of period of limitation, then the period of limitation is extended by one more period from the date of such part payment.

According to section 3 of Limitation Act, a suit cannot be filed for recovery on the strength of a time barred document. Even the provisions regarding condonation of delay in taking appropriate legal action as per section 5 of the Act, is not applicable for filing a suit for recovery of debt. Hence, if the documents are time barred, the bank's right of legal remedy for recovery is lost.

IMPORTANT POINTS:

1. In respect of all types of loans and advances, payable on demand *viz.* Cash Credits, Overdrafts, Demand Loans (whether secured by mortgage or not), the limitation period is 3 years, from the date of document (in respect of personal liability of the borrower). If the documents date is other than that of the date of first debit, the limitation period expires after 3 years from the date of the document or the first debit, whichever is earlier.
2. In respect of Term Loan documents (whether secured by mortgage or not) limitation period in respect of personal liability is 3 years from the date an instalment is defaulted. *e.g.*, Date of document 1-3-2013, repayable in 48 monthly instalments. 1st instalment to commence from 1-3-2014 and expires on 28-2-2017. If the borrower defaults within the above period, the limitation period will be 3 years from the date of first default.
3. Banks are required to obtain revival letter within three years from the date of execution of documents or from date of release of funds, whichever is earlier, so as to safeguard against all the contingencies. Banks should obtain revival letters, before expiry of subsequent period(s) of three years. Revival letters obtained/signed after the expiry of three years period will not revive the documents and are not enforceable.
4. In case of loans secured by mortgage of immovable properties, the limitation period is 12 years when the money sued for becomes due in relation to mortgaged security. But to keep the borrower's personal liability intact (in which case limitation period is only 3 years branches should obtain revival letters from borrowers once in 3 years.
5. In case of mortgage loans, the effect of not obtaining revival letters from the borrower, within 3 years reviving his personal obligation, is that, in case of his default at a subsequent date, the Bank can proceed only against mortgaged security, but cannot sue the borrower, in his personal capacity; and realise the Bank's dues from the other personal assets of the borrower.
6. In case of pledge loans, the expiry of D.P. Note (after 3 years) does not vitiate the Banker's right as a pledge, to dispose off the pledged articles (after giving notice and following other formalities), and recover its dues (even after 3 years).

In such cases, however, the Bank, in case of shortfall (amount recovered from sale of pledged articles being less than the outstanding amount), cannot enforce its claim against the borrower, in a Court of Law.

7. In respect of the documents, where the interest amount is payable at a date other than that of payment of instalment the date for reckoning limitation period starts from the date of failure of payment of either principal instalment amount or interest amount, whichever is earlier.
8. The earliest date, on the various documents, should be taken for the purpose of reckoning limitation period.
9. Revival letters should be obtained from both the borrower(s) and guarantor(s), to extend limitation against both the borrower(s) and guarantor(s). Where there are more than one guarantor, the revival letters should be obtained from all the guarantors, to extend limitation against each one of them. Revival letters can be signed/executed by the borrowers and guarantors on different dates, best within the period of limitation. The next periods of limitation, in such cases, commence, respectively, from the dates on which the borrowers and guarantors have signed the revival letters. Action should be taken, considering the earliest of the revival letters among these, to save limitation both against the borrower and the guarantor.
10. In case of joint borrowers, it is necessary to obtain revival letters from all the joint borrowers, to extend the limitation against each one of them.
11. In cases where the borrower has refused to sign the revival letter or his signature could not be obtained for one reason, or the other, but guarantor has signed revival letter (before the expiry of the limitation period), the guarantor's obligation will continue even though the borrower's obligations are barred by limitation. The *vice-versa* position is also the same.
12. In cases where the documents are already barred by limitation, fresh documents like D.P. Note etc. should be obtained. The D.P. Note should be for the amount outstanding as on that date (*i.e.* on the date of obtention of fresh documents but not for the original loan amount). Along with interest, at a rate applicable as on that date. A fresh D.P. Note can be obtained on any date subsequent to the date of limitation of old set of documents. If the loan is guaranteed, a fresh guarantee deed from the old guarantor, if possible or from a new guarantor should be obtained. In these cases, a link document should also be obtained.
13. Credit vouchers signed by the borrower or his authorized agent (in case of tie-up arrangements the remitter authorized by the borrower, to act as his agent to remit the amount direct to the Bank), has the effect of extending the limitation, against the borrower, provided such credits are made before the expiry of limitation period.

14. Pay-in-slips (Credit vouchers) signed by the guarantors, for depositing the amounts into the account of the borrower, after the guarantee is invoked, but within the period of limitation, may have the effect of extending the limitation, against the guarantor. When pay-in-slips, accompanied by cheques for credit of the borrower's account, duly signed by him or with a covering letter, enclosing a draft, duly signed by him are received, we can treat the liability as revived from the date of payment of cheque or draft. After expiry of three years (*i.e.* after limitation period is over) amounts received for credit of borrower's accounts through pay-in-slips duly signed by him, will not revive his obligation.
15. Balance confirmation letters, obtained from the borrower, will extend the limitation, for a further period of three years, from the date of such obtention/execution.
16. In case, Revival Letters are not available, a simple letter of the borrower, addressed to the Bank in reply to any notice/communication by the Bank; or otherwise referring to the liability and offering to repay the amount, would be sufficient acknowledgement of debt, for the purpose of limitation.
17. In case either the borrower or guarantor dies, within the period of limitation, agreements/acknowledgements from the legal heirs of the deceased along with the guarantors, if any, should be obtained on proper stamp paper, to keep the documents live.
18. Diary Note of due dates of agreements/documents is most important, for timely obtention of revival letters. Any laxity in this regard will jeopardize Bank's interests.

Computation of period of limitation:

(*a*) When the period of limitation expires on a day when the court is closed, the suit, appeal or application may be instituted, preferred or made on the day when the court reopens.

(*b*) Any appeal or any application other than execution petitions may be admitted after the prescribed period, if the appellant or applicant makes out sufficient cause for not preferring the appeal or application within the period of limitation.

(*c*) In computing the period of limitation, the day from which such period is to be reckoned, shall be excluded.

(*d*) For an application for execution of decree, the period during which the institution or execution has been stayed by injunction or order, the day on which the order was issued or made and the day on which it was withdrawn shall be excluded.

(*e*) In computing the period of limitation for any suit, the time during which the defendant has been absent from India and from the territories outside India under the administration of the Central Government shall be excluded, etc.

9.4.7 Renewal of Documents

At the time of renewal or if there is variation in the limit or amount originally sanctioned by the bank, it is necessary to obtain a fresh set of documents or continue the existing set of documents duly supported by supplemental/additional deeds, if required. Cancellation of the existing set of documents would cause a discontinuity in the bank's charge on the security for the credit facility.

It is not mandatory to obtain fresh sets of documents for renewal of the credit facility. A formal letter to the borrower agreeing to continue the credit facility by the bank for a further period of say, one year, at his request would suffice. Acknowledgement of the debt incorporating particulars of the original security document duly signed by the borrower is obtained at the time of renewal and attached to form part of the original set of documents.

9.4.8 Safekeeping and preservation of documents

Now-a-days, banks give loan for a longer period say twenty years or even twenty-five years. Until such time the entire dues are recovered, the documents are to be preserved in good condition.

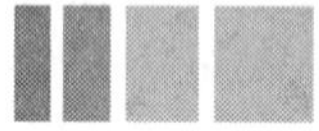

9.5 REGISTRATION OF DOCUMENTS EXECUTED

(*a*) Registration of charge on movables: A deed relating to the mortgage of movables (*i.e.* charge on movables including pledge, hypothecation etc.) does not require registration. A document hypothecating standing corps also do not require registration as it relates to movable property.

(*b*) Registration of Power of Attorney (POA)/General Power of Attorney (GPA): If a Power of Attorney holder is only a duly authorized agent of his principal and the POA does not create and right, title or interest in the immovable properties of the principal in favour of the POA holder, the POA does not require registration. However, if the POA authorizes the holder to recover the mortgage debt, rent or profit accruing from the immovable property for the holder's own benefit, the POA would require registration.

(*c*) Requirement of witness: Two witnesses are required at the time of completing the registration formalities to identify the persons who have executed the document. However, if the parties to the document produce sufficient document for identification (*e.g.* passport etc.), then the presence of witness is not required for registration of document.

(*d*) Registration of mortgage of immovable properties: This is relevant issue from lender's point of view. We have already discussed in earlier chapter that provisions relating to equitable mortgage are governed by section 58 of the Transfer of Provisions Act. Whereas there is no legal necessity to register an equitable mortgage, all other mortgages become effective if the instrument of mortgage (Mortgage deed) duly signed by the mortgagor, is registered and attested by the least two witnesses. Now in most of the states Equitable mortgage is required to be registered and provisions in this regard needs to be ascertained. Any second/supplemental mortgage also requires registration as per the Registration Act.

(*e*) The Companies Act, 2013 (Sec. 77) provides that 'charge' means and includes mortgage/charge over any or all properties of the company within or outside India.

(*f*) The Sec. 77(1) provides that the charge created over the properties of the company shall be registered with the Registrar of Companies within thirty days of creation of charge.

Credit Officials need to be careful about the fact that at the time of creation of equitable mortgage by deposit of title deeds, no memorandum or letter is obtained which states that a mortgage is being created. These accompanying documents are treated as documents of bargain between the mortgagor, and the mortgagee and require registration. Some examples of documents considered as documents of bargain are following:

- The borrower/guarantor acknowledge receipt of the loan against the security of immovable properties in respect of which the title has already been deposited. The acknowledgement has been made in an agreement executed for the purpose. They further agree that they would create a regular mortgage at their own expense as and when required by the bank. The agreement in this situation constitutes a document of bargain and would require registration.
- The mortgagor hands over the title deeds to the bank along with a letter stating that the title deeds are being handed with an intent to create mortgage and in consideration there-against, the loan amount is being provided by executing a document/DP Note on the security of the title deeds. The letter is a document of bargain.
- A document is executed which authorizes the second/subsequent mortgagee to liquidate the dues owned to the prior mortgagee, recover the dues from the latter, and retain the title deeds as additional security. Such a document which embodies the terms of agreement in this manner, may be executed in situations like takeover of loans from other banks/institutions against the security of immovable properties that was mortgaged to the previous lender.

It is important to note that if a particular document requires registration under section 17 of the Registration Act and is not registered, it loses its legal validity. Such a document is rendered inoperative and unenforceable as it becomes inadmissible in evidence. By complying with the registration procedures, a proper legal title passes on to the purchase/transferee and the document also becomes admissible as an evidence. In simple words, the title to the property becomes defective if registration of the document is not done. Besides, if the document is registered, it is possible to obtain a certified copy of such document from the Registrar's office in case of loss or misplaced of the original.

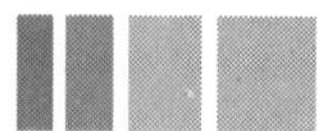

9.6 LET'S SUM UP

Among the various purposes of taking documents, resorting to legal remedies, in case of necessity, is the prime one. The various steps namely, selection of correct set of documents, stamping at right point of time, filling in a proper manner, their execution on observing the legal formalities, keeping the documents alive and preserving the documents till the entire dues are recovered, should be reported to make error-free documentation. Registration of loan documents, wherever it is required by law, should be got done within the stipulated period.

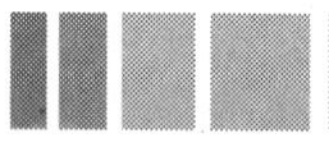

9.7 KEY WORDS

Documentation, Demand Promissory Note, Form, Agreement, Stamping, Execution, Revival, Registration

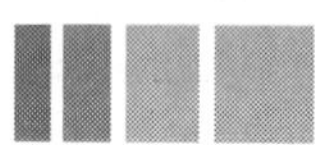

9.8 CHECK YOUR PROGRESS

1. As per the Stamp Act, a document executed in India shall be stamped:
   - (*a*) only before execution
   - (*b*) at any time, but before filing suit
   - (*c*) within 30 days after execution
   - (*d*) before or at the time of execution
2. One of the following statements is not true:
   - (*a*) The Court cannot condone delay in filing suit, if the document is time-barred.
   - (*b*) If a demand promissory note is not stamped before or at the time of execution in India, the defect can be set right by paying penalty.
   - (*c*) When the borrower acknowledges the debt before the expiry of limitation period, the period of limitation is extended by one more period.
   - (*d*) If the borrower makes part payment into the loan account before the expiry of limitation period, the period of limitation is extended by one more period.

3. Under the Companies Act, 2013 a charge includes:
   (*a*) Mortgage
   (*b*) Promissory Note
   (*c*) Bill of Exchange
   (*d*) Letter of credit
4. Charge shall be registered within ------ days from the date of creation of charge:
   (*a*) 60
   (*b*) 30
   (*c*) 15
   (*d*) At the discretion of the Bank
5. Charge means any form of (*i*) Security (*ii*) Debt (*iii*) Deposit:
   (*a*) (*i*)
   (*b*) (*i*) and (*ii*)
   (*c*) (*ii*) and (*iii*)
   (*d*) (*i*), (*ii*) and (*iii*)

9.9 ANSWERS TO CHECK YOUR PROGRESS

1.	(*d*)	2.	(*b*)	3.	(*a*)	4.	(*b*)	5.	(*a*)				

CHAPTER

10 Income Recognition and Asset Classification

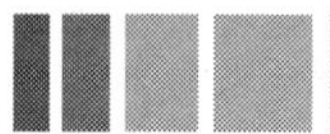

10.1 OBJECTIVES

At the end of the chapter, the student would be able to understand:

(*a*) Definition of Non-Performing Assets (NPA)

(*b*) Standard assets

(*c*) Sub-standard assets

(*d*) Doubtful assets

(*e*) Loss assets

10.2 INTRODUCTION

Loans and advances of banks appear on the asset side of the balance sheet and are classified as assets. It is expected that the banks recover interest on their loans and advances and that the principal amount comes back as stipulated at the time of sanctioning loans. If the payment of interest is delayed or defaulted and the principal amount or the instalments are delayed defaulted an account is said to be over-due. If the accounts remain overdue or past due beyond the stipulated time the accounts are classified as Non-Performing Asset (NPA).

It is important to remember that in the case of NPA accounts the banks cannot recognize the income. Also, if the assets are NPA for some time the banks will have to provide for loan losses. In this regard Banks are required to classify their loan assets as per the regulatory guidelines issued from time to time by Reserve Bank of India (abbreviated as RBI hereafter), namely Standard assets, Sub-standard assets, Doubtful assets, and Loss assets. The definition of these terms and also of Non-Performing Assets (abbreviated as NPA hereafter) will be given as per RBI circulars.

10.3 DEFINITION OF NPA

The under-quoted definition of NPA is self-explanatory. In terms of RBI guidelines - Prudential Norms on Income Recognition, Asset Classification and Provisioning pertaining to Advances are as under:

An asset, including a leased asset, becomes non-performing when it ceases to generate income for the bank. A non-performing asset (NPA) is a loan or an advance where:

(*i*) Interest and/or instalment of principal remains overdue (*unpaid*) for a period of more than 90 days in respect of a term loan,

(*ii*) The account remains 'out of order' * for a period of more than 90 days (*the outstanding balance being in debit or in excess of the limit sanctioned*) in respect of an overdraft/cash credit,

(*iii*) The bills remain overdue (*unpaid*) for a period of more than 90 days in case of the bills purchased and discounted,

(*iv*) The instalment of principal or interest thereon remains overdue for two crop seasons for short duration crops in case of agriculture finance,

(*v*) The instalment of principal or interest thereon remains overdue for one crop season for long duration crops,

Banks should classify an account as NPA if the interest charged during any quarter is not serviced fully within 90 days from the end of the quarter.

*(An account should be treated as 'out of order' if the outstanding balance remains continuously in excess of the sanctioned limit/drawing power. In cases where the outstanding balance in the principal operating account is less than the sanctioned limit/drawing power, but there are no credits continuously for 90 days as on the date of the balance sheet, or credits are not enough to cover the interest debited during the same period, these accounts should be treated as 'out of order').

10.4. INCOME RECOGNITION

Normally banks/NBFC recognizes income on accrual basis. Interest so levied but not recovered is shown as interest receivable. In the case of NPA's, banks cannot recognize income except on cash basis *i.e.*, in respect of NPA account banks will not accrue interest on due basis and will also reverse interest that has accrued in the past and is outstanding *i.e.*, not paid.

Income recognition should be objective and based on the record of recovery. Therefore, the banks/NBFC should not charge and take to income account interest on any NPA. This will apply to Government guaranteed accounts also. In this connection:-

i. Interest on advances against Term Deposits, National Savings Certificates (NSCs), Kisan Vikas Patras (KVPs) and life insurance policies may be taken to income account on the due date, provided adequate margin is available in the accounts.

ii. Fees and commissions earned by the banks because of renegotiations or rescheduling of outstanding debts should be recognized on an accrual basis over the period covered by the renegotiated or rescheduled extension of credit.

iii. In case of loans where moratorium has been granted for repayment of interest, income may be recognized on accrual basis for accounts which continue to be classified as 'standard'.

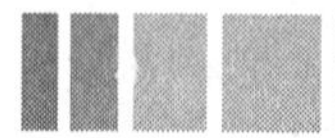

10.5 REVERSAL OF INCOME

i. The entire income that has been recognized should be reversed in case of any advance including bills purchased and discounted becomes NPA. This will apply to Government guaranteed accounts also.

ii. In case of NPA accounts, fees, commission, and similar income that has been accrued should cease to accrue in the current period. Past fee if any should be reversed if uncollected.

iii. Interest realized on NPAs may be taken to income account provided the credits in the accounts towards interest are not out of fresh/additional credit facilities sanctioned to the customer concerned.

iv. In the absence of a clear agreement between the bank and the customer for the purpose of appropriation of recoveries in NPAs (*i.e.*, towards principal or interest due), banks should exercise the right of appropriation of recoveries in a uniform and consistent manner.

v. On an account turning NPA, banks should reverse the interest already charged and not collected by debiting Profit and Loss account and stop further application of interest. However, banks may continue to record such accrued interest in a Memorandum account in their books. To computing Gross Advances, interest recorded in the Memorandum account should not be considered.

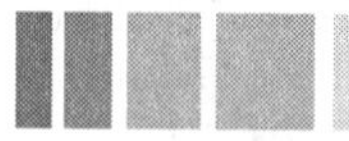

10.6 ASSET CLASSIFICATION

RBI guidelines stipulate that banks must classify assets or loans into four categories:

- Standard Assets
- Sub-standard Assets
- Doubtful Assets
- Loss Assets

An asset is either NPA or non-NPA. Standard Assets are those assets which are performing assets and not NPAs. Therefore, NPA accounts are grouped under three remaining categories and can be further classified into three sub-categories: Sub-standard, Doubtful and Loss assets.

Standard assets are those that service their interest and principal instalments on time. NPAs are characterized by non-servicing of interest and principal as per stipulation as defined later. Standard Assets are called performing assets as they yield regular interest to the bank and return the due principal, thus enabling them to earn profits and re-cycle the repaid portions of loans for further loaning.

The retail loan debtors under performing loans will normally pay the monthly instalments dues (EMI) regularly and in time. It will be seen that if there is some temporary delay the account will not have 3 EMIs remaining unpaid consecutively, as otherwise the loan would fall in the category of NPA (over-dues for more than 90 days), entailing adverse consequences, including levy of higher interest rate and provisioning.

The following three NPA categories of debtors will, however, be marked by delay/avoidance/resistance in payment of the overdue amount, due to their financial difficulty or unwillingness to pay or similar other reasons.

10.7 SUB-STANDARD ASSETS

As per existing guidelines, a Sub-standard asset would be one, which has remained NPA for a period less than or equal to 12 months. Such an asset will have well defined credit weaknesses that jeopardise the liquidation of the debt and are characterised by the distinct possibility that the banks will sustain some loss, if deficiencies are not corrected. To illustrate, if 3 EMIs of a loan remain unpaid for a period of over 90 days but less than 12 months, the account will be treated as a Sub-standard asset.

The collection of Sub-standard assets will become progressively difficult. For example, if the default period is 91 days, it may be less difficult to collect the overdue amount as compared to an account which is in default for longer periods. When the default period increases to, say, 6 months, the overdue amount will increase due to 6 months EMI in default (as compared to 3 months earlier) and also additional interest on the overdue amount added up.

10.8 DOUBTFUL ASSETS

An asset would be classified as doubtful if it has remained in the *Sub-standard category for a period of 12 months.*

Doubtful assets are cause of concern as it is worsening of Sub-standard asset as they have remained unpaid for at least 12 months since they were classified as Sub-standard asset. It would be more difficult to collect the overdue amount in Doubtful assets, as the overdue amount relates to additional 12 months (or more) along with additional interest.

In these cases, it is evident that the financial/liquidity position of the debtor has obviously deteriorated as reflected in the debtor's continued inability to pay the overdue amount despite lapse of 12 months from the time his account was classified as Sub-standard asset. Such assets are rightly called doubtful, since their recovery seems improbable and highly questionable on the basis of the currently known facts, condition and values of the security for the loan.

(If arrears of interest and principal are paid by the borrower in the case of loan accounts classified as NPAs, the account should no longer be treated as non-performing and may be classified as 'standard' accounts).

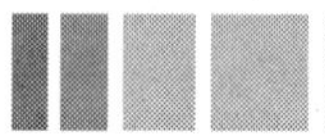

10.9 LOSS ASSETS

A loss asset is one where loss has been identified by the bank or its internal or external auditors, or by the RBI inspection, but the amount has not been written off wholly. Loss assets are considered uncollectible. They are of such little realisable value that their continuance as bankable assets are not warranted. However, there may be some salvage value in the long term, in some cases.

We may conclude the Asset Classification by stating that the probability of repayment of loans in four categories will generally be:

- High in Standard assets,
- Good or fair in Sub-standard assets,
- Doubtful or Questionable in Doubtful assets, and
- Improbable or negligible

Before a loan account turns into an NPA:

Banks are also required to identify incipient stress in the account before a loan account turns into an NPA, by creating three Sub-categories under the Special Mention Account (SMA) category as given in the table below:

For Term Loans:

SMA Sub-categories	FOR LOANS - Basis for classification
SMA-0	Principal or interest payment not overdue for more than 30 days but account showing signs of incipient stress
SMA-1	Principal or interest payment overdue between 31-60 days
SMA-2	Principal or interest payment overdue between 61-90 days

For Cash Credit/OD Accounts:

SMA-0	Basis for classification (FOR CASH CREDIT/REVOLVING CREDIT) Outstanding balance remains continuously in excess of the sanctioned limit or drawing power, whichever is lower, for a period of 0 to 30 days
SMA - 1	31 – 60 days
SMA - 2	61 – 90 days

10.10 IMPORTANT POINTS ABOUT NPA ACCOUNTS

RBI has come up with a Master Circular on Prudential Norms on Income Recognition, Asset Classification and Provisioning pertaining to advances which has laid down the guidelines in detail which need to be followed by banks and all other financial institutions pertaining to policy of Income Recognition, Classification of Assets and Provisioning which should be made on the basis of the Classification of Assets based on the period for which the Asset has remained non-performing and the availability of security and the realisable value thereof.

Few important points are summarized as followed:

i. Accounts with temporary deficiencies: The classification of an asset as NPA should be based on the record of recovery. Bank/NBFC should not classify an advance account as NPA merely due to the existence of some deficiencies which are temporary in nature such as non-availability of adequate drawing power based on the latest available stock statement, balance outstanding exceeding the limit temporarily, non-submission of stock statements and non-renewal of the limits on the due date, etc.

ii. Upgradation of loan accounts classified as NPAs: A loan account classified as NPAs may be upgraded as 'standard' asset only if entire arrears of interest and principal are paid by the customer. In case of customers having more than one credit facility from a bank/NBFC, loan accounts shall be upgraded from NPA to standard asset category only upon repayment of entire arrears of interest and principal pertaining to all the credit facilities.

iii. Accounts regularized near about the balance sheet date: The asset classification of borrowed accounts where a solitary or a few credits are recorded before the balance sheet date should be handled with care and without scope for subjectivity. Where the account indicates inherent weakness based on the data available, the account should be deemed as an NPA. In other genuine cases, bank/NBFC must furnish satisfactory evidence to the Statutory Auditors/ Inspecting Officers about the manner of regularization of the account to eliminate doubts on their performing status.

iv. Asset Classification to be customer-wise and not facility-wise: It is difficult to imagine a situation when only one facility to a customer/one investment in any of the securities issued by the customer becomes a problematic credit/ investment and not others. Therefore, all the facilities granted by a bank/NBFC to a customer and investment in all the securities issued by the customer will have to be treated as NPA/NPI and not the particular facility/investment or part thereof which has become irregular.

v. Accounts where there is erosion in the value of security/frauds committed by customers: In respect of accounts where there are potential threats for recovery on account of erosion in the value of security (erosion being 50% or more) or non-availability of security and existence of other factors such as frauds committed by customers, it will not be prudent that such accounts should go through various stages of asset classification. In cases of such serious credit impairment, the asset should be straightaway classified as doubtful, or loss asset as deemed appropriate. Further if the realizable value of the security, is less than 10 per cent of the outstanding in the borrowed accounts, the value should be ignored, and the asset should be straightaway classified as loss asset.

vi. Provisioning norms in respect of all cases of fraud: Banks/NBFC should normally provide for the entire amount due to them or for which the bank/NBFC is liable (including in case of deposit accounts), immediately upon a fraud being detected. However, to smoothen the effect of such provisioning on quarterly profit and loss, institutions have the option to make the provisions over a period, not exceeding four quarters, commencing from the quarter in which the fraud has been detected.

vii. Advances against Term Deposits, NSCs, Kisan Vikas Patras, etc.: Advances against term deposits, NSCs eligible for surrender, KVPs and life insurance policies need not be treated as NPAs, provided adequate margin is available in the accounts. Advances against gold ornaments, government securities and all other securities are not covered by this exemption.

viii. Agricultural advances by banks: A loan granted for short duration crops will be treated as NPA, if the instalment of principal or interest thereon remains overdue for two crop seasons. A loan granted for long duration crops will be treated as NPA, if the instalment of principal or interest thereon remains overdue for one crop season.

ix. Government guaranteed advances: The credit facilities backed by guarantee of the Central Government though overdue may be treated as NPA only when the Government rejects its guarantee when invoked. This exemption from classification of Government guaranteed advances as NPA is not for the purpose of recognition of income. The requirement of invocation of guarantee has been delinked for deciding the asset classification and provisioning requirements in respect of State Government guaranteed exposures. With effect from the year ending March 31, 2006, State Government guaranteed advances and investments in State Government guaranteed securities would attract asset classification and provisioning norms if interest and/or principal or any other amount due to the bank remains overdue for more than 90 days.

x. Credit Card Accounts: A credit card account will be treated as non-performing asset if the minimum amount due, as mentioned in the statement, is not paid fully within 90 days from the payment due date mentioned in the statement. Banks shall report a credit card account as 'past due' to Credit Information Companies (CICs) or levy penal charges, *viz.* late payment charges, etc., if any, only when a credit card account remains 'past due' for more than three days. The number of 'days past due' and late payment charges shall, however, be computed from the payment due date mentioned in the credit card statement.

10.11 COLLECTION FUNCTION

The role or involvement of DRA begins when the amount of instalment is not paid on date and the account becomes past due. These accounts are based on number of days of default classified into buckets:

i. First bucket: Loans past due from 1 day to 30 days

ii. Second Bucket: Loans past due from 31 days to 60 days

iii. Third Bucket: Loans past due from 61 days to 90 days.

iv. NPA

As a rule, all clients are reminded about the amount due and due date by SMS and closer to the due date by call centers of the financial institutions. Prior to an account falling into the first bucket, based on some technical parameters, close follow-up by call centers is done in the case of clients likely to move in to the first bucket. This has good impact on majority of the customers.

DRAs are introduced into collection once the amount is not paid on due date. DRAs are allotted the clients with Loans Past Due (LPD) based on buckets. Generally, a DRA who is collecting in the first bucket is not allotted second and third bucket in the same area. This is to ensure that DRA does not allow the accounts to move from one bucket to another as fee and commission could vary on account of ageing of LPD. The endeavour of the lender is to collect the dues before an account slips into an NPA.

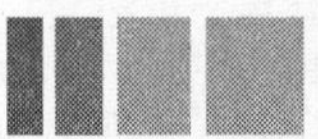

10.12 KEY WORDS

Dues, past dues, NPAs, Standard asset, Sub-Standard asset, doubtful asset, loss asset, Income recognition, Buckets.

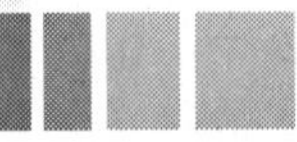

10.13 CHECK YOUR PROGRESS

1. Loans and advances of banks appear in their balance sheets on the side of:
   (*a*) Liabilities
   (*b*) Assets
   (*c*) Income
   (*d*) Expenses
2. A loan or advance of a bank is defined as 'Non-Performing Asset' (NPA) when it remains overdue or out of order for a period of:
   (*a*) 90 days
   (*b*) Less than 90 days
   (*c*) More than 90 days
   (*d*) More than 180 days
3. A loan or advance of a bank is defined as 'Doubtful' when it has remained in Sub-standard category for a period of at least:
   (*a*) 6 months
   (*b*) 12 months
   (*c*) 3 months
   (*d*) 18 months
4. A 'Standard Asset' of a bank is defined as an asset which is:
   (*a*) Not a Non-Performing Asset (NPA)
   (*b*) A Doubtful Asset
   (*c*) A Loss Asset
   (*d*) None of the above

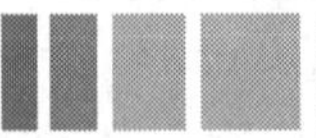

10.14 ANSWERS TO CHECK YOUR PROGRESS

1.	(*a*)	2.	(*c*)	3.	(*b*)	4.	(*a*)						

CHAPTER

11 Legal Aspects of Loan Recovery

11.1 OBJECTIVES

After reading this chapter, you should be able to know:

(*a*) Important aspects of recovery

(*b*) Recovery of loan under SARFAESI Act

(*c*) Recovery of loan through Lok Adalat

(*d*) Recovery of loan through compromises

(*e*) Recovery of loan through Debt Recovery Tribunal

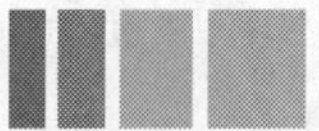

11.2 INTRODUCTION

The most important canon of any lending should be the inherently self-liquidating character of loans. Loan implies repayment. It is very important for the profitability and viability of lending institutions that the funds lent are recycled back. Inadequate recovery of loans not only inhibits the ability of the system to recycle the funds but also denies the benefits of borrowing to the other needy people. Better recovery of loans helps in building confidence of general public in the soundness of the banking system. With the current RBI guidelines relating to income recognition and the concept of Non-Performing Assets (NPAs), recovery of loans has assumed paramount importance in assessing financing strength of banks.

Loan recovery agents are legally bound by certain guidelines about how to collect. They cannot misbehave or mistreat the customers in any way. Lenders must have a diligence process in place when it comes to engaging loan recovery agents and are responsible for all complaints filed against them if enquiry shows that the complaints about harassment or misbehaviour are correct.

11.3 IMPORTANT ASPECTS OF RECOVERY

A. Adequate and timely Loan:

Timeliness is the essence of bank credit. Not only should the loans be granted in time but necessary efforts to recovery the loan should also be initiated at the appropriate time. Even at the time of granting loans, it should be impressed upon the borrowers that loans have to be repaid as per schedule. This will remove the apprehension, if any, in the minds of borrowers that the bank's loan could be repaid conveniently like Government loans. Persuasive efforts like periodical contacts with the borrowers particularly at the time of harvest/marketing of produce, should be made for ensuring prompt repayment.

B. Pre-sanction formalities:

The credit needs of the borrower should as far as possible, be worked out on an integrated basis. The assessment should be made in a rational manner and not arbitrarily, so that over/under financing does not take place. The proper pre-sanction appraisal and counselling should be made. The repayment schedule should be realistically fixed with proper regard to income flow expected out of the activity financed and after allowing for adequate gestation period before actual recovery starts.

C. Post-sanction follow-up:

1. In order to ensure proper end use of credit, the disbursements in respect of various items of inputs, etc. should be made, as far as possible direct to suppliers, where expenditure is incurred in stages, the release of funds should also be suitably phased.
2. Provision of supportive services in the service area villages with the help of appropriate agencies such as arrangements for supply of inputs, store, transport, marketing, etc. should be given due importance.
3. Where the repaying capacity of the borrowers has been adversely affected on account of natural calamities causing loss or damage to crops and other assets of the borrower, the branches should not hesitate in extending conversion/ rescheduling facilities to them. The most crucial stage would be at the time of marketing and the field staff should to the extent possible, guide the borrowers particularly the small producers, about the best ways of marketing their produce. In this context, all efforts should be made to establish tie up arrangements with the appropriate purchasing/processing agencies.

D. Follow-up of recovery:

1. This is the most important factor affecting loan recoveries. Where borrowers are not contacted for months together, the absence of contact increases the default ratio. Branches should arrange widely publicized meeting in centrally located village, which can be a good forum for coming into contact with the farmers

and educating them in regard to timely repayment of bank's loans. It may not be possible to establish contact with individual borrower during visit by field staff in cases the number of borrowers being large. With a view to keep contact with the clientele, frequent visits to villages during Melas (fair) and other functions and Krishi Upaj Mandies at the time of harvest/marketing of produce is needed.

2. Recovery notices to the borrowers should be sent well in advance. Issuance of loan pass-books should be ensured as the repayment schedule is also recorded therein.

3. Qualitative lending ensures timely and regular repayment of loans. Only viable proposals should be sanctioned.

4. Institutional tie-up should be preferred as far as possible. While advancing crop loan for sugarcane and term loan for dairy farming and sheep rearing etc., effective tie-up can be developed with agencies engaged in procurement of produce.

5. In the event of natural calamities like drought/flood, conversion/rescheduling of loans must be done quickly as also in genuine cases where the repayment capacity of the borrowers is affected by calamities other than natural calamities, keeping in view the fact that the period of loan so extended should not go beyond the economic life of the assets charged to the bank. This will not only make the old account regular but also open the way for provision of timely fresh credit without which borrowers and bank will get caught in a vicious circle.

6. Branches should assist farmers in lodging their claims with the insurance companies within a reasonable time and get them settled, which will also improve recoveries. In the case of cattle loans, it must be ensured that they are adequately insured and insurance policies are renewed invariably on due dates.

7. Guarantors must be informed of developments in respect of borrower's account and in extreme cases, issuing/renewals of loans should be linked with the proper conduct of borrowers' account.

8. The revival letters (Acknowledgement of Loans) must be obtained well in time to keep the debt alive and legal course open.

9. Field staff must remain in the fields for maximum days. Overnight stay in the villages should be encouraged as the farmers are mostly available in the late night or early morning in the villages.

10. Borrowers having good repayment records should be appreciated. They may be honoured in Gram Sabha with small gifts. Their names may also be displayed

at the branch premises. Recently, Government of India has decided to provide concession in rate of interest applicable on crop loans where the repayment is made on time.

11. Recovery camps be organized with the assistance of Government officials in the critical areas which will help in creating a favourable climate for recovery of loans. Regional Managers/Controllers of branches should also attend these camps.

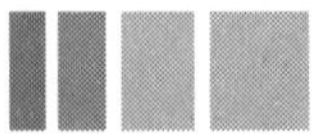

11.4 RECOVERY OF LOANS UNDER SARFAESI ACT

The Securitisation and Reconstruction of Financial Assets and Enforcement of Security Interest (SARFAESI) Act was enacted in 2002 by Government of India. Holding the security is not sufficient to discharge the obligations towards the depositors. The securities are to be liquidated for the purpose. At this juncture the importance of enforcement of securities becomes relevant. For a healthy banking system, well-knit recovery mechanism supported by proper recovery laws are the key factors. Banks prefer movable and immovable properties as security. Movable are accepted as security by way of pledge/hypothecation etc. Securities over immovable properties are created by way of mortgages. It is easy to dispose off pledged items by giving notice to the Pawner as contemplated under the Contract Act. *e.g:* Pledge of gold ornaments. With regard to the enforcement of rights over the immovable properties taken as security, banks face a lot of problems. Mainly, the bottlenecks of the extant civil laws of the Country. The civil laws of the country are too cumbersome that it may take years to get a decree. As far as India is concerned, prior to 2002, there was no option for the banks to recover its dues by enforcing the security other than through a court/Tribunal. By this enactment, banks and financial institutions are empowered to take possession of the secured assets of the borrower including the right to transfer by way of lease, assignment or sale for realizing the secured asset without the interferences of Court/Tribunal.

The Act stipulates four conditions for enforcing the rights by a creditor:

(*a*) The debt is secured

(*b*) The debt has been classified as an NPA by the banks.

(*c*) The outstanding dues are one lakh and above and overdues are more than 20% of the principal loan amount and interest there on.

(*d*) The security to be enforced is not an agricultural land.

11.4.1 Procedure for Enforcement of Rights

(*i*) Under Section 13(2), a notice has to be issued to the borrower/co-borrowers/guarantors/surely giving 60 days' time for settling the liability and also informing the intention of the secured creditor to take action under section 13(4) by taking possession of the assets.

(*ii*) After the expiry of 60 days, in case the amount due is not paid, the bank can take possession of the property and bring it for sale to realize the dues.

(*iii*) The borrower can seek any clarification and the bank is legally bound to answer the queries within 15 days of such request.

(*iv*) As such the Act gives opportunity to a debtor to get whatever details he requires from the creditor thereby avoiding any arbitrary decision by the creditors as to the amount due, interest claimed etc. If there are mistakes or irregularity in the notice, the creditor can issue a fresh notice. However, the reasons so communicated or the likely action of the secured creditor at the stage of communication of reasons shall not confer any right upon the borrower to prefer an application to the DRT.

(*v*) The notice under the Act can be issued only by an 'Authorised Officer' of the bank who will be an official in the rank of Scale IV and above.

(*vi*) After expiry of sixty days from the notice, the bank can proceed under Section 13(4) of the Act for taking possession. It shall be ensured before taking possession that the notice was acknowledged by all the parties. If notice returns from any party, a paper publication of the notice shall be made in two widely published newspapers of which one should be in vernacular language.

(*vii*) After taking possession, the bank has to publish a possession notice in two newspapers for the information of the general public.

(*viii*) Such publication is to be made within 7 days of taking possession of the property. The borrower/mortgagor can approach Debt Recovery Tribunal (DRT) for redressing grievances if any within 45 days from taking possession by the bank. Any party aggrieved by the decision of the DRT can again approach the DRAT by filing appeal within the stipulated time of 30 days.

(*ix*) The property of which possession is taken can be sold only after obtaining valuation through Government approved valuer and thereafter issuing 30 days notice to the parties which shall also be published in two newspapers (one in vernacular). Thus, the property can be sold for maximum price with wide publicity. If the amount realized is not sufficient to cover the dues, the secured creditor can approach the DRT to recover the balance amount.

(*x*) Debts owed to a secured creditor will get priority over all other claims – including other debts and all revenue, taxes, cesses and dues payable to Centre and State Governments and local authorities.

11.5 RECOVERY THROUGH LOK ADALAT

Lok Adalats are organised under the Legal Services Authorities Act, 1987. Lok Adalats shall be guided by the principles of justice, equity, fair play and other legal principles. Lok Adalats are intended to bring about a compromise or settlement in respect of any dispute or potential dispute. Lok Adalats derive jurisdiction by consent of parties or on an application made to the court by one of the parties to the dispute or the court is satisfied that the dispute between the parties could be settled by Lok Adalat. In respect of a potential dispute, any party may request the Authority or Committee organising Lok Adalat to refer the dispute for determination.

Loans up to Rs. 20 Lakh can be amicably settled between the borrower and the lender using the forum of Lok Adalats. Lok Adalats can take cognizance of cases where either two parties to a dispute agree to utilise the services of the forum or one of them makes an application to the court (and the court is *prima facie* satisfied that there are chances of a settlement) for referring the case to the Adalat.

The Lok Adalat is vested with the same powers as are vested in a civil court under the Code of Civil Procedure while trying a suit in respect of the summoning and enforcing the attendance of any witness and examining him on oath; the discovery and production of any document; and the requisitioning of any public record or document or copy of such record or document from any court or office.

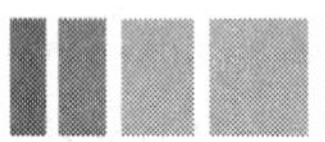

11.6 RECOVERY THROUGH LOCAL RECOVERY ACTS

For recovery of agricultural advances, almost every State Government has passed its own recovery Acts on the lines of Talwar Committee recommendations, yet these are similar in contents. In a "Model Bill of Recovery" through Government agencies, the following procedure is to be adopted:

The bank is required to make an application to the notified/designated authority for recovery of overdues on the prescribed proforma. The Notified Authority under the said Act, will be able to take action against the guarantors also for recovery of bank's dues simultaneously with the borrowers. Therefore, the application should contain full particulars of the guarantor(s), such as name and address together with details of property/assets owned, etc.

11.7 RECOVERY OF ADVANCES THROUGH COMPROMISE SETTLEMENT

Compromise settlement refers to a negotiated settlement where a borrower offers to pay and the Bank agrees to accept in full and final settlement of its dues an amount less than the total amount due to the Bank under the relative loan contract. Thus, the settlement invariably involves certain sacrifice by the Bank (by way of write off and/or waiver) of a portion of the dues from the borrower(s).

However, compromise can be marketed as a strategy in cases where:

- The security coverage back up is questionable less and prospect of recovery out of the borrower's and guarantor's own means are remote.
- Suit is pending in court and may take long time for settlement, ultimately when the amounts are recovered the value of money would be depreciated.
- Court decree awarded in favour of the bank but there are practical difficulties in enforcing the security, due to various reasons.
- Suit may not be maintainable because of improper execution of documents.

Recovery of advances through compromise settlement is accepted as an effective non-legal remedy by the Bank in cases where it is considered most appropriate to adopt this option *vis-à-vis* other resolution strategies.

The basic Objective of a compromise settlement is to minimise loss to the bank or optimise recovery, gaining as much of (uncharged interest) as possible. The ultimate strike point can be arrived at only through negotiation.

RBI Guidelines on "One Time Settlement" (OTS):

(1) Every bank should have a Board approved policy of recovering loans through OTS. The provisions of the OTS may vary in different sectors.

(2) Banks will ensure that:

(*a*) the authority approving the settlement proposal did not sanction the advance in question in his individual capacity. However, the hierarchy level of sanctioning committee may be the same as the approval authority.

(*b*) the sanctioning authority in the case of advances had exercised his powers judiciously, and adhered to the guidelines issued by the Bank in the matter of grant of advances and that normal terms and conditions were stipulated.

(*c*) there was no laxity in the conduct and post disbursement supervision of the advances.

(*d*) there was no act of commission or omission on the part of the staff leading to the debt proving irrecoverable.

(*e*) all possible expedient steps to recover the dues have been taken and there are no further prospects of recovering the debt and that the settlement proposal is in the larger interest of the Bank.

(3) Bank may enter a compromise settlement with wilful defaulters/fraudulent borrowers without prejudice to the criminal case against the borrower and

those cases of compromise settlement should be vetted by appropriate approval authority.

(4) While entering compromise settlements in NPA accounts, the Bank shall ensure that the Net Present Value (NPV) of the settlement amount should generally not be less than the net present value of the realizable value of securities.

(5) In the cases of accounts classified as Sub-standard Assets:

(*a*) In justifiable cases, competent authority can entertain/approve compromise proposals with a reasonable sacrifice, where security deterioration is likely to happen or borrowers have incurred genuine business losses. However, the account should have been classified as Sub-standard assets as at the end of the previous quarter.

(*b*) However, in cases where the provisions of SARFAESI Act cannot be invoked like in case of NPA accounts with outstanding balance of Rs. 1.00 lac and below or where there is no enforceable security or security offered is agricultural lands, etc., compromises can be entertained as per the guidelines immediately on classification of account as NPA.

(*c*) Moreover, where there is a loss of security charged to the Bank on account of natural calamities such as floods, earthquakes, riots, civil commotion, strikes, fire accidents, etc., acquisition of securities by the Government agencies and similar other circumstances, which are beyond the control of the borrower, Competent Authority can entertain/approve compromise proposals with a reasonable sacrifice.

(*d*) Consequent to the issue of notice under SARFAESI Act and taking possession of securities etc., if the borrower comes forward for a compromise settlement, in justifiable cases, compromise can be entertained.

(6) In the cases of Doubtful and Loss Assets:

Both doubtful and loss assets are chronic NPAs by nature as the chances of recovery in these accounts through normal course either by upgradation of the account to standard category or for complete closure of the account are remote/bleak. Continuation of these assets necessitates provision of substantial amounts, which will have a direct bearing on the profitability of the Bank. As a measure to recover the dues out of this category of assets, compromise settlements are preferred. The decision on when to consider the compromise opportunity in order to maximize recovery will be taken by a competent authority.

(7) Technical Written Off Accounts:

(*a*) The write off is only technical in nature and purely for internal accounting purpose only. The spirit behind the write off is transparency and reflecting the true picture of the health of the Bank in an attempt to clean up the Balance sheet of the Bank. The write off is without prejudice to bank's right to recover dues from the borrower. Some of these accounts are backed by sufficient tangible securities and bank has filed suit to recover the dues. As the settlement of cases through legal process is time consuming, banks may prefer negotiated settlements for early recovery of dues, under these guidelines.

(*b*) Realisable Value and Marketability of Securities Charged to the Bank

- Present value of the primary and collateral securities, held by the bank for the advances, should be carefully assessed on a conservative basis. Bank should not purely be guided by the engineer's valuation taken at the time of allowing the advances.
- Bank should ascertain the realizability of securities in letter and spirit, while arriving at the value thereof. This will have a bearing on the settlement amount. If, there is wide variation between the value taken at the time of release of limits and the present realisable value, explanation should be provided and considered as to reasons thereof.
- Properties of huge value though equitably mortgaged to the bank are at times difficult for enforcement even through the process of law, in view of several practical impediments. Bank should look into this aspect and the reasons for the difficulty in enforceability of securities should be duly explained while recommending/considering the proposal. Net Present Value of the Realisable value of the securities should be used as a Benchmark for negotiating the compromise settlement.

(8) While dealing with the settlement proposals of loss asset, overriding consideration will be aggregate worth and perceivable means as per market enquiries of the borrower(s) and the guarantor(s). It should be kept in mind that any recovery under loss asset is a clean profit to the Bank since, the entire outstanding is provided for.

(9) Settlement Proposals from Guarantors:

There are cases, where Guarantors in NPA accounts come forward with settlement proposal so that they can seek release of their guarantees/securities or discharge them from payment of bank dues. Such proposals from guarantors and one of the Directors should be treated at par with proposals received from Borrowers.

(10) Criminal Proceedings/CBI Cases:

In accounts where criminal action is initiated or matter is under investigation by an investigating authority such as Central Bureau of Investigation etc., without prejudice to such proceeding/s action, the Bank should be at liberty to enter a compromise/settlement in such accounts purely on commercial consideration, but only after making an intimation to the controlling authorities and the investigating agency through the Chief Vigilance Officer of the bank. If the Bank initiates the criminal proceedings, it should be open to Bank to pursue or not to pursue the case depending upon the circumstances of each case. But, decision in that behalf shall be taken by the Chief Vigilance Officer of the Bank.

Wherever the borrower has filed any case, or counter claim against the Bank, and in such a case, a compromise/settlement is sought to be made, it should be made a condition of the settlement that the borrower would withdraw the suit/case, or counter claims as the case may be, and that in future also no claim will be raised against the Bank.

(11) Terms of Compromise:

While considering compromise settlement in NPA accounts and technically written-off accounts, the following concessions could be considered as possible sacrifice by the bank considering each and every individual case, outstanding period as NPA/suit, present financial position, availability/non-availability of tangible security, their value, enforceability and opportunity cost of funds:

- Waiver of extra/penal interest could be a simple solution and can be termed as good settlement from Bank's point of view.
- Realising the full outstanding as per the books of the branches plus reasonable interest with effect from the date of NPA or from the date of filing suit.
- Waiver of interest being the difference between negotiated rate and the contracted/debited rate from the date of advance.
- Waiver of interest charged after the date of becoming NPA or the date of suit filing.
- Full waiver of the interest from the date of advance.
- Only in exceptional cases, remission/write-off part of the principal dues.
- General and Operational Principles for compromise and settlements
- Bank may take up a compromise settlement/OTS proposal for consideration, irrespective of the present stage and status of the recovery proceedings. Any compromise will be a negotiated settlement under which the bank should endeavour to recover its dues to the maximum extent possible, with minimum sacrifice. However, it is recognised that amicable settlements are possible only in a win-win situation and sacrifice is a part of settlement.
- The last status of the activity of the borrowing entity which seeks a compromise will be taken into reckoning at the very first stage of the negotiation. An initial deposit of 10-20% of the amount should be taken from the borrower as evidence of his intention to pursue the compromise

settlement with the Bank. In case this is not possible, a waiver should be sought specifically in the approval note by way of deviation. For Consumer Bank Retail loans, a one-instalment settlement or a monthly EMI settlement may be acceptable without an upfront deposit.

- In case the borrower has other group companies, influence of these companies or the parent company may be used for a better settlement and/or for getting additional security, pending realization of the entire amount of compromise. It should be the endeavour of the Bank to get the entire compromise amount within three months from the date of settlement. Where the period of settlement exceeds 3 months and the amount is agreed to be recovered in instalments, as far as possible, a certain portion of the amount say 15% to 25% may be made payable upfront on a best-efforts basis, with balance in instalments spread over reasonable period considering source of repayment.
- At the time of One Time Settlement negotiation when OTS amount is proposed to be paid in instalments seriousness and preparedness of the borrower to honour OTS commitments shall be considered.
- In the case of suit filed account if need be and if practical, the terms and conditions of settlement should be finalized and consent decree from the court should be obtained.
- It is recognised that the OTS amount normally will not be less than the realisable value of securities. While considering the realisable value due consideration will be given to various factors like forced sale value, early realization of money, sale ability of the property, type, effort and cost involved & yield in the account.
- In case of non-receipt of the committed compromise amount as per the terms of the settlement, the recovery proceedings already initiated before the settlement shall be continued.
- The Authority who had approved the compromise settlement earlier may consider the modification in the terms of the settlement.
- In compromise settlements/write off the amount of sacrifice will be determined regarding balance/dues as on the 'settlement date' which shall be indicated in the compromise settlement/write off proposals.

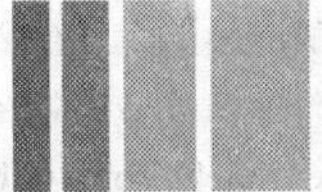

11.8 RECOVERY OF LOANS THROUGH FILING OF SUITS

Filing of suits is resorted to as a last recourse. Sometimes, filing of suits become necessary when the delay may result in the account getting time-barred or when the bank has reasons to apprehend that the borrower is frittering away the assets or is attempting to alienate the securities to the prejudice of the bank.

As earlier stated, sometimes, filing of suits becomes unavoidable to enforce the securities or when no specific security is charged to the bank and the bank seeks to rely upon the personal covenant of the parties. For filing of suits, plaints are prepared by the bank's advocate and presented to the court having pecuniary and territorial jurisdiction to try the case. Plaint should be properly drafted and should contain full particulars of the case besides claim for relief of principal, interest, cost and other relief. As the case progresses, the banker should remain in constant touch with the advocate and provide to him the necessary information/evidence, etc., whenever required. Once the decree is issued by the court, steps should be taken to execute the same expeditiously. In case the decree awarded by the court contains some onerous clauses which are detrimental to the interests of the bank, steps should be taken to file an appeal against the judgment within the prescribed time. In case of mortgage suits, where preliminary decree remains unsatisfied, court should be immediately moved for obtaining the final decree.

Many a times, it is possible to file a suit in summary form under Order 37 of Code of Civil Procedure. A suit under this for may be filed in respect of following:

(*a*) Suits upon bill of exchange, hundies and promissory notes.

(*b*) Suits in which the plaintiff seeks only to recover a debt or liquidated demand in money payable by defendant, with or without interest arising:

  (*i*) on a written contract

  (*ii*) on an enactment, where the sum sought to be recovered is a fixed sum of money or in the nature of a debt other than a penalty, or

  (*iii*) on a guarantee, where the claim against the principal is in respect of a debt or liquidated demand only.

11.9 RECOVERY THROUGH DEBT RECOVERY TRIBUNAL

Debt Recovery Tribunals (DRTs) have been established as per Recovery of Debts Due to Banks and Financial Institutions Act, 1993 to assist the banks in the speedy adjudication of matters relating to recovery of NPAs. The Act came into operation from 24 June, 1993. It is applicable to cases where the amount of debt due to any bank or financial institution defined under the Act or a consortium of banks or financial institutions is Rs. 20 Lakh or more. Debt Recovery Tribunals (DRTs) are the quasi-judicial institutions which have been set up to process the legal suits filed by banks against defaulting borrowers. Limitations as given under the Limitations Act will apply also to the DRT. Appeals filed against the proceedings initiated by secured creditors under the SARFAESI Act can also be taken up by the Debt Recovery Tribunal.

DRT Proceedings:

Following are the proceedings for the Tribunal:

1. An original application along with the documents of evidentiary value and the required fees is filed with the Registry.
2. The Registry reviews the application, checks for any flaws, accepts or rejects it.
3. The file then passes to the Registrar for further scrutiny of the application.
4. If the application is registered, a summon is issued by the Registrar.
5. If the defendant does not appear, the case becomes *ex parte.*
6. Else, the defendant is required to file a Written Statement within 90 days of the summons.
7. Proof-Affidavit is filed by the applicant.
8. A Hearing Date is set by the Registrar under the directions of the Presiding Officer.
9. A Stay Petition may be served by the defendant.
10. Counter-Proof Affidavit is filed by the defendants.
11. Final Hearings on the case will be done.
12. The Final Order/Decree is made by the Presiding Officer.
13. A Recovery Certificate made by the Tribunal will be passed on to the Recovery Officer of the Tribunal who has the responsibility of recovering the amount and hand it over to the bank.

Procedure in Nut-shell:

On receipt of an application, the Tribunal shall issue summons, requiring the defendant to show cause within 30 days of the service of summons as to why the relief prayed for should not be granted.

- A Counterclaim can be filed by the applicant through a written statement against the application and the acts of the applicant, attached with the necessary documents of evidentiary value.
- The Tribunal shall give an interim order in the form of an injunction, stay or attachment.
- The tribunal can appoint a Receiver.

Debt Recovery Appellate Tribunal (DRAT)

Any person aggrieved by the order passed by the Tribunal or deemed to have been passed by the Tribunal under DRT Act, may prefer an appeal to Debt Recovery Appellate Tribunal (DRAT) having jurisdiction in the matter. The DRAT has the appellate jurisdiction on all matters concerning the recovery of debts in India. The Judge in a DRAT is addressed as Chairperson. An appeal can be made against a decision by the DRT within 45 days from the date of passing of the decree, by depositing 50 per cent of the claim or any such amount as fixed by the DRT.

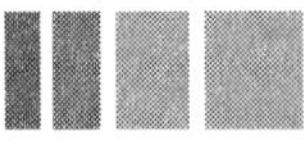

11.10 RECOVERY OF LOAN FROM GUARANTOR

In terms of Section 128 of the Indian Contract Act, 1872, the liability of the surety is co-extensive with that of the principal debtor unless it is otherwise provided by the contract. Therefore, when a default is made in making repayment by the principal debtor, the banker will be able to proceed against the guarantor/surety even without exhausting the remedies against the principal debtor. As such, where a banker has made a claim on the guarantor on account of the default made by the principal debtor, the liability of the guarantor is immediate. It is important to understand that as a guarantor on any form of loan, one is equally responsible to ensure the repayment of the loan. A guarantor pledges to repay a loan on behalf of a third party who has taken the loan. Banks take a signed promissory note jointly signed by the Principal Creditor and his Guarantor. Based on a promissory note, wherein signatories are liable to pay individually or severally, the lending organization can get a decree filed against the Guarantor.

11.11 RECOVERY THROUGH INSOLVENCY AND BANKRUPTCY CODE, 2016

The Insolvency and Bankruptcy Code was formulated with the aim that there be a single framework which resolves the issue of insolvency and bankruptcy for not just firms and companies but also for the individuals. In the event of default by the debtor, recovery proceedings can be started against him or her. To initiate recovery proceedings one can approach the National Company Law Tribunal (NCLT) (this applies to corporate persons) which exercises the authority to dispose cases under the Insolvency and Bankruptcy Code.

The Default is generally defined as non-payment of debt when whole or any part of payment of the amount of debt has become due and payable and is not paid by the debtor.

Who can initiate the recovery proceedings on the admission of a default by the debtor?

(1) Financial Creditor (Financial creditors are those whose relationship with the entity is a pure financial contract, such as a loan or debt security)

(2) Operational Creditor (Operational creditors are those whose liabilities from the entity comes from a transaction on operations)

Before Insolvency and Bankruptcy Code, initiation of a resolution process lied with the debtor, and the creditor may follow separate actions for security enforcement, recovery, and debt restructuring. But Insolvency and Bankruptcy Code make a noteworthy departure from the present resolution regimen by shifting the obligation on the creditor to initiate the insolvency resolution process against the debtor. Under IBC, both the creditors and the debtors can appeal for resolution. Once the application is accepted, the creditors take over the assets of the debtor. The said Committee of Creditors (CoC), which constitutes the lenders to the defaulter, is formed by the officials overseeing the resolution.

What are the steps of the insolvency procedure?

1. Initiation of CIRP.
2. Declaration of Moratorium and Public Announcement.
3. Committee of Creditors.
4. Appointment of Resolution Professional.
5. Preparation of Information Memorandum.
6. Approval of Resolution Plan.

As per the Insolvency and Bankruptcy Code, 2016, the procedure involved in the Corporate Insolvency Resolution Procedure (CIRP) should be completed within 180 days or within the extended period of 90 days and mandatorily be completed within **330 days** including any extension and the time taken in legal formalities.

Central Government through gazette notification dated March 24, 2020 specified one crore rupees as the minimum amount of default for initiation of proceedings under the Insolvency and Bankruptcy Code, 2016. Overall, IBC has been a boon for all entities that are facing bankruptcy. This Code helps in providing not only the best possible solution and resolution but also does so in a speedy and an efficient manner. The essence of the Code is to ensure that no entity or creditor should face any loss or damage while at the same time keeping the best interest of the debtor in mind.

11.12 LET US SUM UP

The most important canon of any lending should be the inherently self liquidating character of loans. Timeliness is the essence of bank credit. Not only should the loans be granted in time but necessary efforts to recover the loan should also be initiated at the appropriate time. Banks prefer movable and immovable properties as security. Movable are accepted as security by way of pledge/hypothecation, etc. Securities over immovable properties are created by way of mortgages. Loans up to Rs. 20 lakh can be amicably settled between the borrower and the lender using the forum of Lok Adalat. In terms of Section 128 of the Indian Contract Act, 1872, the liability of the surety is co-extensive with that of the principal debtor unless it is otherwise provided by the contract. DRTs have been set up to assist the banks in the speedy adjudication of matters relating to recovery of NPAs of Rs. 20 lakh and above. The latest development in recovery process is the INSOLVENCY AND BANKRUPTCY CODE, 2016

11.13 CHECK YOUR PROGRESS

(1) SARFAESI Act is not applicable for loans outstanding upto Rs. ---------:

- (*a*) 10 lakh
- (*b*) 5 lakh
- (*c*) 2 lakh
- (*d*) 1 lakh

(2) Loans upto Rs. ________ can be settled through Lok Adalat:

- (*a*) 2 lakh
- (*b*) 5 lakh
- (*c*) 10 lakh
- (*d*) 20 lakh

(3) DRTs can entertain cases for recovery for Rs. ---------:

- (*a*) 20 Lakh and above
- (*b*) 30 Lakh only
- (*c*) 50 lakh only
- (*d*) 100 lakh only

(4) Under Insolvency and Bankruptcy Code, 2016, the recovery process can be initiated for the amount of loan :

- (*a*) Minimum Rs. 1 crore
- (*b*) Minimum Rs. 5 crore
- (*c*) Minimum Rs. 10 crore
- (*d*) Minimum Rs. 50 crore

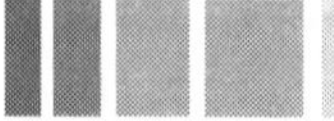

11.14 ANSWERS TO CHECK YOUR PROGRESS

1.	(*d*)	2.	(*d*)	3.	(*a*)	4.	(*a*)							

CHAPTER

12 Collection Operations

12.1 OBJECTIVES

- Debt Recovery Process
- General notion about EMI
- Loan Repayment
- Readiness of Debt recovery agent
- Preparation before meeting the customer
- Things to keep in mind while meeting the customer
- Tips on maintaining anger management

12.2 DEBT RECOVERY PROCESS

The debt recovery process is initiated when a debtor is unable to repay a loan. As per RBI guidelines, the lender needs to ensure that the process to recover the loan is beneficial to it while at the same time the debtor's legal rights and obligations need to be respected.

There are two main ways of debt recovery:

(*i*) Through a non-judicial route (Soft Recovery)

(*ii*) Through judicial route (Hard Recovery)

One of the main criteria for determining the debt recovery process is the reason for loan default.

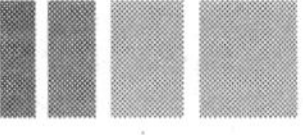

12.3 GENERAL NOTION ABOUT EMI

At the time of taking the loan or purchasing an article/vehicle under EMI, customers are not completely aware of the details of repayment, EMI, its due date, period of EMI etc. When these terms are explained, they generally do not grasp as much, and all specifications of EMI are not very clear. Some of them may not, before taking the loan, even think if they have enough monthly cash flow to meet the EMI. In view of this, at the time of disbursement, customer should be asked to confirm if she/he has read all the conditions and is in acceptance of the same. Once these details are confirmed, it can be agreed that the customer has taken an informed decision.

Once the loan is disbursed, the financial institution should have practice of thanking the customer for starting the relationship with them and mention the full details of loan, period of loan, EMI, due dates and indicate available mode of payments. It will be appropriate if this is done in a language understandable to the customer (local language).

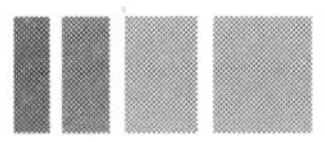

12.4 LOAN REPAYMENT

Collection agents could be involved in collection of all dues *i.e.*, amounts not defaulted and/or amount defaulted. In some NBFC/Banks, the collection agents are used only for collecting the amount defaulted. Generally, DRA or collection agents are used for defaulted amounts as there is no need to pursue amounts which are being paid regularly.

Some of the borrowal accounts will go into default, *i.e.*, there are some customers who will not pay their instalments or EMI on time and hence be called defaulters. These amounts are not paid in normal course and may have to be handled by DRA for collection support.

Once it has been decided to use a DRA, the institution will have to brief the DRA about the collection function, the code of conduct, the collection process and dos and don'ts. Agents are informed that any misbehaviour will have serious implications for the institution and that it is very important to maintain a civil code of conduct. The approach of the agent must be calm, polite, and professional and yet be able to recover as much overdue as possible.

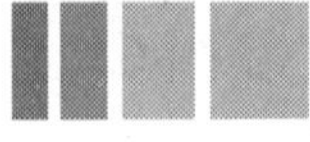

12.5 READINESS OF THE DEBT RECOVERY AGENT

In order that the DRA can meet and discuss with the client and seek repayment, the financial institution must share with the DRA:

(*a*) Authorisation letter to deal with the debtor on behalf of the bank

(*b*) the name of the clients (defaulter)

(c) address and contact details

(*d*) office address if the customer is working

(*e*) terms and conditions of the loan which include type of loan, purpose of loan, instalment amount, total amount due, etc.

It is important that the DRA is clear about the total amount of loan, EMI, period of loan and the amount in default. This information is needed as it may be necessary to answer customer's query, if any, or correct her/him if their perception or information is incorrect. If the DRA knows only about the EMI due, then it could result into some arguments and difficulties in recovery.

DRA should keep all this information confidentially and not with anyone other than the customer and unless customer asks to share the detail. Confidentiality does not mean it should not be shared with the defaulting customer as she/he is aware of the above details. Also, without using this information DRA cannot ask for repayment. This information should not be shared with others.

Approach to collection cannot be same or uniform as customers/clients who has defaulted could be one who has :

i. Borrowed more than his/her capacity to pay.

ii. Paid instalments regularly in the past but defaulted for the first time due to personal exigencies.

iii. Defaulted in the very first instalment after taking the loan

iv. A history of defaulting intermittently with the bank/NBFC or others evidenced by a low credit score

v. Has defaulted in two instalments so far and the account is about to be classified as NPA if the 3rd instalment is also not paid

vi. Has misused credit

vii. Has taken loan for someone else. This is seen happening when people take consumer article loan for family members or friends. Subsequently, the family member or friend stops paying and the client slips into default.

Generally, the client is aware that an instalment or two has been defaulted. Also, they have been reminded about this by the call centres which have reminded them about the amount due and seek payment. Possibly, they are also aware of the consequences. In some cases, they might have been encouraged to default by media or misguided persons. Given this, for the client, the instinct will be to avoid paying and blame the company or DRA about:

(*i*) Harassment

(*ii*) Pursuing recovery knowing well the poor status of the client and

(*iii*) misselling (at the time of loan or while purchasing an item there is no such compliant though. But this cannot be pointed out by the DRA).

Also, there could be cases where they seek time without any indication as to where they will get funds for meeting the commitment.

In this background, the DRA should neither be too optimistic nor pessimistic about the collections in each day or time. The following preparation could help:

The DRA should prepare his pitch to the defaulter by highlighting on the advantages of repaying debt on time viz.

- The credit score will improve by providing the opportunity for availing future loan
- In case the credit score comes down, it may lead to reputation loss
- the bank may initiate legal action against the defaulter
- In the case of mortgage loan, the bank will seize the property and sell it through auction process

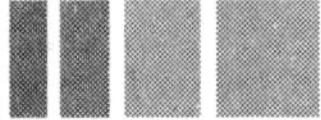

12.6 PREPARATION BEFORE MEETING A CUSTOMER

i. Keep the ID card issued by the company in hand.

ii. Be well groomed.

iii. Be clear about the dues.

iv. Be aware of various payment modes accepted.

v. Check if the customer has given any choice of meeting time.

vi. Not to use personal mobile phone and hence, carry the phone given by the company.

vii. Gather and understand all the details of customers very clearly. DRA should remember and tell the dues to the client without verifying the diary or book. At times, it will be a useful technique to refer the notes and inform the amount due.

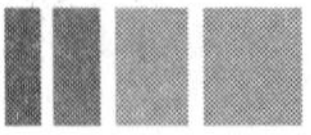

12.7 AT THE MEETING WITH THE CUSTOMER

i. DRA should plan the travel time carefully such that he/she arrives at customer's place at the appointed time.

ii. DRA should be polite and not use rough and/or abusive language.

iii. Address the client as 'Sir' or 'Madam'. Use local language equivalent of 'आप', and do not use 'तू' or its local vernacular equivalent.

iv. Request the customer to pay the instalment mentioning the amount due and that the due date that has passed.

v. If the customer disputes, then say, "let me check" and then if he is correct, apologise for the error and inform the correct figure. If he is not correct, then say "Sir, I have verified and the amount due is......"

vi. If the customer wants to pay, guide him/her for the same with the various options available and facilitate the process.

vii. If the customer does not pay, politely tell him that he has taken the loan for which the EMI payment has been defaulted. If he has paid in the past, he can be told that current instalment is due.

viii. DRA should be patient and listen to what the customer says. If customer asks for more time, he should be politely, informed that payment should be within (as per your company policy) and that, if need be, he will be contacted again.

ix. To keep the conversation going and if the customer is interested to know, he may be told of various methods of payment.

x. Some customers may offer to pay in cash. If the company policy allows cash collection, this may be accepted. This has some issues as some customers may subsequently claim that they paid a higher amount, etc. In view of this, the customer should be encouraged to pay through an electronic channel, failing which, he should be given an official receipt for cash receipt at that instant. That cash has been accepted should be informed to the office immediately-through mobile or other means. Office may be asked to send an immediate confirmation SMS to the client.

xi. DRA can also take the customer to the nearest branch of the company where cash can be accepted.

xii. DRA should not handle transactions by himself. Rather help the customer to do it by himself. In this regard, the DRA should not ask for CVV, OTP, etc., nor handle such information. Support the customer on how to do digital remittances.

xiii. If office mobile has company's QR, then the process can be explained to the customer and he could be asked to pay through it. The debit to the customer account will be instant and message will come in his mobile.

xiv. If the customer pays part of the amount due, it should be accepted. Customer should be asked for the date for paying the remainder. The date *i.e.*, (promise to pay) PTP should be updated the system so as to connect with the customer on that specific day only.

xv. Customer may ask the DRA to come home in the evening or later at time beyond what is officially permitted. Such requests should be politely refused until and unless, there is specific instruction from the bank/NBFC to visit the customer during odd hours.

xvi. In some situations, the customer can be with a group of people when the recovery agent arrives. In such circumstances, the customer could be asked to step aside for some time for pursuing the recovery. These talks are best done in a confidential manner and while maintaining the respect and integrity of both, customer, and the Agent.

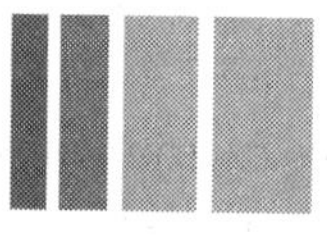

12.8 TIPS ON MAINTAINING DIALOGUE AND ANGER MANAGEMENT

i. DRA should not enter into any verbal duel with the client.

ii. If the customer mentions that he/she does not want to pay, the agent can inform about the consequences of late payments, its impact on the credit score and subsequent legal consequences.

iii. Unnecessary dialogue heating up into an argument might not be the best way to convince the customer to pay as creating pressure could be interpreted differently, as coercion or excessive pressure.

iv. Another scenario could be when the customer says he does not want to make the payment on that day, but he can pay later – in such a scenario, the agent can ask the customer when the next suitable time is that they can make payment. This can be taken as a PTP (Promise to Pay), and the agent can come back on that day.

v. In some residential buildings or complexes, there could be an entry system of customers, where the security could restrict the entry of agents for debt recovery. In such a scenario, the agent should call or send an SMS to the customer, asking him/her to permit entry in the building and then complete the meeting scheduled with the customer.

vi. In the above case, customers could intentionally refuse entry citing vague reasons. In such cases, office should send an official message about the denial of such entry.

vii. Some customers may behave in a disrespectful manner and use provoking language with the Agent, saying "do whatever you want" or "okay, what you are going to do". In such situations, it is preferable for agents to maintain their calm and not get into unnecessary argument with the customer. DRA may politely leave the place at that moment and revisit the customer later.

viii. There could be instances when the customer may dispute the loan or say they took the loan for someone else and ask DRA to meet the other person. In such cases, DRA should inform the office. They should not meet the other person because on record the customer is the person who has taken the loan. This may be informed to the customer as well.

ix. Many customers threaten to complain but they do not go ahead with it as the process of filing a complaint is not easy. They are also aware that they owe the money. Since the agent is also aware of this, he/she may therefore be tempted to take a chance and be aggressive. This must be avoided as the regulatory authorities do not tolerate even one complaint from the customer and it could result in huge penalty for the company.

x. It is best not to be afraid or threatened by the Media. Their intent will be to derive information from the DRA. As such DRA should not give any information to the media. Customer information should not be shared with the media.

xi. Losing one's cool is easy however, the impact this can have on the job is immense. It is easy to be angry. But once anger sets in, it is difficult to be polite and correct. This should be kept in mind. For a DRA, anger has negative consequences for the job in hand.

xii. General courtesy is always appreciated and comes handy. Whether money collected or not, while leaving the customer do not forget to say "Thanks". It could be:

1. Thanks for the payment
2. Thanks for meeting me
3. Thanks for your time

xiii. Collection is important for the DRA. Let that factor not come in the way of maintaining proper behaviour with the client however difficult it is.

RBI *vide* its Circular No. RBI/2022-23/108 DOR.ORG.REC.65/21.04.158/2022-23 dated August 12, 2022 has advised all that all recovery agents do not resort to intimidation or harassment of any kind, either verbal or physical, against any person in their debt collection efforts, including acts intended to humiliate publicly or intrude upon the privacy of the debtors' family members, referees and friends, sending inappropriate messages either on mobile or through social media, making threatening and/or anonymous calls, persistently calling the borrower and/or calling the borrower before 8:00 a.m. and after 7:00 p.m. for recovery of overdue loans, making false and misleading representations, etc.

Important Tips for Anger Management

While negotiating with the client, the DRAs need to keep their anger under control. The defaulter may try to provoke heated situations but the DRAs need to maintain their calmness. Some useful tips for controlling anger are:

(*a*) Listen carefully before speaking

(*b*) Think before you speak

(*c*) Think before you react to any situation

(*d*) Express your concerns after you are calm

(*e*) Take a break and relax

(*f*) Practice Yoga, exercise and meditation

(*g*) Don't hold a biased view or grudge

(*h*) Use humour to diffuse situation

(*i*) Identify possible solutions

(*j*) Be respectful while talking

(*k*) Seek help when necessary

12.9 SUMMARY

Collection operations are functions which are part of Debt management services of any Lending organisation. Most of the times, people are not aware of the EMI that they are taking, the calculated interest of it, how that EMI will affect their gross monthly income, etc.

Once loans are disbursed, the aspect of loan recovery steps in. Some of the accounts will go into default, *i.e.*, there are some customers who will not pay their EMI on time and hence be called defaulters. These may not be collected in normal course and may have to be handled by DRA.

The Debt recovery agent initiates meeting with the customer and collects outstanding dues. There are many things for the DRA to keep in mind before he goes to visit the customer and certain things to keep in mind during a meeting with the customer.

There are situations when the customer may lose their temper seeing the agent or the agent may behave disrespectfully with the customer. Certain tips to maintain calm and keep your temper in control are shared with the agent which can help maintain their cool and make the meeting a useful one.

Common courtesy should be maintained while dealing with the customer along with understanding the customer's point of view while simultaneously sharing the importance of paying on time.

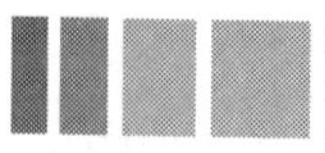

12.10 KEYWORDS

EMI, Debt Recovery Agent, Defaulter, Promise to Pay (PTP)

12.11 CHECK YOUR PROGRESS

1. Which of the following behavioural traits need to be avoided by the recovery agent while dealing with defaulting customer?

   (*a*) Calm

   (*b*) Polite

(*c*) Professional

(*d*) Aggressive

2. Confidential information about the loan details should be shared with ....:

(*a*) Neighbours

(*b*) Borrower

(*c*) Family Members

(*d*) Parents

3. Which of the following can be a possible reason for default by the customer?

(*a*) Borrowed more than his/her capacity to pay.

(*b*) Has misused credit.

(*c*) Paid instalments regularly in the past but defaulted for the first time

(*d*) All of the above

12.12 ANSWERS TO CHECK YOUR PROGRESS

1.	(*d*)	2.	(*b*)	3.	(*d*)							

MODULE

DRA Role in Loan Recovery and Soft Skills

CHAPTER

13 DRA - Meaning, Legal and Regulatory framework

13.1 OBJECTIVE

- Introduction
- Why are debt collection agencies important?
- Meaning of Debt Recovery Agent
- Legal and regulatory framework: Legal aspects of an agent's contract
- Elements of debt recovery arrangement
- Legal and regulatory framework for debt recovery
- Trends in collection systems

13.2 INTRODUCTION

Debt collection is the process of pursuing payments of debts owed by individuals or businesses. An organization that specializes in debt collection is known as a collection agency or debt collector. Most collection agencies operate as agents of creditors and collect debts for a fee or percentage of the total amount owed.

13.3 WHY DEBT COLLECTION AGENCIES ARE REQUIRED

People who borrow money from financial institutions could default in the payment of instalments or interest or both (EMI). This amount must be collected. For this, it is necessary to meet the borrower and pursue collection. Financial institutions that specialize in retail and MSME lending have many borrowers. The government also gives thrust to issue loans under various development schemes. Given the large number of loan/debts accounts, these lenders may find it difficult to involve their own staff for collection because collection work is spread across various localities and the amount collectible may be small to medium in value. In this regard, some lenders have special in-house departments dedicated to debt collection, while others hire third parties to handle collections on their behalf.

Collection agents could be individuals or agencies that are entrusted with the job of collection by lenders. They collect the defaulted debt on behalf of the financial institution that has lent the money to individuals or business entities for various purposes. If an agency were to buy the defaulted loans under some arrangement, then they step into the role of a lender and are no more agents. However, the collection nuances, rules and dos and don'ts apply to them as well.

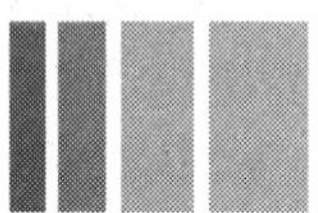

13.4 ADVANTAGES OF ENGAGING COLLECTION AGENCIES

Financial Institutions seek the Debt Recovery/Collection Agencies route as it offers some comfort such as:

- These agencies are experienced in collection work and perform better in recovering debts for lending organizations
- Being a specialist service, a debt Collection Agency is well versed with laws concerned and procedures and can adhere to compliance requirements in this regard.
- Though it is the responsibility of the borrower to repay the loans, forced collections are not allowed and there exist several rules and regulations established to protect the customers or clients from those debt collection/recovery agents who tend to misbehave or use inappropriate methods of recovery.
- Lenders do not pursue collecting small loans through legal processes and a business owner, may not have the time to call and follow-up or write legal notices to collect the debts but the agency associated can help and fulfil these requirements.
- When a Debt Collection agency is hired, focus for the financial institution can remain on the core business because the debt collection aspect is catered by these agencies.

However, there are few disadvantages as well:

- Debt collection does cost money.
- The debt collection agency will be establishing a relationship with the bank customers, which could be potentially harmful if they sour that relationship by not dealing with customers in a courteous manner.

13.5 DEFINITION - DEBT RECOVERY AGENT

Debt Recovery Agents act as agents of Banks/NBFCs. Therefore, Banks/NBFCs are responsible for their behaviour. A debt- recovery agent can be defined as a person or entity engaged by a financial institution or some other entity for the purpose of collecting specified loans *i.e.*, loans past due or loans which are impaired and/or other kinds of debts from the debtors (or customers) as per specific terms and conditions.

The word debt recovery agent comprises of three separate words debt, recovery, and agent. Debt refers to a sum of money owed by one person or business entity to a lender. There are two parties to a debt *i.e.*, debtor (borrower) who receives the money by way of a debt and a creditor (Bank/NBFC/others) who lends money to the debtor. To illustrate, if Mr. A takes a loan of Rs. 3 Lakh from a bank for purchasing a car, he becomes the debtor (or borrower) and the bank is the creditor (or lender) and the loan of Rs. 3 Lakh is the debt (principal). Mr. A would be required to repay the loan in Equated Monthly Instalment (EMI), comprising the principal and interest, spread over the repayment period of, say, 3 years (debt tenor).

The word Recovery means collection or recovery of money from the debtor by or on behalf of the creditor after it has become due for payment in accordance with the terms of credit agreed by both debtor and creditor at the beginning. The repayment could be in the form of instalment to be paid monthly by the debtor to the creditor. In the above example, if Mr. A (debtor) fails to pay the agreed instalment (EMI) on the due date, the bank may send him notice to remind him to pay the agreed amount within a stipulated period. If he does not pay even after receiving the notice the bank may use the service of a collection agent. It is to be noted here that a debt becomes payable by the debtor only on or after the due date, but not before that date. If the debt is not paid on the due date, it becomes overdue or past due.

The word Agent as defined by the Indian Contract Act, 1872 is a person employed to do any act for another or to represent another in dealings with third person the person for whom such acts are done or who is represented is called the principal and agent has an authority to do acts on behalf of the principal within the limits of authority and thereby bind the principal for such acts in relation to third parties. The lender has the contractual right to recover or collect and under this the institution employs an agent to the collection. If an agency were to enter collection it can use its staff to do the collection under this arrangement. In the above example of the car loan to Mr. A, if the bank (creditor) engages XY for collecting dues from Mr. A (and other debtors) after they remain unpaid on the due dates, XY will be called as a Debt Recovery Agent of the bank. The bank may prefer to utilize its resources in terms of staff, time, etc., for its core banking functions like deposits, lending, remittance, foreign exchange business and out-source the debt recovery function by engaging Debt Recovery Agents on certain terms and conditions, including fee or commission for their services.

13.6 COLLECTION AND RECOVERY

Collection includes repayment made by the customer in due course of time without any reminder and initial process of reminders etc.

Recovery starts once the customer defaults in making payment and the amount becomes overdue for payment. Overdue loans are also called as loans past due and reckoned in terms of number of days past due. However, in modern banking collection function encompasses recovery also.

13.7 LEGAL AND REGULATORY FRAMEWORK FOR DEBT RECOVERY

Reserve Bank of India is the regulatory authority for banks and NBFC. Guidelines on debt recovery agents issued by RBI from time to time are required to be complied by the banks/NBFCs and their recovery agents. Failure to comply with the guidelines of RBI or the internal procedures laid by the lender can result in the levy of penalty by RBI. In the recent years there has been substantial media activity in this area and poor compliance results in adverse publicity and reputation risk for the concerned lenders.

Legal aspects of agency contract with reference to the Indian Contract Act as follows:

1. Agency is a relationship that exists between two people, one is called principal and the other agent. The principal, *i.e.*, the financial institution consents that the agent should represent it or act on its behalf. The agent also consents to represent the principal and to act on its behalf.
2. In a contract of agency, both the parties to the contract namely the principal and the agent must be above 18 years of age and of sound mind.
3. Most agency contracts contain a remuneration clause in terms of which the recovery agent will receive appropriate fee for the services rendered to the principal.
4. An agent's authority may be expressed where it is given by word, spoken, or written or implied where it is inferred from circumstances of the case.
5. In respect of the acts which the principal expressly or impliedly has the power or authority to do, the agent has the authority to act. This authority constitutes a power to affect the principal's legal relations with third parties.
6. An agent having authority to do an act has authority to do everything, lawful which is necessary to do such an act. As indicated above, an act of an agent of a bank/NBFC not in conformity with the regulatory guidelines is considered unlawful.

13.8 FEATURES OF DEBT RECOVERY ARRANGEMENT

Definition: An arrangement or agreement between a financial institution and debt recovery agent is a contract of agency. Based on the foregoing paragraphs the essential features of a debt recovery arrangement may be described as:

a. It is a contract between a credit institution and the debt recovery agency. Both the parties in an agency arrangement must be competent to contract. The agent can be a natural person, major and of sound mind or an entity. In the case of an entity which is contracted for DRA work, the bank/NBFC should specifically indicate the role of the employees of such entity.

b. The debt recovery arrangement between the principal and the agent can be created in three ways:

- by an express agreement in writing, specifying the terms and conditions of the arrangement (agency by agreement)
- In cases where there is no express agreement, the relationship between the principal and agent could be ascertained by facts and circumstances of the case (implied agency).
- In some cases, the work done by a person on behalf of the principal and with full knowledge of the principal may not have been authorized by the principal. If the principal subsequently ratifies the actions, such *post facto* ratification will bind the parties concerned (agency by ratification).

c. The debt recovery agreement, like any other contract, requires acceptance by the principal and the agent. The accepted agreement is legally binding on both the parties.

d. The role and tasks of the recovery agents will be mentioned in the debt recovery agreement. These must be lawful, that is, in accordance with the laws of the country and regulations of industry.

e. The acts of an agent performed within the authority delegated by the agency agreement will be legally binding between the principal and the third parties. However, the acts of an agent done outside the delegated authority, or in excess of the authority, will not bind the principal and the responsibility for the consequences will be on the agent exclusively.

The agency agreement regarding debt recovery contains the main terms and conditions agreed by the principal and the agent. These may be called as the main elements of debt recovery arrangement and would generally include:

- Specific tasks to be accomplished, namely collection of dues from the clients of the lending institutions as per details and instruction given by the institution. It will also contain the time frame for the acts to be performed as per contract.

- Details of the debt recovery policy and procedure of the Bank/NBFC such that the agency/agent does not violate the procedures.
- Code of conduct in recovery process which will include dress code, rules to be followed in verbal and written communication with the clients and other rules, confidentiality of the information etc. to be followed by the individuals employed by the agency for the purpose of collection.
- Duties of the agent
- Rights of the agent, including the Commission or fees payable by the principal to the agent for the recovery of debt services.

The Debt Recovery Policy and Code of Conduct in the debt recovery arrangement will be in line with the directives and guidelines of the Reserve Bank of India issued from time to time.

An agreement could be in digital format between the credit institution and the debt recovery agent or agency serves and is legally binding on both the lending institution and the agency. Exact arrangements, however, could vary from institution to institution.

13.9 RBI'S GUIDELINES

Banks were advised by RBI to take into account the following specific considerations while engaging recovery agents:

(*i*) Banks should have a due diligence process in place for engagement of recovery agents, which should be so structured to cover, among others, individuals involved in the recovery process. The due diligence process should generally conform to the guidelines issued by RBI on outsourcing of financial services *vide* circular DBOD.No.BP.40/21.04.158/2006-07 dated November 3, 2006. Further, banks should ensure that the agents engaged by them in the recovery process carry out verification of the antecedents of their employees, which may include pre-employment police verification, as a matter of abundant caution. Banks may decide the periodicity at which re-verification of antecedents should be resorted to.

(*ii*) To ensure due notice and appropriate authorization, banks should inform the borrower the details of recovery agency firms/companies while forwarding default cases to the recovery agency. Further, since in some of the cases, the borrower might not have received the details about the recovery agency due to refusal/non-availability/avoidance and to ensure identification, it would be appropriate if the agent also carries a copy of the notice and the authorization letter from the bank along with the identity card issued to him by the bank or the agency firm/company. Further, where the recovery agency is changed by the bank during the recovery process, in addition to the bank notifying the borrower of the change, the new agent should carry the notice and the authorization letter along with his identity card.

(*iii*) The notice and the authorization letter should, among other details, also include the telephone numbers of the relevant recovery agency. Banks should ensure that there is a tape recording of the content/text of the calls made by recovery agents to the customers, and *vice-versa*. Banks may take reasonable precaution such as intimating the customer that the conversation is being recorded, etc.

(*iv*) The up-to-date details of the recovery agency firms/companies engaged by banks will also be posted on the bank's website.

(*v*) Where a grievance/complaint has been lodged, banks should not forward cases to recovery agencies till they have finally disposed off any grievance/complaint lodged by the concerned borrower. However, where the bank is convinced, with appropriate proof, that the borrower is continuously making frivolous/vexatious complaints, it may continue with the recovery proceedings through the Recovery Agents even if a grievance/complaint is pending with them. In cases where the subject matter of the borrower's dues might be sub-judice, banks should exercise utmost caution, as appropriate, in referring the matter to the recovery agencies, depending on the circumstances.

(*vi*) Bank should have a mechanism whereby the borrowers' grievances with regard to the recovery process can be addressed. The details of the mechanism should also be furnished to the borrower while advising the details of the recovery agency.

Incentives to Recovery Agents

(*vii*) Some banks/NBFCs set very stiff recovery targets or offer high incentives to recovery agents. These have, in turn, induced the recovery agents to use intimidatory and questionable methods for recovery of dues. Banks should ensure that the contracts with the recovery agents do not induce adoption of uncivilized, unlawful and questionable behaviour or recovery process. The incentive may be based on performance and better recovery methods without resorting to questionable methods.

Training for Recovery Agents

(*viii*) Banks/NBFCs have been advised to ensure that, among others, the recovery agents are properly trained to handle with care and sensitivity, their responsibilities, in particular aspects like hours of calling, privacy of customer information, etc.

(*ix*) Financial Institutions should ensure that all their recovery agents undergo proper training and obtain the certificate from Indian Institute of Banking and Finance (IIBF) which has, as per RBI advice, created a certificate course for recovery agents with minimum 100 hours of training for non-graduates and 50 hours training for graduates.

Taking possession of property mortgaged/hypothecated to banks

(*x*) In a recent case which came up before the Honourable Supreme Court, the Honourable Court observed that we are governed by rule of law in the country and the recovery of loans or seizure of vehicles could be done only through legal means. In this connection it may be mentioned that the Securitisation and Reconstruction of Financial Assets and Enforcement of Security Interest Act, 2002 (SARFAESI Act) and the Security Interest (Enforcement) Rules, 2002 framed thereunder have laid down well defined procedures not only for enforcing security interest but also for auctioning the movable and immovable property after enforcing the security interest. It is, therefore, desirable that banks rely only on legal remedies available under the relevant statutes while enforcing security interest without intervention of the Courts.

(*xi*) Where banks have incorporated a repossession clause in the contract with the borrower and rely on such repossession clause for enforcing their rights, they should ensure that the repossession clause is legally valid, complies with the provisions of the Indian Contract Act in letter and spirit, and ensure that such repossession clause is clearly brought to the notice of the borrower at the time of execution of the contract. The terms and conditions of the contract should be strictly in terms of the Recovery Policy and should contain provisions regarding (*a*) notice period before taking possession (*b*) circumstances under which the notice period can be waived (*c*) the procedure for taking possession of the security (*d*) a provision regarding final chance to be given to the borrower for repayment of loan before the sale/auction of the property (*e*) the procedure for giving repossession to the borrower and (*f*) the procedure for sale/auction of the property.

Use of forum of Lok Adalats

(*xii*) The Honourable Supreme Court has also observed that loans, personal loans, credit card loans and housing loans with less than Rs. 10 Lakh (now Rs. 20 Lakh) can be referred to Lok Adalats. In compliance of these instructions, banks have been advised by RBI to use the forum of Lok Adalats organized by Civil Courts for recovery of loans. Banks are now encouraged to use the forum of Lok Adalats for recovery of personal loans, credit card loans or housing loans with less than Rs. 10 lakh (now Rs. 20 lakh) as suggested by the Honourable Supreme Court.

Utilisation of Credit Counsellors

(*xiii*) Banks should have in place an appropriate mechanism to utilise the services of the credit counsellors for providing suitable counselling to the borrowers where it becomes aware that the case of a particular borrower deserves sympathetic consideration.

Complaints against the bank/its recovery agents

(*xiv*) Banks, as principals, are responsible for the actions of their agents. Hence, they should ensure that their agents engaged for recovery of their dues should strictly adhere to the laid down guidelines and instructions while engaged in the process of recovery of dues.

(*xv*) Complaints received by Reserve Bank regarding violation of the above guidelines and adoption of abusive practices followed by banks' recovery agents would be viewed seriously. Reserve Bank may consider imposing a ban on a bank from engaging recovery agents in a particular area, either jurisdictional or functional, for a limited period. In case of persistent breach of above guidelines, Reserve Bank may consider extending the period of ban or the area of ban. Similar supervisory action could be attracted when the High Courts or the Supreme Court pass strictures or impose penalties against any bank or its Directors/ Officers/agents with regard to policy, practice and procedure related to the recovery process.

13.10 RIGHTS OF THE LOAN DEFAULTER WHEN HE OR SHE IS THREATENED BY RECOVERY AGENTS

There are many instances about the high-handed and illegal behaviour of recovery agents, who were trying to recover amounts on behalf of banks. In one instance, an 81-year-old lady was severely harassed by recovery agents—she received 375 threatening calls regarding her son's unpaid bank dues. After she approached the police, a case was filed against these agents. In another instance, a private bus was stopped, and 42 passengers were held hostage for three hours by recovery agents, who wanted to recover money from the travel company which owned the bus.

Recovery agent should be aware of the probable action that may be taken by the borrower on intimidation or harassment. If the borrower is harassed by the bank or the recovery agent, then the borrower can resort to the police station and can file a complaint. This must be a primary move before taking more stringent action. In case, there is no relief from the police or they do not file the complaint, then the client can even move to the civil court and can plead for relief. The court, in this case, can rule in favour of the borrower and can order the agent not to resort to unauthorized and illegal conduct.

Recovery agents should also be aware of the Borrower's Rights which are as follows:

- Right to Notice
- Right to Fair Value
- Right to be Heard

- Right to Claim the Balance
- Right to be Treated Politely

(1) Filing a complaint at a police station:

A formal complaint may be filed against the bank/NBFC and the recovery agency. In case the police refuse to file a case, the magistrate can be approached for the same.

(2) Injunction suit against the bank and recovery agents:

A civil injunction suit with an *ad interim* relief can be filed against the bank and recovery agency in the civil court. This can be done to ensure that bank officials and recovery agents do not visit borrower's home for recovery of dues.

(3) Filing a complaint with the Reserve Bank of India (RBI):

The borrower can also file a complaint at the Reserve Bank of India (RBI) Banking ombudsman where RBI can take strict measures for ensuring that the loan recovery agent should not follow illegal conduct. RBI guidelines state that the complaints received by Reserve Bank regarding violation of the guidelines and adoption of abusive behaviour by recovery agents would be viewed seriously.

(4) Defamation suit:

If the debt recovery is based on erroneous information which led to the loss of borrower's CIBIL score, then he can file a defamation suit against the bank and recovery agency.

(5) Trespass complaint:

If the recovery agents of the bank illegally entered into borrower's house without authorised permission, then a trespass complaint can be filed against them for violating his rights.

(6) Extortion complaint:

If the recovery agents forcefully recovered the amount, an extortion case can be filed against them.

The following norms/guidelines are to be meticulously complied by banks while engaging Recovery Agent:

a. Sufficient bank notices/reminders/phone calls asking for settlement of dues

b. DRA details such as DRA firm/companies, name, telephone number, etc. should be informed to the borrower

c. DRA details should also be provided in bank's website

d. DRA should carry the notice and the authorization letter along with his identity card. DRA to produce the letter and ID to the borrower when he visits him for recovery.

e. Visiting time only 8:00 am to 7:00 pm. Contact at the place of the borrower's choice and in the absence of any specified place, at the place of his residence and if unavailable at the residence, the place of business/occupation. In other words, the DRA is supposed to ask for a place where the borrower is comfortable meeting and only if not, DRA can visit residence and if not there, then the office.

f. During the visit for dues collection, decency and decorum should be maintained. Inappropriate occasions such as bereavement in the family or other calamitous occasions would be avoided for making calls/visits to collect dues.

g. Polite dealing is essential. If borrower refuses to talk to DRA, then oblige.

h. DRA should not resort to intimidation or harassment of any kind, either verbal or physical, against any person in their debt collection efforts, including acts intended to humiliate publicly or intrude the privacy of the debtors' family members, referees and friends, making threatening and anonymous calls or making false and misleading representations. Agents bothering for loan recovery might seem to be a small issue but there are cases where people have committed suicide or suffered mental trauma due to the informal conduct of the agents. The agents harass the clients by their activities. Some of the prominent acts which are regularly committed by the agents are like calling frequently or arriving at the residence of the clients regularly, sending obscene messages either on mobile or through social media, calling or reaching out to neighbours.

i. Banks should ensure that there is a tape recording of the content/text of the calls made by recovery agents to the customers, and *vice-versa*. Banks may take reasonable precaution such as intimating the customer that the conversation is being recorded.

j. DRA should not offer any discount in the repayment amount as DRAs are authorized to make any verbal or written promise to a customer instead just to remind the borrower about non-payment of their dues.

k. For any settlement at lesser amount, direct the borrower to the bank directly. No receipt should be issued for lesser amount.

l. Do not accept any cash and instead accept only cheques if offered cash, direct him to go to the bank.

m. Read thoroughly the authorization letter and show to the borrower. Go strictly as per the authorization letter issued by the bank.

n. If any dispute with the borrower, the same should be intimated by the bank to DRA. The DRA should not visit such borrowers for recovery. Bank should also ensure that such cases should not be forwarded to the DRA. Visit only once, grievances are addressed and resolved and same is intimated by the bank to DRA.

o. Non-compliance of the norms/guidelines, RBI may ban the bank from engaging recovery agents in a particular area either jurisdictional or functional for a limited period of time.

But all such activities if done on a formal basis, will not result in harassment. If the agent sends a message, not frequently but provide an update regularly, like a reminder, or even calling for a reminder, will not result in harassment. Moreover, Indian Courts have been strict on the informal attitude of recovery agents where courts have observed that strong-arm tactics for recovering money are unlawful and authorized fair treatment of law must be resorted.

What is considered harassing by a recovery agent?

If the recovery agent attempts to do any of the following, it could be viewed as harassment to recover the money owed. These actions include:

- reaching people multiple times each day, or promptly in the first part of the day or the late evening;
- seeking people on social media platforms, for example, Twitter and Facebook;
- putting pressure on people to sell their home;
- threatening or continuously contacting relatives of the borrower;
- visiting the borrower with a group of people, in turn, to pursue people for instalment;
- using desk work or business logos that give off an impression of being official when they're not, for instance sending people letters that seem as though they represent court forms;
- pressurizing people to pay all the money, or in bigger instalments when they can't afford to;
- attempting to humiliate people in front of the general public;
- telling another person about your debts or using someone else to pass on messages, for example, a neighbour or a relative.

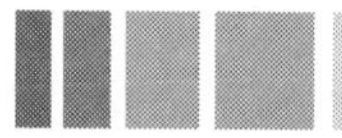

13.11 INTEGRATED OMBUDSMAN SCHEME, 2021

The Integrated Ombudsman Scheme, 2021 applicable to Banks and NBFCs was launched by Hon'ble Prime Minister. The Scheme integrates the existing three Ombudsman schemes of RBI namely,

- **the Banking Ombudsman Scheme, 2006**;
- **the Ombudsman Scheme for Non-Banking Financial Companies, 2018**; and
- **the Ombudsman Scheme for Digital Transactions, 2019**.

The Scheme envisages cost-free redressal of customer complaints involving deficiency in services rendered by entities regulated by RBI, if not resolved to the satisfaction of the customers or not replied within a period of 30 days by the regulated entity.

In addition to integrating the three existing schemes, the Scheme also includes under its ambit Non-Scheduled Primary Co-operative Banks with a deposit size of Rs. 50 crore and above. The Scheme adopts 'One Nation One Ombudsman' approach by making the RBI Ombudsman mechanism jurisdiction neutral.

Some of the salient features of the Scheme are:

i. It will no longer be necessary for a complainant to identify under which scheme he/she should file complaint with the Ombudsman.

ii. The Scheme defines 'deficiency in service' as the ground for filing a complaint, with a specified list of exclusions. Therefore, the complaints would no longer be rejected simply on account of "not covered under the grounds listed in the scheme".

iii. The Scheme has done away with the jurisdiction of each ombudsman office.

iv. A 'Centralized Receipt and Processing' Centre has been set up at RBI, Chandigarh for receipt and initial processing of complaints through post/courier and email in any language.

v. The responsibility of representing the Regulated Entity and furnishing information in respect of complaints filed by customers against the Regulated Entity would be that of the Principal Nodal Officer in the rank of a General Manager in a Public Sector Bank or equivalent.

vi. The Regulated Entity will not have the right to appeal in cases where an Award is issued by the Ombudsman against it for not furnishing satisfactory and timely information/documents.

vii. The Executive Director-in charge of Consumer Education and Protection Department of RBI would be the Appellate Authority under the Scheme.

Complaints can be filed online on https://cms.rbi.org.in. Complaints can also be filed through the dedicated e-mail or sent in physical mode to the 'Centralized Receipt and Processing Centre' set up at Reserve Bank of India, 4th Floor, Sector 17, Chandigarh - 160017 in the prescribed format. Additionally, a Contact Centre with a toll-free number - 14448 (9:30 am to 5:15 pm) - is functioning where complaints can be lodged in Hindi, English and in other regional languages. The Contact Centre will provide information/clarifications regarding the alternate grievance redress mechanism of RBI and to guide complainants in filing of a complaint.

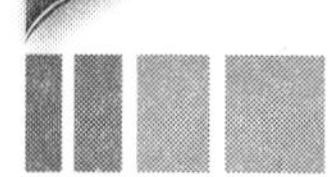

13.12 TRENDS IN COLLECTION SYSTEMS

Traditionally collection was in terms of cash and cheque and cheque variants like draft. In the recent years however many new electronic options for payment have come. These have been covered in previous chapters. However, it must be noted here that payment modes and options are changing, and it is expected that a DRA is fully aware of such changes and adopts the same

Online Payment Options

Other than the traditional recovery options, financial institutions provide various other options for recovery of dues s follows:

(*i*) Payment through net-banking or mobile banking

(*ii*) Payment through debit cards at ATMs or hand held devices

(*iii*) UPI payment through online platforms like BHIM UPI, PayTM, GPay, etc.

(*iv*) Using scan and pay trough customer specific QR codes

(*v*) Bill Payment option through BBPS

(*vi*) Cash payment at designated third party centres for customer convenience

By providing the additional ways to collect a payment, the lender can increase the likelihood of recovering the debt more efficiently.

Automated Compliance Software

Machine learning and artificial intelligence is another development in debt collection. Companies can use machine learning and artificial intelligence specifically for receivables management. These services offer a compliant platform and a suite of optimization models based on each company's specific needs. This will help the team of agents focus on the accounts that have a better chance of success. Also, automated compliance software has been shown to reduce errors from internal and external non-compliance.

Ramp Up Self-Service Options

Financial institutions may also identify how its customers prefer to be contacted. Clients' preference could be SMS, email, or phone. Understanding this helps in reducing person-to-person contact. Financial institutions could build options on their website or apps that allow customers to complete basic tasks like "Make a Payment," "Check my Account," "Register a Dispute," etc., such that customers can quickly address simple repayment issues. And as a best practice, it is advisable to seek feedback from consumers about their experience with the automation process to ensure that system bugs are addressed and fixed.

13.13 SUMMARY

The phrase Debt Recovery Agent comprises three terms - Debt, Recovery and Agent. Debt Recovery/collection agents are employed by Direct Selling/Marketing Agencies or Debt Collection Agencies who work for banks subject to certain terms and condition.

Law of Agency forms the legal basis of the relationship between the debt recovery agent and the financial Institution/bank. Banking Ombudsman scheme aims to facilitate the resolution of complaints relating to Banking services through conciliation and mediation between the bank and the aggrieved parties or, by passing an Award. Ombudsman can reject a complaint where it is without a purpose, beyond jurisdiction of Ombudsman. Customer can appeal against grounds of rejection to Appellate Authority within 30 days of receipt of communication regarding rejection.

Debt recovery arrangement is an arrangement or agreement between a financial institution and covering agent is a contract of agency which requires a final approval of the principal and the credit institution.

Some recent trends in collection systems include - online payment services and automation of repayment of dues.

13.14 KEY WORDS

Debt recovery agent, procedure, process, stages, arrangement, automation of repayment, self-sufficient to pay

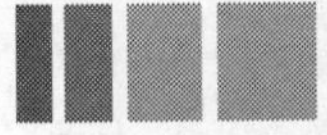

13.15 CHECK YOUR PROGRESS

1. Retail loans include:
   (*a*) Home loans, Auto loans, Corporate loans
   (*b*) Home loans, Auto loans, Bridge loans
   (*c*) Auto loans, Corporate loans, Credit card dues
   (*d*) Home loans, Auto loans, Personal loans
2. Retail loans are generally of:
   (*a*) Large amounts
   (*b*) Medium amounts
   (*c*) Small amounts
   (*d*) Medium and Small amounts

3. Retail loans are generally granted to:
   (*a*) Professionals, individuals, companies
   (*b*) Individuals, institutions, companies
   (*c*) Professionals, salaried employees, corporations
   (*d*) Professionals, salaried employees, individuals
4. Which one constitutes the largest percentage of Retail loans in India?
   (*a*) Auto loans
   (*b*) Home loans
   (*c*) Personal loans
   (*d*) Personal overdrafts
5. The term 'debtor' means:
   (*a*) A person who owes some debt
   (*b*) A person to whom some debt is owed
   (*c*) Lender
   (*d*) None of the above

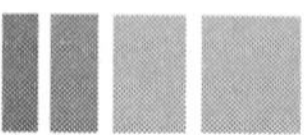

13.16 ANSWERS TO CHECK YOUR PROGRESS

1.	(*d*)	2.	(*d*)	3.	(*d*)	4.	(*b*).	5.	(*a*)				

CHAPTER

14 Functions of Debt Recovery Agents

14.1 OBJECTIVE

By the end of this chapter, you will learn about various functions of Debt recovery agents which include:

- Collecting dues receivable
- Remitting collected funds
- Initiating legal action
- Tracing debtors
- Compiling opinion reports

14.2 INTRODUCTION

The most important function of a debt recovery agent is to collect dues/receivables from the specified debtors of the bank or other financial companies as per the agency agreement entered with the respective financial institution. The agent also must remit the collected funds to the principal and must keep an account of the receivables collected and dues yet to be collected.

Another important function of the debt recovery agent is to report the position and developments regarding client if any to the principal on a time-to-time basis.

Apart from the easily collectible receivables, most banks have on their books overdue receivables from debtors who are not traceable, or who show unwillingness to pay or who resist surrendering the security charged. In such cases, the recovery process is difficult and requires handling by specialized collection agencies that possess the required expertise. The functions of repossessing the security, initiating legal action and tracing the vanished debtors may be called as specialized functions of debt collecting agencies.

Both the normal and specialized collection functions will need to be performed in accordance with the recovery policy and procedure prescribed by the bank (principal) and also the regulatory and legal requirements. The functions of agents will correspond to their duties prescribed by law.

14.3 COLLECTING FUNDS FROM DEBTORS

As mentioned above, collecting dues/receivables is the core function of a debt recovery agent. Receivables refer to the sums of money which have become due in the loan/advances accounts and are payable on due dates by the debtors to the creditors as per the loan/advances agreements entered between the lenders and creditors. Recovery Agent is assigned with the work of recovering/collecting receivable which have become due for payment but not paid by the borrower. Thus, the receivables in a loan/advance account connote the following essential features:

- Existence of loan or advance agreement between the creditor (bank) and debtor
- Repayment obligation of the debtor to repay the loan/advance, in part or whole, to the creditor, as per the loan/advance agreement.
- Due date on or after which the obligation is required to be discharged by the debtor in favour of the creditor.

In terms of the arrangement between the creditor bank (principal) and the debt recovery agency (agent), the former authorizes the agent to collect specified receivables from the named debtors on or after the specified due dates. The required particulars of the debtors and receivables to be collected from them are furnished by the bank to the agent, along with copies of the relative loan agreements.

Thus, the debt recovery agent is legally authorised to collect the specified receivables from the debtors on behalf of the principal (creditor bank), in terms of:

- the loan agreement, and
- the debt collection agency agreement.

The procedure and processes of debt collection, code of conduct in collection process and other regulatory requirements need to be complied by both the principal and agent.

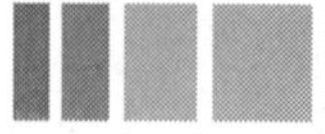

14.4 REMITTING COLLECTED FUNDS

The funds collected through cheque, draft or cash from the debtor should be sent/deposited by the agent to the lending institution immediately or as per accepted periodicity and as per the agency agreement. It should however be ensured that the amount collected is credited to the client's loan account immediately if not within a day's time. Statement of amounts collected should be sent to the financial institution along with the amount, preferably in duplicate. The copy acknowledged by the creditor should be kept on record by the agent in chronological order for future reference.

14.5 BOOK-KEEPING

While each debt recovery agent may devise their own accounting and book-keeping methods, the following would constitute the minimum requirement of book-keeping for any recovery agent:

- **Lists of debtors received from the principal:** Collection of receivables is an on-going activity of a recovery agent who may receive the debtor' lists from the principal (bank) from time to time. The debtors' lists form the basis of the agent's activities and also the book-keeping required. These should therefore be carefully kept on record in chronological order.
- **Lists of remittances to the principal:** "A list of collections made by the agent from the debtors and the proceeds remitted to the principal (bank) be prepared in chronological order and sent to the principal on daily basis or as per the prescribed periodicity."
- **Ledger account of each debtor** - Showing the amounts of receivable due, collected and balance to be collected, should be kept in chronological order. This can be maintained in the computer also. Amounts remitted to the principal out of the collections should also be kept debtor-wise, showing reference of the remittance date and list number. It may be noted that all the collections/recoveries should be remitted to the bank/NBFC. Normally an agent cannot adjust its dues on account of fee against the recoveries made on behalf of the bank.
- **Copies of loan/advances agreements between the debtors and the bank** - A bank is obliged to keep confidentiality of its customer's accounts and records and these should not be divulged to third parties without the customer's consent. As such, a debt recovery agent must take all due care to keep the required privacy and confidentiality as regards the records of each debtor furnished by the bank/NBFC (principal) and also as regards the collections made and remitted by him to the principal.

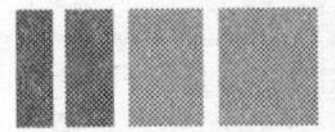

14.6 DOCUMENTING AND REPORTING

A debt recovery agent is required to document the important developments and events in the collection process, particularly in disputed and difficult cases and send reports periodically to the principal in terms of the agency agreement. Some banks/NBFCs may require agents to record conversations they have with the customers during recovery process.

Further, from accounting angle, the receivables collection by the agents would be required to be reported periodically to the principal. The account statement would normally show the due receivable, amount collected and remitted and balance yet to be collected - debtorwise.

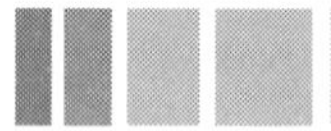

14.7 RE-POSSESSING SECURITY

When the debtor refuses to repay the overdue loan or advance, the bank/NBFC (creditor), in terms of the loan agreement, can take possession of the security charged to it by the debtor by way of hypothecation or pledge of movable assets, and sell the assets without the intervention of the court. Of course, the bank has to follow the legal provisions in this regard, including giving reasonable notice to the debtor (owner of the secured assets). In cases where the creditor's security is by way of mortgage of immovable property, court's intervention is required to repossess and sell the security for adjusting the outstanding loan. Under SARFAESI Act, the bank can enforce the mortgage without intervention of court. In both the cases of repossession (*i.e.*, with or without the intervention of court), the creditor can give authority to a collection agency, which has expertise in this field.

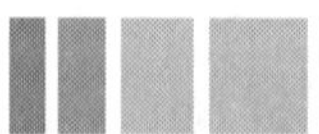

14.8 INITIATING LEGAL ACTION

In case the debtor has means and assets but is unwilling to repay the loan the debt recovery agent can recommend legal action. After obtaining the consent and instructions of the bank or the creditor, the recovery agent can, if it is as per agreed terms, initiate and pursue legal proceedings on behalf of the creditor.

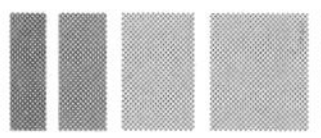

14.9 TRACING DEBTORS

Debt collecting agencies with nation-wide presence and large resources and computerized database also act as tracing agents of defaulters/debtors who have disappeared and are not traceable by the financial institution. Such services save the credit institution considerable time and money, which is otherwise spent in trying to track down the missing debtors.

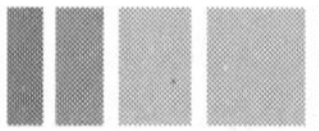

14.10 COMPILING OPINION REPORTS

The information on the means and net worth of the principal debtors/guarantors, who have not paid the dues for a long period, remains unknown to the lender for want of information forthcoming from the defaulters. Debt recovery agents can reach the relevant sources to collect information about such debtors/guarantors, their income and assets, which may be very difficult and cumbersome for the lender. Such information can help the lender decide about the feasibility of taking legal action for recovery against the defaulters. The sources of information to compile opinion reports on the means and assets of the defaulters can be obtained discreetly from:

- Business references
- Bank references
- Credit information agencies
- Chamber of commerce
- Employers
- Credit application forms of the defaulters submitted to the creditors.

14.11 SUMMARY

One of the most important functions of Agents is to remit/collect funds from debtors. The other duties of agents are:

(*a*) Collecting funds from the debtor - debt recovery agent collects funds from customers pertaining to the loan agreement and the debt collection agency agreement.

(*b*) Remitting collected funds - the funds collected through cheque, draft, cash or various online channels from the debtor should be sent/deposited by the agent to the creditor periodically as per the agency agreement.

(*c*) Book-keeping- maintenance of accounts needs to be done for deposits collected, ledger of each debtor, funds deposited, copies of loans/advances of debtors are done.

(*d*) Documenting and reporting - debt recovery agents are required to document the important developments and events in the collection process.

(*e*) Repossessing security- When the debtor refuses to repay the overdue loan or advance, the creditor can take possession of the security charged to it by the debtor.

(*f*) Initiating legal action - in case debtor has means and assets but is unwilling to repay, the DRA can initiate legal action

(*g*) Tracing debtors- Debt collection agencies also act as tracing agents for debtors

(*h*) Compiling opinion reports -rely on business, bank references, credit cards, etc.

Specialized functions of Debt Recovery Agents include - repossessing security, initiating legal action, tracing the vanished orders, etc.

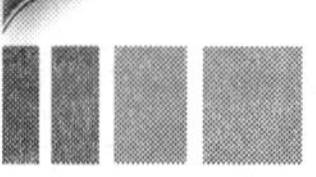

14.12 KEY WORDS

Collection, receivables, remitting, repossessing, tracing, book-keeping, opinion reports, documenting and reporting.

14.13 CHECK YOUR PROGRESS

1. A recovery agent is entitled to collect the specified dues from the debtors on behalf of the principal in terms of the:
   (*a*) Loan agreement between the debtor and the creditor
   (*b*) Authorization letter by the creditor to the agent
   (*c*) Both (*a*) and (*b*) above
   (*d*) None of the above
2. The function(s) of recovery agents under an Agency agreement include:
   (*a*) Only collection of the specified dues from the customers
   (*b*) Only documenting and reporting collections/developments to the principal
   (*c*) Only remitting the collection of dues to the principal
   (*d*) All of the above
3. In a home loan recovery case, the particulars of the property mortgaged (*i.e.*, the security) for the loan can be found from:
   (*a*) The loan agreement between the debtor and the lender and its schedule
   (*b*) The loan application form submitted by the debtor to the lender
   (*c*) Both of the above
   (*d*) None of the above
4. The recovery agents of a bank should follow:
   (*a*) Only the debt recovery policy and procedure of the bank (principal)
   (*b*) Only the directives of RBI on recovery agents engaged by banks
   (*c*) Only the Model Policy on collection of dues etc. framed by IBA
   (*d*) All of the above
5. The laws and regulations which govern debt recovery of a bank's dues apply:
   (*a*) to the bank's employees engaged in recovery process
   (*b*) to the recovery agents engaged by the bank
   (*c*) to the bank's employees and its recovery agents
   (*d*) to borrowers only

14.14 ANSWERS TO CHECK YOUR PROGRESS

1.	(*c*)	2.	(*d*)	3.	(*a*)	4.	(*d*)	5.	(*c*)				

CHAPTER

15 Policy, Processes and Procedure of Debt Recovery

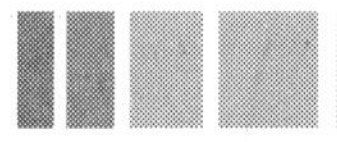

15.1 OBJECTIVE

At the end of this unit, you will learn about :

- Debt recovery policy
- Deb recovery processes
- Debt recovery procedure

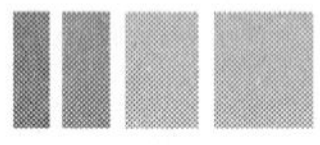

15.2 INTRODUCTION

Financial institutions lay down their policy and procedure for collection of past due debts in conformity with the legal and regulatory framework. The Institution/bank will, abide by:

1. The RBI directives on recovery of debt, including recovery agents engaged by the bank.
2. The model policy on collection of dues and repossession of security frame by the Indian Banks' Association (IBA).

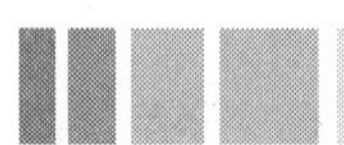

15.3 DEBT RECOVERY POLICY

The debt collection policy of a financial institution/bank provides guiding principles to the employees or authorized agents in their recovery efforts and interaction with the debtors. The procedures laid down for recovery will conform to these guidelines and should be interpreted accordingly in case of doubt. The debt collection policy of financial institutions is generally based on the following principles:

1. Dignity and respect to customers: a customer should be treated fairly and with due respect. This is the cornerstone of collection policy, based on the commitment

of a financial institution to customers, which most of the financial institutions adhere to.

2. Courtesy, fair treatment and persuasion in interactions with customers: These principles also govern the collection policy of most financial institutions. This is not only the right thing to do but is also the most effective way of collection of dues from customers.

3. Appropriate authorization: After entering recovery arrangement with recovery agents, the financial institution/bank will furnish them the authorization letters to collect the dues from the specified debtors. This authority must be carried by the recovery agent and shown to the customers on demand.

4. Due notice to the customers: This is necessary under the general law. The financial institution or the bank should inform, in their website the details of recovery agents engaged for the purpose. The details should include their names and telephone number etc. The recovery agent should call the customers only from the telephone numbers notified to the customer by the financial institution.

5. Document the disputes/resistance/threats of customers in recovery efforts: In order the disputes are settled amicably it should be recorded appropriately by the agent. The relevant details should be recorded by the recovery agent and the copies of communication exchanged with the customers should be kept on record. It could be referred to the bank appropriately for further course of action for recovery.

6. Use simple business language in all verbal or written communications with the customer: the main objective of debt recovery is to be able to share a simple message of when the customer's account is overdue and which agent will be assigned to them to collect the same. Any communication made to the customer must be in simple yet business language that is appropriate for the customer as well as the recovery agent.

7. Keep privacy and confidentiality of customer's dues and other records: this is required as it forms part of an institution/bank's commitment to customer. However, there are exceptional situations when the customer's account may be discussed with third parties. For example, with the customers written permission or otherwise information can be shared with the tax authority or law courts respectively.

8. No misleading statements or misrepresentation be made to the customers: Misleading statements are not permitted under the law. If this happens the agent can be proceeded against by the customer who, acting on such misrepresentation could have suffered certain loss or damage.

9. Read, understand and abide by the policy guidelines: Prior to beginning collections on debts owed by the customers, an agent must read, understand and abide by

the policy guidelines laid out by the authority. Failure to comply may result in termination of employment.

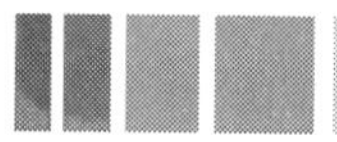

15.4 DEBT RECOVERY PROCESSES

Debt recovery processes can be typically of the following kinds each involving a different procedure:

1. Normal recovery process: This situation is where the debtors are willing to pay the dues smoothly without resistance.
2. Difficult recovery process: This is where the debtors are not willing to pay and are intentionally resisting or avoiding recovery efforts. In these cases, the recovery agent must follow special process of recovery against these reluctant defaulters.
3. Asset's possession process: If the debtor does not eventually pay the dues, the movable assets charged to the financial institution/bank by way of hypothecation or pledge can be possessed by the institution/bank or the recovery agent. Such assets can be sold by auction or otherwise to recover the dues.
4. Legal recovery process: The intervention of the court is required to repossess mortgaged immovable property by the financial institution or bank and/or their recovery agent. Also, if the charged assets do not exist, or the debt is unsecured, the debtor will have to be sued for recovery of the dues.

15.5 DEBT RECOVERY PROCEDURE

Stage of initiation: A normal recovery procedure begins when the recovery agent is notified, by the financial institution of the details as well as the name, the telephone number, and the address of the customer. Two such stages can be the initiation of debt recovery procedure:

1. The recovery agent has been authorized by the financial institution to collect the past due debt from the customer.
2. The customer has been notified by the financial institution of the details (name, telephone number, etc.) of the recovery agent for collection of the past due debt.

Step 1: Making customer calls: this is the first step in recovery procedure and following rules should be followed generally by all recovery agents:

a. Calls are made from the same numbers as advised by the lender/bank to the customer.

b. The caller discloses his/her identity and authority at the first instance.

c. The agent contacts the debtor between **8:00 AM to 7:00 PM** unless the special circumstance of his or her business or occupation requests the lender/bank to contact at a different time.

d. The agent, should, as far as possible, honour the customer's requests to avoid calls at a particular time or at a particular place. Inappropriate occasions such as bereavement in the family or illness should be avoided for making calls or visits to collect dues.

e. All calls where the customer becomes abusive or threatening should be appropriately documented.

f. Customers' questions should be answered in full, and they should be provided with information requested and given assistance in making payment.

g. How often should a call be made to the customer? The purpose of a collection goal is to bring to the customer's notice the obligation and to seek a commitment to pay on a specified date. Once the customer promises, a call on the desired date for payment confirmation should be made.

h. In the event of the commitment not forthcoming from the customer or it has been broken, calls may be made at reasonable frequency, based on amount owed, product, aging of the debt and history. Excessive numbers of calls or calls closely bunched together in the same day could be construed as harassment and should be avoided.

i. If the customer is not available during a few calls made by the agent, a message maybe left to an adult family member. The message should indicate only the name of the agent who had called requesting the customer's name to call back add a given phone number. The agent should not inform them it the customer has any overdue amount, or the call has originated from a recovery agency.

j. In case calls are being made to senior citizens, the discussion should be done in a respectful manner. Enquire about the health before initiating the discussion and avoid discussion in case the borrower is not well.

k. In case calls are being made to Pardanashin woman, it is advisable the discussion is done by a female recovery agent who is conversant with the local language.

i. In case the calls are being made to lady borrower, the calls should be made respectfully considering the sensitivity of the topic. The call needs to be recorded to avoid any kind of future issues. The tone of the voice should be soft and the caller needs to use appropriate and gentle words.

Step 2: Visiting the customer or the debtor

This would be the second step in collection process. The following procedure should generally be followed:

1. A customer should be visited for debt collection only after following conditions are satisfied:

- the debtor has not paid the due amount within the days of grace and the dues are still outstanding against him or her.
- the debtor has been notified of the amount due and of the name of the collection agent.
- the collection agent has taken an appointment from the debtor for the visit (at a particular place and at a particular date and time)

2. During the visit the agent should be dressed appropriately as prescribed by the principal and follow timing and place of visit as per the instructions or as agreed by the debtor expressly.
3. In the initial meeting with the customer, the agent could enter salutation words like Good morning, Good evening, etc. the agent should, thereafter showing his ID card and authority given by the principal for collection of dues from the debtor. Only after these initial formalities, the conversation regarding debt collection should start.
4. The time of visiting the customer will be generally between 8:00 AM to 7:00 PM. Visits earlier or later than the prescribed time may be made only under the following conditions:
   - when the customer has expressly consented to the timing.
   - When attempts to contact the customer have resulted in information that the customer is normally only available outside these hours and no alternate telephone number is available to contact him or her.
   - As per the nature of the customers' employment that is working in shifts in jobs, he or she is usually available outside these hours.
5. The agent should respect the privacy of the debtor. Privacy policy as discussed above for calls would apply during visits also.
6. During the visit due respect and courtesy should be shown to the customer and the interactions should be civil and polite as per the creditors policy.
7. During interactions with the debtor, the agent must not use threats or intimidation verbally or by body language. Under no circumstances, any physical violence can be used in debt collection process.
8. Conversation with the debtor could be recorded audio or video as per the financial institutions policy regarding documentation, particularly when the debtor disputes the dues or does not show proper conduct. This would provide safeguard to the agent against false accusation by the debtor.
9. Caution needs to be exercised while dealing with Senior Citizens. They can be vulnerable, physically fragile and not in good financial health. The client needs to be dealt with respect and empathy and in case of genuine financial reasons, the DRA needs to facilitate settlement of the debt in coordination with the bank/financial institution.

10. In case the customer is a lady borrower or Pardanashin woman, the visit should be done preferably by a female DRA agent and she should directly interact with the borrower. If the borrower wants to involve her immediate family member in the discussion, the same should be allowed. But the consent or final feedback should be always obtained from the Pardanashin woman only.

15.6 IMPORTANT POINTS FOR DEBT RECOVERY

Based on the foregoing procedure for normal recovery process, we may list below certain Don'ts for debt recovery, which are as follows:

i. Don't violate or breach the recovery policy, procedure etc. prescribed by the principal.

ii. Don't exceed the authority given in the recovery arrangement.

iii. Don't make calls to the debtor before 8:00 am or after 7:00 pm.

iv. Don't make anonymous calls or bunched calls to the debtor, which may be perceived as harassment.

v. Don't conceal or misrepresent the agent's identity during calls and visits or other interaction with the debtor.

vi. Don't show uncivil/indecent/dirty (uncouth) behaviour or use such language during calls and visits to the debtor.

vii. Don't harass/humiliate/intimidate/threaten the debtor - verbally or physically

viii. Don't intrude into the privacy of the debtor's family members, friends/colleagues.

15.7 CODE OF CONDUCT (COC) GUIDELINES FOR DEBT RECOVERY AGENTS

COC guidelines for Agents are already set for Agents and these are mentioned below:-

Do's and Don'ts for Debt Recovery Agents

Sr. No.	Description
1.	Customer should be contacted generally at the address of his choice, in case if he is unavailable or unable to meet at his residence, at the place of business/occupation.
2.	Customer's privacy should be respected.
3.	Interaction with the customer and any third party must always be in polite, civilized, and professional manner and they must be treated with dignity at all point in time
4.	Special care and precaution to be taken while dealing with female and elderly customers.
5.	One should not be accompanied by any person not authorized.
6.	Customer request to avoid calls at a particular time or at a particular place should be honoured as far as possible.

Sr. No.	Description
7.	Agent is not allowed to send any communication to customer *via* SMS, Email, Whatsapp or any other social media networks. In case, if customers are required to be communicated on e-mails/letters/electronic messages, the same need to be ensured through authorized communication desk
8.	Customer should be provided with the accurate information regarding his dues and loan details.
9.	Agent should collect customer payments through only authorized payment channels.
10.	Customer must be provided authorized payment acknowledgement and collected amount must be remitted to the financial institution within 24 hours of payment.
11.	Reasonable notice would be given before repossession of security and its realization.
12.	All assistance should be given to resolve disputes or differences in a mutually acceptable way
13.	During visit to customer for collection of dues, decency and decorum must be maintained.
14.	No written or verbal threats, abuse or rudeness is permitted while interacting with customers/third parties (Family members/relatives/friends).
15.	Inappropriate occasions such as bereavement in the family or such other calamitous occasions should be avoided for making calls/visits to collect dues.
16.	Strictly avoid any appearance and action which can be perceived as any criminal intimidation or threatening or violent behaviour.
17.	Agent while interacting with customers and third party should not resort to any false, deceptive, or misleading representation which can imply that he/she is affiliated with any of the governmental or judicial authority such as Police, Advocate, etc.
18.	Agents should be appropriately dressed and well groomed.
19.	Agents should try to interact in the language which the customer understand and is comfortable with.
20.	Agents are required to share, with the financial institution the name of the customer who becomes abusive or threatening. All such instances should be appropriately documented.
21.	Agents should not promise or commit for any type of written communication on behalf of the principal without prior permission.
22.	Agent should not mislead the customer about their true business or organization name
23.	Agent should not mislead the customer on the action proposed and consequences thereof.
24.	Agent should carry his belongings such as Daily Collection Sheet, Receipt Book, Minimal Stationery and Code of Conduct.
25.	Unauthorized information, written or verbal, cannot be divulged to any Customer/competitor/any other person.
26.	Agents must perform their role within the framework of the instructions issued in terms of process notes and specifics of collection action based on the product.
27.	Recovery Agents must strive to maximize the effectiveness of the visits by pre visit preparation and result orientation to improve results. Will also document result in visit/action taken.
28.	Maintain a reasonable distance from the Customer and no physical contact with the Customer/third party and in no scenario obstruct their movement.

Sr. No.	Description
29.	Non-adherence of the above guidelines will lead to strict action against the partner and could lead to penalty and termination of services.

15.8 A CASE STUDY

Based on press reports, we give a case study (name of the bank, debtor and recovery agent concealed) to illustrate the extent of damage eventually caused to the debtor, recovery agent and bank by the undesirable conduct of the recovery agent.

Case Study:

ABC Bank had granted a personal loan of Rs. 60,000 to XY, a lower middle-class individual, for consumption needs. The loan was to be repaid in instalments by XY. The loan was without any tangible security and also without any third-party guarantee. The borrower XY could not repay in time some instalments and therefore the loan became overdue.

ABC Bank gave XY's case to Z recovery agent, along with other overdue loans for recovery. Z recovery agent called XY a couple of times and also visited him at his residence. As XY was not able to repay the amount in default, Z, used abusive and harsh language in front of XY's wife and daughters to make recovery. During one of the visits to XY's house, Z and his colleagues took away forcibly some of the things that were available in XY's house in front of his wife and daughters and also used threatening language for payment of the dues. XY felt very much humiliated and also depressed. Being unable to repay the dues, one day, XY committed suicide. He left a suicide note, blaming Z for harassing him endlessly. He mentioned the abuses he had suffered at the hands of Z before his wife and daughters. He also mentioned the threat Z gave that he would suffer dire consequences if he failed to repay the overdue amount.

Following the suicide of XY, the local police arrested Z and his colleagues (who used to accompany Z during his visits to XY's house) on charges of abetment of suicide. A case was also filed against ABC Bank, which had to pay an *ex-gratia* payment of Rs. 20 Lakh to the deceased's family. The incident was also published in the press and damaged the Bank's reputation in public eye.

Questions:

After going through the case study, please answer the following points:

(*i*) Identify the major deviations of the RBI and IBA rules (*vide* Appendices 1 and 2), committed by Z (recovery agent) in the recovery process.

(*ii*) As a debt recovery agent, how would you have proceeded for recovery against XY (debtor)?

(*iii*) Is it proper for a recovery agent to talk about the dues in front of others or family members?

(*iv*) Is it appropriate for a recovery agent to involve his friends in the recovery process?

(*v*) What is the approved procedure for repossessing items from the debtor? Is it appropriate to take over things which are not funded by the debt?

(*vi*) What measures, if any, ABC Bank (lender) should take to avoid the kind of damages that were eventually caused to all the three parties concerned in the recovery process as mentioned in the case study?

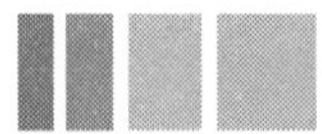

15.9 SUMMARY

Financial institutions lay down their policy and procedure for collection of past due debts in conformity with the legal and regulatory framework. The debt collection policy of a financial institution provides guiding principles to the employees or authorized agents in their recovery efforts and interaction with the debtors. The procedures laid down for recovery will conform to these guidelines and should be interpreted accordingly in case of doubt.

The debt collection policy of a bank provides guiding principles to the bank employees or authorized agents in their recovery efforts and interaction with the debtors. The procedures laid down for recovery will conform to these guidelines and should be interpreted accordingly in case of doubt.

The debt recovery process can be divided into- normal recovery, recover from difficult debtors, asset's possession process and legal recovery.

A normal recovery procedure begins when the recovery agent is notified of the bank details as well as the name, the telephone number and the address of the customer. The DRA can initiate by making customer calls as the first step and the second being, visiting the customer to collect the cash for recovery.

There is also Code of conduct guidelines prescribed by all Banks/NBFCs that must be followed by all Debt recovery agents.

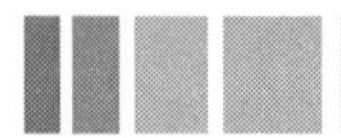

15.10 KEY WORDS

Recovery policy, Recovery procedure, due notice, misleading or misrepresentation, legal recovery process

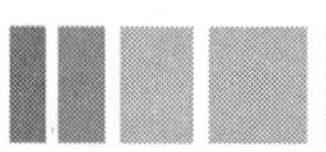

15.11 CHECK YOUR PROGRESS

1. Making a telephone call to the debtor by the recovery agent is:

   (*a*) The first step in recovery process

   (*b*) The last step in recovery process

(*c*) Optional in recovery process

(*d*) Not at all necessary in recovery process

2. Before making a telephone call to a customer, a recovery agent should ensure that:

(*a*) He/she has been authorized by the bank to collect the due debt from the customer.

(*b*) The customer has been notified by the bank of the details (name, telephone number, etc.) of the recovery agent for collection of the due debt.

(*c*) Both the above requirements are followed.

(*d*) None of the above is necessary.

3. While making a first telephone call to a customer for recovery of dues, a recovery agent should:

(*a*) Only disclose his/her identity.

(*b*) Disclose his/her identity and also authority to collect the dues.

(*c*) Discuss with the customer about payment of the dues.

(*d*) Do both (*b*) and (*c*) above

4. As per IBA's model policy on collection of dues, customer calls for recovery of dues should be normally made between:

(*a*) 0800 and 1700 hours

(*b*) 0700 and 1900 hours

(*c*) 0800 and 1900 hours

(*d*) 0700 and 1800 hours

5. As per IBA's model policy on collection of dues, borrower's requests to avoid calls at a particular time or place would be:

(*a*) Rejected outright

(*b*) Rejected politely

(*c*) Ignored and not responded

(*d*) Honoured as far as possible

15.12 ANSWERS TO CHECK YOUR PROGRESS

1.	(*a*)	2.	(*c*)	3.	(*d*)	4.	(*c*)	5.	(*d*)				

CHAPTER

16 Soft Skills and Strategies for Debt Recovery

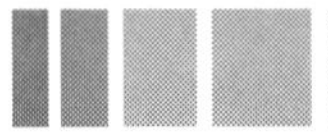

16.1 OBJECTIVE

By the end of this chapter, you will be acquainted with soft skills used for debt recovery:

- Communication Skills
- Listening skills
- Inter-personal skills
- Persuasive skills
- Negotiation skills
- How to deal with difficult debtors
- Strategy for recovery
- Etiquettes for collection through telephone calls

16.2 INTRODUCTION

Success in recovery depends on compliance with the regulatory norms added with soft skills and strategy. Both are complementary to each other. Mere regulatory compliance without soft skills and strategy may not result in recovery. Similarly, collection skills and strategy without regulatory compliance may vitiate recovery atmosphere in the long-term.

Soft skills are intra-personal and inter-personal skills that determine a person's ability to excel or at least fit in a particular social structure. These skills include competencies in areas such as Emotional Intelligence, Communication, Leadership ability, Etiquette, Conflict resolution, Decision making, Self-motivation, Self-discipline, Persuasion, etc.

16.3 COMMUNICATION SKILLS

Communication is a two-way process and is the process of exchanging information, ideas and thought between at least two persons, to create common understanding. In recovery, the communication takes place between the customer and the agent by words, in writing or by body language.

Communication is of two types:

1. **Verbal Communication** Verbal Communication implies oral communication through spoken words. Here, the speaker gives words to his feelings, thoughts, ideas and opinions and expresses them in the form of speeches, discussions, presentations, and conversations. The verbal communication can be made more effective depending on the tone of the speaker, clarity of speech, volume, speed, body language and the quality of words used in the conversation. The feedback is immediate since there are a simultaneous transmission and receipt of the message by the speaker and listener respectively.
2. **Non-Verbal Communication** *e.g.*, facial language (facial expressions, eye contact), voice language (voice tone, voice pitch) and body language (body position, body movement). All or any of these elements of non-verbal language communicate some message (whether intended or unintended by the communicator) to the receiver. The Recovery agent while communicating with the debtor, should observe the main principles of effective communication.
    - The language, verbal as well as body language, should be civil and courteous, as indicated by the financial institution.
    - The language used should be easily understood by the debtor (customer)
    - The agent must be watchful and sensitive to the customer's responses.

The agent must be sure that non-verbal communication (or body language) is not averse to the debtor, though unintentional. The agent must be sure that the debtor has understood the message intended to be conveyed by him; otherwise, he should reiterate and clarify the missing points.

16.4 LISTENING SKILLS

The agent should be a good communicator and a good listener. Listening refers to all the ways in which communication is being received from the other party and includes not only hearing but also facial and body expressions, attentiveness, or lack of it.

The importance of good listening lies in that, it improves the flow of communication by removing the psychological distances between the two parties. Better relations are built between the recovery agent and the debtor through good communications and good listening, than without these two essential skills or lack of them.

Main principles of effective listening:

Stop Talking: One cannot do a good listening job, while he does the talking always. If it is not possible to stop talking, always let the other people do most of the talking. This is a very simple matter. The Agent should also do minimum talking and he should listen to the customer. Listening to others is the strongest weapon. Given the opportunity, the debtor (customer) will tell the agent everything the agent needs to know.

The Agent should listen with empathy. Empathy is a respectful understanding of what others are experiencing. Following are the requisites of good listening, which help improve communication and make it effective:

- The agent should be patient when the debtor talks.
- The agent should remove distractions and create an environment for the listening to occur. Active listening is the art of communicating to the debtor that the agent is hearing every word.
- The agent should try asking more questions.
- The agent should get used to 'listening' for non-verbal messages -- body language.
- The agent should hold his temper.
- The agent should go easy on argument and criticism as argument and criticism puts the debtor (customer) on the defensive and there is break in communication.
- Normally, commence speaking only after the other party has finished speaking or making a point. Normally do not interrupt. In other words, interrupt only when absolutely necessary, *e.g.*, when the points being spoken are irrelevant or becoming unduly lengthy or controversial and time is limited or is being exceeded. Also interrupt softly by saying words like "excuse me".

Other than effective listening skills, few other key skills will be required to be an effective communicator which are as follows:

(*a*) Understand Non-Verbal Communication: Recollect the popular phrase-"Actions speak louder than words". Most of the message is communicated non-verbally. It includes many aspects like body language, tone and pitch of the voice, body movement, eye contact, posture, facial expression, and even physiological changes such as sweating. One can understand other people better by paying close attention to their non-verbal communication. So a message is conveyed more clearly by ensuring that your words and body language are consistent.

(*b*) Emotional Awareness and Management: It is important to manage emotions and express them appropriately in context for clear communication and personal well being. Allowing strong emotions to unnecessarily creep into a professional setting can lead to poor communication and conflict.

(*c*) Questioning Skills: Questioning is a crucial skill to understood someone's message correctly. It is an apt way to obtain more information about a particular topic, or simply starting a conversation and keeping it going. Those with good questioning skills are often also seen as very good listeners, because they tend to spend far more time drawing information out from others than conveying their own opinions.

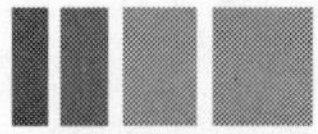

16.5 NEGOTIATION SKILLS

Negotiation skills play a crucial role in debt collection. Debt collectors must be adept at identifying the debtor's ability to pay and negotiate suitable repayment plans. By understanding the debtor's financial constraints, debt collectors can propose realistic payment options that align with the debtor's circumstances. They should choose the right time, place, convenience of the debtor and suitable payment terms in order to negotiate a payment or settlement which is mutually beneficial both for the parties. They should adopt a flexible approach and try to strike a balance between maximizing debt recovery and maintaining a positive business relationship with debtors.

A few examples of interpersonal skills are (*i*) Proper & clear communication (*ii*) Empathic behaviour (*iii*) Active listing (*iv*) Responding positively (*v*) Being positive (*vi*) Building relationships (*vii*) Conflict Management (*viii*) Collaboration (*ix*) Leadership (*x*) Dependability.

Normally, the Debt Recovery Agents are not allowed by the financial institutions to negotiate and compromise with the customers while doing the recoveries. As such, the need for negotiation, will arise only when the agent has been granted specific powers, by the lender/Bank, to negotiate with the debtor in terms of the agency agreement. Further, financial institutions delegate powers of compromise only to those recovery agents who have proven expertise in negotiating and recovering debts, classified in doubtful category, as under:

i. Where the security documents are missing or are impaired and cannot be filed in a law court, *e.g.*, improper execution, or barred by Law of Limitation.

ii. Where the assets charged to the Bank have deteriorated in quantity and quality and do not cover fully the outstanding dues in the debtor's account.

iii. Where the dues are totally unsecured by any security.

Effecting recoveries in doubtful and chronic cases are by no means an easy job for the Agent and he might be required to bring all his negotiating skills to the fore when facing the difficult customer.

The DRA must imbibe all the characteristics of a good negotiator, which are:

- A good negotiator must be a good listener.
- He should be confident but not arrogant.
- He should be focused but not rigid.
- He should follow the simple rule "You cannot give what you do not have."

- As a good negotiator, he must exercise a healthy dose of self-control.
- He should study the terrain before settling into a negotiation.
- He should not assume superior posture and belittle the customer.
- He should shun ego.
- He should not unduly delay the end game.

Before negotiations reach final stage, the recovery agent may need a formal approval on 'case by case' basis by the principal. The negotiated settlement can be signed thereafter and recovery effected by the agent. The agent is given a fixed percentage fee from the amount collected as per the settlement. The fee will be higher than in normal recovery cases, in view of greater work/time and specialized skill of negotiation required in such cases.

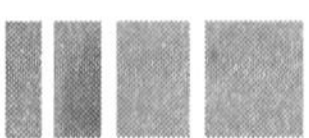

16.6 PERSUASIVE SKILLS

Most skilled negotiators use the power of persuasion. Persuasion is a form of influence. It is a problem-solving negotiation strategy, and it does not rely on force or deceit.

The DRA should bring all his persuasive skills into play when facing the difficult customer. He must imbibe all the characteristics of a good persuasive negotiator, which are:

- **Establish credibility.** Nothing undermines persuasive efforts more than a lack of credibility. People don't want to listen to a person they don't trust and respect.
- **Use a positive, tactful tone.** Assume the customer whom he is trying to persuade is intelligent and mature, the DRA should be respectful, direct, sincere, and tactful while talking to the customer.
- **Present strong evidence to support your position.** The DRA needs to explain why what he wants is important. He should demonstrate with strong supporting evidence. The responsibility for building the case lies with the DRA.
- **Appeal to the customer's self-interest.** To persuade the customer effectively, the Agent needs to understand what makes the customer tick. Then he can put himself into the position of the customer. An individual's behaviour is directed toward satisfying self-interests. The Agent needs to appeal to that self-interest by anticipating, before he makes any demands, that the customer will ask, "What's in it for me?"
- **Appeals**. Presenting clear, rational, and objective evidence are not often enough and DRA needs to appeal to the customer's emotions.
- **Use logic**. Though a logical and reasoned argument may not be a guarantee to persuade the customer, the lack of material facts and reasons to support your argument, will certainly undermine your persuasion.

16.7 INTER-PERSONAL RELATIONS/SKILLS

Inter-personal skill refers to 'Communication Plus skill' that enhances the relationship and understanding between two or more persons. It thus includes communication and listening skills (explained above), plus 'something more'.

Socialization transmits culture. The Recovery Agent should shun any sort of rigidity and should develop professional relationship with the customer. The mutually satisfying and reciprocal interactions between two or more persons is often called interpersonal relationship.

Trust between Agent and the customer is very essential. This may lead to enduring relationships. In the absence of trust, any relationship would be fragile, and the relationship could break-up at minimum strain or provocation.

Recognizing emotions in others is very essential and expressing them in a manner that is appropriate to the circumstances go a long way to cement and foster the interpersonal relations in a big way. Conflict arises only when the other people's inputs or views are not properly valued. When the other person is reached with understanding, compassion and his emotions are recognized and valued, the relations grow.

A few examples of Interpersonal skills are (*i*) Proper & clear communication (*ii*) Empathic behaviour (*iii*) Active listening (*iv*) Responding positively (*v*) Being positive (*vi*) Building relationships (*vii*) Conflict Management (*viii*) Collaboration (*ix*) Leadership (*x*) Dependability

Following are some of the elements of inter-personal skill for a recovery agent:

Compassion: Compassion calls for a sympathetic, listening ear, or for advice, which reflects a positive attitude of the Agent that goes a long way to improve the interpersonal relationship. An Agent who can help the customer's cause and cope with his difficulties, may deflect the cause of grievances of the customer and may end up with recoveries.

Body Language: Body language is the unspoken or non-verbal communication that goes on in every Face-to-Face encounter with another human being. Body language is a term used for communication by way of body movements or gestures instead of or in addition to, sounds, verbal language, etc.

Facial Expression: The face is perhaps the most obvious vehicle for non-verbal communication. Facial expressions mostly convey emotions and attitudes. Consistent eye contact can indicate that a person is thinking positively of what the speaker is saying. Eye contact creates a strong connection between two people and creates an impression of sincerity and trustworthiness. Lack of eye contact can indicate negativity.

DRA should maintain eye contact even while speaking. Eye contact with the customer would show DRA's interest in him. Disbelief is usually indicated by averted gaze. So

is eyestrain. If the customer is not being convinced by what the DRA is saying, the attention invariably wanders, and the eyes will scare away for an extended period.

Shaking Hands: Shaking hands helps DRA create a friendly and professional image. The DRA should make sure that his handshake is prompt and firm. Body language is used specially to express feelings. For instance, if the customer does not like the DRA, who has approached him for recoveries, he may find it difficult to say that directly to the DRA. However, he can make it clear either intentionally or unintentionally through body language. The opposite is also true. The DRA must learn to understand and interpret body language of others.

16.8 EMOTIONAL INTELLIGENCE

Emotional Intelligence (EQ) is an important skill which a DRA needs to develop in order to manage the difficult situations faced in front of the borrowers. It refers to their ability to maintain self-restraint, control moods, empathize with others, and develop self-motivation to face setbacks or handle adverse situations. According to several research reports on human behavior, it has been found out that Intelligence Quotient (IQ) accounts for 20% of our success in life whereas the remaining 80% comes from non-IQ factors such as social skills, emotional intelligence, etc. In order to excel in personal or professional life, it is critical to manage emotional impulses.

At the workplace, stress is unavoidable. Under pressure, employees often lose their cool, become emotional, express their anger, behave abnormally and hurt others estranging relationship with people. However, there are some people who are able to manage their emotions or anger and able to control adverse situations. They don't let tough situations effect their judgment or behaviour. They are able to manage a problem critically and find a solution. They are able to assess themselves honestly, take criticism positively and use it to improve their performance. Such people are considered to be have strong EQ and have good anger management as well as social skills.

Characteristics of Emotional Intelligence

The concept of Emotional Intelligence (EQ) was first coined in 1990 by researchers John Mayer and Peter Salovey and later popularized by Daniel Goleman, an American psychologist in his book "Emotional Intelligence".

The concept of EQ can be understood as a framework of five elements as detailed below:

1. **Self-Awareness:** Self-awareness is the most important quality of people with high emotional intelligence. They are able to control their emotions/anger and they don't let their feelings rule over them. They are able to critically assess themselves and are ready to work on their strengths and weaknesses in order to enhance their performance.

A DRA should know about his personality trait and be aware of own emotions, particularly if he gets frustrated easily and expresses anger in public. He should take feedback from his close people who know him personally and acknowledge their feedback and work on it to control emotions and anger in a tense moment.

2. **Self-Regulation:** The ability to emotional impulse and anger is known as self-regulation. Persons who are able to self-regulate generally don't express anger or jealousy, and they avoid making impulsive or careless decisions. A few characteristics of self-regulation are anger management, thoughtful decision making, open to changes, have high integrity, and have the ability to say 'No' whenever needed.

   A DRA has to develop the ability of self-control in a situation where arguments go out of control. The DRA should only present the bank's views and should not lose temper when a borrower refuses payment. The borrower to be politely explained in decent words about the consequences of not paying the loan. A DRA must keep anger in control and never be a trap to the provocation of the difficult borrowers.

3. **Self-Motivation:** The third important element of people with a high degree of emotional intelligence is self-motivation. These people do not require external influences to motivate them for work. They don't look for instant gratification and are willing to defer immediate results for long-term success. They are high performance oriented, love challenges and are effective in their work.

   Recovery is neither an easy task nor an impossible work. DRAs who are self-motivated and have self-belief make sincere and continuous effort by meeting the borrowers, persuading them and ultimately get success. A DRA should not wait for others to inspire them for making recovery effort and rather motivate themselves to complete the task.

4. **Empathy:** This is another important element of emotional intelligence. Empathy is the ability to identify with and understand the wants, needs, and viewpoints of those around you. People with empathy are able to recognize the feelings of others even in situations when those feelings may not be obvious. Because of this, empathetic people are able to relate to the feelings in a much better way and are able to manage relationships effectively. They are not judgmental and live their lives in a very open and honest way.

   Not all borrowers are wilful defaulters. There are many who want to pay, but situation is beyond their control. Because of COVID like situations, natural calamities, recession etc. Some borrowers close their business or lose their jobs due to which they are unable to pay. A DRA should make effort to understand the person with empathy (going to his position and trying to understand) and in consultation of the bank help such borrowers to improve their position and repay the money gradually.

5. **Social Skills:** Another important element of emotional intelligence is Social Skills which make them easily approachable and likable by others. These people are typically team players and help others develop and shine instead of focusing on their own successes. They can manage disputes, are excellent communicators, and are masters at building and maintaining relationships.

   One must realize, society is interdependent and one can succeed as a DRA only when focus is on building excellent relationship with the borrower, the guarantor, government officials and those who help in recovery of bad debts. Also, it must be remembered that a borrower is not an enemy. Treating the borrower with empathy might bring better result than confrontation and rude behaviour. History of debt recovery is full of examples, where DRAs are immensely benefited by developing friendly relationship with others who have helped in recovery of bad loans.

   Debt Recovery Agents should master the above skills to be emotionally intelligent. They should have control of their anger and practice to stay cool in provocative situations. Along with their IQ, they must develop their EQ to deal with difficult customers who try to create an environment of stress and confrontation by refusing to make payments on some pretext or other. Such a behaviour in a borrower generates frustration and anger in a DRA leading to intense arguments and physical commotion that ends in police station and court cases. This diverts the attention from the real purpose of recovery. Need is to be self- aware, have control on emotions/ anger and manage the situation tactfully.

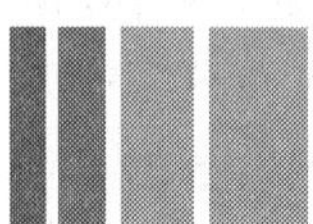

16.9 TELEPHONE ETIQUETTE OR PHONE MANNERS FOR COLLECTIONS

Phone Manners: Telephonic conversations regularly take place, whether at work or for personal reasons. The recovery agents do regularly talk to the customers over phone. The following basic etiquette tips will ensure the recovery agent does not offend anyone (the customer) at the other end of the line! The Do's and Don'ts in phone usage, apply across the board, from answering or placing calls, ending calls, special features as call waiting, answering machines, voicemail etc.

Answering the Phone:

1. While answering a call, the DRA should not scream or use a harsh voice. He should begin softly saying, "Hello" and introduce him.
2. If the phone has caller ID, DRA may avoid greeting a caller by using his name before he says 'Hello' and identifies himself.

3. If the caller has not identified himself, a polite "May I know who is calling please" is a courteous way of answering the call.
4. If the call comes at an inconvenient moment, it is okay to say, "I'll call you back in a few minutes" (DRA should keep his word of calling back) rather than keeping the caller waiting while DRA is busy on an errand of his own.
5. At the receiving end of a wrong number, a direct and polite response would be "I am sorry, you have dialed wrong number".

Placing calls:

1. While placing calls, DRA not to hang up before the phone has rung up at least 5 to 6 times.
2. Once DRA reaches the customer, if he wants, he should ask (if he feels interrupting) "Are you in middle of some work? I can call back again".
3. If the customer whom DRA wants to reach is not there and he wants to leave a message - he should keep the message short but do state his name and number. If DRA wants to leave a voice mail message on the phone, he should repeat his name and telephone number twice, clearly.
4. As a rule, DRA should place his call between 8 A.M to 7 P.M

Calls in progress:

Once a call is on, DRA should try to be brief. And as he/she listens, let the customer know that the DRA is listening with verbal responses like "yes", "of course", "I understand", "I see", etc.

Ending calls:

Traditional telephone etiquette says that the person who originates the call is the one who terminates it. If DRA is having difficulty ending a call, he ought to be polite and firm. At the first pause in the conversation, he should just say, "I am sorry, but I simply must go now".

Some Don'ts when on Phone:

- Conversing with someone nearby while your phone mate is online.
- Busying yourself with other things, suggests that your attention is elsewhere.
- Eating while on phone is not only impolite but also crude.
- Sneezing, coughing into the receiver. If you must, either turn your head away or excuse yourself for a movement and put down the phone.
- Never lay down the receiver with a bang. Set the receiver gently so you won't startle your phone mate.

16.10 DEALING WITH DIFFICULT DEBTORS

There are some debtors who may be termed as 'difficult debtors' *i.e.*, such debtors who 'can pay' but 'do not want to pay'. Such debtors may also be termed as 'wilful defaulters.'

The wilful defaulters show these features:

i. They would avoid responding to the calls of the recovery agents on one pretext or another.

ii. They would avoid meeting the recovery agent, by cancelling the appointment at the last hour and repeat this avoidance.

A pattern of avoidance is discernible from the responses of difficult debtors, who do not want to pay. The Debt recovery agent should collect and preserve the documentary evidence to prove the debtor's negative responses to the collection efforts. He is required to do the following:

i. Documenting every effort made to contact.

ii. Audio recording all the responses of the debtor during calls and personal visits. This should be done in full knowledge of the debtor.

iii. sending letters by registered post, containing full details of the dues and of the efforts made by the recovery agent for containing the debtor by phone calls and visits, which were of no avail, failing which a suit would be filed for recovery of the dues.

If the above efforts do not elicit any positive response from the debtor, the agent should arrange for serving a lawyer's notice on the debtor to repay the dues within a reasonable time.

If the debtor still does not pay the dues, steps should be taken to repossess the charged assets, if any, or to file a suit for recovery of the dues.

Case Study:

Mr. P receives a phone call at 7:00 p.m. from a person who greets him politely and identifies himself as a recovery agent for ABC Bank. "I've had a difficult time locating you, Mr. P he says, "I'm calling you about the money you owe to ABC Bank. You must pay or we will be forced to take strong action against you."

Mr. P objects, stating he has never purchased anything through the credit card.

Question:

Analyse the situation and suggest what the debt recovery agent is required to do at this point?

16.11 STRATEGY FOR RECOVERY

Devising a strategy helps in achieving a set goal or objective. Recovery agents should therefore devise a strategy for debt recovery. The following guidelines would help in preparing proper strategy for debt recovery:

- The collection process should be compliant to the financial institution/bank-specific recovery norms and regulatory guidelines.
- The collection timing should be synchronized to the cash inflow pattern of the debtors. For example, recovery from salaried employees should be timed when salary is received by or credited to, the debtor's account, normally at the month-end (where salary is paid monthly).
- In case of MSME customers, the effort should coincide with cash flow on account of sales.

This will call for knowledge of lenders/banks' products on the part of agents. It should be the endeavour of the agent that collection should be made well before the cash inflows are spent away by the debtor for meeting other expenses. Adopt different collection strategy for different debtor types. This is based on the dictum that one size does not fit all.

In the foregoing paragraphs, three types of debtors have been described and they need different strategies for recovery success:

- Normal debtors, *i.e.*, who can pay and will pay if reminded or/and persuaded to pay.
- Difficult debtors, *i.e.*, those who can pay, but will not pay.
- Doubtful debtors, *i.e.*, those who can pay the reduced amount as negotiated with them.

While different strategies are required for different types of debtors, the following are the common points to be followed in all kinds of recovery strategies:

- Recovery effort should start with establishing a good rapport with the debtor.
- Communication, listening and persuasive skills should be applied in building good interpersonal relations.
- Go through the 'Know Your Customer' (KYC) papers furnished by the bank and know the customer's identity and personal profile (carry the copy during visit to the debtor).
- Go through the copy of the loan agreement of the debtor furnished by the lender/bank and note down the financial position, cash flow pattern, and assets charged to the lender/bank (carry this note for reference during recovery process).
- Record in notebook recovery efforts in chronological order for each debtor.

This would help:

(*a*) as evidence in court in cases where a suit has been filed

(*b*) in sending periodic report

16.12 POSITIVE ATTITUDE TOWARDS RECOVERY

As a Debt Recovery Agent (DRA) you need to recover bad debts from defaulting borrowers. It is a challenging task and needs a lot of expertise on:

- Knowledge about general banking and loans/advances;
- Communication skill, interpersonal skills, persuasion and negotiation skill;
- Positive attitude towards such type of works.

Dealing with difficult customers is often frustrating. It has been observed that, DRAs who succeed in such difficult assignments like to do such challenging job and enjoy the work because they develop a positive attitude for debt recovery.

How to develop Positive Attitude towards the job

(1) Developing Self:

When you have decided to take the assignment as a DRA, accept the challenges and prepare yourself to handle possible challenges.

At first, be informed from the bank officials about the work and what etiquettes/ qualities are required to handle such tasks. Make a SWOT (Strength/Weakness/ Opportunity and Threat) analysis of yourself in relation to debt recovery. The major areas of improvement are as follows:

i. Remaining Physically Fit:

A DRA needs to meet borrowers, bank officials, guarantors, and many others as and when required. Hence, it's imperative that he should be physically fit by:

- Take balanced diet
- Do regular exercise
- Learn to stay relaxed in stressful situations and
- Be presentable (well groomed)

ii. Having Adequate Knowledge: A DRA should have adequate knowledge about loans and advances, NPA (Non-Performing Assets) concepts, Interest calculation on loan accounts, RBI & IBA guidelines on recovery process, DRA's Duties and Rights, Fair practices code, etc. He should be equipped enough to explain the borrowers when questions are raised by them.

iii. Proficiency in Soft Skills: Soft skills along with hard skills are the hall mark of a DRA's success in recovery process. Sharpening communication skills, both verbal and non- verbal, having capacity to persuade the borrower to repay, negotiate in case of need, able to stay cool in tense situations, dealing with difficult customers are all skills a DRA needs to master.

iv. Being emotionally Intelligent: IQ is necessary but not sufficient to deal with people. A DRA should be aware about his impulses and emotions that propels him to emotional outburst when the borrower does not agree with his view points. In a tense situation a DRA should keep himself cool and not react with the same negative intensity as the borrower does. All borrowers are not willful defaulters. Some have genuine problems. The DRA should be empathetic towards such people to win over them and facilitate recovery.

v. Building Character: A DRA should love his profession as it is. Remember, all works in this world have their inherent challenges, not just your works only. If you have accepted, it as your profession love the challenges. This positive attitude towards your job will motivate you to learn the techniques of recovery. Never be unwilling to discharge your responsibility. Your bank or agency is depending on you for such recovery and you must give your best in an honest manner and success will eventually happen.

(2) Understanding Others: A DRA needs to understand the viewpoints of others to be effective in his job role. A few important aspects of this critical element are as follows:

i. Try to understand your principal, the bank, who has engaged you for recovery. You may not agree with the viewpoints and strategy of the concerned bank authority. In such cases, you may ask for some explanation or express your concern and opinion politely. A banker has profound experience on loan disbursement and recovery. It is always helpful to listen to them, take ask for guidance and execute your plan.

ii. The same may happen while interacting with the borrowers. Some borrowers who have money and do not pay are marked as difficult borrowers. They take all pretexts not to pay the loan. That will naturally frustrate you as you are giving so much efforts. But remain positive and cool in such challenging situations. Never insult such a borrower. Any act of aggression – verbal or non- verbal, most certainly ends up in a police station. This is undesirable, illegal and must be avoided at any cost. You get diverted from your impending goal and also will be blamed for such deeds. Persuade such people to repay public money. Politely but assertively convey the consequences of not paying bank loans.

Yet, there are many borrowers who are willing but unable to pay back. Reasons might differ from borrower to borrower- failed business venture, less revenue generation, natural calamity, family problems etc. Use empathy, understand their positions and suggest remedies in consultation with your bank officials.

iii. A DRA should be in touch with the guarantors of loans and persuade him to be a part of recovery process. At times, village sarpanches, cooperators and local leaders in towns/cities and other local activists can come to your rescue in the recovery process. Build rapport with them. Success will embrace you.

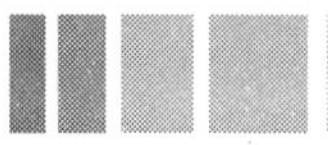

16.13 CREDIT COUNSELLING

a. **Credit counselling** is the process of educating the borrowers about how to avoid incurring debts that cannot be repaid and also how to manage the debt burden and repayment commitments in respect of a number of debts. This process is actually more about debt counselling than a function of credit education.

Credit counselling often involves negotiating with banks to establish a **Debt Management Plan (DMP)** for a customer. A DMP may help the debtor repay his/her debt by working out a repayment plan with the bank. DMPs, usually offer reduced payments, fees and interest rates to the borrower. Recovery agents refer to the terms dictated by the bank to determine payments or interest reductions offered to customers in a debt management plan.

b. **Debt Management Programs**: Once a customer has come under a DMP, the bank will close/merge the customer's various accounts and restrict any future charges in the accounts. The most common benefit of a DMP is the consolidation of multiple monthly payments into one monthly payment, which is usually less than the sum of the individual payments previously paid by the customer. This is because credit card banks will usually accept a lower monthly payment from a customer in a DMP than if the customer were paying the account on their own. Some DMPs advertise that payments can be cut by 50%, although a reduction of 10-20% is more common.

c. **Rephasement**: The second feature of a DMP is a reduction in interest rates charged by creditors. A customer with a defaulted credit card account will often be paying an interest rate approaching 30% to 42.5%. Upon joining a DMP, credit card banks sometimes lower the annual percentage rates charged to 15-20%, and a few eliminate interest altogether.

Example:

A customer owes money with a monthly payment of Rs. 15,000/- which has not been paid in two months. This will be considered by the creditor to be 60 days past due. After joining the DMP and making three consecutive monthly payments, the creditor could reage the account to reflect a current status. Thereafter, the monthly payment due on the statements would be the monthly payment negotiated by the DMP which gives a fresh start and an opportunity for the customer to begin building a positive credit history.

Case Study:

A customer is heavily indebted. How can the recovery agent counsel him to manage his debt?

1. Borrower to prioritise his debts:

List all his debts, ranking them according to the rate of interest. Concentrate on paying off the higher interest debts first. Once the highest-rate debt is paid-off, add the total he was paying on this debt, to the next one on his list. This way, he will have more to pay off each debt on his list, with the benefit that these payments are already built into his budget. Be sure to continue to pay the minimum amount owing on his remaining debts.

2. Talk to bank:

Most banks would rather find a suitable repayment plan for the borrower, than have his payments overdue or worse, lose a debt altogether. If a debtor cannot make his payments or struggling to make the payments on time, it is important that he contacts the bank.

Explain to the bank that he wants to pay in full, but needs more time to pay. Provide full details of his situation, and emphasize the positives. Explain that he is taking steps to reduce his spending, and show his budget plus a suggested repayment plan showing a specific amount allocated to repaying each bank.

It is likely that bank will revise his repayments and/or extend the time he has to pay.

3. Consolidate debts:

Debt consolidation involves combining all debts into one loan. This can have many advantages including reducing minimum monthly repayment, establishing a payment structure that will see the loan paid-off in a structured way, setting a fixed monthly payment that helps with budgeting.

16.14 LET US SUM UP

Success in recovery depends on compliance with the regulatory norms added with collection skills and strategy. Both are complementary to each other, In the recovery process, communication takes place between the debtor and the agent by words, in writing, eye contact or by body language (during personal meetings).

Listening is another skill which is essential in recovery process. A good recovery agent should be a good communicator and a good listener. Establishing good inter-personal relationship with a person means establishing a 'rapport with that person'.

The persuasive skill is built on establishing a good rapport and winning the trust of the debtor. The need for negotiation for a recovery agent will arise only when the agent has been granted specific power to negotiate with the debtor in terms of the agency agreement. In such cases, the extent of authority and parameters of compromise (*e.g.*, reduction of interest or principal or both and its percentage to the total dues) will be adhered to by the agent.

Interpersonal skills are very important for Agents. The Recovery Agent should remove any sort of rigidity and should develop relations with the customer. The mutually satisfying and reciprocal interactions between two or more persons are often called interpersonal relationship. He/she must also have telephone etiquettes and display the same while interacting with the customer on call.

Credit counselling is another skill that must be present in DRA. It provides consumers with guidance on consumer credit, money management, debt management, and budgeting. The goal of most credit counselling is to help a debtor avoid bankruptcy if they find themselves struggling with debt repayment.

16.15 KEY WORDS

Communication Skills, Listening skills, Inter-personal skills, Persuasive skills, Negotiation skills, difficult debtors Strategy for recovery, Telephone collection etiquettes

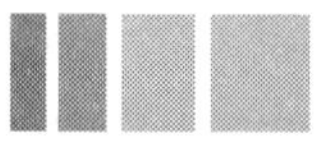

16.16 CHECK YOUR PROGRESS

1. Persuasive skill means-----------:
   (*a*) A person should be a good listener
   (*b*) Inter-personal relationship
   (*c*) Negotiating
   (*d*) Establishing a good "rapport" and winning the trust of another person
2. Debt recovery agent---------:
   (*a*) can exceed the delegated authority
   (*b*) should not exceed the delegated authority
   (*c*) can partially exceed the delegated authority
   (*d*) are not given any authority for compromise
3. DMP means:
   (*a*) Debt Management Plan
   (*b*) Delegated Monetary powers
   (*c*) Derived Monetary Powers
   (*d*) Diligent Management of Property

16.17 ANSWERS TO CHECK YOUR PROGRESS

1.	(*d*)	2.	(*b*)	3.	(*a*)								

CHAPTER

17 Rights and Duties of Recovery Agents

17.1 OBJECTIVES

By the end of this chapter, you will learn about:

- The rights and duties available for agents
- Right to remuneration
- Right to retainer
- Right to compensation
- Right to indemnity
- Duty to follow instructions
- Duty to exercise care and skill
- Duty to communicate
- Duty to render accounts
- Duty to remit money
- Duty not to delegate

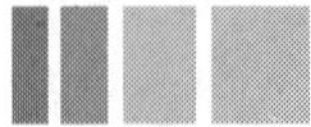

17.2 INTRODUCTION

Rights and duties of agents are governed by the Contract Act. The Act defines an 'agent' and related matters relating to agents. Recovery Agents act as 'agents' for and on the authority of the Principal (bank or other institution). The rights and duties of Recovery Agents will therefore be essentially those of an 'agent' and governed by the Contract Act provisions and also the regulatory guidelines of RBI and IBA. In view of this, the rights and duties described herein are as per the general provisions of the law. However, these can be modified by a specific agreement between the Principal and Recovery Agent to the extent permitted by the law. The reason is that if two adult persons/entities agree to certain things and enter into a formal contract as per the provisions of the law, the specific provisions of the agreement will prevail and be enforceable between them. The Contract Act contains the general provisions of the law, which will apply where the agreement is silent (*i.e.*, not specific), or doubtful.

In terms of the Contract Act, an agent has some rights as enumerated below:

17.3 RIGHT TO REMUNERATION

Contract of Agency under the Contract Act does not provide a mandatory duty on the principal to remunerate the agent for the work done on behalf of the principal and it does not specifically provide for an agent's right to remuneration. For the agent to get any remuneration, the agency agreement must expressly or impliedly provide for the same.

Since specific provisions of the agreement will prevail and be enforceable, the financial institution and the Agency can agree to scale of fees for various kinds of debt recovery and when the fees would be payable by the institution/Bank. If the agreement does not provide for any fee or other remuneration, the principal is liable to pay to the Agent fee as per the customary practices of the industry.

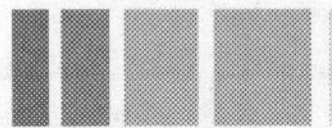

17.4 RIGHT TO COMPENSATION

In terms of Sec. 225 of the Contract Act, the Principal is liable to compensate the agent in respect of any injury caused to him either because of the principal's neglect or want of skill.

17.5 RIGHT TO INDEMNITY

Sec. 222 of the Contract Act states that the employer of an agent is bound to indemnify the agent against the consequences of all lawful acts done by such agent in exercise of the authority conferred upon him. In view of the provisions, there are two essential conditions that are to be satisfied by an agent, to claim indemnity from the principal:

i. The agent must have acted lawfully when the injury was sustained.

ii. The act should have been done during the agency business.

However, Section 224 of the Act, states that "where one person employs another to do an act which is criminal, the employer is not liable to the agent, either upon express or implied promise, to indemnify him against the consequences of that act."

17.6 RIGHT TO RETAINER

The right to retainer means that an agent can retain the money belonging to the principal, for meeting the following kinds of expenses, and thereafter remit the balance amount to the principal:

- The expenses incurred during the course of agency,
- Any sum due to the agent as remuneration.

This right is given under section 217 of the Contract Act. An agent can retain money only for the expenses incurred during the transaction in question, and not for the previous dues for services rendered.

However, this right is practically of little consequence where debt recovery agency agreements provide for the agent's remuneration and also the manner and timing of the payment obligation of the principal. The agreement may also provide a duty on the agent to remit the debt collections at the stipulated time intervals, without any deduction towards the agent's remuneration and other expenses. As the money collected represents payment by a customer to the bank towards dues it would be ideal if the money is remitted in full and not adjusted towards the dues of the bank to the agent.

17.7 DUTIES OF AGENTS

There are various duties of Agents which are mentioned below:

(1) DUTY TO FOLLOW INSTRUCTIONS

The foremost duty of a recovery agent is to follow the instructions of the principal who has engaged him for stipulated tasks and pays remuneration for doing so. In this regard, following points should be noted:

1. The instructions of the principal must be clear, unambiguous, and lawful
2. It is the duty of the agent to follow only the lawful instructions. Where the acts which the agent has undertaken to perform are unlawful or void in law, the principal cannot compel the agent to perform, and the principal also cannot claim damages against the agent for failure to perform such acts.
3. If an agent acts contrary to the instructions/directions of the principal, he may be held liable to the principal for the loss suffered by the principal due to such default.

In this regard the financial institution's policy towards customers and the code of conduct of the agents as prescribed by the bank/IBA should be kept in mind and adhered to by the DRA.

(2) DUTY TO FOLLOW TRADE CUSTOMS

A recovery agent must discharge his duties according to the terms of the agency agreement with the principal. Where the instructions are not given in detail, the agent must follow the commercial customs and industry practice. For instance, for debt collection for banks, RBI and IBA have laid down some guidelines which have to be followed in recovery process. If an agency agreement does not provide any behaviour code in collection process, the RBI/IBA code or guidelines would require to be followed by the recovery agent while collecting dues from the debtors. Most of these guidelines are applicable to NBFCs as well.

(3) DUTY TO EXERCISE CARE AND SKILL

A recovery agent has a duty to keep care and skill in discharging his duties as he is managing his own affairs. An agent is bound to act with reasonable diligence and to use his skill. He is else liable to compensate the principal in respect of the direct consequences of his own act.

No hard and fast rule can be laid down as regards the degree of care and skill required by the recovery agent. It will vary on the facts of each case. The tests of reasonableness and acting for one's own business are applied in determining the degree of skill and care.

(4) DUTY TO COMMUNICATE

It's the duty of on agent "to use all reasonable diligence in communicating with his principal in case of a difficulty and obtaining its instructions" (*vide* section 214 of the Contract Act). Whenever there is some doubt or difficulty, the agent must act according to the principal's wishes, rather than to do whatever he feels like. Thus, a recovery agent should seek instructions from his principal on all those points where the agency arrangement is silent.

(5) DUTY TO RENDER ACCOUNTS

An agent is bound to render proper accounts to his principal on demand (*vide* section 213 of the Contract Act). He should keep his principal's accounts up to date, so that they can be furnished to the principal on his demand. Further, an agent is required to keep his principal's money separate from his own. Generally, the accounting method, format and other requirements will be prescribed by the lender/bank (principal) to harmonize them with their own accounting system.

(6) DUTY TO REMIT MONEY

Section 218 of the Contract Act provides that an agent is bound to pay all sums received by him on behalf of the principal. This is called the agent's duty to remit money to the principal. The recovery agent has to periodically remit the collected moneys to the principal as per the agency agreement.

(7) DUTY NOT TO DELEGATE

An agent cannot further delegate his authority unless he is so permitted by the specific contract with the principal, or established trade practice. This is based on the Common Law principle of *'delegatus non protest delegare'* which means what is delegated cannot be further delegated. Normally the recovery agency agreement will provide such a clause. If DRA is an agency and it employs persons to do recovery it is not in the nature of delegation. An agency can use its employees for recovery duty as it has to be specifically provided in the agreement.

(8) DUTY OF CONFIDENTIALITY

This duty of recovery agent is based, not on the provisions of the Contract Act, but on the IBA Code for Debt Recovery and the customary practice in the banking industry. As per this, financial institutions are obliged to keep confidentiality of the affairs of the customers' accounts and their recovery agents have also to follow their principal's duty in recovery process.

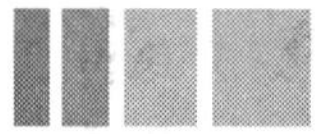

17.8 ETHICS AND CORPORATE GOVERNANCE

Banks and financial institutions play a vital role in a country's economy, and it is based on being just and truthful. The financial business depends on various moral codes like truthfulness, honesty, integrity, transparency etc. that are vital given the nature of business of accepting deposits for lending.

Need and Importance of Ethics

Ethics is moral dependability, punctuality of fulfilling obligations and honouring the terms of contracts. It creates credibility for the banks. They need to deliver high quality services, driven by high ethical standards, and maintain the same in its work culture, management, and the quality of its employees. Banks can only work well when the public trusts them. Warranting safety of banking activities is certainly a challenging task.

Along with global integration, the ongoing financial innovations have brought the possibilities of minimum direct intervention of governments and regulators on banking operations. Therefore, the safety of banking activities is largely dependent on the attitude and confidence of market players.

Ethics helps in dealing with dilemmas - A bank, at times, may have to confront with moral dilemmas in course of business. Banks have to deal with complex dilemmas between right versus less right. Hence the need for a set of strong moral principles, to enable employees navigating through complex ethical choices.

Guards Reputation/Goodwill - Banks' ethical practices aid in safeguarding depositors' interest, thus, maintain stability of the system and preserve the reputation of the bank.

Ethical practices prevent legal breaches and corrupt activities, protects other stakeholders' interest and enhances brand image.

Helps avoid risk – A well-defined code of ethics followed by the superiors ensures high ethical standards and preventive and corrective measures against unethical practices by staff. This will refrain the staff members from committing an offence due to temptation of some gratification, like approving unqualified loan application, granting credit at unjustifiable terms and delaying the process of loan application deliberately, etc.

As the DRAs are the extended arms of banks ensuring recovery of debt, adherence to ethical principles is important for them.

Corporate Governance

Directors of a firm are responsible for creating wealth and happiness for all the stakeholders of an organization and improvising by using corporate governance. It is the duty of directors to avoid ethical misconduct in their director role and also to provide leadership in decisions to prevent ethical misconduct in the organization. To remove the opportunity for employees to make unethical decisions, most companies have developed formal systems of accountability, oversight, and control- known as corporate governance.

Some of the benefits that are achievable having sound corporate governance practices are:

Creates conducive environment that enables incentive to the owners, various stakeholders including Business Correspondents to achieve objectives which are in the interest of the organization.

Minimises corruption, delays, risks and mismanagement.

Good corporate governance ensures building and maintenance of trust between banks and their customers. Being agents of banks, the business correspondents have a significant role to ensure that the trust with their customers is always maintained.

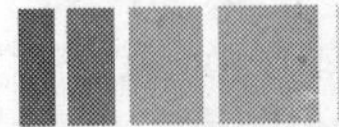

17.9 LET US SUM UP

- The various sections of the Contract Act, containing provisions regarding the rights and the duties of an 'agent'. The agent's rights to remuneration, right to retainer, right to compensation and more such rights are important to know as they help in understanding the legal aspects of agent's rights and duties.
- Rights and duties of agents are governed by the Contract Act. The Act defines an 'Agent and related matters relating to agents'. Recovery Agents act as 'agents' for and on the authority of the principal (bank or other institution).
- The rights and duties of recovery agents can be modified by a specific agreement between the Principal and Recovery Agent to the extent permitted by the law. The reason is that if two adult persons/entities agree to certain things and

enter a formal contract as per the provisions of the law, the specific provisions of the agreement will prevail and be enforceable between them.

- Where an agency contract does not provide for any fee or other remuneration, the principal may be liable to pay to the agent only the fee as per the customary practices of the industry.
- Duties of an agent include the duty to follow instructions, Duty to exercise care and skill, Duty to communicate, Duty to render accounts, Duty to remit money & Duty not to delegate.

17.10 KEY WORDS

Rights, duties, confidential, remuneration, indemnity, render account, remit money

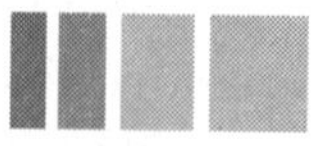

17.11 CHECK YOUR PROGRESS

1. The generic provisions for rights and duties of agents are contained in:
   (*a*) The Constitution of India
   (*b*) The Contract Act
   (*c*) The Companies Act
   (*d*) None of the above
2. The generic rights and duties of agents contained in relevant Act:
   (*a*) Cannot be modified by the specific agreement between the agents and the bank
   (*b*) Can be only modified by the agreement between the agents and the bank
   (*c*) Can be modified, altered and deleted by the specific agreement between the agents and the bank
   (*d*) None of the above is correct
3. The generic duties of agents contained in the relevant Act, include:
   (*a*) Duty to follow lawful instructions of the principal
   (*b*) Duty to follow lawful and unlawful instructions of the principal
   (*c*) Duty to follow customs of the trade/industry, where instructions of the principal are silent.
   (*d*) Both (*a*) and (*c*) above

4. Recovery agents have a duty to exercise reasonable care and skill in recovery functions, in terms of:
   (*a*) The Contract Act
   (*b*) The IBA's Model Policy on Collection of dues
   (*c*) The RBI's guidelines on recovery agents engaged by banks
   (*d*) All of the above

17.12 ANSWERS TO CHECK YOUR PROGRESS

1.	(*b*)	2.	(*c*)	3.	(*d*)	4.	(*d*)						

CHAPTER

18 Fair Practices Code for Lenders

18.1 OBJECTIVE

By the end of this chapter, you will learn about:

- Loan appraisal-terms and conditions
- Disbursement
- Supervision

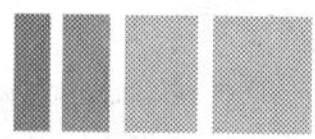

18.2 INTRODUCTION

The Reserve Bank of India, in consultation with Government of India and some banks finalized a set of codes, called, 'the fair practices code for lenders' and advised financial institutions to adopt the guidelines individually.

18.3 APPLICATIONS FOR LOANS AND THEIR PROCESSING

a. Loan application forms in respect of priority sector advances up to Rs. 2 lakh should be comprehensive. It should include information on fees/charges, if any, payable for processing and amount of such fees refundable in the case of non-acceptance of application, pre-payment option and any other matter, which affects the interests of the borrower.

b. Banks and financial institutions should give acknowledgement for receipt of all loan applications.

c. Financial institutions/financial intermediaries should verify the loan applications within a reasonable period. If additional details/documents are required, they should intimate the borrowers immediately.

d. In the case of small borrowers seeking loans up to Rs. 2 lakh, the lenders should convey in writing, the main reason/reasons which, in their opinion after due consideration, have led to rejection of the loan applications within stipulated time.

18.4 LOAN APPRAISALS AND TERMS/CONDITIONS

a. Lenders should ensure that there is proper assessment of loan application by borrowers. They should not use margin and security stipulation as a substitute for due diligence on credit worthiness of the borrower.

b. The lender should convey to the borrower the credit limit alongwith the terms and conditions given with his full knowledge on record.

c. Terms and conditions and other caveats governing credit facilities given by financial institutions arrived at after negotiating by lending institution and the borrower should be given in writing and duly certified by the authorized official. A copy of the loan agreement along with a copy each of all enclosures quoted in the loan agreement should be furnished to the borrower.

d. The loan agreement should clearly stipulate credit facilities that are solely at the discretion of the lenders. These may include approval or disallowance of facilities, such as, drawings beyond the sanctioned limits, honouring cheques issued for the purpose other than specifically agreed to in the credit sanction, and disallowing drawing on a borrower account of non-compliance with the terms of sanction. It may also be specifically stated that the lender does not have an obligation to meet further requirements of the borrowers on account of growth in business, etc. without proper review of credit limits.

e. In case of lending under consortium arrangement, the participating lenders should evolve procedures to complete appraisal of proposals in a time bound manner to the extent feasible and communicate their decisions on financing or otherwise within a reasonable time.

18.5 DISBURSEMENT OF LOANS INCLUDING CHANGES IN TERMS AND CONDITIONS

Lenders should ensure timely disbursement of loans sanctioned in conformity with the terms and conditions governing such sanction. Lenders should give notice of any change in the terms and conditions including interest rates, service charges, etc. Lenders should also ensure that changes in interest rates and charges are effective only prospectively.

18.6 POST DISBURSEMENT SUPERVISION

Post Disbursement Supervision by lenders, particularly in respect of loans up to Rs. 2 lakh, should be constructive with a view to taking care of any 'lender related' genuine difficulty that the borrower may face.

Before taking a decision to recall/accelerate payment or performance under the agreement or seeking additional securities, lenders should give notice to borrowers, as specified in the loan agreement.

Lenders should release all securities on receiving payment of loan or realization of loan subject to any legitimate right or lien for any other claim lenders may have against borrowers. If a right of set off is to be exercised, borrowers shall be given notice about the same with full particulars about the remaining claims and the documents under which lenders are entitled to retain the securities till the relevant claim is settled/paid.

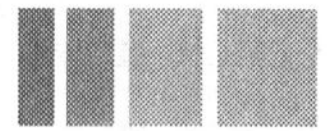

18.7 GENERAL

1. Lenders should restrain from interference in the affairs of the borrowers except for what is provided in the terms and conditions of the loan sanction documents.
2. Lenders must not discriminate on the grounds of gender, caste, region, language and religion in the matter of lending.
3. In the matter of recovery of loans, the lenders should not resort to undue harassment that is, persistently bothering at odd hours, or use of physical strength for recovery of loans, etc.
4. In case of receipt of request for transfer of a loan account, either from the borrower or from a bank/financial institution, which proposes to take over the account, the consent or otherwise, *i.e.*, objection of the lender, if any, should be conveyed within 21 days from the date of receipt of request.
5. Apart from the fair practices code, every lender/bank have laid down appropriate grievance redressal mechanism within the organization to resolve disputes arising in this regard. Such a mechanism ensures all disputes arising out of the decision of functionaries of lending institutions are heard and disposed off at least at the next higher level.

18.8 LET US SUM UP

The Reserve Bank of India, in consultation with Government of India and some banks and financial institutions finalized a set of codes called "the Fair Practices Code for Lenders" and advised banks to adopt the guidelines individually.

These fair practices are applicable for lenders for loan application, its processing and appraisal of loans. These are guidelines which all lending companies follow to remain compliant with the regulatory board. Lenders should ensure timely disbursement of loans sanctioned in conformity with the terms and conditions governing such sanction.

Lenders should restrain from interference in the affairs of the borrowers except for what is provided in the terms and conditions of the loan sanction documents.

Lenders should release all securities on receiving payment of loan or realization of loan subject to any legitimate right or lien for any other claim lenders may have against borrowers.

In the matter of recovery of loans, the lenders should not resort to undue harassment that is, persistently bothering at odd hours, or use of physical strength for recovery of loans, etc.

Apart from the above, lenders should (*a*) ensure timely disbursement of loans sanctioned; (*b*) should give notice of any change in the terms and conditions including interest rates, service charges, etc., (*c*) should also ensure that changes in interest rates and charges are effective only prospectively.

18.9 KEY WORDS

Loan appraisal, releasing securities, honouring cheques, loan disbursement, appraisal of loans

18.10 CHECK YOUR PROGRESS

1. In case of a 'wilful defaulter', the recovery agent should:
   (*a*) Collect the documentary evidence to prove the debtor's negative responses to his collection efforts
   (*b*) Preserve the documentary evidence
   (*c*) Collect and send the documentary evidence to the principal
   (*d*) Collect, preserve and send copies of the documentary evidence to the principal for further action.

18.11 ANSWER TO CHECK YOUR PROGRESS

1.	(*d*)												

MODULE D Additional Reading on NBFCs

CHAPTER 19 Non-Banking Financial Companies (NBFCs)

19.1 LEARNING OBJECTIVES

- About NBFCs
- Types of NBFCs
- Loan companies
- Broking companies
- Housing finance companies
- Functions of a loan company

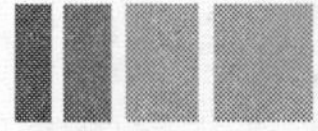

19.2 INTRODUCTION: WHAT IS AN NBFC?

A Company that carries the business of a financial institution and is not a bank is called a Non-Banking Financial Corporation or NBFC. Non-Bank Finance Companies (NBFCs) could be in the form of government/public/private limited companies. Government companies in India are known as All India Financial Institutions and State Level Financial Institutions. NBFCs are engaged in providing credit in the form of loans and advances or investments to several sectors ranging from infrastructure to financially excluded population of the economy. Non-Banking Financial Companies are registered as companies under the Companies Act, 2013.

Based on registration with the regulator and financial focus there are a variety of NBFCs. But primarily NBFCs could be engaged in the business of

i. Loans and advances,

ii. Investment i.e., acquisition of shares/stocks/bonds/debentures/securities issued by Government or local authority or other marketable securities of a like nature, *iii.* Leasing, Hire-purchase,

iv. Insurance business,

v. Chit-fund business

Historically, NBFCs started in the early 60's as an alternative institution for savers and investors whose financial needs were not met or not fully met by banks. Banks, being conservative were also difficult to reach.

The NBFCs initially operated on a limited scale without making much impact on the financial industry. They accepted fixed deposits from investors and issued loans and worked out leasing deals for big industrial firms. In the initial stages there was no formal regulation. In recent years many NBFCs have been formed. However, the spate of new NBFCs and other complexities brought the NBFCs under RBI and other regulators. Initially RBI started regulating deposit-taking NBFCs, and later initiated measures to regulate the entire NBFC sector. In the meantime, due to aggressive marketing and ease of access, NBFCs attracted a huge number of investors.

In January 1997 there were huge changes in the RBI Act, 1934, especially the Chapters III-B, III-C, and V of the Act seeking to put in place a complete regulatory and supervisory structure, which would protect the interests and ensure the smooth functioning of NBFCs. By mid-90's NBFCs had grown significantly in terms of operations, range of products and instruments and have also started using technological solutions in their operations. Currently there are many types of NBFCs, the latest being Fintech-NBFCs who are using technological solutions and innovative credit appraisal methods to finance Micro, Small & Medium Enterprise, and other activities.

The growth and development of NBFCs have led to the classification of NBFCs based on various sectors or classes. The classification is based on

(I) Based on Liabilities

(II) Based on Activities

Based on Liabilities, they can be classified into

- **Deposit taking Non-Banking Financial Company (NBFC-D)**
- **Non Deposit taking Non-Banking Financial Company (NBFC-ND)**

Additionally, Non Deposit taking Non- Banking Financial Company (NBFC-ND) can be sub-categorised into-

- **Systematically Important NBFC-ND**
- **Other NBFC-ND**

Based on Business Activities, the NBFCs can be further classified as follows:

i. **Investment and Credit Company (NBFC-ICC)** whose main business will be lending and investment. Under this category, RBI has merged three different categories of NBFCs- asset finance, loan companies, and investment companies into one named "NBFC – Investment and Credit Company (NBFC-ICC)". An Asset Finance Company is a type of financial institution which is involved in the financing of physical assets which supports productive/economic activity like automobiles, tractors, lathe machines, generator sets, earthmoving, material handling equipment, and industrial machines. An Investment Company is a type of company which is involved in carrying out its principal business of the acquisition of securities. A loan company is a type of financial institution which carries its principal business of providing finance in the form of loans or advances other than its own. All the above three types are categorised as NBFC – Investment and Credit Company (NBFC-ICC).

ii. **Infrastructure Finance Company (NBFC-IFC)** whose main business will be financing infrastructure projects/sector. Infrastructure loans are extended to borrowers for exposure in the infrastructure categories like transport, energy, water & sanitation, communication and social & commercial infrastructure which are further divided into further sub-categories.

iii. **Investment Company (Core Investment) (NBFC-CIC)** whose activities will be investment in shares, debt, or lending to group companies. These businesses primarily invest in their own group firms' shares for stake holding. However, they are not permitted to trade these instruments or engage in any other type of financial activity.

iv. **Infrastructure Debt Fund (NBFC-IDF)** involved in arranging long term debt for infrastructure projects which are operational. IDFs are investment vehicles for channelizing investment into the infrastructure sector. They are sponsored by commercial banks in which domestic/offshore institutional investors, specially insurance and pension funds can invest through units and bonds issued by the IDFs.

v. **Microfinance Companies (NBFC-MFI)** for financing small ticket loans (repayable on weekly, fortnightly, or monthly installments) to groups and under microfinance methodology. A microfinance loan is defined as a collateral-free loan given to a household having annual household income up to □3,00,000. For this purpose, the household shall mean an individual family unit, i.e., husband, wife and their unmarried children.

vi. **Non-Operative Financial Holding companies (NBFC-NOFHC)** are companies which facilitate promoters/promoter groups in setting up new banks.This is a non-deposit taking NBFC which holds the shares of a banking company and the shares of all other financial services companies in its group, whether regulated by Reserve Bank or by any other financial regulator, to the extent permissible under the applicable regulatory prescriptions.

vii. **Factoring Companies (NBFC Factor)** engaged in acquisition of receivables of an assignor or extending loans against the security interest of the receivables at a discount. The Factoring Regulation Act, 2011 defines the 'Factoring Business' as "the Business of acquisition of receivables of assignor by accepting assignment of such receivables or financing, whether by way of making loans or advances or in any other manner against the security interest over any receivables". Those NBFCs whose financial assets in the factoring business constitute at least 75 percent of its total assets will be categorised as NBFC Factor.

viii. **Mortgage Guarantee Companies (NBFC-MGC)** undertake mortgage guarantee business. These companies undertake the business of repayment of outstanding housing loan and interest accrued thereon up to the guaranteed amount to the creditor institution, on the occurrence of a trigger event. A trigger event means classification of the account of a borrower as non-performing asset in the books of the creditor institution.

ix. **Account Aggregator Companies (NBFC-AA)** involved in Collecting and providing information about a customer's financial assets in a consolidated, organized, and retrievable manner to the customer or others as specified by the customer. An Account Aggregator (AA) helps an individual securely and digitally access and share information from one financial institution they have an account with to any other regulated financial institution in the AA network. Data cannot be shared without the consent of the individual. There will be many Account Aggregators an individual can choose between.

x. **Housing Finance Companies (NBFC-HFC)** extending home loans, including affordable housing finance. Primarily, the HFCs are engaged in the business activity of providing loans or finance for housing purposes through direct or indirect means. Earlier regulated by National Housing Bank (NHB), HFCs' regulation was transferred to the Reserve Bank of India (RBI) in 2019 through amending the statutes by the government. However, a few of their regulatory powers are still with NHB.

xi. **NBFC–Peer to Peer Lending Platform (NBFC-P2P)** who provide an online platform to bring lenders and borrowers together to help mobilize funds. Peer to Peer lending (P2P lending) is one of the methods of obtaining finances for business. P2P functions as an online platform offering ease of access, flexibility and choice of lending and borrowing for lenders and borrowers. P2P model aggregates lenders and borrowers, facilitates the matching of lenders with borrowers. Lenders can get earn interest higher than from bank savings, while the borrowers can obtain funds at competitive and easier terms.

xii. **Residuary Non-Banking Company (RBNC):** A residuary Non-Banking Company is an NBFC which whose main business is receiving of deposits. It could be under any scheme. A RNBC must maintain liquid assets and investments as per directions of RBI. Prudential Norms are applicable to these companies. Deposits can be received either in lump sum or in instalments by way of contributions or subscriptions or by sale of units or certificates or other instruments, or in any other manner. The functioning of RBNCs is different from NBFCs in terms of method of mobilisation of deposits and requirement of deployment of depositors funds as per directions.

Further there could be some NBFCs which are involved in Merchant banking, Venture Capital funding, Stock Broking and involved in collective investment schemes. These are regulated by SEBI. Insurance companies are regulated by IRDAI; Chit Fund companies by the respective State Governments and Nidhi companies are regulated by Ministry of Company Affairs. PDs, regulated by RBI, ensure subscription to primary issuances of government securities (G-secs), besides acting as market makers in the G-sec market.

19.3 FRAMEWORK FOR SCALE BASED REGULATION FOR NON-BANKING FINANCIAL COMPANIES

RBI has issued Scale Based Regulation (SBR)-A revised regulatory framework for NBFCs *vide* Circular No. RBI/2021-22/112 DOR.CRE.REC. No.60/03.10.001/2021-22 dated October 22, 2021. The NBFC sector has undergone major growth in terms of size, complexity, and interconnectedness within the financial sector due to which a need was felt to align the regulatory framework for NBFCs keeping in view their changing risk profile.

Regulatory structure for NBFCs shall comprise of four layers based on their size, activity, and perceived riskiness:

1. **NBFC - Base Layer (NBFC-BL)**: NBFCs in the lowest layer known as NBFC - Base Layer (NBFC-BL) shall comprise of:
   (*a*) non-deposit taking NBFCs below the asset size of Rs. 1,000 crore and
   (*b*) NBFCs undertaking the following activities-
      (*i*) NBFC-Peer to Peer Lending Platform (NBFC-P2P),
      (*ii*) NBFC-Account Aggregator (NBFC-AA),
      (*iii*) Non-Operative Financial Holding Company (NOFHC) and
      (*iv*) NBFCs not availing public funds and not having any customer interface
2. **NBFC - Middle Layer (NBFC-ML)**: NBFCs in middle layer known as NBFC - Middle Layer (NBFC-ML) shall consist of:
   (*a*) all deposit taking NBFCs (NBFC-Ds), irrespective of asset size,
   (*b*) non-deposit taking NBFCs with asset size of Rs. 1,000 crore and above and
   (*c*) NBFCs undertaking the following activities:
      (*i*) Standalone Primary Dealers (SPDs),

(*ii*) Infrastructure Debt Fund - Non-Banking Financial Companies (IDF-NBFCs),

(*iii*) Core Investment Companies (CICs),

(*iv*) Housing Finance Companies (HFCs) and

(*v*) Infrastructure Finance Companies (NBFC-IFCs).

In line with the existing policy on consolidation of assets of the NBFCs in a Group, the total assets of all the NBFCs in a Group shall be consolidated to determine the threshold for their classification in the Middle Layer. If the consolidated asset size of the Group is Rs. 1,000 crore and above, then each Investment and Credit Company (NBFC-ICC), Micro Finance Institution (NBFC-MFI), NBFC-Factor and Mortgage Guarantee Company (NBFC-MGC) lying in the Group shall be classified as an NBFC in the Middle Layer and consequently, regulations as applicable to the Middle Layer shall be applicable to them.

3. **NBFC - Upper Layer (NBFC-UL)**: NBFCs in upper layer known as NBFC - Upper Layer (NBFC-UL) shall comprise of those NBFCs which are specifically identified by the Reserve Bank as warranting enhanced regulatory requirement based on a set of parameters and scoring methodology. The top ten eligible NBFCs in terms of their asset size shall always reside in the upper layer, irrespective of any other factor.

4. **NBFC - Top Layer (NBFC-TL):** The Top Layer will ideally remain empty. This layer can get populated if the Reserve Bank is of the opinion that there is a substantial increase in the potential systemic risk from specific NBFCs in the Upper Layer. Such NBFCs shall move to the Top Layer from the Upper Layer.

   As the regulatory structure envisages scale based as well as activity-based regulation, the following prescriptions shall apply in respect of the NBFCs:

   a. NBFC-P2P, NBFC-AA, NOFHC and NBFCs without public funds and customer interface will always remain in the Base Layer of the regulatory structure.

   b. NBFC-D, CIC, IFC and HFC will be included in Middle Layer or the Upper Layer (and not in the Base layer), as the case may be. SPD and IDF-NBFC will always remain in the Middle Layer.

   c. The remaining NBFCs, *viz.*, Investment and Credit Companies (NBFC-ICC), Micro Finance Institution (NBFC-MFI), NBFC-Factors and Mortgage Guarantee Companies (NBFC-MGC) could lie in any of the layers of the regulatory structure depending on the parameters of the scale based regulatory framework.

   d. Government owned NBFCs shall be placed in the Base Layer or Middle Layer, as the case may be. They will not be placed in the Upper Layer till further notice.

19.4 WHY NBFCs ARE REQUIRED?

With so many banks with huge volume of funds, a question arises as to why we need NBFCs. Obviously, banks are saddled with larger responsibilities and are also closely regulated. Banks may also find many small loans unviable and may not have the reach as well. There are areas and pockets of population where credit flow is urgently required and hence NBFCs could make an impact in the financial sector. NBFCs could also partner with banks and extend credit to hitherto excluded areas. Following points are worth noting:

- NBFC can contribute to the growth of sectors like infrastructures and transport.
- These institutions could help in augmenting employment potential across India.
- Non-banking financial institutions could render easy financial credit to the economically weaker sections of society.
- NBFCs are growing due to their facility to innovate and customize their products based on the needs of their clients.
- Non-NBFCs are possibly close to customer's place and have a detailed understanding of customers' profiles hence able to offer products suitable to customers.
- Though rate of interest and fees on loans is higher than that charged by banks, Non-Banking Financial companies offer flexible repayment schemes, extended loan tenure, and better service.
- NBFCs require loan seekers to submit minimal documentation as compared to the extensive paperwork required by banks. Applicants also have flexible eligibility criteria against banks that require loan seekers to fulfil stringent and uniform eligibility criteria.

NBFCs have therefore carved a niche in the finance sector. These alternative lenders also offer quick and efficient services to Micro Small and Medium Enterprise (MSMEs), the backbone of Indian economy. As Non-Banking Financial Companies have continuously played a critical role in encouraging the development of the Indian economy, this sector is expected to grow in the years to come.

Acceptance of Deposits by NBFCs

Only those NBFCs which are approved by RBI can accept deposits.

An NBFC including a residuary NBFC (RNBFC) must be registered with the Reserve Bank of India (RBI) and should be specifically authorized to accept deposits from the public. In the case of these NBFCs the Certificate of Registration or a certified copy should be displayed at the Registered office and other offices/branches.

Registration of an NBFC with the RBI is just an authorization to conduct the business of NBFC and is not a guarantee for the repayment of deposits accepted by

NBFCs. NBFCs cannot use the name of the RBI in any manner while conducting their business.

NBFCs which accept deposits should have minimum investment grade credit rating (BBB or above) granted by an approved credit rating agency.

Regarding deposits, NBFCs excluding Residuary Non-Bank Company (RNBC):-

i. Cannot offer a rate of interest on deposits more than that approved by RBI from time to time.

ii. Cannot accept deposit for a period less than 12 months and more than 60 months.

iii. Cannot offer any gifts/incentives to solicit deposits from public.

RNBCs should offer a rate of interest of not less than 5% per annum on term deposits and 3.5% on daily deposits, both compounded annually.

RNBCs cannot accept deposits for a period less than 12 months and more than 84 months.

RNBCs cannot offer any gifts/incentives to solicit deposits from public.

NBFCs including RNBCs can:-

- Accept deposit only against issue of proper receipt.
- The receipt should bear the name of the company and should be signed by an authorized official of the company.
- The receipt should mention the name of the depositor, the amount in words as well as figures, the rate of interest payable on the deposit amount and the date of repayment of matured deposit along with the maturity amount.

In the case of brokers/agents etc. collecting public deposits on behalf of NBFCs there should be verifiable mechanism to ensure that the brokers/agents are duly authorized by the NBFC.

If a deposit taking NBFC fails to repay the deposit or the interest accrued thereon in accordance with the terms and conditions of acceptance of such deposit, redressal of grievance can be through the Regional Bench of the Company Law Board at Chennai/Delhi/Kolkata/Mumbai.

RBI has issued detailed regulations to NBFCs on deposit acceptance. This indicates the quantum of deposits that can be collected, that NBFC should be credit rated, should maintain liquid assets as per norms, etc. NBFCs have also been advised about the way its deposit accounts/books should be maintained. Prudential regulations such as maintenance of adequate capital, limitations on exposures have been issued. NBFCs are also subject to inspection by RBI. The focus of inspection is to verify whether NBFC is complying with RBI guidelines.

RBI will initiate prompt action, including imposing penalties and taking legal action against companies which are found to be violating its instructions/norms on basis of Market Intelligence reports, complaints, exception reports from statutory auditors of the companies, information received through SLCC meetings, etc.

To create awareness among the public on the need to be careful while investing their funds/money, RBI issues cautionary notices in print media. It also publishes informative and educative brochures/pamphlets about NBFCs.

19.5 DISTINGUISHING FEATURES OF AN NBFC

To be an NBFC, a financial company must fulfil the criteria that:

(*a*) Companies' financial assets should constitute more than 50 per cent of the total assets (netted off by intangible assets) and

(*b*) Income from financial assets should be more than 50 per cent of the gross income.

Though NBFCs issue loans and invest funds but they are not banks. They are distinct from banks because:

a. They cannot accept demand deposits.

b. They are not part of the payment and settlement system and cannot issue cheques drawn on self.

c. They cannot issue debit cards.

d. Deposit insurance cover of Deposit Insurance and Credit Guarantee Corporation is not available to depositors of NBFCs

19.6 FUNCTIONS OF A LOAN COMPANY

Loan is an agreement wherein the lender funds to the borrower with a condition that the borrower will return it along with the interest as per the terms and conditions as agreed upon. NBFCs offer several kinds of loans such as -term loan, secured loan, unsecured loan, industrial loan, commercial loan, etc. NBFCs are not allowed to lend for agriculture possibly because the rate of interest is high and collection through DRAs not permitted in the case of agricultural loans. NBFCs cannot give working capital loan except in the form of term loan repayable on an EMI basis.

NBFC is a finance company - not a bank- that lends money to individuals and businesses. The revenue source for these companies is interest on the loan amount and other charges (fee) for loan processing, appraisal, etc. Normally the loans are issued to individuals but some NBFCs issue loans for businesses as well. These companies borrow money from banks and other sources and lend it to their customers.

The interest rate at which they borrow is lower than the rate at which they lend. This is the reason the interest rates charged by finance companies are higher than banks. Generally, proponents and individuals seek funds from finance companies when they do not qualify for bank loans. Also, NBFCs are quicker in taking credit decisions. Finance companies offer both unsecured and secured loans to individuals and companies.

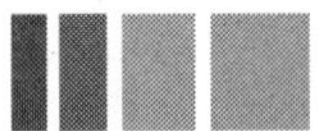

19.7 TYPES OF LOANS

Unsecured Loans

Unsecured loan could be a loan to meet a borrower's immediate financial needs for personal purposes such as house renovation, wedding, medical emergency, or vacation. Personal loans are generally unsecured loans *i.e.*, loans without any collateral. In this regard it should be observed that whereas banks extend such loans only to persons who have a good credit score or history and meet other eligibility criteria, finance companies could offer personal loans to people with poor credit history but at a higher rate of interest. It is expected that the additional rate of interest will take care of the possible defaults. However, to ensure that defaults are lower if not NIL, NBFCs have well organized collection system and employ collection agents.

Secured Loans

A loan for which collateral is demanded is a secured loan. If such loan is not repaid, then the company can sell the collateral and recover its dues. Collateral is in addition to primary security.

Primary security is the asset created out of the credit facility extended to the borrower and/or which are directly associated with the business/project of the borrower for which the credit facility has been extended. Collateral security is any other security offered for the said credit facility. In the case of vehicle loans, the loan is secured because the vehicle is hypothecated to the lender. In this case the vehicle is a primary security though in common parlance it is referred to as collateral. If the borrower does not repay the loan, the lender takes possession of the vehicle. NBFCs prefer to offer secured loans to people because they present much lower risks than unsecured personal loans. If the borrower does not repay the money as per the agreed terms, the finance company can seize the collateral and sell it in open market.

NBFCs do look at credit score while offering both unsecured and secured loans. The rate of interest may be higher if the credit score is lesser than the threshold or could vary as per the range of acceptable credit score.

Business Loans

NBFCs extend loans to meet the gaps in funds of businesses. This could be for meeting working capital requirement (on a term loan basis) or purchase of assets for business or meeting some emergency requirements such as repairs to machinery, etc. These loans are similar to term loans offered by banks. NBFCs cannot sanction cash credit even if the borrowed funds are used for working capital. NBFCs issue business loans to MSME units as well.

There are specialized NBFCs which offer factoring services to businesses.

Other loans offered by NBFCs and the type of security are:–

i. Retail loans to customers for purchasing consumer articles like a refrigerator, TV, Laptop, etc. which are also called **consumer loans** or **consumer durable loans**. These loans are normally arranged in collaboration with companies selling these products. The articles are hypothecated to the NBFC.

ii. Vehicle loans for purchase of two wheelers and cars and also tractors, etc., for own use of the customer (when salary or other income is sufficient to meet the repayment requirement) and for being used for hire-lease or transport business. These loans are offered with or without tie-up with vehicle manufacturing companies. NBFCs ask for hypothecation of the vehicle and registering the charge with the RTO.

iii. Jewellery or gold loans subject to LTV norms as indicated by the regulator. These loans could be for personal use or business use. The gold ornaments are pledged with the NBFC.

iv. Loans against property, insurance policies, fixed deposits, shares, etc. These loans are sanctioned against a percentage of the value of property or percentage of the surrender value of the insurance policy or a percentage of the face value or cumulative maturity value of the deposit or a percentage of the market value of the share respectively. In these cases, the securities are pledged with the NBFC. In the case of shares, NBFC will get it transferred in its name. All securities will be returned once the loan is fully repaid.

v. NBFCs sanction home loans for purchase of land or house, construction or renovation of houses, repair of houses, etc. Some of the NBFCs offer to take over existing loan with other financiers/banks. There are NBFCs which are specialized housing finance companies for financing affordable housing. These are regulated by National Housing Bank and RBI.

vi. Some specialized NBFCs sanction education loans also.

These loans can be issued to individuals or sole proprietors and also other business entities like companies, partnerships, LLP, etc. Generally, the appraisal by NBFCs is quicker and disbursements are faster. NBFCs appraise bigger loans in the traditional manner *i.e.*, through audited financial statements and transaction record and volumes. NBFCs use technology to appraise the loans quickly and without many visits to the place of business to the applicant's place. Applications are accepted on-line and borrowing limits are communicated quickly. Once the terms are accepted documentation takes place.

Interest charged by NBFC on loans could be somewhat higher. As retail loans are given in tie-up with manufacturers, NBFCs offer cashback to reduce the impact of the rate of interest.

In most of the loans NBFCs stipulate equated monthly instalment (EMI) plans to repay the loans. This is because customers for retail loans mostly come from salaried class. Businesses (MSME etc.,) have regular cash flows and paying EMI should not be difficult unless the EMI amount is a very high percentage of borrowers' income. In order to arrive at reasonable EMI, NBFCs appraise the loan limits based on salary slips, bank account statements, GST statements, POS transaction details (retail shops), etc. This appraisal is fast and makes use of available and relevant data. Customers can choose an appropriate EMI plan based on his/her monthly earnings and available disposable income.

NBFCs can offer loans to persons who invest in shares and stock. They also finance persons who are interested in investing in IPOs and take advantage of listing price v. IPO price.

The rate of interest on loans could vary based on purpose, amount of credit, credit score and other details.

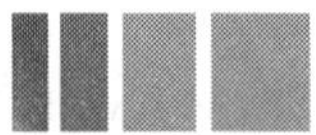

19.8 LET US SUM UP

NBFCs carry on the business of a financial institution and are not banks. NBFC could be in the form of government/public/private limited companies. NBFCs are engaged in different kind of businesses.

NBFCs can be classified into two broad categories namely- NBFCs accepting public deposit (NBFCs-D) and NBFCs not accepting/holding public deposit (NBFCs-ND). Based on size and volume of business, NBFCs are also declared systemically important. NBFCs whose asset size is of Rs. 500 crore or more are considered as systemically important NBFCs.

NBFCs contribute to growth of sectors like infrastructure and transport, could render easy financial credit to the economically weaker sections of society, and offer loans as per the needs of the customers and sanction loans with minimal documentation. To be an NBFC its financial assets should constitute more than 50 per cent of the total assets and income from financial assets should be more than 50 per cent of the gross income.

19.9 KEY WORDS

NBFCs - leasing, hiring, chit business, systematically important, financial assets, impact, secured loan, unsecured loans, business loans

19.10 CHECK YOUR PROGRESS

1. NBFCs can be divided into following categories:
   (*a*) NBFCs accepting public deposit (NBFCs-D) and
   (*b*) NBFCs not accepting/holding public deposit (NBFCs-ND)
   (*c*) Both (*a*) and (*b*)
   (*d*) None of the above
2. NBFC can be divided as a:
   (*a*) Loan company
   (*b*) Investment company
   (*c*) Asset finance company
   (*d*) All of the above
3. NBFC offer the following functions:
   (*a*) Reject loans and advances
   (*b*) Do not innovate customize products
   (*c*) Lend to Micro Small and Medium enterprises
   (*d*) None of the above
4. NBFCs have certain restrictions from Banks, they:
   (*a*) Cannot accept deposits
   (*b*) They are not a part of payment and settlement system
   (*c*) They do not have a central regulatory authority
   (*d*) All of the above
5. Investment Company (IC): IC is a financial institution carrying on as its principal business investments in or the acquisition of securities:
   (*a*) True
   (*b*) False
6. Which kind of needs can an Unsecured loan meet?
   (*a*) Loan for collateral security
   (*b*) Immediate personal needs of the customer
   (*c*) Vehicle purchase
   (*d*) None of the above

7. Business loans are required for which purpose?
   (*a*) To meet the gaps in funds
   (*b*) Working capital requirement
   (*c*) Purchase of assets
   (*d*) All of the above
8. Which are the other loans NBFCs offer to customers?
   (*a*) Refrigerator
   (*b*) TV
   (*c*) Laptop
   (*d*) All of the above
9. What is the criteria to become an NBFC?
   (*a*) company's financial assets should constitute more than 50 per cent of the total assets
   (*b*) income from financial assets should be more than 50 per cent of the gross income:
   (*c*) Both (*a*) and (*b*)
   (*d*) None of the above

19.11 ANSWERS TO CHECK YOUR PROGRESS

1.	(*c*)	2.	(*d*)	3.	(*c*)	4.	(*b*)	5.	(*a*)	6.	(*b*)	7.	(*d*)
8.	(*d*)	9.	(*c*)										

CHAPTER

20 Fair Practices Code (FPC) for NBFCs

20.1 LEARNING OBJECTIVES/CONTENT

1. Fair Practice Code of NBFCs
2. Compliance to guidelines on FPC
3. Details that must be shared with the proponent/borrower in the case of various loans
4. Collection function and FPC

At the end of this lesson the agent will have a clear understanding of Fair Practice Code, policies behind it and how it is implemented and monitored and also the need to adhere to the codes.

20.2 INTRODUCTION

Customer service by regulated institutions is closely monitored by the regulator. Customer complaints are pursued to find if the NBFC has indulged in unfair practices and if it has rendered correct service irrespective of the size, purpose, and the type of client. Customers complain about price, product, etc. One of the important areas of complaint is pressure or harassment at the time of collection. Fair Practice code aims to render transparent and fair customer service and, in the process, avoid customer complaints.

What is Fair Practices Code and what is their purpose?

Fair Practices Codes are regulatory and board guidelines on practices to be used in companies while dealing with customers.

The main purpose of using Fair Practices Code is to ensure that lenders/NBFCs adopt fair practices while dealing with the customer. The objective is to ensure customer satisfaction by setting good standards and achieving them. For this purpose, companies follow methods of operations that are transparent, fair, ethical, legal and justifiable. It is also important that business-related information should be shared to the public which is in their interest. Following FPCs will help promote mutually beneficial long-term relationship. Needless to add that companies should avoid adopting unfair practices.

Fair Practices Code:

Fair practices code is built around the following processes:

1. Receipt and scrutiny of application,
2. Appraisal of the loan proposal and the applicant and security offered if any,
3. Arriving at terms and conditions of credit
4. Sanction, execution of documents and disbursement of loan
5. Monitoring of credit during the loan period
6. Receipt of repayment and or collection and closure of loans.

Responsibilities of Recovery Agents

NBFCs shall ensure that the DSA/DMA/Recovery Agents are properly trained to handle their responsibilities with care and sensitivity, particularly aspects such as soliciting customers, hours of calling, privacy of customer information and conveying the correct terms and conditions of the products on offer, etc.

NBFCs shall put in place a board approved Code of conduct for DSA/DMA/Recovery Agents, and obtain their undertaking to abide by the code. In addition, Recovery Agents shall adhere to extant instructions on Fair Practices Code for NBFCs as also their own code for collection of dues and repossession of security. It is essential that the Recovery Agents refrain from action that could damage the integrity and reputation of the NBFC and that they observe strict customer confidentiality.

The NBFC and their agents shall not resort to intimidation or harassment of any kind, either verbal or physical, against any person in their debt collection efforts, including acts intended to humiliate publicly or intrude the privacy of the debtors' family members, referees and friends, making threatening and anonymous calls or making false and misleading representations.

20.3 APPLICATIONS FOR LOANS AND THEIR PROCESSING

Dealings of the lender/company with the customer in all the above processes should be transparent and clear. All communication to the customers should be in the vernacular language or in the language understood by the customer.

Documents required to be submitted by the customer should be listed or detailed in the application form. All documents, unless a requirement arises on account of some information submitted, should be asked for at the time of application.

NBFCs should acknowledge receipt of the application. It would be appropriate if the time taken for sanction/disposal of the application is indicated while accepting the application. Applicant should be informed about the process and the need for submitting correct and detailed information which will help the bank adhere to the time schedule.

Before application customer should be made aware of general terms and conditions of the loan with all relevant information affecting the interest of the customer. All information about loan should be given to the customer enabling him to understand the same and to make a meaningful comparison with the terms and conditions of other NBFCs. The details in the information brochure on loans should be such that the customer can take an informed decision.

Visit to the applicant's office or residence for the purpose of appraisal should be pre announced and done professionally. If the NBFC desires references, the customer should be asked for the same, instead of making enquiries without customer's knowledge.

20.4 LOAN SANCTION TERMS/CONDITIONS

The NBFC should convey in writing all the terms of sanction including the (*i*) amount of loan sanctioned (*ii*) annualized rate of interest including how it is calculated and applied. This communication should be, preferably in the vernacular language as understood by the customer. Proponent should be asked to read and understand the terms fully and then asked to sign the duplicate of the sanctioned letter as having accepted the terms of sanction and the same should be held on record by the NBFC. Issues such as penal interest, loans past due date and others may be included in the sanction letter or specifically indicated to the proponent. It is a matter of record that there are many complaints against NBFCs more particularly on charging higher rate of interest/penal interest, NBFCs shall mention the penal interest charged for late repayment in bold letters in the loan agreement.

NBFCs should furnish a copy of the loan agreement preferably in the vernacular language as understood by the customer. NBFC should also share all relevant information quoted in the loan agreement in the form of enclosures at the time of sanction/disbursement of loans.

Interest Rates charged by NBFCs

As per Notification No. DNBS. 204/CGM (ASR)-2009 dated January 2, 2009 RBI has issued directions to NBFCs regarding interest rate to be charged to borrowers. The key points are as follows:

(*a*) The Board of each NBFC shall adopt an interest rate model taking into account relevant factors such as, cost of funds, margin and risk premium, etc and determine the rate of interest to be charged for loans and advances. The rate of interest and the approach for gradations of risk and rationale for charging different rate of interest to different categories of borrowers shall be disclosed to the borrower or customer in the application form and communicated explicitly in the sanction letter.

(*b*) The rates of interest and the approach for gradation of risks shall also be made available on the web-site of the companies or published in the relevant newspapers. The information published in the website or otherwise published should be updated whenever there is a change in the rates of interest.

(*c*) The rate of interest should be annualised rates so that the borrower is aware of the exact rates that would be charged to the account.

The rates of interest being charged by the NBFCs beyond a certain level may be excessive and can neither be sustainable nor be conforming to normal financial practice. Boards of NBFCs have been advised to lay out appropriate internal principles and procedures in determining interest rates and processing and other charges.

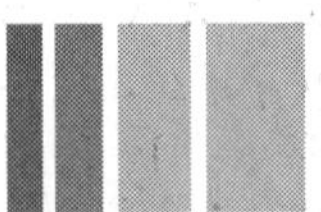

20.5 DISBURSEMENT OF LOANS INCLUDING CHANGES IN TERMS AND CONDITIONS

Disbursement should be as per sanction and timely. After sanctioning the loan and completing the document delaying disbursement is not a fair practice. Except where the loan envisages disbursement in instalments, loan should be disbursed in one go. Wherever disbursement is to be made to the seller of machinery to be purchased it should be informed to the customer.

NBFC should give adequate notice to the customer of change in terms of sanction more particularly interest rates, disbursement schedules, service charges, prepayment charges, etc.

It should be ensured that changes, if any in interest rates and other charges are implemented prospectively and never with retrospective effect. It is important that suitable conditions in this regard are incorporated in the loan agreement. Any decision or change in the repayment period or instalment or accelerated repayment or recall of the advance ahead of time or on default should be in consonance with the loan agreement.

Once the loan is repaid in full or when the dues are paid, NBFCs should release all securities subject to any legitimate right or lien for any other claim it may have against the customer. If the NBFC wants to exercise the right of set-off, it must give a notice to the customer about the same with full particulars about the remaining claim and the conditions under which the NBFC is entitled to retain the securities till the relevant claim is settled.

NBFCs must refrain from interference in the affairs of the customer except for those included in the terms of sanction.

Further if the customer requests for transfer of his/its account to other lenders (NBFCs or banks) the consent or refusal of the same should be conveyed within 21 days from the date of receipt of the request.

Collection or recovery should be done following normal practices and NBFCs should not resort to any undue harassment or muscle power for recovery of loans etc. Staff members of the NBFCs and DRAs should be adequately trained for this purpose and should not bother the customer at odd hours *i.e.*, other than hours permitted as per NBFC's code of conduct. DRA and staff should not be rude to the customers.

Board of Directors of NBFCs should lay down the appropriate grievance redressal mechanism within the organization to resolve disputes arising with reference to the dealing with customers/defaulters. NBFC must ensure that all disputes are heard and disposed of at least one level above the level at which the dispute has occurred. The Board of Directors should also ensure that these issues *i.e.*, having a grievance procedure and follow-up of complaints, their redressal is reviewed periodically and whether company follows Fair Practices Code. NBFC must ensure that the grievances redressal mechanism at various levels of management is functioning efficiently and with correct outcome.

Fair Practices Code (in the local vernacular and English) should be displayed or put in place by the NBFCs. Companies may add other fair practices based on its experience and need.

Considering complaints from the customers of NBFCs regarding charging of excessive interest and other fees and charges by them, RBI has advised Boards of NBFCs to layout appropriate internal principles and procedures for determining interest rates and levy of processing fee and other charges. NBFC may have to arrive at the interest for various products and terms considering cost of funds, margin, risk premium etc. The rates of interest and the approach for gradation of risks should be shared transparently in the website of the NBFC. Rates of interest should be charged on an annualized basis so that the customer is aware of the exact rate of interest charged to the account.

It is likely that NBFC may have to repossess certain assets like vehicles financed by it. In view of this, the agreement should contain a repossession clause in the contract/loan agreement with the customer. The repossession clause should consider existing law on the subject and must be legally enforceable. NBFC should transparently share details such as, circumstances when repossession will be done, the extent of notice period before taking possession, circumstances under which the notice period can be waived, and procedure for taking possession of the security. NBFC may also indicate the method of giving a final chance to the customer for repayment of the loan before sale/auction of the security along with, procedure for giving repossession to the customer. The procedure for sale/auction of the security must be made available to the customer.

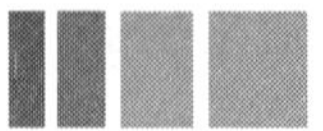

20.6 NBFC-MICRO FINANCE INSTITUTIONS

In addition to the general principles as above, NBFC-Micro Finance Institutions (MFIs) shall adopt the following fair practices that are specific to their lending business and regulatory framework.

20.6.1 General Fair Practices - NBFC-MFI

(*a*) NBFC-MFI shall formally declare its commitment to FPC which shall be displayed in local vernacular language in all the premises of MFI

(*b*) NBFC-MFI loans are given to the poor and needy. It is likely that NBFC-MFI customers might have taken loans from other NBFC-MFI or informal sources. Field staff should make necessary enquiries about existing debt of the customers and arrive at credit decisions as per company's rules. NBFC-MFI must train the staff for this purpose.

(*c*) Customers of NBFC-MFI may require knowledge and skills in use of credit and other financial services. MFI shall arrange for financial literacy and related training of its customers. Training should be free of cost.

(*d*) Details about the effective rate of interest charged by the NBFC-MFI and the grievance redressal system should be prominently displayed in its local vernacular in its offices and in the website. Website may cater to the need of all languages.

(*e*) The loan agreement shall contain a clause that the MFI will prevent inappropriate behaviour of staff and timely redressal of grievances. That MFI is accountable for any lapses in this regard made in the loan agreement and in the FPC displayed in the office or branch premises.

(*f*) NBFC-MFI should follow KYC guidelines for identifying its customers. It shall carry out due diligence to ensure the repayment capacity of the customer.

(*g*) It must be ensured that the application form and procedure of application is not cumbersome.

(*h*) Complete sanctioning and disbursement of loan should be done at a central location convenient for the customers. Generally, several people will assemble at such centers. Yet it must be ensured that more than one individual should be involved in the function. NBFC -MFI should have appropriate systems for supervision of the disbursement functions.

20.6.2 Disclosures in loan agreement/loan card of NBFC -MFI

NBFC should have a standard form of loan agreement in a vernacular language. In the loan agreement the following shall be disclosed:

- All the terms and conditions of the loan,
- Components of pricing will include only three components *viz.*, the interest charge, the processing charge, and the insurance premium,
- There will be no penalty charged on delayed payment,
- No security deposit/margin is being collected from the customer,
- Client cannot be a member of more than one SHG/ILG
- The moratorium between the grant of the loan and the due date of the repayment of the first instalment will be specified. This moratorium shall be as per RBI guidelines.
- Assurance that the privacy of the customer data will be respected.

The loan card should reflect the following details:

- The effective rate of interest charged
- Details of terms and conditions of the loan
- Information which adequately identifies the customer
- Acknowledgements by the NBFC-MFI of all repayments including instalments received and the final discharge.
- Non-credit products issued shall be with full consent of the customers and fee structure shall be communicated in the loan card itself.
- All entries in the loan card should be in vernacular language

The loan card should prominently mention the grievance redressal system set up by the MFI and the name and contact number of the nodal officer.

20.6.3 Non-Coercive Methods of Recovery

In the case of MFI's recovery should normally be made only at a central designated place. Field staff should make recovery at the place of residence or work of the customer only if the customer fails to appear at the central designated place on 2 or more successive occasions.

NBFC-MFIs shall adopt a code of conduct approved by the Board. It shall have a policy about the recruitment, training, and supervision of the field staff. In the case of MFI's employees make the collection or recovery and not the outsourced agents.

20.6.4 Internal control system

NBFC-MFIs should assign the responsibility for compliance to various regulations and guidelines to designated individuals within the company. The compliance official will also be responsible to establish systems of internal control including audit and periodic inspection and follow-up compliance thereof.

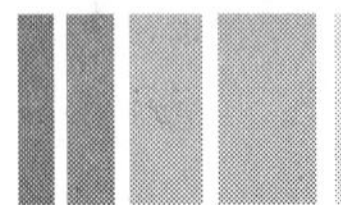

20.7 LENDING AGAINST COLLATERAL OF GOLD JEWELLERY

In the case of gold loans, NBFCs shall adopt the following points in addition to general guidelines indicated above:

- Proper assessing procedure for the jewellery pledged as security for loan.
- Internal systems to satisfy that ownership of the gold jewellery vests with the customer.
- NBFC should have appropriate and adequate storing place (safes/safe custody) and storing system for the jewellery. Loans against gold jewellery should not be extended by a branch that does not have adequate secure storage facility. This system must be reviewed periodically.
- NBFC should have a periodic inspection by the internal auditors to ensure that the gold/Jewel loan procedures are strictly adhered to.
- Jewellery accepted as collateral should be properly insured.
- NBFC may have to auction the jewellery in case the loan is defaulted and cannot be recovered. For such cases the NBFC should have:
    - A well calibrated policy for auction of jewellery. The policy must be transparent. Also, adequate prior notice must be given to the customer before the auction.
    - NBFC must ensure that there is no conflict of interest and the auction process is smooth.
    - It must be ensured that there is arm's length relationship in all transactions during the auction including with group companies and related entities.
    - Auction should be announced to the public by issue of advertisement in at least two newspapers, one in vernacular language and the other in a national daily newspaper.
    - As a rule, the NBFC or its staff shall not participate in the auction held.

- Gold pledged should be auctioned only through auctioneers approved by the Board.

- Loan agreement shall also disclose full details of auction procedure.

20.8 COMPLIANCE

NBFCs have been advised by the regulator to have internal compliance officials to ensure that it complies with all regulations and also that the Board reviews compliance in regular periodicity. Adherence to fair practices code, review and follow-up of customer grievances, etc., are among the duties of compliance officials. The result of grievance redressal gives an indicator about how serious the NBFC is about Fair Practices Code. If the grievances are found correct then it is necessary to review the adherence to and the implementation of Fair Practices Code.

20.9 LET US SUM UP

Fair Practice Code of financial institutions indicates the functioning of that industry in compliance with the guidelines of the Reserve Bank of India and they are not carrying out any activities which is prohibited/barred/forbidden by the RBI.

Fair practices code for NBFCs are concerned with transparency, fair dealings and good customer service in various stages of loan processing such as application, sanction, follow-up, monitoring, collection and closure. The codes encourage NBFCs to share all the relevant information with the borrowers and also not to harass or put the borrower into difficulties. The need to transparently inform the borrower of all critical details is highlighted. Customer service is the focus of FPC.

Fair Practice Code related to Gold Loan:

- The NBFC should complete adequate KYC procedure due diligence of the customer.
- To satisfy the owner of the gold to the borrower the NBFC will conduct internal procedures.
- NBFC shall ensure adequate systems for storage of gold.
- Gold insurance and other validation checks should be done.

NBFC-MFI must also follow similar fair practices code for their processes and provide disclosures in the stage of loan processing. Their recovery should be at a designated place and field staff to visit their residence or place of work only if the customer does not meet them in the decided designated place.

NBFC-MFIS should assign the responsibility for compliance to various regulations and guidelines to designated individuals within the company. Compliance to FPC should be reviewed by the Board.

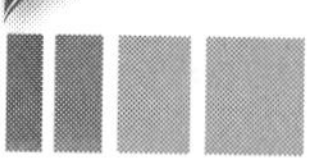

20.10 KEY WORDS

Fair practices Code, NBFCs, Loan processing, Loan appraisal, Pricing, NBFC-MFI, Non-coercive recovery, gold loans, regulations and Compliance

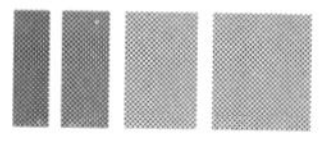

20.11 CHECK YOUR PROGRESS

1. What is the meaning of fair practices code?
   (*a*) Regulatory guidelines issued by RBI
   (*b*) Regulatory guidelines on practices to be used in companies while dealing with customers.
   (*c*) Guidelines for Agents
   (*d*) All of the above
2. All application in loans should be done in ________ language.
   (*a*) One
   (*b*) Many
   (*c*) Vernacular
   (*d*) None of the above
3. ________ required from the customer should be listed in the Application form:
   (*a*) Securities
   (*b*) Documents
   (*c*) Policies
   (*d*) None of the above
4. NBFCs should declare all details of annualized rate of interest in which step?
   (*a*) Applications for Loan
   (*b*) Loan disbursal
   (*c*) Appraisal of loan and terms & conditions
   (*d*) Loan Sanction
5. NBFCs should release all ________ once the loan is repaid in full:
   (*a*) Documents
   (*b*) Securities
   (*c*) Advances
   (*d*) All of the above

6. Which mechanism helps in resolving disputes?
   (*a*) Grievance redressal mechanism
   (*b*) Raise a request
   (*c*) Help and support
   (*d*) None of the above
7. Lending against gold jewellery should be properly ______?
   (*a*) Assayed
   (*b*) Tested
   (*c*) Analysed
   (*d*) None of the above
8. Adequate infrastructure for storage is required for which type of lending?
   (*a*) Vehicles
   (*b*) Gold jewellery
   (*c*) Silver jewellery
   (*d*) None of the above
9. Who manages responsibility of compliance for NBFC-MFI?
   (*a*) External team
   (*b*) Internal team
   (*c*) RBI
   (*d*) None of the above

20.12 ANSWERS TO CHECK YOUR PROGRESS

1.	(*d*)	2.	(*c*)	3.	(*b*)	4.	(*d*)	5.	(*b*)	6.	(*a*)	7.	(*a*)
8.	(*b*)	9.	(*b*)										

APPENDICES

APPENDIX 1 : RBI CIRCULAR ON RECOVERY AGENTS ENGAGED BY BANKS

APPENDIX 2 : IBA - MODEL POLICY ON COLLECTION OF DUES AND REPOSSESSION OF SECURITY

APPENDIX 3 : CASE LAWS ON PAYMENT OF CHEQUES AND LIABILITY OF PAYING BANKER

APPENDIX 4 : RBI GUIDELINES ON MANAGING RISKS AND CODE OF CONDUCT IN OUTSOURCING OF FINANCIAL SERVICES BY BANKS

APPENDIX 5 : CASE LAWS ON REPOSSESSION AND ENFORCEMENT OF SECURITIES

APPENDIX 6 : GLOSSARY OF BANKING TERMS

APPENDIX 7 : SOME OF THE IMPORTANT CASES DEALT BY THE BANKING OMBUDSMAN OFFICES

APPENDIX 8 : OUTSOURCING OF FINANCIAL SERVICES-RESPONSIBILITIES OF REGULATED ENTITIES EMPLOYING RECOVERY AGENTS

RBI CIRCULAR ON RECOVERY AGENTS ENGAGED BY BANKS

Mid-Term Review of the Annual Policy for the year 2007- 08 – Recovery Agents engaged by banks

Please refer to the paragraph 172 and 173 of the mid-term review of the Annual Policy for the year 2007-08, a copy of which is enclosed. In view of the rise in the number of disputes and litigations against banks for engaging recovery agents in the recent past, it is felt that the adverse publicity would result in serious reputational risk for the banking sector as a whole. A need has therefore arisen to review the policy, practice, and procedure involved in the engagement of recovery agents by banks in India. In this backdrop, Reserve Bank issued draft guidelines which were placed on the web-site for comments of all concerned. Based on the feedback received from a wide spectrum of banks/individuals/organizations, the draft guidelines have been suitably revised and the final guidelines are as follows:

Engagement of Recovery Agents

Banks are advised to take into account the following specific considerations while engaging recovery agents:

(*i*) 'Agent' in these guidelines would include agencies engaged by the bank and the agents/employees of the concerned agencies.

(*ii*) Banks should have a due diligence process in place for engagement of recovery agents, which should be so structured to cover, among others, individuals involved in the recovery process. The due diligence process should generally conform to the guidelines issued by RBI on outsourcing of financial services vide circular DBOD. No.BP.40/21.04.158/2006-07 dated November 3, 2006. Further, banks should ensure that the agents engaged by them in the recovery process carry out verification of the antecedents of their employees, which may include pre-employment police verification, as a matter of abundant caution. Banks may decide the periodicity at which reverification of antecedents should be resorted to.

(*iii*) To ensure due notice and appropriate authorization, banks should inform the borrower the details of recovery agency firms/companies while forwarding default cases to the recovery agency. Further, since in some of the cases, the borrower might not have received the details about the recovery agency due to refusal/non-availability/avoidance and to ensure identification, it would be appropriate if the agent also carries a copy of the notice and the authorization letter from the bank along with the identity card issued to him by the bank or the agency firm/company. Further, where the recovery agency is changed by the bank during the recovery process, in addition to the bank notifying the borrower of the change, the new agent should carry the notice and the authorization letter along with his identity card.

(*iv*) The notice and the authorization letter should, among other details, also include the telephone numbers of the relevant recovery agency. Banks should ensure that there is a tape recording of the content/text of the calls made by recovery agents to the customers, and vice-versa. Banks may take reasonable precaution such as intimating the customer that the conversation is being recorded, etc.

(*v*) The up to date details of the recovery agency firms/companies engaged by banks may also be posted on the bank's website.

(*vi*) Where a grievance/complaint has been lodged, banks should not forward cases to recovery agencies till they have finally disposed of any grievance/complaint lodged by the concerned borrower. However, where the bank is convinced, with appropriate proof, that the borrower is continuously making frivolous/vexatious complaints, it may continue with the recovery proceedings through the Recovery Agents even if a grievance/complaint is pending with them. In cases where the subject matter of the borrower's dues might be sub judice, banks should exercise utmost caution, as appropriate, in referring the matter to the recovery agencies, depending on the circumstances.

(*vii*) Each bank should have a mechanism whereby the borrowers' grievances with regard to the recovery process can be addressed. The details of the mechanism should also be furnished to the borrower while advising the details of the recovery agency as at item (iii) above.

Incentives to Recovery Agents

(*viii*) It is understood that some banks set very stiff recovery targets or offer high incentives to recovery agents. These have, in turn, induced the recovery agents to use intimidatory and questionable methods for recovery of dues. Banks are, therefore, advised to ensure that the contracts with the recovery agents do not induce adoption of uncivilized, unlawful and questionable behaviour or recovery process.

Methods followed by Recovery Agents

(*ix*) A reference is invited to (a) Circular DBOD.Leg.No.BC.104/09.07.007/2002-03 dated May 5, 2003 regarding Guidelines on Fair Practices Code for Lenders (b) Circular DBOD.No.BP. 40/21.04.158/2006-07 dated November 3, 2006 regarding outsourcing of financial services and (c) Master Circular DBOD.FSD.BC.17/24.01.011/2007-08 dated July 2, 2007 on Credit Card Operations. Further, a reference is also invited to paragraph 6 of the "Code of Bank's Commitment to Customers" (BCSBI Code) pertaining to collection of dues. Banks are advised to strictly adhere to the guidelines/code mentioned above during the loan recovery process.

Training for Recovery Agents

(*x*) In terms of Para 5.7.1 of our Circular DBOD.NO.BP. 40/21.04.158/2006-07 dated November 3, 2006 on guidelines on managing risks and code of conduct in outsourcing of financial services by banks, banks were advised that they should ensure that, among others, the recovery agents are properly trained to handle with care and sensitivity, their responsibilities, in particular aspects like hours of calling, privacy of customer information etc.

(*xi*) Reserve Bank has requested the Indian Banks' Association to formulate, in consultation with Indian Institute of Banking and Finance (IIBF), a certificate course for Direct Recovery Agents with minimum 100 hours of training. Once the above course is introduced by IIBF, banks should ensure that over a period of one year all their Recovery Agents undergo the above training and obtain the certificate from the above institute. Further, the service providers engaged by banks should also employ only such personnel who have undergone the above training and obtained the certificate from the IIBF. Keeping in view the fact that a large number of agents throughout the country may have to be trained, other institutes/bank's own training colleges may provide the training to the recovery agents by having a tie-up arrangement with Indian Institute of Banking and Finance so that there is uniformity in the standards of training. However, every agent will have to pass the examination conducted by IIBF all over India.

Taking possession of property mortgaged/hypothecated to banks

(*xii*) In a recent case which came up before the Honourable Supreme Court, the Honourable Court observed that we are governed by rule of law in the country and the recovery of loans or seizure of vehicles could be done only through legal means. In this connection it may be mentioned that the Securitisation and Reconstruction of Financial Assets and Enforcement of Security Interest Act, 2002 (SARFAESI Act) and the Security Interest (Enforcement) Rules, 2002 framed thereunder have laid down well defined procedures not only for enforcing security interest but also for auctioning the movable and immovable property after enforcing the security interest. It is, therefore, desirable that banks rely only on legal remedies available under the relevant statutes while enforcing security interest without intervention of the Courts.

(*xiii*) Where banks have incorporated a re-possession clause in the contract with the borrower and rely on such re-possession clause for enforcing their rights, they should ensure that the repossession clause is legally valid, complies with the provisions of the Indian Contract Act in letter and spirit, and ensure that such repossession clause is clearly brought to the notice of the borrower at the time of execution of the contract. The terms and conditions of the contract should be strictly in terms of the Recovery Policy and should contain provisions regarding (*a*) notice period before taking possession (*b*) circumstances under which the notice period can be waived (*c*) the procedure for taking possession of the security (*d*) a provision regarding final chance to be given to the borrower for repayment of loan before the sale/auction of the property (*e*) the procedure for giving repossession to the borrower and (*f*) the procedure for sale/auction of the property.

Use of forum of Lok Adalats

(*xiv*) The Honourable Supreme Court also observed that loans, personal loans, credit card loans and housing loans with less than Rs.10 lakh can be referred to Lok Adalats. In this connection, banks' attention is invited to Circular DBOD.No.Leg. BC.21/09.06.002/2004-05 dated August 3, 2004 wherein they were advised to use the forum of Lok Adalats organized by Civil Courts for recovery of loans. Banks are encouraged to use the forum of Lok Adalats for recovery of personal loans, credit card loans or housing loans with less than Rs.10 lakh as suggested by the Honourable Supreme Court.

Utilisation of credit counsellors

(*xv*) Banks are encouraged to have in place an appropriate mechanism to utilise the services of the credit counsellors for providing suitable counselling to the borrowers where it becomes aware that the case of a particular borrower deserves sympathetic consideration.

Complaints against the bank/its recovery agents

Banks, as principals, are responsible for the actions of their agents. Hence, they should ensure that their agents engaged for recovery of their dues should strictly adhere to the above guidelines and instructions, including the BCSBI Code, while engaged in the process of recovery of dues.

Complaints received by Reserve Bank regarding violation of the above guidelines and adoption of abusive practices followed by banks' recovery agents would be viewed seriously. Reserve Bank may consider imposing a ban on a bank from engaging recovery agents in a particular area, either jurisdictional or functional, for a limited period. In case of persistent breach of above guidelines, Reserve Bank may consider extending the period of ban or the area of ban. Similar supervisory action could be attracted when the High Courts or the Supreme Court pass strictures or impose penalties against any bank or its Directors/Officers/agents with regard to policy, practice and procedure related to the recovery process.

It is expected that banks would, in the normal course ensure that their employees also adhere to the above guidelines during the loan recovery process.

Periodical Review

Banks engaging recovery agents are advised to undertake a periodical review of the mechanism to learn from experience, to effect improvements, and to bring to the notice of the Reserve Bank of India suggestions for improvement in the guidelines.

Yours faithfully

(Prashant Saran)

Chief General Manager-in-Charge

Extracts of Paragraphs 172 and 173 of the Mid-term review of the Annual Policy for the year 2007-08

Recovery Agents Engaged by Banks

In view of the rise in the number of litigations against banks for engaging recovery agents in the recent past, it is felt that the adverse publicity could result in serious reputational risk for the banking sector as a whole. An urgent need has, therefore, arisen to review the policy, practice, procedure involved in the engagement of recovery agents by banks in India. Accordingly, banks are urged to follow prescribed specific considerations while engaging recovery agents.

Complaints received by the Reserve Bank regarding abusive practices followed by a bank's recovery agents would invite serious supervisory disapproval. The Reserve Bank would consider imposing a temporary ban (or even a permanent ban in case of persistent abusive practices) for engaging recovery agents on those banks where strictures have been passed/ penalties have been imposed by a High Court/Supreme Court or against its Directors/Officers with regard to the abusive practices followed by their recovery agents. An operational circular in this regard would be issued by November 15, 2007.

IBA - MODEL POLICY ON COLLECTION OF DUES AND REPOSSESSION OF SECURITY

1. INTRODUCTION

The debt collection policy of the bank is built around dignity and respect to customers. Bank will not follow policies that are unduly coercive in collection of dues. The policy is built on courtesy, fair treatment and persuasion. The bank believes in following fair practices with regard to collection of dues and repossession of security and thereby fostering customer confidence and long-term relationship.

The repayment schedule for any loan sanctioned by the bank will be fixed taking into account paying capacity and cash flow pattern of the borrower. The bank will explain to the customer upfront the method of calculation of interest and how the Equated Monthly Instalments (EMI) or payments through any other mode of repayment will be appropriated against interest and principal due from the customers. The bank would expect the customers to adhere to the repayment schedule agreed to and approach the bank for assistance and guidance in case of genuine difficulty in meeting repayment obligations.

Bank's Security Repossession Policy aims at recovery of dues in the event of default and is not aimed at whimsical deprivation of the property. The policy recognizes fairness and transparency in repossession, valuation and realization of security. All the practices adopted by the bank for follow-up and recovery of dues and repossession of security will be inconsonance with the law.

2. GENERAL GUIDELINES

All the members of the staff or any person authorized to represent the bank in collection or/and security repossession would follow the guidelines set out below:

1. The customer would be contacted ordinarily at the place of his/her choice and in the absence of any specified place, at the place of his/her residence and if unavailable at his/her residence, at the place of business/occupation.
2. Identity and authority of persons authorized to represent bank for follow-up and recovery of dues would be made known to the borrowers at the first instance. The bank staff or any person authorized to represent the bank in collection of dues or/ and security repossession will identify himself/herself and display the authority letter issued by the bank upon request.
3. The bank would respect privacy of its borrowers.
4. The bank is committed to ensure that all written and verbal communication with its borrowers will be in simple business language and bank will adopt civil manners for interaction with borrowers.

5. Normally the bank's representatives will contact the borrower between 0700 hrs. and 1900 hrs., unless the special circumstance of his/her business or occupation requires the bank to contact at a different time.
6. Borrower's requests to avoid calls at a particular time or at a particular place would be honoured as far as possible.
7. The bank will document the efforts made for the recovery of dues and the copies of communication set to customers, if any, will be kept on record.
8. All assistance will be given to resolve disputes or differences regarding dues in a mutually acceptable and in an orderly manner.
9. Inappropriate occasions such as bereavement in the family or such other calamitous occasions will be avoided for making calls/visits to collect dues.

3. GIVING NOTICE TO BORROWERS

While written communications, telephonic reminders or visits by the bank's representatives to the borrower's place or residence will be used as loan follow-up measures, the bank will not initiate any legal or other recovery measures including repossession of the security without giving due notice in writing. Bank will follow all such procedures as required under law for recovery/repossession of security.

4. REPOSSESSION OF SECURITY

Repossession of security is aimed at recovery of dues and not to deprive the borrower of the property. The recovery process through repossession of security will involve repossession, valuation of security and realization of security through appropriate means. All these would be carried out in a fair and transparent manner. Repossession will be done only after issuing the notice as detailed above. Due process of law will be followed while taking repossession of the property. The bank will take all reasonable care for ensuring the safety and security of the property after taking custody, in the ordinary course of the business.

5. VALUATION AND SALE OF PROPERTY

Valuation and sale of property repossessed by the bank will be carried out as per law and in a fair and transparent manner. The bank will have right to recover from the borrower the balance due if any, after sale of property. Excess amount if any, obtained on sale of property will be returned to the borrower after meeting all the related expenses provided the bank is not having any other claims against the customer.

6. OPPORTUNITY FOR THE BORROWER TO TAKE BACK THE SECURITY

As indicated earlier in the policy document, the bank will resort to repossession of security only for the purpose of realization of its dues as the last resort and not with intention of depriving the borrower of the property. Accordingly, the bank will be willing to consider handing over possession of property to the borrower any time after repossession and before concluding sale transaction of the property, provided the bank dues are cleared in full. If satisfied with the genuineness of borrower's inability to pay the loan instalments as per the schedule which resulted in the repossession of security, the bank may consider handing over the property after receiving the instalments in arrears. However, this would be subject to the bank being convinced of the arrangements made by the borrower to ensure timely repayment of remaining instalments in future.

CASE LAWS ON PAYMENT OF CHEQUES AND LIABILITY OF PAYING BANKER

1. Liability of paying banker when customer's signature on cheque is forged.

   When the customer's signature on the cheque is forged there is no mandate to the bank to pay. As such a banker is not entitled to debit the customer's account on such forged cheque. In *Canara Bank* v. *Canara Sales Corporation* [(1987) 2 Supreme Court Cases 666] the company had a current account with the bank which was operated by the Company's Managing Director. The Company's accountant in whose custody the cheque book was, forged the signature of the Managing Director in 42 cheques totalling Rs. 3,26,047.92 over a period of time. This was detected by another accountant. The company immediately on detection of the fraud demanded the amount from the bank. The bank refused payment and therefore the company filed a suit against the bank. The bank lost the suit and took the matter up to the Supreme Court. The Supreme Court dismissed the appeal of the bank and held that:

   Since the relationship between the customer and the bank is that of a creditor and debtor, the bank had no authority to make payment of a cheque containing a forged signature. The bank would be acting against the law in debiting the customer with the amount of the forged cheque as there would be no mandate on the bank to pay. The Supreme Court pointed out that the document in the cheque form on which the customer's name as drawer was forged was a mere nullity. The bank would succeed only when it would establish adoption or estoppel.

2. In a joint account if one of the signatures is forged then there is no mandate and banker cannot make payment.

   In the case of *Bihta Co-operative Development and Cane Marketing Union Ltd.* v. *Bank of Bihar* (AIR 1967 Supreme Court 389), the Co-operative Marketing Union had an account with the bank which was authorised to be operated by the joint secretary and treasurer of the Co-operative Marketing Union. On 16 April, 1948 the bank made payment of Rs. 11,000 on a loose leaf cheque and not on a cheque from the cheque book issued to the Society. Though the two signatures appeared on the cheque, one of them, the signature of the Joint Secretary was forged. The bank made payment, whereupon the Co-operative Marketing Union sued the bank for recovery of the money. Though the bank admitted negligence on its part, it argued that the employees of the Co-operative Marketing Union were dishonest in the discharge of their duties and as such it cannot succeed. The matter went up to the Supreme Court and the Supreme Court while allowing the case of the

Co-operative Marketing Union held that"one of the signatures was forged so that there never was any mandate by the customer at all to the banker and the question of negligence of the customer in between the signature and the presentation of the cheque never arose."

3. Payment to be in due course for bank to seek protection

The Supreme Court in *Bank of Bihar* v. *Mahabir Lal* (AIR 1964 Supreme Court 397) held that a banker can seek protection under Section 85 only where payment has been made to the holder, his servant or agent, *i.e.* payment must be made in due course.

In this case the Bank had agreed to grant to the firm cash credit facility against pledge of cloth bales on the firm fulfilling certain conditions, one of which was that the money for purchasing the cloth would not be directly given to the firm, but instead the supplier would be paid the amount by the bank and the cloth bales would be kept by the Bank as pledge for the loan. The firm thereafter was required to draw a cheque on itself which was handed over to the bank. The bank instead of handing over cash to the firm's partner, to be paid over to the wholesalers, entrusted it with one of the bank's employees (Potdar) who accompanied the partner to the wholesalers. However, before the money could be paid to the wholesalers the Potdar absconded. The bank sought repayment of the money which was refused by the firm. The bank therefore sued the firm for the money relying on Sections 85 and 118 of the Negotiable Instruments Act, 1881. The matter reached the Supreme Court and it was held that before the provisions of Section 85 can assist the bank it had to be established that payment had in fact been made to the firm or to a person on behalf of the firm. Payment to a person who had nothing to do with the firm or a payment to an agent of the Bank would not be a payment to the firm.

4. Payment in good faith, without negligence of an instrument on which alteration is not apparent.

The effect of Sections 10 and 89, and Section 31 was considered by the Supreme Court in *Bank of Maharashtra* v. *M/s Automotive Engineering Co.* (1993) 2 SCC 97.

The question which arose for consideration in this appeal was whether the paying bank was bound to keep an ultraviolet ray lamp and to scrutinize the cheque under the said lamp even if no infirmity on the face of the said cheque on visual scrutiny was found.

There was no evidence to hold that the payment was not made in good faith. Simply because the ultraviolet ray lamp was not kept in the branch and the said cheque was not subjected to such lamp, would not be sufficient to hold the appellant bank guilty of negligence more so when it has not been established on evidence that the other branches of the appellant bank or the other commercial banks had been following a practice of scrutinizing each and every cheque or cheques involving a particular amount under such lamp by way of extra precaution.

In such circumstances, it is not correct legal proposition that the bank, in order to get absolved from the liability of negligence, was under an obligation to verify the cheque for further scrutiny under advanced technology or for that matter under ultraviolet ray lamp apart from visual scrutiny even though the cost of such scrutiny was only nominal and it might be desirable to keep such lamp at the branch to take aid in appropriate case.

The Courts below were not justified in holding that the bank had failed to take reasonable care in passing the cheque for payment without subjecting it for further scrutiny under ultraviolet ray lamp because the branch was in the industrial area where such forgery was rampant and other branches of the appellant bank were provided with such lamp.

The appeal was, therefore, allowed and the Suit of the appellant bank was decreed only for the principal amount without any interest on the same.

5. In *Bareilly Bank Ltd.* v. *Naval Kishore* (AIR 1964 All 78) N opened an account with the bank by making a cash deposit of Rs. 19,900. N was issued a cheque book containing 25 cheques. 17 months after the opening of the account N drew a cheque for the first time for Rs. 5,900 which was dishonoured by the bank. On enquiries N was informed that 11 months back three cheques aggregating Rs. 19,500 were paid by the bank and the present balance in the account was a mere Rs. 437. N denied issuing of the cheques and sued the bank. In evidence it came out that 3 cheques used to withdraw the amounts were not from the cheque book issued to N and were from a different cheque book. Though bank was not in a position to explain this lapse, they made an attempt to counter the contentions of N by producing his specimen signature which appeared to be similar to the ones on the cheques. N however denied that the specimen signature was his and the Court concluded that the alleged specimen signature was totally different from N's regular signature. Evidence also was led to show that the bank's own employees were involved in the forgery since the ledger page of N's account showed that certain erasures and scorings were made and the signature of N missing in the cheque book issue register. Therefore, the court refused to accept the bank's contention.

6. In the case of *Tanjore Permanent Bank* v. *S.R. Rangachari* (AIR 1959 Madras 119) the High Court was called upon to decide a case in which cheque was materially altered and the bank sought protection under Section 89. In this case R had an overdraft account with the bank and requested the Manager to advance him Rs. 16,000 to debit of his account. The Manager asks R to send him three blank cheques signed.

   R accordingly did the same. However, of the three cheques only one was utilised for the payment of Rs. 16,000. The other two cheques were alleged to have been filled by the accountant of the Bank for Rs. 7,600 and Rs. 4,200 and the names of two clerks were written as the payees. In both the cheques the alteration was apparent and visible but the bank paid these cheques. On R not clearing the debit because of his overdraft account, the bank sued him. R contended that the two debit entries for Rs. 7,600 and 4,200 were made by the Bank wrongly and as such he cannot be held liable.

The Court in coming to the above conclusion relied on the following paragraph of Bhashyam and Adiga's Negotiable Instruments Act:

The bank has also to see whether there are any alterations in the cheque and whether they have been properly authenticated. Therefore, where an alteration in a cheque is initialled not by all the drawers but only some of them, the bank will be paying the amount on the said cheque at its own risk. In this connection it is necessary to notice that under Section 89 protection is afforded to the bank paying a cheque where the alteration is not apparent.

It is to be noted as per Section 89 the bank can seek protection only if there is material alteration in the cheque and does not appear to have been altered. This, however, does not protect a banker in case the signature of the customer is forged. As stated earlier a forged cheque is no mandate of the customer and as such the bank cannot make payment on a cheque where the signature of the customer is forged. The question whether a signature is forged or not depends on the evidence and the court in coming to a conclusion that the signature is forged would look into the facts and circumstances that led to the payment of the cheque.

7. Payment by bank under mistake whether recoverable

The question whether a bank paying a forged cheque can recover the same from the payee was considered by the Calcutta High Court in *United Bank of India* v. *AT Ali Hussain & Co.* (AIR 1978 Calcutta 169).

In this case a cheque for Rs. 5,000 purported to have been drawn by a company was presented by the collecting bank to the paying bank, and was paid. The signature, as well as all other writings on the cheque, were forged. The forgery was so perfect that it was not possible even for a trained eye to detect it. The paying bank, having subsequently come to know of the forgery, filed a suit against the collecting bank and the payee of the cheque, for recovery of the amount paid, on the ground of payment under mistake. Defending the suit, the collecting bank contended that it received the cheque in the ordinary course of its business, and presented the same for encashment in good faith. The payee contended that he received the cheque from some persons claiming to be representatives of a company, in the ordinary course of business, towards payment of the price of the goods to be supplied by him, that he acted in good faith having no reason to suspect that the cheque was forged, and that he parted with the goods only on receipt of intimation from the collecting bank that the cheque had been encashed.

The Trial Court having dismissed the suit on the ground that the paying bank had no cause of action, an appeal was preferred to the High Court.

Decision: The High Court dismissed the appeal and held that both from the point of view of equitable principles and the doctrine of estoppel, the paying bank was disentitled to recover the money either from the collecting bank or the payee.

Appended below are legal cases on various aspects of the "Dishonour of cheques" and its implications under Section 138 of N.I. Act, 1881:

I. INGREDIENTS AND REQUIREMENTS OF THE PENAL PROVISIONS:

In '*Harman Electronics (P) Ltd.* v. *National Panasonic India Ltd.* (2008) 16 SCALE 317, the Court opined that the offence under Section 138 of the Act can be completed only with the concatenation of a number of acts, namely:

1. Drawing of the cheque;
2. Presentation of the cheque to the bank;
3. Returning of the cheque unpaid by the drawee bank;
4. Giving of notice in writing to the drawer of the cheque demanding payment of the cheque amount;
5. Failure of the drawer to make payment within 15 days of the receipt of the cheque.

It is not necessary that all the above five acts should have been perpetrated at the same locality. It is possible that each of those five acts could be done at five different localities. But a concatenation of all the above five is a sin qua non for the completion of the offence under Section 138 of the Code......." (*emphasis supplied*)

In section 142 of the Act it has however, provided that such complaint is made within ONE MONTH (In '*Shivakumar* v. *Natarajan*' - (2009) 27 CLA -BL Supp 62 (SC)) of the date on which the cause of action *i.e.,* failure by the drawer of cheque in question to make payment of the said amount to the payee or as the case may be to the holder in due course of a cheque within 15 days of the receipt of the said notice.

Where the Complaint lacks necessary ingredients of the offence under Section 138: Hon'ble Supreme Court in *Jugesh Sehgal* v. *Shamsher Singh Gogi* 2009 (3) CC Cases (SC) 2004. The Hon'ble Supreme Court noted that the cheque alleged to have been issued by the petitioners to the complainant was issued from an account pertaining to some other person. The Hon'ble Court also noted that one of the essential ingredients of the offence punishable under Section 138 of Negotiable Instruments Act is that the cheque must have been drawn on an account maintained by the accused. Since the cheque in the case before the Hon'ble Supreme Court was not issued from the account maintained by the petitioner, it was held that one essential ingredient of offence under Section 138 of Negotiable Instruments Act was not.

II. CONSIDERATION:

Mallavarapu Kasivisweswara Rao v. *Thadikonda Ramulu Firm.*, 2008 (8) SCALE 680, wherein it was observed:

> "Under Section 118(*a*) of the Negotiable Instruments Act, the court is obliged to presume, until the contrary is proved, that the promissory note was made for consideration. It is also a settled position that the initial burden in this regard lies on the defendant to prove the non-existence of consideration by bringing on record

such facts and circumstances which would lead the Court to believe the non-existence of the consideration either by direct evidence or by preponderance of probabilities showing that the existence of consideration was improbable, doubtful or illegal. ..."

This decision then proceeded to cite an extract from the earlier decision in *Bharat Barrel & Drum Manufacturing Company* v. *Amin Chand Pyarelal,* (1993) 3 SCC 35 (Para. 12):

> "Upon consideration of various judgments as noted hereinabove, the position of law which emerges is that once execution of the promissory note is admitted, the presumption under Section 118(*a*) would arise that it is supported by a consideration. Such a presumption is rebuttable. The defendant can prove the non-existence of a consideration by raising a probable defence. If the defendant is proved to have discharged the initial onus of proof showing that the existence of consideration was improbably or doubtful or the same was illegal, the onus would shift to the plaintiff who will be obliged to prove it as a matter of fact and upon its failure to prove would disentitle him to the grant of relief on the basis of the negotiable instrument. The burden upon the defendant of proving the non-existence of the consideration can be either direct or by bringing on record the preponderance of probabilities by reference to the circumstances upon which he relies. In such an event, the plaintiff is entitled under law to rely upon all the evidence led in the case including that of the plaintiff as well. In case, where the defendant fails to discharge the initial onus of proof by showing the non-existence of the consideration, the plaintiff would invariably be held entitled to the benefit of presumption arising under Section 118(*a*) in his favour.
>
> The court may not insist upon the defendant to disprove the existence of consideration by leading direct evidence as the existence of negative evidence is neither possible nor contemplated and even if led, is to be seen with a doubt. The bare denial of the passing of the consideration apparently does not appear to be any defence. Something which is probable has to be brought on record for getting the benefit of shifting the onus of proving to the plaintiff.
>
> To disprove the presumption, the defendant has to bring on record such facts and circumstances upon consideration of which the court may either believe that the consideration did not exist or its non-existence was so probable that a prudent man would, under the circumstances of the case, act upon the plea that it did not exist."

III - CAUSE OF ACTION:

A. Presentation of Cheques any number of times:

A cheque may be presented any number of times during the period of validity. The cause of action, however, arises only once. The cause of action arises, after the issue of statutory notice and non-compliance with demand. (The Hon'ble Supreme Court in *Sadanandan Bhadran* v. *Madhavan Sunil Kumar,* JT 1998 (6) SC 48), It was also held that while the payee was free to present the cheque repeatedly within its validity period, once notice had been issued and payments not received within 15 days of the receipt of the notice, the payee has to avail the very cause of action arising thereupon and file the complaint. Dishonour of the cheque on each representation does not give rise to a fresh cause of action. This view was reiterated in *Prem Chand Vijay Kumar* v. *Yashpal Singh* [(2005) 4 SCC 417]. Also refer *Central Bank of India* v. *M/s. Saxons Farms* 1999 Crl.L.J. 4571.

B. Notice:

(*a*) Notice - returned unclaimed - again send to another address after 15 days – valid –complainant sent notice on 29-5-1999 – returned on 9-6-1999 as unclaimed - complainant on coming to know that accused was available elsewhere sent copy of same notice on 24-6-1999 – period of limitations start after 15 days from second Notice. 2002 (4) CTC 335.

(*b*) Communication: Issuance of Notice would not by itself give rise to a cause of action but communication would (Para 14 of *Harman Electronics Private Limited* v. *National Panasonic India Ltd.*, reported in (2009) 1 SCC (Cri) 610)/[2011] 3 taxmann.com 67 (SC)-While issuance of a notice by the holder of a negotiable instrument is necessary, service thereof is also imperative. Only on service of such notice and failure on the part of the accused to pay the demanded amount within the period of 15 days thereafter, commission of an offence completes.

(*c*) Notice to the Company's MD: The Supreme Court in *Rajneesh Agarwal* v. *Amit J Bhalla* (2001 AIR SCW 124) has held that notice for payment under section 138 of the Negotiable Instruments Act (the Act) to the director who has signed the cheque is notice to the drawer company and that the notice cannot be construed in a narrow technical way.

(*d*) Service of Notice: Supreme Court in the *State of Madhya Pradesh* v. *Hiralal*, JT 1996 (1) S.C. 669, where, postal remarks to the effect "not available in the house," "House Locked" and "shop closed", were held to be service of notice upon the respondent. In *Subodh S.Salaskar* v. *Jayaprakash M. Shah*, AIR 2008 SC 3086, the Hon'ble Supreme Court held that presumption of service under Section 114 of Evidence Act would also arise if the notice is received back with an endorsement that the party had refused to accept it. In the present case, this is petitioner's own case in paragraph 5 of the complaint that it had served registered notice upon the respondent *vide* postal receipt No.8288. Thus, the petitioner/complainant itself claims service upon the respondent on account of the endorsement of the postal department on the registered cover.

What are the requirements of service of a notice is no longer *res integra* in view of the recent decision of this Court in C.C. *Alavi Haji* v. *Palapetty Muhammed* [JT 2007(7) SC 498].

Notice - Cheque issued for part payment of outstanding bills - Cheque dishonoured - By issuing notice demand made of payment of pending bills and not cheque amount - Held, notice is not valid. (*M/s.Rahul Builders* v. *M/s. Arihant Fertilizers & Chemical.*) 2007(3) Apex Court Judgments 554 (S.C.): 2007(4) Criminal Court Cases 990 (S.C.)

IV - REPRESENTATIVE/AUTHORISED REPRESENTATIVE:

In AIR 2002 SC 182, the Hon'ble Supreme Court made the following observations, "Section 142 of the Negotiable Instruments Act provides that a complaint under Section 138 can be made by the payee or the holder in due course of the said cheque. The two complaints, in question, are by the appellant company who is the payee of the two cheques. This Court has as far back as, in the case of *Vishwa Mitter* v. *O.P. Poddar* reported in (1983) 4 SCC 701, held that it is clear that anyone can set the criminal law in motion by filing a complaint of facts constituting an offence before a Magistrate entitled to take cognizance.

V- POWER OF ATTORNEY:

Supreme Court judgment passed in case of *Janki Vashdeo Bhojwani* v. *Indusind Bank Ltd.* I (2005) BC 399 (SC) : 2004 AIR SCW 7064, has submitted that a general or special power of attorney holder can appear, plead and act on behalf of the party but he cannot become a witness on behalf of the party.

In the case of '*Shankar Finance Investments* v. *State of Andhra Pradesh*' (2008) 24 CLA-BL Supp 62 (SC) the appeal was filed against the order passed by the Andhra Pradesh High Court in a criminal petition holding that the complaint signed by a power of attorney holder was not maintainable. The payee of the cheque is 'Shankar Finance & Investments, a proprietary concern of Shri Atmakumari Sankara Rao, represented by its power of attorney holder of Shri Thamada Satyanarayana. The Supreme Court observed the requirements of Sec. 142 of the Act are that the complaint should be in writing and the complaint should be made by the payee or holder in due course. The payee in this case is Shanker & Finance Investments. Once the complaint is in the name of the 'payee' and is in writing, the requirements of Sec. 142 are fulfilled.

In *Jimmy Jahangir Madan* v. *Bolly Cariyappa Hindley* – 2004(12) SCC 509 the Supreme Court ruled that the application under Sec. 302 CrPC to continue the prosecution could not be filed by the power-of-attorney holder of the heirs of the deceased complainant in a prosecution under Sec. 138 of the N.I. Act. It was held that the permission in that regard should be sought by the heirs of the deceased complainant.

VI - DEATH OF THE COMPLAINANT:

S. Reddappa v. *M. Vijaya* (High Court of Karnataka- 1996). It is held in Reddappa's case, *supra*, that in a proceeding under Section 138 of the Act, the death of the complainant does not *ipso facto* terminate the criminal proceedings.

Not necessary that legal heirs or legal representatives only can continue the proceedings - A fit and proper person can be permitted to prosecute the petition.

Ashwin Nanubhai Vyas v. *State of Maharashtra* in which case the Court was dealing with a case under Section 495 of the Code of Criminal Procedure, 1898, which is corresponding to Section 302 of the Code. In that case, it was laid down that upon the death of the complainant, under the provisions of Section 495 of the said Code, mother of the complainant could be allowed to continue the prosecution. It was further laid down that she could make the application either herself or through a pleader.

VII - DEATH OF THE ACCUSED:

The legal heirs cannot be prosecuted under section 138 of N.I. Act. If at all any claim is against them by the complainant, he has to proceed only under the civil law for recovery of the amount against the properties in the hands of the legal heirs.

VIII - COMPANY/PARTNERSHIP FIRM:

Authorization afresh valid – authorization -need for substitution to represent company – filing of complaint - authorised resigning from company – company can be represented by person authorized afresh. 1997 (2) CTC 675.

Offences by company - Expression, 'in-charge of, and was responsible to the company for the business of the company - *K. K. Ahuja* v. *V. K. Vora* [SUPREME COURT OF INDIA, 06 Jul, 2009] [2009] 94 SCL 140 (S.C.). Whether DGM comes within the expression? - Held, No-Apart from the company two kinds of persons are deemed to be guilty of the offence and shall be liable to be proceeded against and punished, they are, one, who was in charge of and was responsible to the company for the conduct of the business of the company, two, any director, manager, secretary or other officer of the company with whose consent and connivance, the offence u/s. 138 has been committed, or whose negligence resulted in such offence being committed by the company - First category person is vicariously liable by reason only of his fulfilling the requirements of sub-section (1) of section 141 - Court observed that if the person responsible to the company for the conduct of business of the company, was not in charge of the conduct of the business of the company, then he can be made liable only if the offence was committed with his consent or connivance or as a result of his negligence - Second category persons as mentioned in sub-section (2) of section 141, are liable not on account of any legal fiction but on account of the specific part played *i.e.* consent and connivance or negligence - Court pointed that if a person is to be made liable under sub-section (2) of section 141, then it is necessary to aver consent and connivance, or negligence on his part - (ii) Who are the persons who are responsible to the company for the conduct of the business of the company, and who could be said to be in charge and was responsible to the company for the conduct of the business of the company?- Settled position, a MD is *prima facie* in charge of and responsible for the company's business and affairs and can be prosecuted for offences by the company; but insofar as other directors are concerned, they can be prosecuted only if they were in charge of and responsible for the conduct of the company's business.

Proprietorship concern - An employee of a proprietorship concern cannot be proceeded against u/s 138 of the Act. (*Raghu Lakshminarayanan* v. *Fine Tubes*) 2007(2) Apex Court Judgments 001 (S.C.) [2007] 76 SCL 25 (S.C.) : 2007(2) Civil Court Cases 641 (S.C.): 2007(2) Criminal Court Cases 709 (S.C.)

IX - DISMISSAL OF COMPLAINT:

(*a*) For default and restoration: The order of dismissal of a complaint by a criminal court due to the absence of the complainant is a proper order (AIR 1986 SC 1440). A second complaint is permissible in law if it could be brought within the limitation imposed by the Supreme Court in the case reported in AIR 1962 SC 876.

(*b*) Dismissal of complaint and appeal thereof: Dismissing complaint due to non-appearance of complainant resulting in acquittal of accused. Revision is not maintainable and only appeal lies to High Court u/s. 378 (4) of CrPC. (II 2003 CCR 387 HP).

In the *Associated Cement Co. Ltd.* v. *Keshvanand* (1998) 1 SCC 687. Justice K.T. Thomas (as he then was) speaking for the court has observed that the purpose of conferring power

on the Magistrate under Section 256 of the CrPC. is to deter dilatory tactics on the part of the complainant once he sets in motion criminal proceeding by instituting a complaint. The purpose being that accused is perforce required to attend court proceedings on dates fixed by the court and is thus, put to harassment if the complainant does not turn up in the court on dates when his presence is necessary. This provision affords protection to the accused against such tactics being adopted by the complainant. This, however, does not mean that if the complainant is absent the court is duty bound to acquit the accused. If the situation mandates the Magistrate has the power to adjourn the hearing. On the other hand, if the Magistrate considers that the personal appearance of the complainant is not necessary it has the power to dispense with his attendance and proceed with the case. It is for the court to consider whether the presence of the complainant is necessary for the progress of the case on the day when the complainant is absent or the situation is such that the case be adjourned to another date. If the situation mandates that there is no reason to adjourn the case, the Magistrate is free to dismiss the complaint and acquit the accused. The ratio of Associated Cement (*supra*) has been followed in a later judgment of the Supreme Court in the case entitled *S. Anand* v. *Vasumathi Chandrasekar* (2008) 4 SCC 67.

X - CIVIL & CRIMINAL LIABILITY:

JURISDICTION:

Territorial jurisdiction: *Musaraf Hossain Khan* v. *Bhagheeratha Engg. Ltd.* (SC) *Smt. Shamshad Begum* v. *B. Mohammed*, reported in AIR 2009 SC 1355, (Court followed the earlier view of the Hon'ble Supreme Court in the case of *K. Bhaskaran* v. *Sankaran Vaidhyan Balan*). In the case of *K. Bhaskaran* v. *Sankaran Vaidhyan Balan* (*supra*), a Division Bench of the Apex Court in paragraph 14 held the following of the Acts which are the components of the offence punishable under Section 138 of the Negotiable Instruments Act:

(*a*) Drawing of the cheque.

(*b*) Presentation of the cheque to the bank.

(*c*) Returning the cheque unpaid by the drawee bank.

(*d*) Giving notice in writing to the drawer of the cheque demanding payment of the cheque amount.

(*e*) Failure of the drawer to make payment within 15 days of the receipt of the notice.

In *Harman Electronics Private Limited* v. *National Panasonic India (P) Ltd.*, reported in (2009) 1 SCC (Cri) 610 (*State of Punjab* v. *Amar Singh Harika* AIR (1996) SC 1313 followed) sending of notice from a particular place would not give rise to cause of action but communication of notice would. Therefore, no Court has the territorial jurisdiction to hold a trial of an offence punishable under Section 138 of the Negotiable Instruments Act merely because the notice was sent from a place situated within its territorial limit.

Belated Complaint:

Nataraj @ T. Natarajan v. *P. Venkatachalam* (2008) 1 CTC 503- Practice and Procedure - Dishonour of Cheque case - Necessity to file condone delay Application with affidavit in case of belated Complaint - Proper procedure to be followed - If there is any delay in filing Complaint complainant should file condone delay Petition that on such filing Magistrate should issue notice to accused – After giving opportunity of hearing to accused, cause shown for delay to be considered – Magistrate should satisfy himself first and pass appropriate order by accepting or rejecting condone delay Petition – Failure to follow such procedure affects valuable right of accused.

XI - APPEARANCE:

Either admitted to bail on furnishing a personal bond and the surety of a like amount. Or file an application for exemption from personal appearance

XII - COMPOUNDING OF OFFENCE:

Damodar S. Prabhu v. Sayed Babalal H. SC 2010 (Crl Appeal No. 963 of 2010) [2010] 101 SCL 27 (SC): Compounding of the Offense is possible under Section 147 of the NI Act. In January 2010 the Supreme Court held that the offence of issuing cheque, which is dishonoured for want of funds can be compromised between the parties. The Supreme Court stated that under Section 147 of the Negotiable Instruments Act, the parties can compromise as the offence is listed as 'compoundable'.

XIII - ACCOUNT CLOSED:

When the cheque is returned by a bank with an endorsement 'account closed', it would amount to returning the cheque unpaid because "the amount of money standing to the credit of that account is insufficient to honour the cheque" as envisaged in Section 138 of the Act. (*NEPC Micon Ltd.* v. *Magma Leasing Ltd.*) 1999(2) CIVIL COURT CASES 471 (S.C.).

Cheque issued when account had already been closed –

Provision of Section 138 will apply. (*N.A.Issac* v. *Jeemon P.Abraham*) 2005(1) CIVIL COURT CASES 690 (S.C.) : 2005(1) CRIMINAL COURT CASES 119 (S.C.)

XV - STOP PAYMENT: Many a times the drawer, to escape his debt or liability has used it (Stop Payment) as an instrument of deception. "the object of the provision cannot be allowed to be defeated by such ingenious action". Observed Kerala High Court in *Calcutta Sanitary Wares* v. *C. T. Jacob.*

M.M.T.C. Ltd. v. *Medchl Chemicals & Pharma (P) Ltd.*, (2002) 1 SCC 234 [2002] 39 SCL 270 (S.C.) (Para. 19):

> "... The authority shows that even when the cheque is dishonoured by reason of stop payment instruction, by virtue of Section 139 the Court has to presume that the cheque was received by the holder for the discharge in whole or in part, of any debt or liability. Of course this is a rebuttable presumption. The accused can thus show that the 'stop payment' instructions were not issued because of insufficiency or paucity of funds. If the accused shows that in his account there was sufficient funds to clear the amount of the cheque at the time of presentation of the cheque for encashment at the drawer bank and that the stop payment notice had been issued because of other valid causes including that there was no existing debt or liability at the time of presentation of cheque for encashment, then offence under Section 138 would not be made out. The important thing is that the burden of so proving would be on the accused. ..."

The Supreme Court observed in 'Modi Cements' case.

> "Even when the cheque is dishonoured by reason of 'stop payment' instructions, by virtue of Section 139 of the Act, the court has to presume that the cheque was received by 'the holder' for the discharge, in whole or in part, of any debt or liability," a Bench said.

Of course, this is a rebuttable presumption and the accused (the drawer) can thus show that the 'stop payment' instructions were not issued because of insufficiency or paucity of funds," the Bench added.

> "If the accused shows that there were sufficient funds in his account to clear the amount of the cheque at the time of its presentation for encashment and that the stop payment notice had been issued because of other valid causes, including that there was no existing debt or liability, then offence under Section 138 would not be made out," the Bench said citing an early Apex Court ruling in the 'Modi cements case' (1998).

In *M/s. Electronics Trade & Technology Development Corpn. Ltd., Secunderabad* v. *M/s. Indian Technologists & Engineers (Electronics) Pvt. Ltd.* Hon'ble Supreme Court Said that:

> "It would thus be clear that when a cheque is drawn by a person on an account maintained by him with the banker for payment of any amount of money to another person out of the amount for the discharge of the debt in whole or in part or other liability is returned by the bank with the endorsement like (1) in this case, "I refer to the drawer" (2) "instructions for stoppage of payment" and (3) "stamp exceeds arrangement", it amounts to dishonour within the meaning of Section 138 of the Act. On issuance of the notice by the payee or the holder in due course after dishonour, to the drawer demanding payment within 15 days from the date of the receipt of such a notice, if he does not pay the same, the statutory presumption of dishonest intention, subject to any other liability, stands satisfied".

Hon'ble Supreme Court in *Jugesh Sehgal* v. *Shamsher Singh Gogi* 2009(3) CC Cases (SC) 2004-The Hon'ble Supreme Court noted that the cheque alleged to have been issued by the petitioners to the complainant was issued from an account pertaining to some other person. The Hon'ble Court also noted that one of the essential ingredients of the offence punishable under Section 138 of Negotiable Instruments Act is that the cheque must have been drawn on an account maintained by the accused. Since the cheque in the case before the Hon'ble Supreme Court was not issued from the account maintained by the petitioner, it was held that one essential ingredient of offence under Section 138 of Negotiable Instruments Act was not satisfied

XVI - SECURITY CHEQUE:

Hon'ble Bombay High Court in *Ramkrishna Urban Cooperative Credit Society (RUCCS)* v. *Rajendra Varma* (2000), held that banks cannot prosecute borrowers if the blank post-dated cheque issued by them (Borrowers) as collateral security is dishonoured', sending a sense of disappointment across commercial and business circle.

Cheque was issued in terms of a compromise agreement: The Supreme Court has ruled that criminal proceedings for issuing a cheque without sufficient balance in the account would be valid only if it is drawn for discharging a debt or liability. If it is issued to satisfy the terms of a compromise or settlement, Section 138 of the Negotiable Instruments Act could not be used to proceed against the drawer of the cheque.

Loan - No instrument executed though a huge loan was advanced - Even no interest thereon charged - Earlier accused did not pay instalments in respect of the prized amount of chitties - Loan advanced inspite of the fact that three civil suits for recovery of money against accused were pending - Complainant not approaching Court with clean hands and his conduct not that of a prudent man - Held, accused has discharged his burden to rebut the presumption available under section 139 of the Act - Order of acquittal, upheld. (*John K.John* v. *Tom Varghese*) 2007(3) Apex Court Judgments 655 (S.C.) : 2007(4) Civil Court Cases 690 (S.C.) : 2007(4) Criminal Court Cases 974 (S.C.)

XVII - EXPERTS OPINION:

Disputed cheque, to be sent for comparison Ms. Kalyani Baskar, (2007) 1 MLJ (Crl) 1020 (SC),

FORGED CHEQUE: Negotiable Instruments Act, 1881 - Section 138 -Criminal Procedure Code, 1973 - Section 195 - Section 195(1)(*b*)(*ii*) - Dishonour of cheque - Cheque alleged to be forged before filing complaint - Held, if offence is committed pertaining to document prior to its production in Court and when it was not in custody of Court then bar under section 195(1)(*b*)(*ii*) of Cr.P.C. does not arise and complainant is at liberty to file complaint and take action as per law.

Negotiable Instruments Act, 1881 - Section 138 - Dishonour of cheque - Complaint under section 138 of the Act - Cheque alleged to be forged before filing complaint - Accused lodged complaint under sections 464, 468, 389, 420 r/w section 511 IPC - Bar under section 195(1)(*b*)(*ii*) is not applicable - In the interest of justice both matters ordered to be heard and disposed by same Court together and at the same time (*Bombay HC Court Ramanand* v. *Kailasnath*)

RBI GUIDELINES ON MANAGING RISKS AND CODE OF CONDUCT IN OUTSOURCING OF FINANCIAL SERVICES BY BANKS

RBI/2006/167

DBOD.NO.BP. 40/21.04.158/2006-07

November 3, 2006

1. INTRODUCTION

1.1 The world over, banks are increasingly using outsourcing as a means of both reducing cost and accessing specialist expertise, not available internally and achieving strategic aims. 'Outsourcing' may be defined as *a bank's use of a third party (either an affiliated entity within a corporate group or an entity that is external to the corporate group) to perform activities on a continuing basis that would normally be undertaken by the bank itself, now or in the future.*

'Continuing basis' would include agreements for a limited period.

In keeping with this international trend, it is observed, that banks in India too have been extensively outsourcing various activities. Needless to say, such outsourcing, results in banks being exposed to various risks as detailed in para 1.3. Further, the outsourcing activities are to be brought within regulatory purview and the interests of the customers have to be protected.

It is against this background, that Reserve Bank of India has deemed it appropriate to put in place a set of guidelines to address, the risks that bank would be exposed to in a milieu of growing outsourcing activity and to ensure that the bank concerned and the Reserve Bank of India have access to all books, records and information available with service provider. The guidelines also cover issues relating to safeguarding of customer interests.

Typically outsourced financial services include applications processing (loan origination, credit card), document processing, marketing and research, supervision of loans, data processing and back office related activities, etc.

1.2 The Joint Forum, a tripartite body comprising Basel Committee on Banking Supervision, International Organization of Securities Commission and International Association of Insurance Supervisors had issued guidelines on outsourcing in financial services in February 2005. The Joint Forum has developed a set of Guiding Principles. These Guiding Principles have been suitably incorporated in the guidelines now being issued by RBI. Internationally, several countries have also put in place, guidelines on outsourcing in financial services. These include USA, UK, Germany, Hong Kong, Australia and Singapore. The guidelines of RBI are based on international best practices.

1.3 Outsourcing brings in its wake, several risks. Some key risks in outsourcing may be Strategic Risk, Reputation Risk, Compliance Risk, Operational Risk, Legal Risk, Exit Strategy

Risk, Counter party Risk, Country Risk, Contractual Risk, Access Risk, Concentration and Systemic Risk. The failure of a service provider in providing a specified service, a breach in security/confidentiality, or non-compliance with legal and regulatory requirements by either the service provider or the outsourcing bank can lead to financial losses or loss of reputation for the bank and could also lead to systemic risks within the entire banking system in the country. It would therefore be imperative for the bank outsourcing its activities to ensure effective management of these risks.

1.4 These guidelines on managing risks in Outsourcing are intended to provide direction and guidance to banks which choose to outsource financial services to adopt sound and responsive risk management practices for effective oversight, due diligence and management of risks arising from such outsourcing activities. The guidelines are applicable to outsourcing arrangements entered into by a bank with a service provider located in India or elsewhere. The service provider may either be a member of the group/conglomerate to which the bank belongs, or an unrelated party.

1.5 The underlying principles behind these guidelines are that the regulated entity should ensure that outsourcing arrangements neither diminish its ability to fulfil its obligations to customers and RBI nor impede effective supervision by RBI. Banks, therefore, have to take steps to ensure that the service provider employs the same high standard of care in performing the services as would be employed by the banks, if the activities were conducted within the banks and not outsourced. Accordingly, banks should not engage in outsourcing that would result in their internal control, business conduct or reputation being compromised or weakened.

1.6 (*i*) Banks which desire to outsource financial services would not require prior approval from RBI whether the service provider is located in India or outside India.

(*ii*) In regard to outsourced services relating to credit cards, RBI's detailed instructions contained in its circular on credit card activities *vide* DBOD. FSD. BC. 49/24.01.011/2005-06 dated 21st November, 2005 would be applicable.

2. ACTIVITIES THAT SHOULD NOT BE OUTSOURCED

Banks which choose to outsource financial services should however not outsource core management functions including Internal Audit, Compliance function and decision-making functions like determining compliance with KYC norms for opening deposit accounts, according sanction for loans (including retail loans) and management of investment portfolio.

3. MATERIAL OUTSOURCING

During Annual Financial Inspections, RBI will review the implementation of these guidelines to assess the quality of related risk management systems particularly in respect of material outsourcing. Material outsourcing arrangements are those, which if disrupted, have the potential to significantly impact the business operations, reputation or profitability. Materiality of outsourcing would be based on:

- The level of importance to the bank of the activity being outsourced
- The potential impact of the outsourcing on the bank on various parameters such as earnings, solvency, liquidity, funding capital and risk profile;
- The likely impact on the bank's reputation and brand value, and ability to achieve its business objectives, strategy and plans, should the service provider fail to perform the service;
- The cost of the outsourcing as a proportion of total operating costs of the bank;
- The aggregate exposure to that particular service provider, in cases where the bank outsources various functions to the same service provider.

4. BANK'S ROLE AND REGULATORY AND SUPERVISORY REQUIREMENTS

4.1 The outsourcing of any activity by bank does not diminish its obligations, and those of its Board and senior management, who have the ultimate responsibility for the outsourced activity. Banks would therefore be responsible for the actions of their service provider including Direct Sales Agents/Direct Marketing Agents and recovery agents and the confidentiality of information pertaining to the customers that is available with the service provider. Banks should retain ultimate control of the outsourced activity.

4.2 It is imperative for the bank, when performing its due diligence in relation to outsourcing, to consider all relevant laws, regulations, guidelines and conditions of approval, licensing or registration.

4.3 Outsourcing arrangements should not affect the rights of a customer against the bank, including the ability of the customer to obtain redressal as applicable under relevant laws. Since the customers are required to deal with the service providers in the process of dealing with the bank, banks should incorporate a clause in the product literature/ brochures, etc., stating that they may use the services of agents in sales/marketing etc. of the products. The role of agents may be indicated in broad terms.

4.4 Outsourcing, whether the service provider is located in India or abroad should not impede or interfere with the ability of the bank to effectively oversee and manage its activities nor should it impede the Reserve Bank of India in carrying out its supervisory functions and objectives.

4.5 Banks need to have a robust grievance redressal mechanism, which in no way should be compromised on account of outsourcing.

4.6 The service provider if it is not a subsidiary of the bank should not be owned or controlled by any director or officer/employee of the bank or their relatives having the same meaning as assigned under Section 6 of the Companies Act, 1956.

5. RISK MANAGEMENT PRACTICES FOR OUTSOURCED FINANCIAL SERVICES

5.1 OUTSOURCING POLICY

A bank intending to outsource any of its financial activities should put in place a comprehensive outsourcing policy, approved by its Board, which incorporates, *inter alia,* criteria for selection of such activities as well as service providers, parameters for defining material outsourcing based on the broad criteria indicated in para 3, delegation of authority depending on risks and materiality and systems to monitor and review the operations of these activities.

5.2 ROLE OF THE BOARD AND SENIOR MANAGEMENT

5.2.1 The Board of the bank, or a Committee of the Board to which powers have been delegated should be responsible *inter alia* for: -

- Approving a framework to evaluate the risks and materiality of all existing and prospective outsourcing and the policies that apply to such arrangements;
- Laying down appropriate approval authorities for outsourcing depending on risks and materiality.
- Undertaking regular review of outsourcing strategies and arrangements for their continued relevance, and safety and soundness and
- Deciding on business activities of a material nature to be outsourced, and approving such arrangements.

5.2.2 SENIOR MANAGEMENT WOULD BE RESPONSIBLE FOR

- Evaluating the risks and materiality of all existing and prospective outsourcing, based on the framework approved by the Board;
- Developing and implementing sound and prudent outsourcing policies and procedures commensurate with the nature, scope and complexity of the outsourcing;
- Reviewing periodically the effectiveness of policies and procedures;
- Communicating information pertaining to material outsourcing risks to the Board in a timely manner;
- Ensuring that contingency plans, based on realistic and probable disruptive scenarios, are in place and tested;
- Ensuring that there is independent review and audit for compliance with set policies.
- Undertaking periodic review of outsourcing arrangements to identify new material outsourcing risks as they arise.

5.3 EVALUATION OF THE RISKS

The key risks in outsourcing that need to be evaluated by the banks are: -

(*a*) Strategic Risk - The service provider may conduct business on its own behalf, which is inconsistent with the overall strategic goals of the bank.

(*b*) Reputation Risk - Poor service from the service provider, its customer interaction not being consistent with the overall standards of the bank.

(*c*) Compliance Risk - Privacy, consumer and prudential laws not adequately complied with.

(*d*) Operational Risk - Arising due to technology failure, fraud, error, inadequate financial capacity to fulfil obligations and/or provide remedies.

(*e*) Legal Risk - Includes but is not limited to exposure to fines, penalties, or punitive damages resulting from supervisory actions, as well as private settlements due to omissions and commissions of the service provider.

(*f*) Exit Strategy Risk - This could arise from over-reliance on one firm, the loss of relevant skills in the bank itself preventing it from bringing the activity back in-house and contracts entered into wherein speedy exits would be prohibitively expensive.

(*g*) Counter party Risk - Due to inappropriate underwriting or credit assessments.

(*h*) Country Risk - Due to the political, social or legal climate creating added risk.

(*i*) Contractual Risk - Arising from whether or not the bank has the ability to enforce the contract.

(*j*) Concentration and Systemic Risk - Due to lack of control of individual banks over a service provider, more so when overall banking industry has considerable exposure to one service provider.

5.4 EVALUATING THE CAPABILITY OF THE SERVICE PROVIDER

5.4.1 In considering or renewing an outsourcing arrangement, appropriate due diligence should be performed to assess the capability of the service provider to comply with obligations in the outsourcing agreement. Due diligence should take into consideration qualitative and quantitative, financial, operational and reputational factors. Banks should consider whether the service providers' systems are compatible with their own and also whether their standards of performance including in the area of customer service are acceptable to it. Banks should also consider, while evaluating the capability of the service provider, issues relating to undue concentration of outsourcing arrangements with a single service provider. Where possible, the bank should obtain independent reviews and market feedback on the service provider to supplement its own findings.

5.4.2 Due diligence should involve an evaluation of all available information about the service provider, including but not limited to:-

- Past experience and competence to implement and support the proposed activity over the contracted period;
- Financial soundness and ability to service commitments even under adverse conditions;
- Business reputation and culture, compliance, complaints and outstanding or potential litigation;
- Security and internal control, audit coverage, reporting and monitoring environment, Business continuity management;
- External factors like political, economic, social and legal environment of the jurisdiction in which the service provider operates and other events that may impact service performance;
- Ensuring due diligence by service provider of its employees.

5.5 THE OUTSOURCING AGREEMENT

5.5.1 The terms and conditions governing the contract between the bank and the service provider should be carefully defined in written agreements and vetted by bank's legal counsel on their legal effect and enforceability. Every such agreement should address the risks and risk mitigation strategies. The agreement should be sufficiently flexible to allow the bank to retain an appropriate level of control over the outsourcing and the right to intervene with appropriate measures to meet legal and regulatory obligations. The agreement should also bring out the nature of legal relationship between the parties - *i.e.* whether agent, principal or otherwise. Some of the key provisions of the contract would be:

- The contract should clearly define what activities are going to be outsourced including appropriate service and performance standards.
- The bank must ensure it has the ability to access all books, records and information relevant to the outsourced activity available with the service provider.
- The contract should provide for continuous monitoring and assessment by the bank of the service provider so that any necessary corrective measure can be taken immediately.
- A termination clause and minimum periods to execute a termination provision, if deemed necessary, should be included.
- Controls to ensure customer data confidentiality and service providers' liability in case of breach of security and leakage of confidential customer related information.
- Contingency plans to ensure business continuity.
- The contract should provide for the prior approval/consent by the bank of the use of sub-contractors by the service provider for all or part of an outsourced activity.
- Provide the bank with the right to conduct audits on the service provider whether by its internal or external auditors, or by agents appointed to act on its behalf and to obtain copies of any audit or review reports and findings made on the service provider in conjunction with the services performed for the bank.
- Outsourcing agreements should include clauses to allow the Reserve Bank of India or persons authorised by it to access the bank's documents, records of transactions, and other necessary information given to, stored or processed by the service provider within a reasonable time.
- Outsourcing agreement should also include clause to recognise the right of the Reserve Bank to cause an inspection to be made of a service provider of a bank and its books and account by one or more of its officers or employees or other persons.
- In cases where the controlling/Head offices of foreign banks operating in India outsource the activities related to the Indian operations, the Agreement should include clauses to allow the RBI or persons authorized by it to access the bank's documents, records of transactions and other necessary information given or stored

or processed by the service provider within a reasonable time as also clauses to recognise the right of RBI to cause an inspection to be made of a service provider and its books and account by one or more of its officers or employees or other persons.

- The outsourcing agreement should also provide that confidentiality of customer's information should be maintained even after the contract expires or gets terminated.
- The outsourcing agreement should provide for the preservation of documents and data by the service provider in accordance with the legal/regulatory obligation of the bank in this regard.

5.6 CONFIDENTIALITY AND SECURITY

5.6.1 Public confidence and customer trust in the bank is a prerequisite for the stability and reputation of the bank. Hence the bank should seek to ensure the preservation and protection of the security and confidentiality of customer information in the custody or possession of the service provider.

5.6.2 Access to customer information by staff of the service provider should be on 'need to know' basis *i.e.*, limited to those areas where the information is required in order to perform the outsourced function.

5.6.3 The bank should ensure that the service provider is able to isolate and clearly identify the bank's customer information, documents, records and assets to protect the confidentiality of the information. In instances, where service provider acts as an outsourcing agent for multiple banks, care should be taken to build strong safeguards so that there is no commingling of information/documents, records and assets.

5.6.4 The bank should review and monitor the security practices and control processes of the service provider on a regular basis and require the service provider to disclose security breaches.

5.6.5 The bank should immediately notify RBI in the event of any breach of security and leakage of confidential customer related information. In these eventualities, the bank would be liable to its customers for any damage.

5.7 RESPONSIBILITIES OF DSA/DMA/RECOVERY AGENTS

5.7.1 Code of conduct for Direct Sales Agents formulated by the Indian Banks' Association (IBA) could be used in formulating their own codes for Direct Sales Agents/Direct Marketing Agents/Recovery Agents. Banks should ensure that the Direct Sales Agents/ Direct Marketing Agents/Recovery Agents are properly trained to handle with care and senstivity, their responsibilities particularly aspects like soliciting customers, hours of calling, privacy of customer information and conveying the correct terms and conditions of the products on offer, etc.

5.7.2 Recovery Agents should adhere to extant instructions on Fair Practices Code for lending (Circular DBOD. Leg. No. BC.104/09.07.007/2002-03 dated 5th May, 2003) as also their own code for collection of dues. If the banks do not have their own code they should, at the minimum, adopt the Indian Banks Association's code for collection of dues and repossession of security. It is essential that the Recovery Agents refrain from action that could damage the integrity and reputation of the bank and that they observe strict customer confidentiality.

5.7.3 The bank and their agents should not resort to intimidation or harassment of any kind either verbal or physical against any person in their debt collection efforts, including acts intended to humiliate publicly or intrude the privacy of the debtors' family members, referees and friends, making threatening and anonymous calls or making false and misleading representations.

5.8 BUSINESS CONTINUITY AND MANAGEMENT OF DISASTER RECOVERY PLAN

5.8.1 A bank should require its service providers to develop and establish a robust framework for documenting, maintaining and testing business continuity and recovery procedures. Banks need to ensure that the service provider periodically tests the Business Continuity and Recovery Plan and may also consider occasional joint testing and recovery exercises with its service provider.

5.8.2 In order to mitigate the risk of unexpected termination of the outsourcing agreement or liquidation of the service provider, banks should retain an appropriate level of control over their outsourcing and the right to intervene with appropriate measures to continue its business operations in such cases without incurring prohibitive expenses and without any break in the operations of the bank and its services to the customers.

5.8.3 In establishing a viable contingency plan, banks should consider the availability of alternative service providers or the possibility of bringing the outsourced activity back in-house in an emergency and the costs, time and resources that would be involved.

5.8.4 Outsourcing often leads to the sharing of facilities operated by the service provider. The bank should ensure that service providers are able to isolate the bank's information, documents and records, and other assets. This is to ensure that in adverse conditions, all documents, records of transactions and information given to the service provider, and assets of the bank, can be removed from the possession of the service provider in order to continue its business operations, or deleted, destroyed or rendered unusable.

5.9 MONITORING AND CONTROL OF OUTSOURCED ACTIVITIES

5.9.1 The bank should have in place a management structure to monitor and control its outsourcing activities. It should ensure that outsourcing agreements with the service provider contain provisions to address their monitoring and control of outsourced activities.

5.9.2 A central record of all material outsourcing that is readily accessible for review by the Board and senior management of the bank should be maintained. The records should be updated promptly and half yearly reviews should be placed before the Board.

5.9.3 Regular audits by either the internal auditors or external auditors of the bank should assess the adequacy of the risk management practices adopted in overseeing and managing the outsourcing arrangement, the bank's compliance with its risk management framework and the requirements of these guidelines.

5.9.4 Banks should at least on an annual basis, review the financial and operational condition of the service provider to assess its ability to continue to meet its outsourcing obligations. Such due diligence reviews, which can be based on all available information

about the service provider should highlight any deterioration or breach in performance standards, confidentiality and security, and in business continuity preparedness.

5.9.5 In the event of termination of the agreement for any reason, this should be publicized so as to ensure that the customers do not continue to entertain the service provider.

5.10 REDRESSAL OF GRIEVANCES RELATED TO OUTSOURCED SERVICES

(*a*) Banks should constitute Grievance Redressal Machinery within the bank and give wide publicity about it through electronic and print media. The name and contact number of designated grievance redressal officer of the bank should be made known and widely publicised. The designated officer should ensure that genuine grievances of customers are redressed promptly without involving delay. It should be clearly indicated that banks' Grievance Redressal Machinery will also deal with the issue relating to services provided by the outsourced agency.

(*b*) Generally, a time limit of 30 days may be given to the customers for preferring their complaints/grievances. The grievance redressal procedure of the bank and the time frame fixed for responding to the complaints should be placed on the bank's website.

(*c*) If a complainant does not get satisfactory response from the bank within 60 days from the date of his lodging the complaint, he will have the option to approach the Office of the concerned Banking Ombudsman for redressal of his grievance/s.

5.11 REPORTING OF TRANSACTIONS TO FINANCIAL INTELLIGENCE UNIT (FIU) OR OTHER COMPETENT AUTHORITIES

Banks would be responsible for making Currency Transactions Reports and Suspicious Transactions Reports to FIU or any other competent authority in respect of the banks' customer related activities carried out by the service providers.

6. CENTRALISED LIST OF OUTSOURCED AGENTS

If a service provider's services are terminated by a bank, IBA would have to be informed with reasons for termination. IBA would be maintaining a caution list of such service providers for the entire banking industry for sharing among banks.

7. OFF-SHORE OUTSOURCING OF FINANCIAL SERVICES

7.1 The engagement of service providers in a foreign country exposes a bank to country risk - economic, social and political conditions and events in a foreign country that may adversely affect the bank. Such conditions and events could prevent the service provider from carrying out the terms of its agreement with the bank. To manage the country risk involved in such outsourcing activities, the bank should take into account and closely monitor government policies and political, social, economic and legal conditions in countries where the service provider is based, during the risk assessment process and on a continuous basis, and establish sound procedures for dealing with country risk problems. This includes having appropriate contingency and exit strategies. In principle, arrangements should only be entered into with parties operating in jurisdictions generally upholding confidentiality clauses and agreements. The governing law of the arrangement should also be clearly specified.

7.2 The activities outsourced outside India should be conducted in a manner so as not to hinder efforts to supervise or reconstruct the Indian activities of the bank in a timely manner.

7.3 The outsourcing related to overseas operations of Indian banks would be governed by both, these guidelines and the host country guidelines. Where there are differences, the more stringent of the two would prevail. However, where there is any conflict, the host country guidelines would prevail.

8. OUTSOURCING WITHIN A GROUP/CONGLOMERATE

The risk management practices expected to be adopted by a bank while outsourcing to a related party (*i.e.* party within the Group/Conglomerate) would be identical to those specified in Para 5 of this guidelines.

9. SELF-ASSESSMENT OF EXISTING/PROPOSED OUTSOURCING ARRANGEMENTS

Banks may conduct a self-assessment of their existing outsourcing agreements within a time bound plan and bring them in line with the above guidelines expeditiously.

CASE LAWS ON REPOSSESSION AND ENFORCEMENT OF SECURITIES

1. The complainant had availed loan for purchasing a tractor and the tractor was hypothecated to the bank. When the complainant committed default in payment of the instalment, the bank seized the tractor in accordance with the terms and conditions subject to which the loan was advanced. Held that there was no deficiency in service. *M.V. Krishna Reddy* v. *Andhra Bank Guder* 1992 (1) CPR 456 (SCRDC - Hyd.)
2. The complainant's case against the bank was that the Bank had locked and sealed two rooms in the premises where the stocks were stored. The Banks contention was that it is within its discretion to consider whether the stock is sufficient to meet obligations of the borrowers and take appropriate action to safeguard its interest. The decision of the banking authorities is not subjected to review by the forums constituted under Consumer Protection Act. The State Commission held that when the bank loan has been advanced primarily at the stock of goods, it is for the bank to consider whether the stock is sufficient to meet obligations of the borrowers. *Babu Ranganathan* v. *Manager, State Bank of Saurashtra* 1994 (3) CPR 149 (SCDRC - Tamil Nadu)
3. The non-return of title deeds pledged with the bank by the borrower would amount to deficiency of service on the part of the bank and the bank was directed to pay compensation of Rs. 1,00,000 for the loss caused to the complainant and cost quantified at Rs. 25,000. *C.L. Khanna* v. *Dena Bank* - judgment dated September 2, 2005 of the National Consumer Disputes Redressal Commission.
4. Bank can call in the said provisions of the Securitisation Act, 2002 even though Civil Suit are pending concerning the subject matter.

   FACTS:

   Appellant, writ petitioner, was served with Notice dated 10.2.2004 by the Punjab National Bank under Section 13(4) of the Securitisation Act calling upon him to pay within a period of 60 days from the date of receipt of the notice the amount of Rs. 6,17,058/ towards the outstanding amount under the loan availed of by him in the account of M/s M.s. Oils and Rs. 7.11,708 towards the outstanding amount under the loan availed by him in the account of M/s S. B. Bricks, failing which it was informed that the secured assets would be proceeded with for realization of the amounts due to the Bank. The contention raised by the appellant was that the suits filed by him in civil courts against the Bank for settlement of accounts in respect of account of M/s S.B. Bricks and in respect of Account of M/s M.S. Oils of which he is the proprietor and the suit filed by the bank for recovery of money with interest against the appellant in civil court, in respect of the account

of M/s M.S. Bricks & M/s Oils are still pending. The Bank had also secured an order of attachment in those suits and hence at his juncture provisions of Section 13(4) of Securitisation Act cannot be imported.

HELD:

Dismissing the appeal, the Hon'ble Court held that section 13(1) of the Act confers power of the creditor for enforcement of security interest without the intervention of the court or Tribunal. Nowhere it is stated in the statute that once the jurisdiction of the civil court has been invoked the provisions of the Securitisation Act would not apply. Before the coming into force of the Securitisation Act, the remedy upon the Bank was to approach the civil court or Debt Recovery Tribunal, as the case may be. The expression "without the intervention of the court or the Tribunal" was used to show that the option is on the Bank to move to the civil court or the Tribunal under the Act but there is no bar under the statute that having approached the Civil Court Section 13(1) of the Act cannot be invoked. The provisions of the Act or the rules made thereunder shall be in addition to, and not in derogation of the other laws, remedy which is unless barred by the statute can be enforced at any point of time.

(*Abdul Azeez* v. *Punjab National Bank 2005* (1) KLT 243)/[2005] 64 SCL 44 (Ker.).

5. Bank holding decree against the appellant and execution petition pending, whether notice by Bank under enforcement of security Act permissible - Held- Yes.

FACTS:

The Punjab National Bank secured a decree and filed the execution petition against the petitioner for the amount due from him. The petitioner later sought for one-time settlement with the respondent bank. But the Bank issued a notice Under Section 13(2) of the Securitisation and Reconstruction of Financial Assets and Enforcement of Security Interest Act, 2002 wherein the Bank stated that, if the petitioner failed to comply with the requirements of the notice it would proceed to take possession of the property. Upon receipt of the notice, the petitioner Filed a writ petition before the High Court at Kerala contending that the Bank had no power to proceed under the Act, as it had already obtained a decree and filed an execution petition against the petitioner.

HELD:

The Hon'ble High Court observed that Section 14 of the SARFAESI Act enabled the Bank to seek assistance in getting possession and that it was enacted to ensure that the financial institution does not forcibly disposes the person in possession. The Hon'ble Court holding that the notice issued by the Bank is valid dismissed the writ petition. However, the court also observed that the dismissal of the writ petition shall not stand in the way of the petitioner approaching the bank for settling the dues.

(*Aboobacker* v. *Punjab National Bank* (2005) 127 Comp. Cases 519/64 SCL 42 (Kerala High Court).

6. When a service of notice by post is refused by the addressee to accept the same, knowledge of the contents of the notice must be imputed to him.

FACTS:

The respondents were the landlords of the premises in which the appellant was the tenant. They have sent a notice to the tenant demanding payment of arrears and seeking ejectment on termination of tenancy which was refused by the latter. On his failure to comply with the requisitions contained in the notice, the respondents filed a suit against the tenant seeking eviction as well as recovery of rents and mesne profits. The suit was resisted by the tenant *inter alia* on the grounds that there was no default and that no notice of demand and ejectment was served on him and consequently prayed for dismissal. The trial Court decreed the suit for arrears but dismissed the same insofar as the relief of eviction was concerned after finding that no notice for eviction was served on the tenant. On appeal to the District Court, it found that there was service of notice by refusal, but no knowledge of the contents of the notice could be imputed to him, and consequently there was no wilful default in the payment of rent. The Court therefore dismissed the appeal. On further appeal to the High Court, it was held that when notice was tendered to the tenant and when the latter refused to accept the same, knowledge of the contents of the notice must be imputed to him. The High Court accordingly allowed the appeal and ordered eviction of the tenant. Aggrieved by the said decision, the tenant took up the matter to the Supreme Court by special leave and vehemently contended that no presumption as drawn by the High Court could be made especially when the envelope was not opened and the contents were not read by the tenant before it was returned to the postman.

DECISION:

The learned Judges of the Supreme Court by a majority judgment, after discussing the case-law cited before them by both sides, had rejected the contention of the appellant-tenant, and while doing so held as under:

> "Section 27 of the General Clauses Act, 1897 deals with the topic-'Meaning of service by post' and says that where any Central Act or Regulation authorizes or requires any document to be served by post, then unless a different intention appears, *the service shall be deemed to be effected by* properly addressing, pre-paying and posting it by registered post, a letter containing the document, and unless the contrary is provided, to have been effected at the time at which the letter would be delivered in the ordinary course of post. The section thus raises a presumption of *due service or proper service* if the document sought to be served is sent by properly addressing, prepaying and posting by registered post to the addressee and such presumption is raised irrespective of whether any acknowledgement due is received from the addressee or not."

NOTES:

The presumption of knowledge would arise under Section 114 of the Indian Evidence Act that the refusal was with the knowledge of the contents of the registered envelope.

Indian Evidence Act, 1872.

Section 114. Court may presume existence of certain facts – The Court may presume the existence of any fact which it thinks likely to have happened, regards being had to the common course of natural events, human conduct and public and private business, in their relation to the facts of the particular case. (Citation of the case may be given for easy reference)

7. Payment of deficit stamp duty.

FACTS:

Applicant Bank granted letter of credit facility of Rs. 30 crores and cash credit (hypothecation) facility of Rs. 10 crores, total amounting to Rs. 40 crores to the respondent firm. In order to secure the said credit facilities, the respondent No. 2 firm through its partners, respondent Nos. 4 to 7 created equitable mortgage of their immovable properties by executing memorandum of deposit of title deeds at Bombay. The respondent failed to repay the amount and, therefore, the applicant bank filed application before the DRT, Ahmedabad in the State of Gujarat & sought for recovery of Rs. 9,10,46,271 and also for realization of that amount by sale of the mortgaged property. The respondents/original defendants contended that the documents relied upon by the applicant bank were insufficiently stamped & hence, they were not admissible in evidence unless the applicant ban paid stamp duty in terms of the Bombay Stamp Act, 1958 and they also prayed that the various documents relied upon by the applicant bank in the application may also be impounded for the reason that they are insufficiently stamped. The Presiding Officer DRT, Ahmedabad rejected the contention of the respondents/defendants with respect to other documents but partly allowed the application by observing that memorandum of deposit of title deeds was not sufficiently stamped and as such was not admissible in evidence unless the Bank made payment of deficit stamp duty as per provisions of the Bombay Stamp Act as applicable in the State of Gujarat. Aggrieved by the said order of the Debt Recovery Tribunal applicant bank filed the appeal before the Debts Recovery Appellate Tribunal, Mumbai.

HELD:

Dismissing the appeal, the Appellate Tribunal held that an adhesive stamp of Rs. 50,000 was affixed on memorandum for deposit of title deeds executed by the defendants/respondents at Mumbai. The copy of the said document had been brought in Ahmedabad in the State of Gujarat and in terms of Article 6 of the schedule of the Bombay Stamp Act, the stamp duty payable was Rs. 1 lakh and

thus there was and is a shortfall of the remaining amount. Therefore, when the applicant bank is relying upon the memorandum of deposit of title deeds, they have to pay deficit stamp duty, as applicable in the State of Gujarat and on payment of required stamp duty, they should file affidavit enclosing therewith proof of such payment, then only the said document will be admissible in evidence otherwise it will be hit by provision of Section 34 of the Bombay Stamp Act.

(*State Bank of Saurashtra* v. *N.C.K. Sons Export* 2004 (2) 1SJ (Banking) 13 DRAT, Mumbai).

8. Cancellation by writing the signature or initials is not the only way of cancelling the stamp. There can be other effectual ways in which stamps can be cancelled. Drawing two lines across the stamps is one such effectual way of cancellation. The purpose of cancellation is to see that the stamps are not used again.

FACTS:

Two suits have been filed for recovery of monies due under 3 promissory notes executed by the third defendant, Managing Partner of the first defendant firm, for and on behalf of the firm, the second defendant being the other partner. The amounts remained unpaid inspite of demand and notices. The suits were contested by the defendants on the ground *inter alia* that the third defendant had no authority to borrow money so as to bind the firm, that the suit pronotes were mere letters but not promissory notes that they were not properly stamped and they were not supported by consideration. In the second suit, an additional plea was taken that the endorsement made by the fourth defendant in favour of the plaintiff was not valid since the said pronote was not negotiable for want of words 'or order' on the note. The trial Court held on consideration of the entire evidence adduced by both the parties that the promissory notes were not mere letters but promissory notes only, that they have been materially altered by affixing and cancelling stamps subsequently, that they have been executed by the third defendant for and on behalf of the firm and he had no power to contract debts so as to bind the firm and that they were collusive and without consideration. Accordingly, the Court dismissed the suits. Being aggrieved by the said decision, the matters were taken in appeal by the plaintiffs to the High Court.

DECISION:

Repelling each of the contentions raised by the defendants in defense to the suits, the learned Judges of the High Court held as under:

> "It is true that the documents do not say that the payment will be made to any promise named in the body of the documents or to his order. Going by the definition in Section 4 of the Negotiable Instruments Act, it is not necessary that the promise should be to pay the money to the "order" of a certain person. Even without such a clause a document could be a promissory note. Section 13 of the Negotiable Instrument Act defines a negotiable instrument as a promissory note, bill of exchange or cheque payable either to order or bearer. Expln. 1 states that such a documentation is payable to order if it

is expressed to be so payable to a particular person and does not contain words, prohibiting transfer or indicating an intention that it shall not be transferable. A reading of Sections 4 and 13 of the Negotiable Instruments Act makes it clear that a document, if it otherwise satisfies the definition of promissory note, will not cease to be so merely because the words "to order" are absent in the document. Even without such an expression, the document could be a promissory note. It is also negotiable in case the document does not contain words or expressions prohibiting negotiation".

"The other ground urged that the documents do not show the name of the payee and therefore cannot be treated as promissory notes does not appear to be correct. Section 4 of the Negotiable Instruments Act only requires that the document must show that the amount is to be paid to or to the order of "a certain person". If a document clearly states that it is so payable to a certain person specifically described therein as such in the body of the document, the matter is clearly beyond controversy. The question of interpretation arises only where a document is not so clearly expressed".

"In each of these documents the stamps are seen affixed on the fact of the documents by the side of the signature. *Prima facie* there are not suspicious circumstances on the face of these documents. In the case of negotiable instrument, the court is entitled to draw an initial presumption that it is properly stamped, though where the instrument itself appears suspicious or bears marks of alteration on the face of it, the plaintiff will have to be required to make out that there was no alteration after its execution".

9. A promise to pay a time-barred debt to be valid must be an express promise and there must be some indication in the writing itself to show that the writer agreed to pay the debt although the same is barred by time.

FACTS:

A Promise was executed by the appellant for Rs. 1,300 on 5th January, 1963 in favour of the respondent and promised to pay the amount with interest at 1% per mensem on demand. The amount was not paid. On 10th July, 1966, the appellant made an endorsement in Hindi, the translation of which reads in English to the effect that 'I accept this promote and it is valid for the next three years'. The suit was later filed on 2nd March, 1968 by the respondent and contended that it was within time as the endorsement made on the pronote was not a mere acknowledgement but a promise to pay in writing within the meaning of clause (*3*) of Section 25 of the Contract Act and therefore he was entitled to recover the same on the basis of the said endorsement. The trial Court accepted the said contention and decreed the suit. The said decree was confirmed by the first appellate Court on appeal. Being aggrieved by the said decisions, the defendant (appellant) took up the matter of the High Court by way of second appeal and contended *inter alia* that if no express promise to pay was spelt. It was however contended by the respondent that if there was something more than mere acknowledgement and promise to pay could be spelt out from such a writing, the suit would be covered by clause (3) of Section 25.

DECISION:

Considering the arguments advanced by both the parties, the learned Judge, after the review of the existing case law cited before him, held as follows:

(1) The clause (2) of Section 25 of the Contract Act requires that there should be promise in writing, that it should be signed by the debtor or his agent and that this promise should be to pay wholly or in part a debt barred by time. If these conditions are fulfilled, an agreement made without consideration amounts to a contract.

(2) The contracts that are made in words are known as express contracts and if they are made otherwise than in words, such contracts are known as implied contracts. Clause (3) of Section 25 of the Act uses the words "promise made in writing to pay". Thus, there should be an express promise to pay a barred debt to constitute a contract which may be the basis of the suit.

(3) Reading of Section 9 and clause (3) of Section 25 of the Act, it makes clear that though the word "express" is not used in clause (3) of Section 25, it is essential that the promise to pay must be clear and express. In other words, an implied promise is not sufficient to satisfy the condition of clause (3) of Section 25 of the Act.

(4) The endorsement on the back of the pronote amounts to only an admission of the pronote and that it is valid for next 3 years. There are no words expressing any promise to pay by the defendant to the plaintiff. The endorsement is meaningless. At best it can mean that the defendant has acknowledged the existence of the purpose. In other words, it may amount to an acknowledgement for purpose of limitation but admittedly this endorsement was not made within the period of limitation. Hence this endorsement is not a promise to pay within the meaning of Section 25 of the Act.

Accordingly, the decree of the Courts below was set aside and the suit of the plaintiff-respondent was dismissed.

No force, recovery of bank loans only through legal means, says SC

In the case of *ICICI Bank* v. *Shanti Devi Sharma a Bench of the Supreme Court comprising Dalveer Bhandari, J. and Tarun Chatterjee, J. warned ICICI* (on May 15, 2008) against the use of musclemen to recover loans.

The Supreme Court went on to remind financial institutions that they are bound by law. The recovery of loans or seizure of vehicles can only be done through legal means; we live in a civilized country and are governed by the rule of law.

The Supreme Court, while emphasising that banks and other financial institutions cannot resort to muscle power for recovery of their loans, strongly expressed its intent of "putting an end" to this practice.

The Bench was hearing an appeal filed by ICICI Bank, against an Allahabad High Court order, rejecting its plea to quash the criminal cases registered by the Uttar Pradesh Government against the managing director and other top officials for allegedly using criminal force against a loan defaulter. The case was registered at the instance of the High Court there on a complainant from an owner that the bank had sent musclemen to seize the vehicle for non-payment of loan instalments.

GLOSSARY OF BANKING TERMS

Acceleration clause: A provision in a loan agreement which enables a lender to recall the entire amount of loan in case there is a default in even a single instalment payment by the borrower.

Account: A record of financial transactions in the books of account for an asset or individual, such as at a bank. For example, a savings account would show all deposits and withdrawals of moneys by the account holder over a period of time.

Accrued interest: Interest that is due on a bond or other fixed income security since the last interest payment was made. This is an example of accrued income.

Affidavit: A statement written and sworn to in the presence of someone authorized to administer an oath, such as a notary public. The document may be required for legal purposes.

APR : Annual Percentage Rate. The yearly cost of a loan, including interest, insurance, etc., expressed as a percentage.

Asset : Any item of economic value owned by an individual or corporation, especially that which could be converted to cash. Examples are cash, securities, accounts receivable, inventory, equipment, real estate, a car, and other property.

ATM : Acronym for automated teller machine, a machine at a bank branch or other location which enables a customer to perform basic banking activities (checking one's balance, withdrawing or transferring funds) even when the bank is closed.

Attachment : The act of seizing a debtor's property and placing it under a court's control. This is in case of default in repayment of debt.

Bank reconciliation : The process of adjusting balance in an account reported by a bank to reflect transactions that have occurred since the reporting date. For instance cheque issued by account holder may not yet reflect in the bank's books, but accounted for by the issuer. Hence the need to know the likely balance.

Banking : In general terms, the business activity of accepting and safeguarding money owned by other individuals and entities, and then lending out this money in order to earn a profit.

Bankrupt : A person, firm, or corporation that has been declared insolvent through a court proceeding and is relieved from the payment of debts (or allowed to do so) after the surrender of all assets to a court-appointed trustee.

Bearer : The holder of a negotiable instrument. That is, a person who is entitled to receive payment on the instrument.

Bounced cheque : A cheque which a bank returns because it is not payable due to insufficient funds in the account of the drawer of the cheque.

Cash credit : A short-term loan to a company to meet working capital requirements.

Chequebook : A booklet of blank cheques which enable a bank account holder to draw money from his/her deposit account.

Collateral : Assets pledged/mortgaged by a borrower to secure a loan or other credit, and subject to seizure in the event of default. Also called security.

Collecting banker : Bank which collects the negotiable instrument on behalf of its customer.

Commitment fee : A charge by a lender for holding credit available for a borrower.

Compound interest : Interest which is calculated not only on the initial principal but also the accumulated interest of prior periods. Compound interest differs from simple interest in that simple interest is calculated solely as a percentage of the principal sum.

Credit agency : Is a company which collects information about the creditworthiness of individuals and corporations and provides it for a fee to interested parties.

Credit analysis : The process of evaluating an applicant's loan request or a corporation's debt issue in order to determine the likelihood that the borrower will live up to his/her obligations.

Credit card : A card that may be used repeatedly to borrow money or buy products and services on credit. Issued mostly by banks.

Credit limit : The maximum amount of credit that a bank or other lender will extend to a customer, or the maximum that a credit card company will allow a card holder to borrow on a single card.

Credit rating : A published ranking, based on detailed financial analysis by a credit bureau, of one's financial history, specifically as it relates to one's ability to meet debt obligations.

Credit risk : The possibility that a bond issuer/borrower will default, by failing to repay principal and interest in a timely manner.

Crossed cheque : A form of cheque which has two parallel or transverse lines across the face so that the bank on which it is drawn may not pay to any other party than to a bank where the payee has an account.

Current account : A deposit account at a bank which does not pay interest, but can be withdrawn any time. It is basically for running business.

Debit card : A card which allows customers to access their funds immediately, electronically.

Debt : An amount owed to a person or organization for funds borrowed.

Default : Failure to make required debt payments on a timely basis or to comply with other conditions of an obligation or agreement.

Demand deposit : An account balance which can be drawn upon on demand, *i.e.* without prior notice. Savings deposit is an example.

Disclosure : The release of relevant information.

Drawee : The party directed to pay the amount of a draft or cheque or a bill of exchange.

Drawer : The party who draws the draft, cheque or bill of exchange upon another party for payment.

Due date : Date on which an obligation must be paid.

Endorsement : A signature used to legally transfer a negotiable instrument.

Equated Monthly instalment (EMI) : An equal amount repaid periodically comprising of interest and principal over the period of the loan or debt.

Floating rate : Any interest rate that changes on a periodic basis. The change is usually tied to movement of an outside indicator, such as the prime interest rate.

Garnishee order : Monetary judgment by the court against defendant by ordering 3rd party (garnishee) to pay, money owed to the defendant (judgment debtor), to the plaintiff (judgment creditor). This is so when there is default in debt repayment.

Guarantee : To accept responsibility for an obligation if the entity with primary responsibility for the obligation does not meet it. That is the guarantor pays when the debtor fails to do so.

Guarantor : One who guarantees an obligation and has a legal duty to fulfil it.

Holder in due course : Is a person who is in possession of an instrument for which consideration has been paid and who believes that there is no defect in the title.

Introduction : Introduction of a potential customer to a bank by an account holder, employee, or a well known person. It is necessary for a bank seeking protection under section 131 of the N.I. Act. This formality is necessary for opening of accounts.

Joint and several liability : An obligation for which multiple individuals are liable for payment as in case of obligations of a partnership concern.

Law of limitation : Law that sets out a period after which a legal document cannot be enforced unless revalidated before the said date.

Lien : A legal claim against an asset which is used to secure a loan and which must be paid when the asset is sold.

Mandate : Power given to a person or group of persons for carrying out certain jobs/activities/obligations.

Margin : Margin refers to an amount required to be brought in by a borrower, as specified by the lender, as his own contribution (equity) to the business.

Marketable security : Security that could be converted into cash quickly and easily.

Material alteration : Any alteration that changes the tenor of an instrument. To validate a material alteration the drawer must authenticate.

Maturity date : The date on which a debt becomes due for payment.

Moratorium : A period of time during which a certain activity is not allowed or required. For instance when repayment on a loan starts only after a lapse of a certain period after its disbursement, then that period is called the moratorium on the loan.

Negligence : Failure to act during the normal course of business in an usually accepted manner.

Negotiable instrument : A transferable, signed document that promises to pay the bearer a sum of money at a future date or on demand. Examples include cheques, bills of exchange, and promissory notes.

Non-performing asset : A loan that is not meeting its stated principal and interest payments. More generally, an asset which is not producing income.

Notary public : A person authorized by the state to notarize certain documents.

Online banking : A system allowing individuals to perform banking activities at home, *via* the internet

Order nisi : To freeze all transactions in debtors' account and use the amount to pay off the judgment debt.

Passbook : Book issued by a bank to record deposits, withdrawals, and interest earned in a deposit account.

Payee : One who receives a payment, such as through cash, cheque, money order, bill of exchange etc.

Paying banker : Bank on whom the negotiable instrument is drawn and which is sent for collection.

Personal guarantee : Promise made by an entrepreneur which obligates him/her to personally repay debts his/her corporation defaults on.

Personal Identification Number : PIN Code used by an individual so that he/she can access his/her bank account at an ATM machine.

Post-date : To put a future date on a document or cheque, postponing the effective or negotiable date.

Power of Attorney : A legal document that enables an individual to designate another person, called the attorney, in fact, to act on his/her behalf as long as the individual does not become disabled or incapacitated.

Secured Loan : A loan which is backed by assets belonging to the borrower in order to decrease the risk assumed by the lender. The assets may be forfeited to the lender if the borrower fails to make the necessary payments.

Set off : Adjusting debit in one account of a borrower with credit in another.

Simple interest : The interest calculated on a principal sum, not compounded on earned interest.

Stop payment : An order to a bank not to honour the payment of a cheque after it has been delivered but before it has been cashed.

Time deposit : Money kept as deposit in a bank, for a fixed term or with the understanding that the customer can withdraw only by giving advance notice.

Transfer : A movement of funds from one account to another

Vicarious Liability : Liability that arises out of the responsibility of a superior for the acts of his subordinate. As in case of a bank which is liable to the acts of its employees in the natural discharge of duties.

Waiver : The act of voluntarily giving up a right or covenant. Covenants are certain clauses in an agreement.

Wire Transfer : An electronic transfer of funds.

Write-off : To charge an asset amount to expense or loss, in order to reduce the value of that asset and one's earnings. An example, is of receivables not recoverable being charged to the profit and loss account in order to offset the income that has already accrued to the account.

APPENDIX 7

SOME OF THE IMPORTANT CASES DEALT BY THE BANKING OMBUDSMAN OFFICES

Case 1: Charging usurious and unsustainable interest rates on unsecured personal loans

Two complainants preferred two separate complaints against the exorbitant interest rates being charged by a bank, without transparency, on unsecured small ticket personal loans. The first complainant stated that the bank had charged 48% p.a. for the personal loan of Rs. 30,000 as against the initial intimation of interest at 18% p.a. and the bank had also not disbursed the loan amount in full. The second complainant had availed a personal loan of Rs. 35,000. The bank had not specified the interest rate, despite repeated enquiries and had only informed that it would be slightly high. Later, it was observed that the bank had been charging interest at 52% p.a., and along with the various other charges levied, it worked out to about 60% p.a., on the disbursed amount. On taking up the matter with the bank, the bank provided a copy of the terms and conditions of the loan duly acknowledged by the borrowers, which left room for doubt relating to transparency in charging of rates. The bank explained that they had charged processing fee as per their norms and disbursed the loan amount after deducting the processing charges and hence there was difference in the loan amount disbursed to the complainants. The bank insisted that they charged interest at 48% p.a. and 52% p.a., respectively as per the terms and conditions of the bank, duly accepted by the complainants and took refuge under the extant RBI guidelines, according to which banks could charge an interest rate as deemed appropriate based on the risk profile associated with each segment, their operating costs and other charges as determined by the bank. The Banking Ombudsman observed that the effective cost of the loan was 60% p.a. taking into consideration the impact of charging the processing fees upfront and the actual amount disbursed. On detailed enquiry and intervention by the Banking Ombudsman, the bank contacted the complainants and agreed to reduce the interest rate to 18% p.a. diminishing, upon which the first complainant withdrew the complaint and the same was closed. In the case of the second complaint, since the complainant had not paid any amount in the loan account, the bank informed the complainant that the re-schedulement would be effected on upfront payment of the overdue interest at 18% p.a., diminishing, from the date of the loan till the date of settlement. The complainant, while acknowledging the reduction in interest rate, refused to pay the overdue interest demanded upfront and sought further intervention of Banking Ombudsman, which was denied and the case was closed.

Case 2: Insurance premium debited to credit card account without cardholder's consent

The complainant represented to the Banking Ombudsman that although he had surrendered the credit card of XYZ Bank in May 2006 after repaying card dues, the bank had been harassing him by demanding payment of the dues. However, the bank had not provided to him the details of the payments demanded from him. After protracted correspondence, the bank informed him that they had reversed the finance charges and late fees charged to the credit card account totalling Rs. 4,676 as a good service gesture and after the reversal there was an outstanding amount of Rs. 6,236 which he was asked to pay to avoid levy of further charges.

In the conciliation meeting convened by the Office of the Banking Ombudsman to facilitate an amicable settlement of the complaint, the bank reported that the outstanding amount in the card account was on account of insurance premium and consent for insurance policy had been obtained from the cardholder at the time of submitting the application for the credit card. The bank further informed that the insurance product for which the premium was levied was not an add-on feature on the card but a 'sold product', which was offered to the customer. The bank agreed to produce documentary evidence within a week to prove that cardholder's consent had been obtained for the insurance product. However, the bank could not produce the documentary evidence within the time frame agreed to at the meeting and reversed premium charged to the customer.

Case 3: Wrongly classifying a card holder as a defaulter

The complainant, a Credit Card holder, was paying the dues regularly as per the statements. He received a letter from the card issuers informing him that he was a defaulter and that legal action will be taken if the overdues were not cleared. Immediately after a week, the Card Issuer had advised that the earlier letter was sent inadvertently to him and had also apologized for the mistake. Meanwhile, as per the data reported to CIBIL, the complainant was implicated as a defaulter. Though an apology letter was issued immediately thereafter, no steps were taken to rectify the wrong information reported. When the complainant approached another bank for a credit facility, they refused to grant the loan for the above reason. In spite of written representation by the complainant, the card issuer did not take steps to do the rectification required. On taking up the complaint with the card issuers, they submitted that data of all card holders are reported to CIBIL and the Card Holder's name was reported under Standard Category. In response to the detailed enquiries of the Banking Ombudsman, they conceded that their service providers would have entered the data erroneously in one of the fields. The same was rectified subsequently as directed by the Banking Ombudsman. The conciliatory efforts of the Banking Ombudsman to settle the complaint did not elicit the desired response from the card issuers. The details furnished by the card issuer revealed that the list of mandatory fields in the CIBIL datasheet submitted by the card issuer included *inter alia* the amount overdue, asset classification and suit-filed wilful default status. As stated by CIBIL, members use the CIBIL data for credit decisions and wrong reporting in any of the fields such as amount overdue or under suit-filed wilful default status could have a direct bearing on the credit decision and could also result directly in an unfavourable decision for no fault of the individual customer.

It was observed that the complainant's name was not reported as a defaulter and had been shown under standard category. At the same time, his liability under cards was reported as 'overdue'. The terms Due and Overdue had different connotations. The first term denotes only the liability outstanding which is payable, whereas the second term denotes the amount in default. Though, the cardholder was not reported as a defaulter, the fact that there was wrong reporting in one of the fields in the CIBIL database resulted in his being considered as a defaulter, thereby denying him access to credit from institutional sources. It was clearly established that there had been deficiencies on the part of the card issuer in classifying the complainant's liability under the card as overdue and measures were taken only belatedly in rearranging the data correctly. The mental agony experienced by the complainant and the reputational loss could not be quantified in monetary terms.

After taking into account all the facts of the case, the Banking Ombudsman issued an Award directing the Credit Card Issuer to pay Rs. 25,000 as compensation for the inconvenience, mental agony and loss of prestige caused by their error in reporting.

Case 4: Ambiguous clause in Loan Agreement for levy of pre-closure charges

The complainant wanted to close his loan account with the respondent bank prematurely. The bank, on enquiry informed him the amount payable by him would include the pre-closure charges. The complainant paid the amount and the account was closed. The bank provided the complainant the statement of the closed account wherein the pre-closure charge mentioned was lower than the amount actually paid by him. The complainant claimed refund of the excess amount recovered from him towards pre-closure charges. The bank, in response, claimed that in terms the loan agreement, it can recover the pre-closure charges at a rate which can range between 0 to 5% of the outstanding amount of the loan. As regards the higher amount of the above charge advised to the complainant, the bank contented that it advised only the approximate amount as a pre-term quote. Since the bank can recover the charge in the range of 0 to 5%, the bank's act of recovering an amount, which is different from the amount advised earlier, is justified.

The efforts of conciliation made by the Banking Ombudsman did not yield results. Perusal of the records relating to the case revealed that the bank had advised different amounts towards pre-closure charges in its various correspondences. The complainant relied on the information given to him by the bank and paid accordingly. The bank's act of recovering the higher amount from the complainant and appropriating the lesser amount towards the pre-closure charges, which it subsequently increased, cannot be considered justified. Further, though the banks enjoy freedom to decide charges for various services, they are required to intimate the charges to the customers, in advance, in an unambiguous manner. The clause of the agreement referred to by the bank provides for the charge in the range of 0 to 5%. The above clause may be considered as ambiguous as it does not intimate the exact charge recoverable in case of pre-closure of the loan account.

Based on the above consideration the bank was directed to restore the amount recovered by it in excess of what was originally intimated to the complainant for closure of the loan account. The bank has since implemented the order.

Case 5: Charges on a credit card

The complainant lodged the complaint alleging that the credit card issuing bank has not credited the payment of Rs. 5,600 made in October 2005 despite the complainant's bank

account being debited to that effect. The bank levied several charges for non-accounting of the same including the over limit charges. The complainant informed the bank several times over phone and made written representation with three reminders for rectification of the above error by providing the documentary evidence of his bank pass book entry wherein the disputed cheque amount debited to his bank account was reflected. But no response was received from the respondent bank. The complainant approached the Banking Ombudsman and sought relief of Rs. 5,600 along with interest @ 2% for the delayed period, reversal of over limit fee charged as the credit limit exceeded because of non-crediting of the payment made and compensation of Rs. 10,000 for wasting his valuable time and for the harassment meted out on him. The bank credited only Rs. 5,600 and other charges levied thereon. Despite giving the bank sufficient opportunity it had not addressed the issue completely and satisfactorily. Therefore, a hearing of the complaint with the bank and the complainant was conducted on 14-6-2007 for conciliation and settlement as provided under Clause 11 of the Banking Ombudsman Scheme, 2006. An amicable settlement was arrived in the conciliation meeting. The bank agreed to reverse over limit fee levied Rs. 330/60, pay interest of Rs. 1,232 and Rs. 7,500 as compensation for loss of time and harassment.

Source: RBI Website

"*Disclaimer:* The Reserve Bank of India does not vouch the correctness, propriety or legality of orders and awards passed by Banking Ombudsman. The object of placing this compendium is merely for the purpose of dissemination of information on the working of the Banking Ombudsman Scheme and the same shall not be treated as an authoritative report on the orders and awards passed by Banking Ombudsman and the Reserve Bank of India shall not be responsible or liable to any person for any error in its preparation."

APPENDIX 8

OUTSOURCING OF FINANCIAL SERVICES - RESPONSIBILITIES OF REGULATED ENTITIES EMPLOYING RECOVERY AGENTS

RBI/2022-23/108

DOR.ORG.REC.65/21.04.158/2022-23

August 12, 2022

Outsourcing of Financial Services – Responsibilities of Regulated Entities employing Recovery Agents

The Reserve Bank of India has from time to time advised Regulated Entities (REs) that the ultimate responsibility for their outsourced activities vests with the mand they are, therefore, responsible for the actions of their service providers including Recovery Agents (hereafter referred to as 'agents').

2. It has been observed that the agents employed by REs have been deviating from the extant instructions governing the outsourcing of financial services. In view of concerns arising from the activities of these agents, it is advised that the REs shall strictly ensure that they or their agents do not resort to intimidation or harassment of any kind, either verbal or physical, against any person in their debt collection efforts, including acts intended to humiliate publicly or intrude upon the privacy of the debtors' family members, referees and friends, sending inappropriate messages either on mobile or through social media, making threatening and/or anonymous calls, persistently[1] calling the borrower and/or calling the borrower before 8:00 a.m. and after 7:00 p.m. for recovery of overdueloans, making false and misleading representations, etc.

3. The instructions contained in para 2 above shall supplement and be read in conjunction with the existing guidelines/directions issued by the Reserve Bank of India, as amended from time to time, including those tabulated in **Annex.**

4. Any violation in this regard by REs will be viewed seriously.

Applicability

5. This circular shall apply to the following REs:

(*a*) All Commercial Banks (including Local Area Banks, Regional Rural Banks, and Small Finance Banks) excluding Payments Banks;

(*b*) All All-IndiaFinancial Institutions (viz. Exim Bank, NABARD, NHB, SIDBI, and NaBFID);

1. For example-calling repeatedly

(*c*) All Non-Banking Financial Companies including Housing Finance Companies;

(*d*) All Primary (Urban) Co-operative Banks, State Co-operative Banks, and District Central Co-operative Banks; and

(*e*) All Asset Reconstruction Companies.

6. This circular shall not apply to microfinance loans covered under 'Master Direction –Reserve Bank of India (Regulatory Framework for Micro finance Loans) Directions, 2022', dated March 14, 2022.

ANNEX

Existing Guidelines/Directions issued by the Reserve Bank of India referring to/ governing the 'Outsourcing of Financial Services' and 'Recovery Agents'

Sl. No.	Circular No.	Date	Subject
1.	DBOD.Leg.No.BC.104/09.07.007/2002-03	May 5, 2003	Guidelines on Fair Practices Code for Lenders
2.	DBOD.NO.BP.40/21.04.158/2006- 07	November 3, 2006	Guidelines on Managing Risks and Code of Conduct in Outsourcing of Financial Services by banks
3.	DBOD.No.BL.BC.59/22.01.010/2006-2007	February 21, 2007	Section 23 of Banking Regulation Act, 1949 - Doorstep Banking
4.	DBOD.NO.BP.64/21.04.158/2007-08	March 03, 2008	Guidelines on Managing Risks and Code of Conduct in Outsourcing of Financial Services by banks
5.	DBOD.No.Leg.BC.75/09.07.005/2007-08	April 24, 2008	Mid-Term Review of the Annual Policy for the Year 2007-08 - Recovery Agents Engaged by Banks
6.	DBOD.No.BP.97/21.04.158/2008-09	December 11, 2008	Guidelines on Managing Risks and Code of Conduct in Outsourcing of Financial Services by banks
7.	DBS.CO.PPD.BC. 5/11.01.005/2008- 09	April 22, 2009	Guidelines on Managing Risks and Code of Conduct in Outsourcing of Financial Services by banks-Compliance Certificate
8.	DBOD.No.BAPD.BC.7/22.01.001/201 4-15	July 1, 2014	Section 23 of the Banking Regulation Act, 1949 - Master Circular on Branch Authorisation
9.	DBR.No.BP.BC.76/21.04.158/2014- 15	March 11, 2015	Guidelines on Managing Risks and Code of Conduct in Outsourcing of Financial Services by banks
10.	DBR.No.Dir.BC.10/13.03.00/2015-16	July 1, 2015,	Master Circular - Loans and Advances - Statutory and Other Restrictions
11.	DBR.CO.RRB.BL.BC.No.17/31.01.00 2/2015-16	July 1, 2015	Master Circular on Branch Licensing

Sl. No.	Circular No.	Date	Subject
12.	DNBR.PD.004/03.10.119/2016-17	August 23, 2016	Master Direction - Standalone Primary Dealers (Reserve Bank) Directions, 2016
13.	DoR(NBFC).PD.003/03.10.119/2016- 17	August 25, 2016	Master Direction - Core Investment Companies (Reserve Bank) Directions, 2016
14.	DNBR.PD.007/03.10.119/2016-17	September 1, 2016	Master Direction - Non-Banking Financial Company - Non- Systemically Important Non-Deposit taking Company (Reserve Bank) Directions, 2016
15.	DNBR.PD.008/03.10.119/2016-17	September 1, 2016	Master Direction - Non-Banking Financial Company - Systemically Important Non-Deposit taking Company and Deposit taking Company (Reserve Bank) Directions, 2016
16.	DNBR.PD.009/03.10.119/2016-17	September 2, 2016	Master Direction - Non-Banking Financial Company - Account Aggregator (Reserve Bank) Directions, 2016
17.	DNBR.(PD).090/03.10.124/2017-18	October 4, 2017	Master Directions - Non-Banking Financial Company - Peer to Peer Lending Platform (Reserve Bank) Directions, 2017
18.	DNBR.PD.CC.No.090/03.10.001/201 7-18	November 9, 2017	Directions on Managing Risks and Code of Conduct in Outsourcing of Financial Services by NBFCs
19.	DOR(NBFC)(PD)CC.No.112/03.10.00 1/2019-20	June 24, 2020	Loans Sourced by Banks and NBFCs over Digital Lending Platforms: Adherence to Fair Practices Code and Outsourcing Guidelines
20.	CEPD.CO.PRD.Cir.No.01/13.01.013/2020-21	January 27, 2021	Strengthening of Grievance Redress Mechanism in Banks
21.	DOR.FIN.HFC.CC.No. 120/03.10.136/ 2020-21	February 17, 2021	Master Direction - Non-Banking Financial Company - Housing Finance Company (Reserve Bank) Directions, 2021
22.	DOR.ORG.REC.27/21.04.158/2021- 22	June 28, 2021	Guidelines for Managing Risk in Outsourcing of Financial Services by Co-operative Banks
23.	DOR.SIG.FIN.REC 1/26.03.001/2022-23	April 1, 2022	Master Circular - Asset Reconstruction Companies
24.	DOR.ACC.REC.No.20/21.04.018/2022-23	April 19, 2022	Disclosures in Financial Statements-Notes to Accounts of NBFCs

Sl. No.	Circular No.	Date	Subject
25.	DoR.AUT.REC.No.27/24.01.041/202 2-23	April 21, 2022	Master Direction - Credit Card and Debit Card - Issuance and Conduct Directions, 2022
26.	DOR.REG.No.45/19.51.052/2022-23	June 8, 2022	Section 23 of the Banking Regulation Act, 1949 - Doorstep Banking